Meaning in Architecture

Meaning in Architecture

Edited by

Charles Jencks

and

George Baird

George Braziller   New York

Produced by Design Yearbook Limited, 21 Ivor Place, London N.W.1, with the cooperation of the Architectural Association, London.

Art Director: Ian Cameron
House Editor: Elizabeth Kingsley-Rowe
Designer: Tom Carter

We are indebted to all those who gave material and photographs for this book. In particular we should like to thank the authors for providing their photographs, work and commentary over a period of a year, without all which such an enterprise would not have been possible. In addition we should like to thank the following for their aid and for permission to reproduce their work:
Cedric Price and Reyner Banham; Aldo van Eyck, Martin Pawley, Folon and Françoise Choay; Geoffrey Broadbent, Gillo Dorfles, Kenneth Frampton, Christian Norberg-Schulz, Joseph Rykwert, Nathan Silver and Alan Colquhoun. C. Albisetti, American Geographical Society of New York, Architectural Press, Atlantis, Baltic Press, Camera Press, Scott Hyde and Damora for CBS, Peter Cook, Curzon Museum of Archæology, François Dallegret, Simon Dell, Richard Einzig, Buckminster Fuller, Gallerie Denise René, Bernard Gay, HT Bild, Herman Haan, Ernst Haas, Lucien Hervé, Hot Car Magazine, Italian State Tourist Office, Martti i. Jaaninen, Charles Jencks, Sam Lambert, F. Maki, John Maltby, Roy E. Petersen, Press Association, Port of London Authority, O. Rajsky, Reuters, Cervin Robinson, Mrs Schräder-Schröder, Tate Gallery, United States Information Service, Dr A. Von Gerkau, Wates Advertising, John Weeks, Shadrach Woods.
Finally we should like to thank those at the Architectural Association who have been of great help in lending their time and aid: Dennis Sharp, Wendy Fenton and Josephine Reid.

Contents

Preface   7

PART 1: SEMIOLOGY & ARCHITECTURE
Semiology & Architecture   Charles Jencks   11
Urbanism & Semiology   Françoise Choay   27
Structuralism & Semiology in Architecture   Gillo Dorfles   39
Meaning into Architecture   Geoffrey Broadbent   51

PART 2: PUBLIC & PRIVATE
'La Dimension Amoureuse' in Architecture   George Baird   79
The Architecture of Wampanoag   Reyner Banham   101
The Time House   Martin Pawley   121
Labour, Work & Architecture   Kenneth Frampton   151
The Interior of Time   Aldo van Eyck   171
A Miracle of Moderation   Aldo van Eyck, with essays by Paul Parin &
     Fritz Morgenthaler   173
Meaning in Architecture   Christian Norberg-Schulz   215

PART 3: FORMS OF MEANING
The Sitting Position - A Question of Method   Joseph Rykwert   233
History as Myth   Charles Jencks   245
Typology & Design Method   Alan Colquhoun   267
Architecture without Buildings   Nathan Silver   279

Index   286

Preface

'A book is a machine to think with' – so opened I. A. Richards in 1924 echoing sentiments heard throughout Europe at that time and raising the question 'what kind of book, what kind of machine, is adequate to the present?' While our notion of what a machine is has undergone a radical change since then, our idea and ideal of a book has not changed considerably – it is an instrument along with which a reader thinks. Thus the ideal book might possess at the end of this mutual endeavour as much marginal comment from the reader as written text from the writer. To be more precise then, a book is a machine to communicate with and the better the book the more insertions and qualifications it will continue to generate all the time. One can't help thinking here of the recent machines which have made this ideal of interaction even more possible, and thus the metaphor more apt.

But there is another equally valid reason for the metaphor which also derives from the present situation. This, if one may balance generalities, is the present lack of consensus on important issues coupled with its joint benefit – the rich plurality of views. No book seems adequate or relevant to this condition unless it acknowledges the crisis and its attendant possibilities. On the one hand, there is a general crisis over such issues as revolution and change within architecture (some authors wishing to jettison 'architecture' altogether) and on the other hand there is a specific crisis over what 'meaning in architecture' (or rather 'meanings') is relevant. Because these issues are current and by no means settled, we have pursued a course different from other books. Instead of isolating traditions from one another to produce one monolithic and consistent statement, we have consciously sought out views which contradict our own and each of the others. It is one thing to discuss pluralism and the open society and quite another to actively engage incisive criticism and continuously expose one's dearest views to the onslaughts of the opponent; the former is an agreeable enough exercise in reasonable sense, whereas the latter is an object lesson in realigning one's ego. Here all of the contributors have at least allowed this latter possibility to occur by letting their work be published with an accompanying critical commentary.

Hence the book is in the form of a controversy or debate. It is divided into three main sections, each of which debates a general area from different points of view. The first section contains four articles differing over the possibility of applying semiology to architecture or urbanism. Semiology, literally the theory of signs, has been postulated as the fundamental science of human communication, so it is naturally central or at least relevant to all the following disputes over meaning in architecture. Françoise Choay and I put forward this relevance and Gillo Dorfles qualifies it, while Geoffrey Broadbent shows some of its dangers.

The second section continues this debate over semiology. George Baird in a sense applies it to two buildings which he finds do not acknowledge a wide enough scope of meaning. This conclusion is then questioned by Reyner Banham while he puts forward the idea of a homeostatic architecture responsive to the individual. The implications of this view are then challenged by Kenneth Frampton who explores the possibilities for a public architecture and public realm, and by Martin Pawley who returns to the idea of an architecture responsive to the private realm. His view gives the question a new twist as he explicitly attacks both previous positions and substitutes the idea of an architecture which records actual, individual time ('The Time House'). If Pawley sees private time as authentic and opposed to public time, this whole opposition receives a new phrasing with Van Eyck's essay on the Dogons starting 'The Interior of Time', for here the collective and individual memory of time are seen to be resolvable. Whether this resolution is possible today in historical societies remains an open question – Françoise Choay having previously argued that it is next to impossible, while Van Eyck and Norberg-Schulz argue that it is absolutely necessary. Thus in this section we are posed with a series of antinomies: public vs. private, place vs. space and at least in one author's view monumental vs. responsive. Whether these are real antinomies offering an

7

either/or choice or only complementary aspects of a larger phenomenon ('twinphenomenon' in Van Eyck's words) is at the very center of battle.

Finally the last section, less a debate, discusses different forms of meaning in the environment: those coming from 'the sitting position' (i.e. such things as chairs) to those which come simply from any activity or use (such things as ceremony). Joseph Rykwert shows how sitting generates the same symbolic pressures as other environmental forms; I show how the history of recent architecture can be considered in semiological terms as undergoing a dialectical transformation; Alan Colquhoun shows how some of these terms or 'typologies' underlie all architecture; and Nathan Silver argues that the particular typology 'use' is the most important determinant of form and how thus we could have 'Architecture without Buildings'.

The last title again underscores the polemical nature of the issues and hence brings me back to the form of the book. So that each writer can attack and defend a position, there is a running commentary alongside the articles and where possible a response from the author. This not only allows a deeper, more explored view of any issue, but also a quick, sometimes vitriolic, response also unusual in books. However, it does place a certain burden on the reader because it means that he must keep several contradictory views in his mind at the same time, while weighing their relative merits. Yet it also allows that rare possibility open to the explorer and anthropologist of occupying several positions at once and seeing an event go through a series of reflected permutations without having to immediately limit himself to one. Thus the book resembles that other kind of machine which can control a series of ideas and send them through a cybernetic cycle until they are less obviously in error.

Three of the articles in this book derived from an issue of *Arena* (Journal of the Architectural Association) entitled 'Meaning in Architecture' which was primarily compiled by George Baird with my assistance. Subsequent to this, he helped me compile this volume with the remaining articles and critical commentary. The contributors, to whom I am indebted for their patient effort particularly on the commentary, come from different parts of the world. George Baird is a Canadian architect teaching both in Toronto and at the University of Essex, England; Reyner Banham teaches at University College London and has just finished *The Architecture of the Well-Tempered Environment;* Geoffrey Broadbent is Head of the Portsmouth School of Architecture.

Françoise Choay is a critic of art and architecture in Paris whose most recent book explores issues related to those in her article here – an anthology of theories and manifestoes on urbanism called *L'Urbanisme, Utopies et Réalités.* Alan Colquhoun, a British architect, alternates between teaching in the United States and England; Gillo Dorfles, aesthetician and art critic, is a former editor of *Domus,* teaches in Milan and has written many books on architecture, communication and taste; Kenneth Frampton is a former editor of *Architectural Design,* a practicing British architect and teacher at Princeton; Christian Norberg-Schulz is a Norwegian architect whose recent books include *Intentions in Architecture* and *Kilian Ignaz Dientzenhofer e il Barocco Boemo;* Martin Pawley is a technical editor at *The Architects Journal* and one founder of the Progressive Architecture movement; Joseph Rykwert is Professor of Art at the University of Essex and presently at work on a book: *Adams House in Paradise;* Nathan Silver is an American architect and architectural correspondent for the *New Statesman,* and author of *Lost New York;* presently he has a Guggenheim Fellowship to continue study along the lines suggested in his article; Aldo Van Eyck is a Dutch architect, a member of Team Ten, sometime editor of the Dutch Forum, and a teacher at Delft.

CHARLES JENCKS

Part 1 Semiology and Architecture

GLOSSARY OF SEMIOLOGICAL TERMS

The first five articles apply semiology, the theory of signs, to architecture. Since this theory is still in a nascent stage there is a relative plurality of terms which cover roughly the same meaning. Unless otherwise specified in the context, the following generalized definitions and synonyms hold.

Signifier/Signified. The signifier is a representation for an idea or thought which is signified. In language, the sound would be the signifier and the idea the signified, whereas in architecture, the form would be the signifier and the content the signified. The fact that every sign has at least this double nature is called 'double articulation'. See pages 15, 53, 86.

Context/Metaphor. There are two basic ways a sign achieves meaning – both through its relation to all the other signs in a context or chain, and through the other signs for which it has become a metaphor by association, or similarity. The synonyms for context are chain, opposition, syntagm, metonymy, contiguity, relations, contrast; for metaphor they are association, connotation, similarity, correlation, paradigmatic or systemic plane. See pages 21-4, 29-30, 52, 91.

Langue/Parole. All the signs in a society taken together constitute the langue or total resource. Each selection from this totality, each individual act, is the parole. Thus the langue is collective and not easily modifiable, whereas the parole is individual and malleable. See pages 81-84.

Semiology and Architecture

Charles Jencks

Once, when travelling in France, I had a rather unnerving experience which I am unlikely to forget. A French companion turned to me suddenly and pointed toward the spire of a cathedral which had just come into view: 'Jetez un coup d'oeil sur cette flèche!' The glance was painfully exquisite; literally, 'Throw a blow of eye on top of that spire!' I could suddenly see my eyeball wrenched from its socket and thrown across the field to be impaled on that pin-sharp point. But my companion was completely laconic. He had just meant 'look at that spire' and no such ludicrous sensations were reverberating through his head, because to him the metaphor was almost dead. The signs which were deeply embedded in the French language were partially asleep and inaccessible to him. Whereas to myself suddenly they were awake in that raw state of freshness, even wetness, of the newly born.

Later it occurred to me, on hearing further metaphors, that every Frenchman was a natural genius; particularly so because his creative talent was conveyed with such complete insouciance and candour. But then on further thought it became clear that the whole environment, including language, is always in this ambiguous state of limbo—somewhere between life and death. Every dead form that one can perceive is a sign waiting to be resuscitated. As Braque said: 'Reality only reveals itself when illuminated by a ray of poetry. All around us is asleep.' But the problem may well be that 'human kind cannot bear very much reality'. One could not stand the pressure of noticing how every particular object is capable of being revived, of being placed in a new context whether poetic or not. The possibility is too challenging; it would lead to a radical restructuring of every act down to the habitual grasp of a cup of tea. The laboratories which depend on depersonalized objects, green walls and abstract concepts would suddenly explode in a fit of anthropomorphism. Even such stable abstractions as Desoxyribosenucleic Acid would stir into life. The act of posting a letter would become too complex with significance: a walk down the stair-way, over the door-step, on to the side-walk, across the pave-ment and over to the mail-box. Common objects would dissolve into their primal states, each having an independent life.

The most striking of these dissolutions occurs when an object has been put together through an *ad hoc* joining of parts. When we look at Picasso's 'Bull's Head' (Fig. 1), the fact that the figure can work as a bull's head is always threatened by the parts which start to work as a bicycle seat and handlebars. Or to take another example of using the bicycle seat in an *ad hoc* way, the surgeons have created an 'Operating Chair-Stool' out of pre-existing parts: an architect's chair back, a bar-rail, an hydraulic pump, bed casters, car springs and so on. Picasso is taking advantage of the fact that the form of a bicycle seat happens also to work as the face of a bull, whereas the surgeons are using it for stability during the operation. One use is metaphorical, the other functional. Yet clearly, because of the multivalence of any object, the uses of this bicycle seat are hardly exhausted, although they are finite and non-arbitrary.

This is perhaps the most fundamental idea of semiology and meaning in architecture: the idea that any form in the environment, or sign in language, is motivated, or capable of being motivated. It helps to explain why all of a sudden forms come alive or fall into bits. For it contends that, although a form may be initially arbitrary or non-motivated as Saussure points out,[1] its subsequent use is motivated or based on some determinants. Or we can take a slightly different point of view and say that the minute a new form is invented it will acquire, *inevitably*, a meaning. 'This semantization is inevitable; as soon as there is a society, every usage is converted into a sign of itself; the use of a raincoat is to give protection from the rain, but this cannot be dissociated from the very signs of an atmospheric situation'.[2] Or to be more exact, the use of a raincoat can be dissociated from its shared meanings if we avoid its social use or explicitly decide to deny it further meaning.

It is this conscious denial of connotations which has had an interesting history with the avant-garde. Annoyed either by the glib reduction of their

BAIRD: It need not even be 'invented'; all it has to do is get noticed.

BAIRD: I don't agree about the efficacy of these 'explicit decisions'. Meanings are not 'voted down', or controlled by elites (Barthes is wrong about that, I feel, even for the elite world of haute couture). The only way meanings dissolve is through atrophy, across a whole social totality.

I
Three Uses of the Bicycle Seat.

work to its social meanings or the contamination of the strange by an old language, they have insisted on the intractability of the new and confusing. 'Our League of Nations symbolizes nothing' said the architect Hannes Meyer, all too weary of the creation of buildings around past metaphors. 'My poem means nothing; it just is. My painting is meaningless. Against Interpretation: The Literature of Silence. Entirely radical.' Most of these statements are objecting to the 'inevitable semantization' which is trite, which is coarse, which is too anthropomorphic or old. Some are simply nihilistic and based on the belief that any meaning which may be applied is spurious; it denies the fundamental absurdity of human existence. In any case, on one level, all these statements are paradoxical. In their denial of meaning, they create it. This may account for the relative popularity among the avant-garde of the Cretan Liar Paradox, the Cretan who says 'All Cretans are liars'. It seems as if the statement is true, then it is false; if false then true. A very enjoyable situation, to some the essence of life. Yet by expanding the statement and avoiding its self reference the paradox can be avoided. Thus Hannes Meyer's statement might read: 'Our League of Nations symbolizes something, and that something is nothing'. I say might read, because it is quite apparent from the context in which he made the remark that he meant that his building symbolized not all

◀ BROADBENT: See also Stravinsky: '. . . I consider that music is, by its very nature, powerless to *express* anything at all, whether a feeling, an attitude of mind, a psychological mood, a phenomenon of nature, etc. . . .' An Autobiography, 1936.

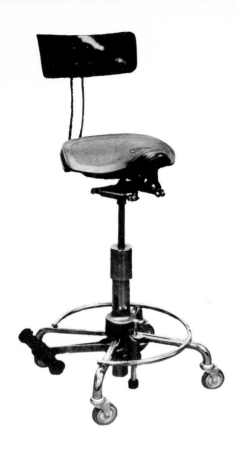

the previous ideas of government, but new ones based on utility.[3] In any case, two points are relevant to my purpose: (1) that every act, object and statement that man perceives is meaningful (even 'nothing') and (2) that the frontiers of meaning are always, momentarily, in a state of collapse and paradox.

The first point is the justification for semiology, the theory of signs. It contends that since everything is meaningful, we are in a literal sense condemned to meaning, and thus we can either become aware of how meaning works in a technical sense (semiology), or we can remain content with our intuition. This dichotomy is probably a false antithesis since, *ex hypothesi*, semiology holds that we cannot be aware of, or responsible for, everything at once. Yet the goal of semiology, even if ultimately vain, is to bring the intuitive up to the conscious level, in order to increase our area of responsible choice.

The second point seems at variance with the first, for it appears to deny the existence of ultimate meanings (in its nihilistic stance) and it certainly undercuts the responsibility toward past, social meanings (except to upset them). To give an example, the position of Reyner Banham is relevant. In one book he starts a sentence 'The Dymaxion concept (of Fuller) was entirely radical . . .' in another, he says 'Given a genuinely functional approach such as this, no cultural preconceptions . . .'[4] Now these three avant-garde ideas, from a semiological (and factual) viewpoint, are demonstrably false. There simply cannot be anything created which is *entirely* radical, *genuinely* functional and with *no* cultural preconceptions (see below). Yet if re-qualified these statements would be semiologically acceptable and, more important, highly relevant. Because they point to that underlying experience where new meanings are actively generated and it seems as if one were totally free from preconceptions. Since there is a real sense in which this is true, one can agree with the emphasis on the radical and undomesticated. Except that, if taken as absolutely true, this tends to discourage a more radical creativity; because it limits the area of criticism and active re-use of the past. It is one of the basic assumptions of semiology that creation is dependent on tradition and memory in a very real sense and that if one tries to jettison either one or the other, one is actually limiting one's area of free choice.

Some of the main ideas of semiology will be outlined below showing their relevance to meaning in architecture. What should be emphasized at this primitive stage of the subject is that the scope should be broad and inclusive. Semiology has to cover very general positions by necessity ranging from epistemology to physiology. (Fig. 2) This is necessary not only because there are pertinent assumptions right across the field, but also because such pursuits tend to fall victim to one limited orthodoxy or another (behaviourism for instance). But again, *ex hypothesi*, one is encouraged to use the various constructions of other semiologists to build a broad picture of how signs relate to meaning.

THE SIGN SITUATION

The first point on which most semiologists would agree is that one simply cannot speak of 'meaning' as if it were one thing that we can all know or share. The concept meaning is multivalent, has many meanings itself; and we will have to be clear which one we are discussing. Thus in their seminal book *The Meaning of Meaning*, Ogden and Richards show the confusion of philosophers over the basic use of this term. Each philosopher assumes that his use is clear and understood, whereas the authors show this is far from the case; they distinguish sixteen different meanings of meaning. To further underline this ambiguity another author has written 'The Meaning of the "Meaning of Meaning" ' and one could imagine that inquiry being justifiably extended in length. But the point is clear: each use of meaning is different from any other and the particular case has to be understood from the context.

Thus, a doctor might say the meaning of a stomach-ache is hunger; a poet that the meaning of truth is beauty; a literalist that the meaning of 'table' is that sort of object to which he is pointing. It is this, apparently simple, kind of meaning which is the bastion of common sense and the tough-minded. Samuel Johnson, in a typically pugilistic mood, kicked a stone and thought he was thereby refuting the idealism of Berkeley. But as Yeats pointed out:

'. . . this preposterous pragmatical pig of a world,
  Its farrow that so solid seem,
  Must vanish on the instant did the mind but change its theme'.

This is of course a debatable point of epistemology.

For Plato, the object 'table' existed as a copy of some ideal, absolute table which itself existed in some absolute realm of ideas. As such, the object was at one remove from the ideal table. Moreover, the painter who drew the table was copying a copy or creating a double lie (of sorts). Continuing Plato's epistemology and morality for the moment we can see how many more times the word 'table' is removed from the ideal. Consider what happens in the sign situation in which we say 'I see the table'. There is (1) the ideal table of Plato, or the 'thing in itself' of Kant, or the 'concrete set of events' of the scientist—particles in motion at a certain moment in time and space, (2) the 'phenomenon' of the table made up of light waves, (3) of a certain spectrum which man can see, (4) coming at a certain angle (5) just from the surface of the table (not the set of events), (6) which make an image on the retina, (7) which is more or less adequate to our thought or expectation of a table, (8) which is called by an arbitrary convention, the word, table.

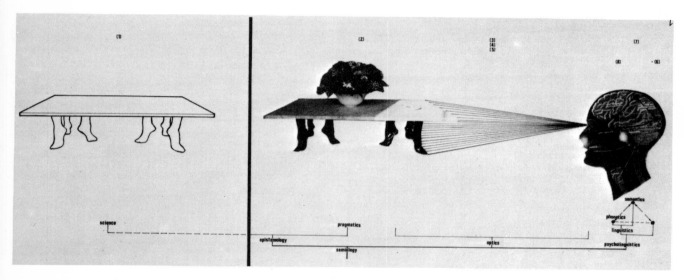

2
The Sign Situation.

Thus if we take this simple breakdown of the sign situation, we see that the word table is at least eight times removed from the thing in itself. Instead of saying merely 'I see the table', we should, less ambiguously, say something like: 'I have an hypothesis about certain light waves out there which come from a surface which stand for an object we socially call a table'. Of course this sounds ridiculous and we would be regarded as quite mad if we avoided the common and understandable contraction. But for speaking in such contractions and regarding words as part of things, we often pay a heavy price; as in the Cretan Liar Paradox, or the scientists' hypostatization of concepts.

This 'abuse' of language is really quite prevalent and can be traced from the politicians cliché to the astronomer who said: 'What guarantee have we that the planet regarded by astronomers as Uranus really is Uranus.' Or the architects who search for the essence of architecture, or the aesthetician who scoured the British Museum looking for what by definition all the objects must have in common: 'beauty'. Perhaps the most convincing example of the power of signs is that of the shaman cited by Levi-Strauss.[5] By the effective use of signs in a social situation the shaman can destroy another man without touching him: the sympathetic nervous system is upset, the blood pressure drops, food and drink are rejected, the capillary vessels become more permeable and the man dies without a trace of damage or lesions. All because a sign was effectively coordinated with a strong belief and social situation. Naturally most sign situations are less extreme than that of the sorcerer, but they are similar in theory and may even reach the same pitch as in religion, or on a mundane level, hypnotic trauma. In addition, the nausea due to misunderstanding a language, the fear due to unfamiliarity with a style, the conflict of generations, are all mild examples of sign shock.

Historically, semiology has been concerned with the right part of Figure 2; that is, basically, what happens when man perceives a sign through one of his five senses. Obviously most perception, particularly that of architecture and the new multi-media which are prevalent today, is a compound of several senses. In fact the present interest in unusual combinations makes semiology almost an inevitable study. It would grow from the happening, if not the laboratory. Yet, in any experience, one or two of the senses are bound to predominate, and for the present purpose we may discuss them together in general terms.

Thus in the usual experience there is always a percept, a concept and a representation. This is irreducible. In architecture, one sees the building, has an interpretation of it, and usually puts that into words. In each sign situation we can see language immediately entering and thus understand why semiology first grew out of linguistics. Following this course and using the model developed by Ogden and Richards, we can further articulate the right side of Figure 2.

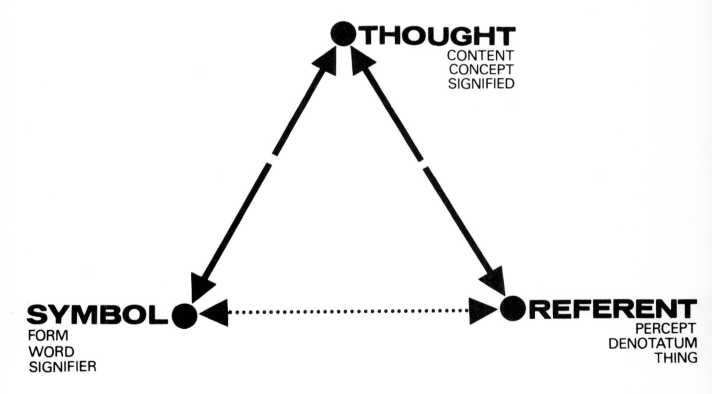

3 *The Semiological Triangle.*

The first point the authors make, is that in most cases there is no direct relation between a word and a thing, except in the highly rare case of onomatopoeia. That most cultures are under the illusion that there is a direct connection has to be explained in various ways. One explanation (see below) is neo-platonic; another is psychological. In any case, everyone has experienced the shock of eating a thing which is called by the wrong name, or would question the adage that a rose 'by any other name would smell as sweet'. It would not smell as sweet if called garlic.

But the main point of the semiological triangle is that there are simply *relations* between language, thought and reality. One area does not determine the other, except in rare cases, and all one can really claim with conviction is that there are simply connections, or correlations.[6] Unfortunately more is claimed, much more. In fact the behaviourists hold that reality determines both thought and language and the Whorfians that language determines the other two, whereas the Renaissance Platonists claimed that thought is determinant. Each semiologist points the arrows in the direction he believes in, but, as the diagram shows, the relations are always two-way and never absolute.

A moment's reflection on the history of architecture will elicit the relative autonomy of one area from another. Gothic form, for example, evolved and changed over two hundred years without the content drastically altering. Then the Renaissance reinterpreted the content of Gothic—calling it barbaric, ugly, irrational—without changing either the form or the objects. Or, in our own age, the correlations have undergone an equally radical inversion. For instance the Pop theorists and artists decided to change the pre-existing relation between form and content, calling all the previous detritus and trivia significant and vice versa. In any new movement, by definition, the pre-existing relations have to be destroyed and also, by definition, the older generation annoyed (even repulsed). The new generation must be confused. If there is not repulsion and confusion in the face of the new, then either it is not new or the viewer is uncomprehending. There is no third alternative if the semiological triangle is correct. What is interesting in the present situation (since this has always been known) is that the avant-garde has become addicted to the notion of change and the animated state of muddled suspension. They change the conventions faster than they can be learned or used, either in the belief that 'that's life' or that it's enjoyable. The logic seems binding. If one assumes that the artist must operate 'in the gap between life and art', and then that life is ultimately pointless and based merely on changing fashions, the result will naturally be an art which approaches fashionable life and sensuous appearance as a limit. One has to grant Pop Art and Neo-Dada their consistent logic.

Returning to the semiological triangle, we can see that if an over-all interpretation is to be at all correct it will have to coordinate these multiple relations (which is by no means easy). Something may go wrong at any point. As Panofsky shows (*Meaning in the Visual Arts* p. 34), we may be confronted with two similar objects floating in space which have two different interpretations. In one case this hovering, or rescinding the law of gravity, is meant to be an apparition or vision; in the other case, a real thing. Without knowing the conventions which support these different meanings we might reverse the intended relations and come up with the wrong interpretations. This is precisely what happened to Gothic forms in Europe for five hundred years. They were very fruitfully misunderstood. Yet if correct understanding is our momentary goal, then we must be able to correlate correctly form, content and percept or, as Panofsky points out, the formal level of meaning with the iconographical (concepts, allegories) into a whole interpretation (what he calls iconology or study of the underlying symptoms and symbols of a culture). This sounds unwieldy and complex. In fact it would destroy an experience if we explicitly isolated meanings in this way. For instance the 13th century semiologist, Durandus, might insist that each representation of Jerusalem be viewed in the following way: 'Jerusalem in the historical sense is the town in Palestine to which Pilgrims now resort; in the allegorical sense it is the Church Militant; in the Tropological it is the Christian Soul; and in the anagogical it is the Celestial Jerusalem, the Home on High.' An academic *tour de force* that, and yet the average pilgrim was meant to be able to do it. In fact in every age some such distinctions have to be made, since experience without abstractions is impossible. Thus in one way or another we are all condemned to academicism as well as meaning. The question is which and how? Postponing this for a moment we might speculate on one possible course.

If the study of how architecture communicates meaning proceeds in

◀ BAIRD: The 'semiological triangle' strikes me as a brilliant construction, in the way it accommodates and explains so many historical positions so clearly. And I know of no observer previous to Jencks, who has seen the three corners of the triangle as having equal weight.

◀ BROADBENT: This will only disturb us if, for the sake of our own security, we *need* to find simple absolutes in aesthetic matters. But stylistic changes of the kind which Jencks describes suggest that such absolutes do not, in fact, exist. Nor need they; all men, presumably, are born with similar appetites and instincts, but even these can be sublimated and there is not the slightest reason to suppose that they are also born with the same interests and ideals. Provided, say, that one's need for food and shelter are satisfied the actual *kind* of food, or *form* of shelter, is a very secondary matter. One's response to it will depend very much on one's previous experience, the things to which one has become habituated, and so on. Certainly the physiology and psychology of perception bear this out. What one perceives is a *transaction* between a pattern of stimuli on the senses and one's previous experience. Each modifies the other and is also modified by the other. The Pop artists, following Duchamp, have merely demonstrated the fact of 'cultural relativity'; what one perceives in art depends entirely on one's frame of reference, But again, why should one *want* it to be otherwise?

JENCKS: This may have a little truth in it, but it misses the points I was trying to make which were that 1) the speed of change is faster than the new conventions can be learned (i.e. fashion is the model for art and technology etc.) 2) the explicit nihilism on which *some* Dada and Pop is based carries with it the consistent drive toward sensuous appearance. Apparently Broadbent, like some early Dadaists, believes in a 'cultural relativity' that depends 'entirely on one's frame of reference'. With this absolute relativism one can, of course, justify any sort of flap-doodle or atrocity. Perhaps the best way to refute those impaled on the apex of the semiological triangle is to kick a stone *à la* Samuel Johnson, or even better tickle their feet and tell them it is merely their 'frame of reference' which is laughing.

BAIRD: No. I fail to see the parallel ▶ between the basic units of linguistics and these proposed architectural ones. Like the 'rational/aesthetic' dichotomy used by Broadbent, 'form, function and technique' in architectural theory seem to me hopelessly overworked, and intellectually exhausted. I don't want to see the tedious and gratuitous warfare among them to be fought all over again within architectural semiology. (See my answer to Broadbent's last question. Jencks)

BROADBENT: The *Gestalt* concept of an ▶ isomorph, or literal model of the perceived object in the electrical field of the brain, really is untenable in the light of recent physiological studies into the electrical *and* chemical action of the brain. And in any case, if one is going to be so literal, the encephalograph trace of a brain in repose is remarkably jagged.

BAIRD: This oversimplification is unfair, ▶ I think, to both Rousseau and Freud, both of whom took more ironic views of man's 'inherent nature' than Jencks allows for.

BROADBENT: But these universals and absolutes, as Plato himself said, have to be ▶ *imposed* on the world by the brain which is trying to comprehend it.
JENCKS: But Plato believed that universals and absolutes existed quite independently of man and his perception. What's more, given the proviso that we can never know these absolutes with *certainty* (see black barrier between 1 and 2 in the Sign Situation), he was right. Broadbent's conceptual pragmatism has all the dangers which Karl Popper has pointed out – the chief being an absolute relativism because one man's 'imposition' is as good as any other's, when there is no third court of appeal, reality.

accordance with past traditions and linguistics, then we might imagine the following set of abstractions. First, in every usual architecture there is always a form, function and technic.[7] We may happily exclude for the moment all artificial exceptions to this rule, just as linguists exclude artificial from natural languages (the former being logic, mathematics etc.). In most architecture there has to be a form (comprising such things as colour, texture, space, rhythm), a function (purpose, use, past connotations, style, etc.) and a technic (made up of structure, materials and mechanical aids, etc.). Now, if the linguist tries to discover what basic units communicate verbal meaning and finds such things as phonemes and morphemes, then it would be highly appropriate if the architectural explorer found 'formemes, funcemes and techemes'—those fundamental units of architectural meaning. Whereas any usual language is doubly articulated, any usual architecture is triply articulated. The new field, naturally following linguistics, would be called architistics. Some such analysis would be absolutely necessary if one were to analyse how architecture can communicate, and the only warning to be made about such a study is that it might well degenerate into academic formulae. The fictions might become rules; the function, 'functionalism' or the form, 'formalism'. Since this is exactly what has happened in any case, it will have to be understood and explained.[8]

INTRINSIC AND EXTRINSIC EXPLANATIONS OF MEANING
Our explanation of meaning is meaningful depending on whether we concentrate on the left or right side of Figure 2. The intrinsic theory of meaning (the right side) posits a direct connection between ourselves and the universe. For instance the *Gestalt* psychologist Arnheim contends that because we are a part of the world it is conceivable that our nervous system shares a similar structure (or isomorphism) to forms. Thus a jagged line intrinsically means activity, whereas a flat line means inactivity or repose. The Platonists supported this kind of meaning and thus it is not surprising to find Renaissance architecture based on simple, absolute forms which were believed to carry intrinsic meaning (such as the circle which signified harmony and repose). By the same line of reasoning the expressionist painter could claim that an all blue canvas meant sadness and a poet that the sound 'bang' meant the concept bang. However, in order to explain the all blue canvas which strangely signified joy, the painter would have to resort to conventions, or the extrinsic theory of meaning.

In spite of this apparent limitation, the intrinsic theory has had an extraordinary influence throughout history as the continual resurgence of Platonism shows. No sooner is it squelched than it sprouts another head. Rousseau wanted to re-align man with his intrinsic nature, Freud hoped to reconcile him with his natural drives, Jung with his inherent archetypes, psychologists with the structure of perception, genetic codes, common instincts and even reflex actions. This tradition has continually sought to find those universals and absolutes in man which determine meaning (*Purism* of Corbusier being the most recent case in architecture). And quite recently, the Psycholinguists have posited various inherent limitations in the mind which make certain language forms universal.[9] If one puts the theory in its strongest form it would claim that a certain pattern intrinsic to man exists prior to and in more strength than a pattern in the environment. One only has to close one's eyes and press hard on the eyeballs to see that this has a certain truth. But one would like to know how much. If there are certain favourable forms in man, then through some principle of psychic economy, extrinsic meanings should tend toward these forms. We would find that all languages and architectures had certain common attributes. For instance, in most cultures, the red light, being intrinsically active, would mean 'go'.

Since however the red light usually means 'stop' one has to resort to another theory. The extrinsic theory contends that it is stimuli from the environment which form meaning—the primary stimuli being language. Thus the way we perceive any object is determined by the concepts we have, or in Gombrich's terms, schemata. And instead of these schemata being an intrinsic part of the nervous system, they are slowly created through language and other cultural sign systems (or alone). A very convincing example of the way they work to create different styles (and thus 'art history') is outlined in Gombrich's *Art and Illusion*. He shows the well known example of the duck-rabbit which according to the schema of the viewer is either a duck or a rabbit, or both, separately—never together. A further interesting proof of the influence of schemata in perception arises when we try to see it as a third thing, a thingummy-bob, neither duck nor rabbit (Fig. 4).

4
Duck-Rabbit – etc. ?

This is actually quite hard to do because the schema, thingummybob, is not nearly so expected as the other two. Our language has stabilized the other two interpretations, which will not budge under such a puny assault. Yet supposing we wanted to start a new art movement and see the old duck-rabbit in an 'entirely radical' new way. We have the form, we want to change the caption. First we might muddle around in that animated state of suspension with the inadequate word 'thingummybob'. Naturally this would bring cries of derision and contempt from everyone else who knew what it 'really' was, but we could bolster our courage by calling them all victims of their preconceptions. We could invoke a little manifest destiny and historical inevitability and show how Hamlet gets a new reading every year. The defenders of the two ancient concepts would be hindering progress, clearly anachronistic and out of touch with the present situation when all things are in flux. We strain, we half close our eyes trying all sorts of improbable combinations, until we hit upon a possible solution. Turned one way the figure might be a hand making the V sign for victory; another way a key-hole or bellows. Unfortunately, none of these new inter-pretations are as plausible as the first two, so they are rejected by society and we have to postpone our revolution. But any successful movement does find the new, plausible meanings; such as Archigram.

Consider some of the successful metaphors they have introduced into archi-tecture. Cities which look like computer nets, robots, pneumatic tubes, bowels, telescopes, soap bubbles, comic books, space capsules, oil refineries, molehills and even the flexing tentacles of the Octopus. (Fig. 5).

Returning for a moment to the extrinsic theory of meaning, it contends, in its strongest form, that schemata determine perception. That is, we are anything but passive receptors of outside stimuli, but always perceive them according to a former expectation. These expectations may be inborn, but mostly they are acquired. The most emphatic of these views is that of Whorf who states that language shapes both thought and our knowledge of reality.[10] While it is difficult if not impossible to prove this, there is a good deal of evidence which seems to suggest that it might be true. There is the test for colour perception on those who speak two different languages. The Englishman sees green, blue and purple, whereas the Navaho cuts up the same spectrum differently into /thatl-it/ and /tootl-iz/. He cannot distinguish the three colours (although he can be taught to), because he uses another language. Each language being different from all others, it stands to reason that each culture sees the world differently. The only problem with this theory is that, like the behaviourist one, it is nicely circular. We see the world differently because we speak a different language and vice versa. Which came first—language, thought, or reality?

The answer, I believe, is a little bit of all three. We form schemata by constant bombardment from outside stimuli, but also by relatively pure thought (logic, chess) and language. The hypothesis is the following: man has certain inborn dispositions to expect recurrent patterns, or to be more exact, he is always asking the environment questions. It is this curious purposeful side, which so completely permeates his nature, that makes the passive, behaviourist position so ridiculous. This active, probing nature extends from concepts in the mind right down to perceptual schemata in the eye, or other receptors. Each level of this hierarchy acts as a sieve, only allowing those stimuli to pass for which it

◄ BROADBENT: These are not metaphors, but simple and direct analogies. And how does one judge their 'success' in the absence of evidence that they actually work?
JENCKS: Their 'success', as the context makes clear, is that they are 'plausible', whereas the Duck-Rabbit creations are not. I take it that any new creation is metaphorical in the sense that it unites past matrices which were previously separated.

5
Archigram Robot II, 1968. An example of finding the possible new meanings in old forms which no one else has found. Here the architectural metaphors come from tele-scopes, blow-ups and umbrellas; bugs, amoebae and pneumatic skins; tubes, capsules, pills and plastic baggies; electronic circuits, transistors and even the Early Warning System for Nuclear Attack.

FOR AN INSTANT

MOMENT-VILLAGE

THE PARTS SLOWLY BUT CONTINUOUSLY EVOLVING—A SENSORY AND RESPONSIVE ROLE AND IT ALL GETS CLEARER

has a (figurative) hole—or schema.[11] Initially these are fairly open and undiscriminating, allowing any old stimulus to pass, but soon they learn. Thus the stimulus is continuously stripped of all its irrelevance and so we arrive at greater and greater generalizations.

The determination of what constitutes an adequate stimulus depends then on its relevance for the schema—how it is coded. For instance there are many examples all up and down the hierarchy of relevance selection: 'women were known to sleep soundly through an air-raid but to awake at the slightest cry of their babies'. This slightest cry for an anxious mother constitutes an adequate stimulus; an air raid does not, so it is filtered out at a low level and repressed (the actual sounds do not reach the brain). Thus perception is partially goal oriented even at this level, although usually the higher centres determine the goals.

To give a very rough idea of how this may work in perceiving for instance, a pyramid, the rather simplistic trip of a multiple stimulus may be traced up the schematic ladder. Start with the first abstraction, that of the eye. The eye strips the image of its irrelevancies of retinal position. Because of colour and size constancy, other accidents of light and shadow are disregarded for more important *Gestalt* forms (such as outline and unity). Yet even here the image may be modified by attitude and we might see the pyramid as larger and brighter if it is of great value to us.

On the next level, the experience of motion may effect the image. Our eye adapts to uniform motion and, supposing we are moving at a constant foot rate toward the pyramid and stop, it will tend to back up: this because of our adapting schemata relevant to movement. Suppose then we suddenly close our eyes. The after-image of the three-dimensional pyramid will slowly collapse into a triangle. Or, if we are a particularly gifted people capable of seeing eidetic images, we could suddenly look to the blank ground and project a near perfect trace of the object—picking out all its salient features. Again, this is a short term example of memory schemata but it is on a higher level than the after-image, because it is more detailed. In some cases it even approaches 'photographic memory'. Yet such total recall, if relatively possible, can only exist with filling in by higher conceptual levels which are more abstract and symbolic.

About these it is hard to generalize except to say they are the most important. They may extend from some vivid image (the brilliant desert light shining on polished limestone) all the way to our attitude about Pharaohs and mass production. Lewis Mumford, who has criticised the pyramid builders for their bureaucratic subterfuge, no doubt tends to diminish and darken his view. In a partial sense then, knowledge and language determine what we see. But so do all the lesser levels of memory. What they have in common is their mutual interdependence and reliance on previous schemata.

We may say, along with Craik and Koestler, that the main function of the nervous system is 'to model or parallel external events' and that 'this process of paralleling is the basic feature of thought and explanation'. We slowly build up our schemata through a cyclical process of hypothesis and correction, all the time making our 'model or parallel' more habitual and closer to 'reality'. Soon this schema may well become a habit or a skill. Perhaps a memory which is so well learned that it is as automatic as driving a car or playing with the rules of chess. In both these cases the rules of the game (or the 'code') have become so habitual that we can use them unconsciously while we attend to something more important (or the 'message'). Or, to put it in Koestler's terms, each schema is a flexible matrix with fixed rules which allows us to perceive each unique situation with a fair amount of flexibility. The more we look and concentrate, the closer our concept will approach reality. But the 'reality' that these schemata approach is still only relevant to the rules of the game. In Kant's terms our schemata only allow us to see 'phenomena' not 'things in themselves'. When they work as an overall whole and are shared by a society or group, we have a 'climate of opinion' or 'myth'.[12]

In short, contrary to 19th century thought, it is impossible to see 'brute facts' or 'things, as in themselves they really are'. Contrary to what Marx, Gropius and Banham wished, it is impossible to get rid of all preconceptions. All we can do is substitute one pre-concept for another and bring it closer to a percept. This has very important implications as Karl Popper has pointed out. It simply means that we can never know with certainty 'absolute truth'. Not surprisingly the way science increases the scope of knowledge is through the same process of schema and correction, always testing a concept against a referent. The only time it comes in touch with the absolute is when it is proved definitely wrong; when an hypothesis is falsified. Otherwise, all the scientific laws and truths which we hold to be true are only unfalsified myths (which may however be in the privileged position of high corroboration). This view of knowledge coupled with Figure 2 helps to explain why the movement from Newtonian schema to Einsteinian was such a traumatic affair: the determinists of the 19th century thought they were in touch with '*das Absolut*'.

CONTEXT AND METAPHOR

There are two primary ways to cut through the environment of all sign behaviour. For instance fashion, language, food and architecture all convey meaning in two similar ways: either through opposition or association. This basic division receives a new terminology from each semiologist,[13] because their purposes differ: here they will be called context and metaphor.

It is evident, as a result of such things as Morse Code and the computer, that a sign may gain meaning just from its opposition or contrast to another. In the simple case of the computer or code it may be the opposition between 'off-on' or 'dot-dash'; in the more complex case of the traffic light each sign gains its meaning by opposition to the other two. In a natural language each word gains its sense by contrast with all the others and thus it is capable of much subtler shades of meaning than the traffic light. Still one could build up a respectable discourse with only two relations, as critics have found. The perennial question of whether a good, bad symphony is better or worse than a bad, good symphony is not as it appears an idle pastime—simply because one adjective acts as the classifier *while* the other acts as the modifier and vice versa.

A similar analysis of architectural forms through simple opposition has been occurring over the last century. For instance Wölfflin has analysed the opposition between Renaissance and Baroque in terms of five polar concepts, whereas Panofsky has analysed Gothic architecture (both over time and within a building) through the contrast of horizontal and vertical emphasis.

Developing this very simple model, we can show that the amount of meaning conveyed by a message is proportional to the unexpectancy of its occurrence in a context. Or to put it differently, the more a message is expected the less its information: 'clichés, for example, are less illuminating than great poems'. If the expectancy of everyone is slightly different, because of their differing memories, then it is natural that their experience of meaning will differ. Thus 'one man's meat is another man's poison' gains support from information theory.

We can see this if we watch our reaction to the generation of a quasi-ridiculous sentence. Start with the word 'Twiggy'. We expect something like a verb to follow: 'is'. Then the words 'as busty as' are not unexpected, all for reasons of sound, sense and syntax. We now have the highly probable beginning 'Twiggy is as busty as . . .' which because of its probability and triteness amounts to something of a boring cliché. Suppose we add the word 'Billy'. This is rather a surprise in terms of sense, but not in terms of grammar because we expect a noun and a rhyming noun at that. Then if we finish 'Twiggy is as busty as Billy is lusty', we're rather shocked because the comparison is odd. If we now substitute 'spring' for 'lusty' and 'crashing' for 'Billy', we have increased the information almost to the point of incomprehension. In an analogous way we can plot the surprise or meaning of a sign in any generative context which has a certain probability: a street sequence for example.

Thus:

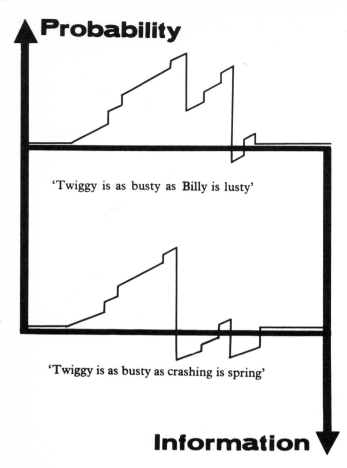

Probability

'Twiggy is as busty as **Billy** is lusty'

'Twiggy is as busty as crashing is spring'

Information ▼

6
Degree of Surprise.

The two obvious things to be noted about the way information is conveyed in such a sequence are that the amount of supporting cues or redundancy is high, so that we can miss a word and still understand the sense, and that information, or great poetry, always hovers on the edge of total incomprehensibility. For instance, some people might have mapped the second example as conveying no information at all, because they would fail to see how Twiggy could be as busty as a crashing spring (what kind of 'spring'?). Thus, on the paradoxical question of value, what information theory can do very well is make the paradox clear. Cocteau caught this conundrum when he said 'Tact is knowing how far too far you can go'.

The other dimension of meaning is conveyed through associations, metaphors or the whole treasure of past memory. This is often built up socially, when a series of words conveys the same connotations in a language. But it also occurs individually through some experience of relating one sign to another: either because of a common quality, or because they both occurred in the same context (which would *be* the common quality, *pace* behaviourists). Thus an individual might associate blue with the sound of a trumpet either because he heard a trumpet playing the blues in an all blue context (the expressionist ideal), or because they both have a common synaesthetic centre; they both cluster around further metaphors of harshness, sadness and depth. The behaviourist Charles Osgood (*Measurement of Meaning*) has thus postulated a 'semantic space' for every individual which is made up by the way metaphors relate one to another. Thus he asks a Republican voter to plot his reactions on one issue (for instance Dwight Eisenhower) against fifty-three key oppositions (good-bad, active-passive, etc.). These oppositions are further differentiated into seven parts so that one can answer 'very good, moderately good . . . very bad'. In this very rough way Osgood can measure one reaction to various issues and plot a sort of frozen map of one's current attitudes and the relation between them. He does not claim that we carry around such a semantic iceberg in our head, since our brain resembles that as much as a filing cabinet. But he does claim, with some legitimacy, that *connotative* meaning is relational.

To imagine what this might mean for architectural criticism, I have plotted a semantic space for certain architects, not because my judgement is important but because a critical consensus is formed through such overlapping of many semantic spaces and mine was the only one available at the moment. The immediate objections to the following diagram are obvious (Fig. 7). Why just the three traditional polar terms (form, function and technic)? We should know there are simply no rules or standards for good architecture, and all I have

7
Semantic Space of Current Architects.

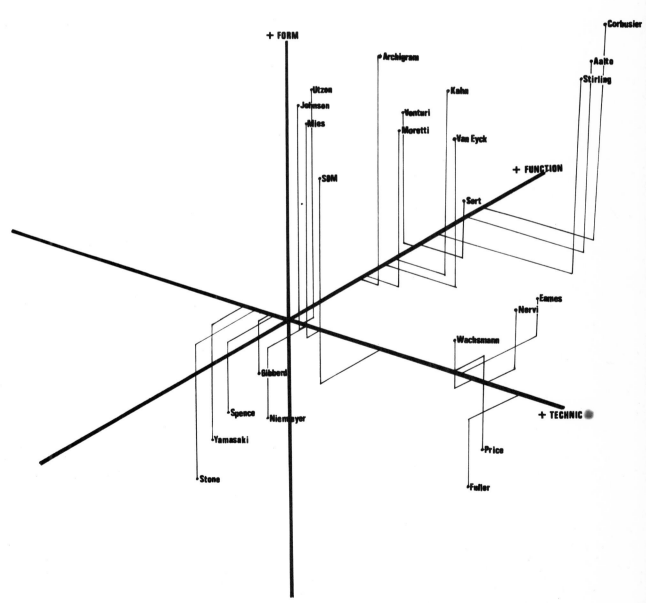

done is frozen my own prejudice and, as if this were not bad enough, had the naivety to make it clear. But this reaction rests on a mistake. If the *past* meaning of a word or sign is determined by all the matrices of which it is a part, and if these matrices must have fixed rules with flexible strategies, then the rules can be translated into a physical model and re-presented. It does not claim to show the present, immediate experience of meanings or those of the future. Furthermore, the model could represent a much larger, more important set, and the main reason I have settled on these three is that they are rather inclusive and can be shown in three-dimensions (one could construct a hyperspace).

MULTIVALENCE AND UNIVALENCE

The first point to be noted about Figure 7 is, as the activist would be quick to object, that it is static and dissociated. But this is the positive point: it is a univalent diagram where the whole (architect) has been analysed into a few isolated parts so that each one may be scrutinized. Whereas the experience of architecture is an indissolubly fused whole, the analysis is a fragmented, controlled separation. To insist on multivalence at the expense of univalence is to insist on enjoyment at the expense of science. A completely false alternative, since one can have both.

To concentrate first on the univalence of the diagram, one can see how architects tend to cluster around similar areas, which to my mind constitute groups or traditions. Secondly, my preference for the technical school is shown by comparing it with my distaste for the formalists. The latter is shown on the negative side of all three poles, not because it does not make positive efforts, but because in my judgement they fail (this *is* a diagram of pre-judice). Lastly, Corbusier, Aalto and Archigram are far out on the positive side and thus explicitly show my preference. But this is not all. What it also indicates is that my experience of the latter inextricably links matrices which are normally dissociated. Actually it does not indicate, but implies this.

When one sees an architecture which has been created with equal concern for form, function and technic, this ambiguity or tension creates a multivalent experience where one oscillates from meaning to meaning always finding further justification and depth. One cannot separate the method from the purpose because they have grown together and become linked through a process of continual feedback. And these multivalent links set up an analogous condition where one part modifies another in a continuous series of cyclical references. As Coleridge and I. A. Richards have shown in the analysis of a few lines from Shakespeare,[14] this imaginative fusion can be tested by showing the mutual modification of links. But the same could be done for any sign system from Hamlet to French pastry. In every case, if the object has been created through an imaginative linkage of matrices (or bisociation in Koestler's terms), then it will be experienced as a multivalent whole. If, on the other hand, the object is the summation of past forms which remain independent, and where they are joined the linkage is weak, then it is experienced as univalent. This distinction between multivalence and univalence, or imagination and fancy, is one of the oldest in criticism and probably enters any critic's language in synonymous terms. For it is an obvious division of experience at two ends of a continuous spectrum, the total involvement of all one's faculties and the careful control of just one. Multivalence is of the greatest value in imaginative works and hence architecture, and univalence is of equal value in science. No doubt there are relevant qualifications to this, but in the main I think it is true.

What is disputable is the method of achieving it. The avant-garde insists on the destruction of all past preconceptions and matrices. But certain of them would go further. Having become committed to the quicker cycles of fashion and technology (in the name of 'reality') they would try to escape preconceptions altogether and approach random change and programmed noise as a positive limit. Often democracy, freedom and individuality are equated with this state of total mixed-upness. Yet this is the extreme of univalence, and if one does

BROADBENT: There seems to be a slight misunderstanding here of Osgood's methods and intentions. He was very careful, in working out his 'concept scales' to choose adjectives which, at first sight, had no direct relevance to the concepts being plotted. Thus he would not plot buildings, say, against a scale of plain/decorated, which describes specific, physical characteristics, but he might use friendly/unfriendly, which can only be applied to buildings metaphorically. In fact buildings, architects, even briefing information on activities, can be plotted very successfully within Osgood's three dimensions of evaluation, potency and activity with much less foregone conclusions than Jencks's form, function and technic would impose. (See Osgood et al. The Measurement of Meaning.)

JENCKS: But I have just mentioned 'a much larger more important set . . . a hyperspace', if one wants to plot more relevant meanings. The question of whether the three dimensions I have used are the right ones, whether they are general and inclusive enough, is so large that it cannot be fully answered in the margin. But a convincing answer would show the *locus classicus* of *past* architecture and how it could be reduced to the three poles I propose and not to those of Broadbent; he would be 'measuring' people's reactions not the architect's general intentions.

value creation or the 'entirely radical' (of which multivalence is an index), then one sees it as an entirely relative concept dependent on the past as well as its destruction. For the only way one can create a new matrix is by active use of those past codes, schemata, conventions, habits, skills, traditions, associations, cliches, and stock responses (even rules) in the memory. To jettison any one of these decreases creation and freedom.

[1] *Course in General Linguistics*, Saussure, McGraw-Hill, 1966, pp. 67–9.
[2] *Elements of Semiology*, Roland Barthes, Cape, 1967, p. 41.
[3] *The humanist vs. the utilitarian ideal*, Ken Frampton, *AD*, March 1968.
[4] *Theory and Design*, p. 326, *The New Brutalism*, p. 68.
[5] *Structural Anthropology*, C. Lévi-Strauss, Basic Books, 1963, Chapter IX.
[6] See for instance *What is Language?* R. M. W. Dixon, Longmans, 1965, p. 170.
[7] One point on which architectural theorists have some sort of consensus from Vitruvius to Norberg-Schulz. See for instance the latter's *Intentions in Architecture*, Allen & Unwin, 1964.
[8] See below under 'schemata', or *History as Myth*, printed here.
[9] *Psycholinguistics*, Osgood and Sebeok, Indiana University Press, 1965, p. 301.
[10] *Language, Thought and Reality*, B. L. Whorf, M.I.T. Press, 1956.
[11] For this theory, the quotes and a similar analysis, see *The Act of Creation*, A. Koestler, Pan Books, 1966, pp. 520–48, p. 624.
[12] See *History as Myth*.
[13] For context other semiologists use syntagm, metonymie, chain, relations, contiguities, contrasts, opposition; for metaphor they use association, connotation, correlation, similarities, paradigmatic or systemic plane.
[14] *Coleridge on Imagination*, I. A. Richards, Routledge, 1934.

Urbanism & Semiology

Françoise Choay

Contemporary man entertains with all of his products a reflexive sort of relationship: language progressively draws a screen between them and himself. Thus literature becomes a reflection upon literature, painting upon painting and as a matter of fact, pop art (even happenings or minimal art) exists only with reference to a reflexive, previous and original stage. The symbol of this situation can be found in the ubiquitous presence (in all fields of present human activities) of communication and information theory; and the same reflexive background exists also in city planning: 'new towns', 'new cities', 'villes nouvelles' appear to us as essentially questionable. And this reflection, this questioning of city planning represents a mutation compared to the situation when cities were derived from rules and principles which (explicit or not) were taken for granted. But in the field of city planning we are confronted with a paradoxical state of things: the reflexive approach is not usually understood as such. Instinctively the study of urbanism, whether it leads to a nostalgic kind of answer or a futurist, anti-aesthetic one, tends to present itself as spontaneous. It tends to ignore this reflexive 'detour'. Thus Dr Banham and Cedric Price and other proponents of a container paradise are just as naïve as were the leaders of the Bauhaus. Both of their situations may be explained in psychoanalytic terms by the concept of repression. For actually, since the beginning of the industrial revolution, we have definitely become the sons of what we still very improperly call the city, and, at the same time, we have been in various ways unconsciously doing our best to disguise its enormity and its powerful grip on us.

It is a necessity for our present architect-planners to free themselves from this repression and accede to their own hidden unconscious: by no means a simple task. One can imagine several ways of getting to it. One would be to analyse the urban scene with the help of present epistemological tools. This is the method which I will follow here. But I would like to stress that the structuralist method which I will employ is used simply as a tool and without any of the metaphysical implications which may have become attached to it. My problem in this article will be to examine whether the urban environment can be considered, as have other human products, as a semiological system.[1] In other words, whether we can study the urban scene with a method derived from general linguistics and consider it as a non-verbal system of meaningful elements, the structure of which in a given society is linked to that of the other cultural systems. I shall conclude with several questions and tentative answers which can be drawn from such an approach.

I. PURE SYSTEMS

Before we come to the problem of the city or urban environment, we must on a more general basis show that some built-up agglomerations are relevant material for semiological analysis; that the crude materiality of their elements and their practical destination do not make them unfit for welcoming systems of meaning, unfit for elaborate symbolic expression.

Evidence of this has been given by Claude Lévi-Strauss in some memorable pages devoted to the 'villages' of a few South American a-historical societies.[2] I shall briefly remind the reader of his example of the Bororo village. This settlement is composed of a number of cabins laid out in groups of three, so as to form a circle around a vacant space the centre of which is occupied by a bigger cabin called the men's house. Two imaginary axes N–S and E–W divide the central circular surface into twice two halves, each of which is given a special name. The various elements of the village (cabins, house and the parts of the central space) together form a system: each of which, while lacking individual autonomy, still becomes meaningful precisely because of its mutual connections. These connections (or relationships) are determined by a series of rules which refer to and involve all the aspects of the Bororo life, from cosmology and religious rituals to social obligations, work organisation, systems of kinship and rules of marriage. Among the Bororo, the position of my cabin in the village circle determines once and for all the nature of my economic activity,

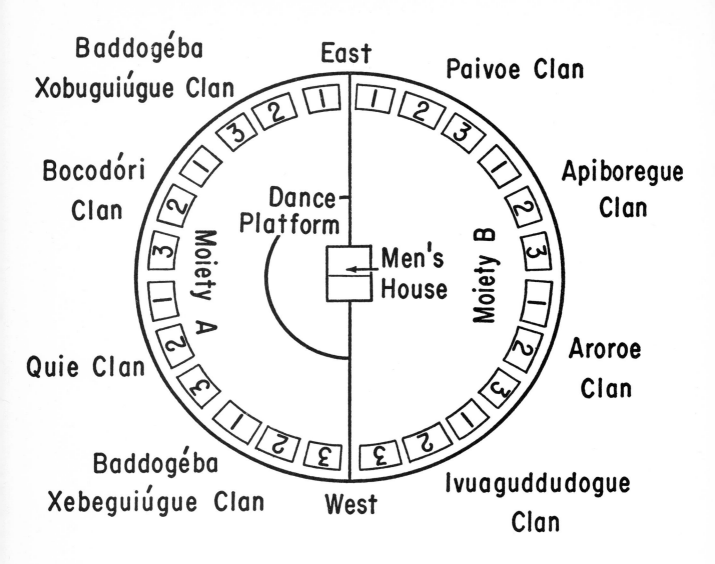

Baddogéba Xobuguiúgue Clan

East

Paivoe Clan

Bocodóri Clan

Apiboregue Clan

Dance-Platform

Men's House

Moiety A

Moiety B

Quie Clan

Aroroe Clan

Baddogéba Xebeguiúgue Clan

West

Ivuaguddudogue Clan

Plan of a Bororo village.

my participation in religious ceremonies and my possible choice of a mate. Moreover, the 'structure of the village not only permits the subtle play of institutions, it also renews and assures the intercourse between man and the universe, between society and the supernatural and between the living and the dead'.[3] In a word, it involves and determines the totality of social behaviour; the constructed system is saturated with meanings.

The proof of this is given in a negative way by the example of what the Salesian missionaries do to the Bororo when they wish to convert them to Christianity. They do nothing more than lay out the round village in a rectilinear plan. C. Lévi-Strauss' analysis is clear: 'Disoriented from their contact with the cardinal points, stripped of their plan which furnished an argument for understanding, the natives rapidly loose the sense of their traditions as if their social and religious systems had become too complicated to accept the scheme, which had been rendered obvious by the plan of their village, the outlines of which the daily gestures perpetually refreshed'.[4]

Thus, full volumes and empty volumes (emptiness as we conceive it does not exist, it is significant in itself and by its relatedness) combine in a way quite fascinating for us, citizens of industrialized countries, because they give roots to the inhabitants. It doesn't matter that the Bororo village is precarious and demolished every three years (after the surrounding land is exhausted) and rebuilt further in the forest on virgin ground; its slight structure succeeds in linking the inhabitants to the ground in a way we have never been able to achieve, in spite of our concrete monoliths which sink much deeper physical roots in the earth. A built-up system such as the Bororo's thus appears to us as both homologous and antithetic to the system of writing: the latter actually tends to cut the individual's roots and liberates him from the grip of his physical surroundings.

Convincing as this may sound, the question remains as to whether we can transfer such an analysis to the case of societies which are involved in the historical process. I shall now proceed to analyse a few examples of so-called 'cities' which actually, in spite of their common denomination, belong to quite different historical contexts.

The first example is the Greek City at the end of the 6th century B.C.,[5] the moment when the *agora* appears and the individual hearth disappears ('the ancient incommunicability of the hearth rooted in a definite place in the ground'). The *agora* holding the *Hestia Koine* is the sanctified place, the centre, the major element which gives meaning and in connection to which a new type of organization is given to the minor elements, the houses (which are from then on identical and loaded with an identical semantic meaning). This structure of the city system is the same as that of the political system: i.e. *isonomia* (the citizens' juridico-political egality) and is related to and conditions its functioning. J. P. Vernant remarks: 'the organization by the city of a homogenous political space, the centre of which alone owns a privileged value because in their connection to it all the various positions occupied by the *citizens*, appear systematic and reversible'. He also describes the *Hestia Koine* as the new hearth which 'from then on will express the centre as the common denominator of all the houses constituting the *polis*'.[6]

But space organization does not refer to political custom alone. Not only is it connected with religious ritual but it also refers to a pattern of knowledge, to a mathematical experience which has then elaborated the concepts of egality, symmetry, reversibility and to a cosmology derived from Ionian philosophies. 'In spite of their seeming disorder, the earth, the seas and the river are in their figuration on the map, organized in a pattern following strict rules of correspondence and symmetry',[7] writes Vernant. And he also points out that the homology of these various structures is confirmed by the use, 'both in the physical and political thought, of the same vocabulary, the same conceptual tools'.[8]

A second example can be borrowed from the mediaeval city which was the framework of a cruder social and political organization. This type of agglomeration can be characterized by the double connection binding the fundamental elements with one another, and with the semantically weighted elements of the church, castle and protecting walls. As far as the first type of connection is concerned, the basic (though minor) elements, i.e. the individual houses, are differentiated from one another especially by their fronts with their various roofs, gables and window patterns; their heterogeneity displays itself along the street in a relationship of proximity that will here be called syntagmatic.[9]

This analysis is of course nothing but a gross schema which does not take into consideration the various types of mediaeval cities which have appeared in time and space; furthermore, the mediaeval city has yet to be studied from a semiological viewpoint.[10] Nevertheless it is clear that the mediaeval, urban system gave its framework to daily life both by crystallizing the forms of church and feudality and by organizing in a syntagmatic structure the emotional relationship of proximity which is still alive today in so many Western villages.

In spite of their striking differences, one still has to note a number of *traits* which these two types of historical agglomerations and the Bororo village have in common.

In spite of the fact that one example is a-historical and the other two are

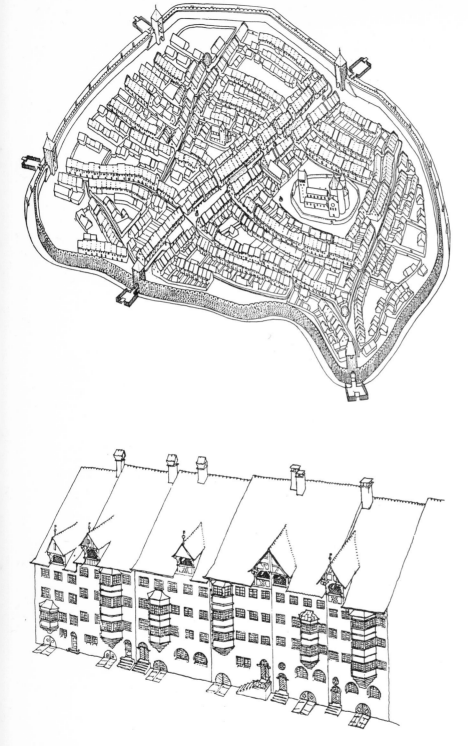

Freiburg in 1200.

Rottweiler Bürgerhäuser.

historical, they can all be considered as closed systems, showing either no transformation, or a slow one.

These built-up systems are as such specific and pure, but they interfere and are interfered with, condition and are conditioned by, an important number of other systems. Thus they refer to global behaviour including mental and spiritual responses, and therefore will here be called hypersignificant.

BROADBENT: Certainly Archytas used the word *topos* to describe the place in which matter can be located, but Democritus was much concerned with the void, he used the word *kenon* 'the empty' – as a kind of infinite space in which his atoms existed. He was concerned, too, with the *relationships* in space between his atoms, and once one considers space as a matter of such relationships, it comes very close to the space of modern physics. Not only that, but it also lends itself, by analogy, to analysis in linguistic terms, using systematic or syntagamatic *relationships*.

JENCKS: I find this argument extraordinarily relevant, particularly because it is not made by other critics who tend to fault architecture for being a poor sort of technology or fashion (just as one could criticise a cow for being a poor sort of horse). This basic confusion has no doubt served a polemical purpose as, for instance, society is continually criticised by Marxists for not progressing as fast and as purposefully as technology. My only difference with Françoise Choay's thesis and conclusion is that she also tends to favour 'fast evolving' speeds over slow ones – as if one had to choose and as if one could not combine the advantages from both 'hot and cold societies' as Lévi-Strauss insists.

FRAMPTON: Given the initial 'mythic' structure of cities the exclusion or inclusion of past syntagmatic forms must surely depend upon their initial essence. Thus the street structure of a linear Zahringer town such as Berne has been successfully incorporated as a living infrastructure in the modern development of the city, whereas the Parisian barrières were totally devalued by Hausmannisation.

FRAMPTON: It is true of course that these supplementary systems now predominate over the built forms of Western urbanism. Whether they are adequate to fulfill the symbolic role of providing synthetic 'schema' by which to perceive complex wholes acausally integrated is totally another matter. In this sense, Lynch's thesis verges on the picturesque.

In such built-up systems any empty space is nonetheless meaningful. Evidence of this is given by the Greek language, which has no word corresponding to our abstract concept of space. There exists only the word place, *topos*, which means, as will become clearer, that only 'places' can provide pure semiological systems.

2. MIXED SYSTEMS

The above examples served two purposes: first they were meant to illustrate the concept of semiology as applied to built-up agglomerations and secondly to demonstrate the richness and abundance of meanings which can become embedded in built-up areas—their social power, the way they help the individual to integrate himself in a society the structures of which are redrawn or reactivated in space. Under such conditions the functioning of the built-up systems could almost be compared to a kind of psychodrama.

Now let us turn to examples closer in relevance to our own situation and study the fast evolving, open systems which appear to be the cities of 'modern times'. We immediately notice that, contrary to the former, there is not much to be deciphered in the new urban developments, that they are hyposignificant and that they have lost their former purity.

The acceleration of history reveals the vice inherent in all built-up systems: a permanence and a rigidity which make it impossible for them to continually transform themselves according to the rhythm set by the less 'rooted' systems such as language, technology, clothing, or painting. Unable to change at the same pace or with the same subtlety as the other social structures, the urban system is threatened in its very existence (i.e. its openness to meaning) and hence partly doomed to continual anachronism.

Against this permanent threat, the modern city's own means allow it but one meagre defence: partial restructuring, or in other words the inclusion of worn-out syntagms in the new, up-to-the-minute syntagms. Concerning such a process, the architectural history of Paris is relevant. For instance, the Portes St Denis and St Martin have lost their former meaning as gateways to Paris and have become landmarks related to the festive atmosphere of their districts. The Parc Monceau rotunda, once a *barrière* for the payment of taxes on imported goods, has lost its economic meaning and become the gate to the Haussmann-designed park and has hence become essentially connected with leisure. In the same manner, a sequence of small, varied houses may have their street level unified by exterior painting and inside renovation, in order to mirror the transformations of capitalism and the exigencies of the new, giant corporations. For the same reason also, in the 19th century the fortifications of Paris were transformed into boulevards, and thus a system of defense became a traffic system. Often this restructuring has been made unconsciously (as it is in language) but the opportunity remains for planners to consciously envisage such a process.

However, in the best of cases, the use of such a method is restricted mostly to ancient and anachronistic parts of the urban fabric. Actually the fundamental weapon that modern society has at its disposal against the obsolescence threatening its cities belongs to other 'unrooted' symbolic systems, such as traffic codes and graphic signs, which began to invade the Western cities at certain stages of their development[11]: we shall call them systems of supplementation. To some present theorists like Kevin Lynch they appear as the means of giving the city a new legibility. But the fact that the legibility of our present urban agglomerations is mostly due to the efficiency of such graphic systems (whether designed or not) must not hide the bare, inescapable fact that from now on the built-up systems in Western society have lost their autonomy: if left to themselves and their specific elements, they do not carry symbolic weight any more.

But here we are driven in a circle: the more the built-up system makes demands upon supplementary systems, the more it proves itself obsolete and its former task of information is carried via printing and telecommunications, through other systems of information, the development of which appears at the same time as cause and result of the obsolescence of the built-up system. It is precisely

at the time when this system ceases to refer to the whole range of social behaviour that the transition from place to space occurs.

The first stage of this may be found in the Baroque city. Here the spatial organization is contaminated by pictorial space which corresponds to an analysis of sight. In the process of acquiring this aesthetic quality and becoming a show, the city also acquires a play dimension, and is lived at a distance which is the exact opposite of the intimate and constraining relationship characterizing the pure systems.

Of course the Baroque space was only a first step towards the much less constraining and more abstract space of present Western agglomerations. But before discussing the latter, we must note that with the Baroque city sociological ambiguity of meaning was born. More exactly, it could be said that the Baroque city was lived as a show by only a fraction of its inhabitants. The others, the majority, clung to an archaic state of the system, that is the ancient framework which was still standing. Here again we find ourselves in a circle: less advanced people cling to an archaic built-up system but the archaic system favours archaic behaviour.

Ever since the Baroque time the city has displayed this ambiguity of meaning. I called it sociological because it appears that whether or not people use the systems of supplementation, or cling to the built-up systems as a set of global references depends on their social class and sociological determinants. Thus the archaic behaviour is mostly adopted by the upper and lower classes either through nostalgia or because of an economically engendered inability to restructure their patterns of behaviour. Regarding another symbolic system in our society, the system of scientific thought, the French philosopher Gaston Bachelard was struck by the variety of levels at which science could be approached at one and the same time by the members of the same society; he also noticed that an individual referred to different levels according to his particular scientific interest. To describe this situation, he coined the expression *niveaux épistemologiques*.[12] To describe the homologous situation which has arisen in the field of urban space, I will use a corresponding concept *niveau politologique*: 'politological level'.

The existence of these various semantic levels among various classes of a population is fundamental for the understanding and tackling of urban planning (showing that as far as urban semiology is concerned, we cannot borrow the concept of synchrony from general linguistics since the physical synchrony actually displays a semantic diachrony). Presently, we get clear evidence of these various levels in two crucial situations—situations which may be clarified by the concept of politological levels. First is the case of urban renewal when it deals with minorities (economic or ethnological) still living in syntagmatic systems, the pattern of which is given by the village. In a recent and remarkable study of the renewal of the thirteenth *arrondissement* of Paris,[13] the investigators notice that the word 'village' came back, like a litany, again and again, in the declarations of the 'renewed' population when they were questioned about their arrondissement before renewal. For the same reasons, Herbert Gans called his book on American slums 'The Urban Villagers'. And this situation was also foreseen by Spengler when he remarked: 'each large city has conserved corners where there are living, in the lanes like the country, the fragments of a humanity almost rural which is maintained on that side of the street by an intercourse which is almost rustic'.[14] In every western town we could find such villages which, in Paris, are called rue Harvey, rue Clisson, L'Impasse de L'Avenir.

The second situation occurs when underdeveloped countries become industrialized. We are then dealing with cultures or micro-cultures which possess their own built-up systems linked to the totality of their cultural structures and customs. Town planning, in the Western manner, deprives these populations of their behavioural framework, it leaves them at a loss. Their only way of coping with such a situation is to master the Western symbolic systems, insert themselves in its cultural structures, learn to use its abstract, supplementary systems of information and communication and to disengage themselves from place and its non-verbal spell—which is by no means an easy task. It is equally hard for the Western planner who not only has to confront a pre-industrial system, but one belonging to an alien culture—and thus has to learn to decipher it like a foreign language. This is the case with some French sociologists and planners who are at present studying the urban communities of Magreb. Such Moroccan cities cannot 'be understood except as a social framework of egocentric space (there are no plazas, no avenues, in a word, no projective space) itself linked to a circular structure of time. . . . In spite of apparent similarity, this example has no connection with the mediaeval syntagm. There are analogies in the town plans, although the mosque or the castle (Kasba) bear a smaller semantic load. But the fundamental difference consists in the lack of differences among the Moroccan façades. A façade, once built, will never be altered or repaired even if it falls to pieces. Poor and rich have the same façades and doors, so that a foreigner has no means of identifying the district where he strolls (he would have to be able to decipher the symbolic positions of the women standing on the thresholds of the houses). This visual homogeneity corresponds to the fact that in Arab society there is no pattern of authority comparable to the one working in our societies or in the WASP societies . . . There is nothing but "chains" of influence connected with polyfunctional individuals whose powers and abilities are numerous and not clearly defined. The city . . . protects itself from country people by its labyrinth: no axis, no monuments; . . . meaning here accompanies motional habits'.[15]

FRAMPTON: The phenomenon of the ▶ 'show' Baroque City cited by Choay and of these cultural differences of economic and ethnic origin, tend to suggest once again that present architectural responsibility must turn upon a conscious cultural determination of the building task.

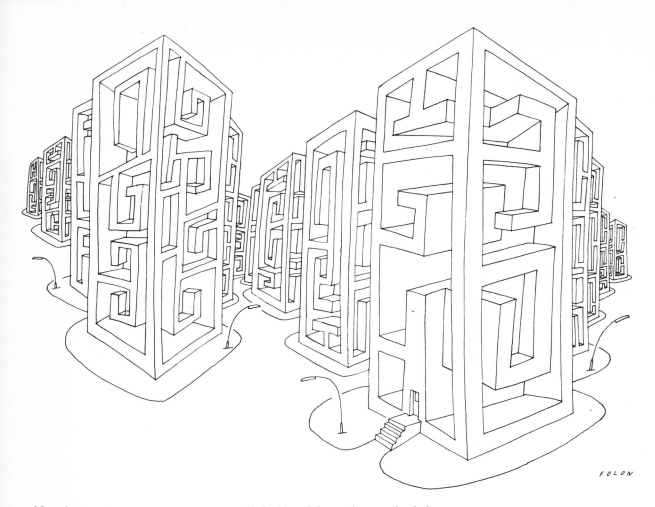

FOLON

Now let us return to our present so-called cities. I have characterized them by a series of concepts such as hyposignificant and semantic reduction which may lead to some misunderstanding. But by these words I do not intend any judgement of value. They only seemed to describe an historical situation. It must be understood that they have been written without the slightest touch of nostalgia. Hyposignificant does not mean without signification, but only that the built-up system no longer refers to the totality of cultural behaviour. Actually it seems to me that in freeing ourselves from the former spatial framework, we have gained mobility, subtlety and richness for our symbolical devices—that is we have increased our liberty and possibility of choices. Because the appeals of written material or images do not exert in matters of behaviour (beliefs, habits, etc.) the same kind of pressure as spatial structures—the determinism of which insect societies give us an extreme example.

More precisely, hyposignificant means that the built-up system has retained a precise and limited meaning; since the industrial revolution it has been exclusively linked with the new type of production, both under its technological and economic aspects. Thus in the course of the 19th century, the new type of production determined the split of industrial towns into two parts, one pertaining to the economic function of production and the social class of producers, the other to the economic function of consumption and the social class of consumers. This was the new, exclusive, single meaning—the system of economic efficiency.

One cannot give enough emphasis to the semantic reduction implied: it was so drastic (even with respect to the forerunning Baroque city) that it must be considered as a mutation. This mutation has had a traumatic and frustrating

effect in two complementary ways. On the one hand, frustration was suppressed and concealed behind an imaginary construction, and '*imaginaire urbain*' which we can trace back to Rousseau.[16] From the end of the 18th century the *imaginaire urbain* gave birth to a new mythology in which the city played the part formerly played by nature. In pre-industrial times, the built-up agglomeration—hamlet, village, town—was experienced as the reassuring element where man discovers himself and builds himself in opposition to nature. Since the industrial revolution, the urban fabric itself, the big cities, conurbations, etc., have appeared to the collective consciousness as another nature, a mysterious wilderness, threatening man's existence. How else can we explain the violence of the new images and myths? According to the descriptions of Marx, the human world of artifacts has truly become a new nature; but the urban environment as artifact has lost its previous implicit (if not unconscious) intelligibility. We are here facing the fundamental contradiction of our modern cities—hence Nietzsche and Baudelaire (and so many others), hence the famous Spenglerian descriptions, hence the Corbusian metaphors ('the modern city is a flourishing cancer').

On the other hand, at a less emotional level, the proliferation of urban agglomerations expressing nothing but the elementary, single-meaning new order gave birth to a compensating phenomenon: an endless rationalization of urban space to which discursive analysis attributed a diversity of purposes and significations. Thus a commentary (i.e. *logos*) inserted itself between the urban agglomerations and its inhabitants, like a screen, creating between them an insurmountable distance. The semantic reduction finally meant an irreversible contamination of the built-up system by the verbal language, the *logos*, and the complete and definitive loss of its former purity. The very idea of a non-verbal

BROADBENT: But may it not be that ▶ many people find the city hostile *because* critics like Ruskin, Morris, Wright, Howard, Mumford and others have *told* them it is. A perception-based theory of meaning could certainly account for that – what they perceive of the city is a transaction between its physical 'reality' and these inherited opinions. And naturally, in the light of those opinions, the City seems hostile.

35

system (which the appearance of supplementary systems still permitted to subsist) was finally destroyed by this metalanguage. This inescapable verbal screen drawn between us and our present urban space explains the abstract quality of the latter much more than does the privilege given to sight, alleged by McLuhan.

I have shown elsewhere[17] that the rationalization, the process of theorizing about the urban system, developed from the very first along two lines of thought, following two basic 'models'. The 'culturalist' one, inspired by nostalgia, aims at recreating a syntagmatic system. The other, the 'progressivist' one, is actually less Utopian than it appears. Its aim is to promote a new building pattern; inside the framework of a neutral, meaningless space the elements of urban space will be classified and associated following functional similarities. I shall here call this structure paradigmatic or metaphoric.

This metaphoric approach has progressively substituted for the original bi-partite 19th century industrial town, a 'more rational' tripartite classification which tends to eliminate from the meaning of the space system social references, in favour of an operative analysis of the economic field. Social segregation ceases to be a principle of structuring; the opposition between living and working areas is transcended by a 'centre'. The three metaphoric poles of the new system, housing, industry, centre, are linked by a complex set of 'circuits' the meaning of which is efficiency. The urban system then becomes an operational space. The information given by this network of connections—its hidden spirit—is the transformation of nature, its metamorphosis in the course of a production process, the sequences of which are inscribed in the ground. In this way the progressivist system is even more monosemic[18] than the pseudo disorder of the 19th century. But such a monosemy is in harmony with our fast evolving world and a society geared to production and consumption. There is no point in criticising or even fighting this monosemy in the name of a so-called humanism. The times of polysemic, built-up systems, referring to an immediate 'total man' are gone for Western man. His world is and has been for some time *en miettes*, crumbled into pieces, and his fate may well be to face up to this situation. If he does not, he cannot expect any aid for his lost unity in the tendency of present built-up systems.

*   *   *

Now let me try to sum up what we have gained through the semiological approach. Undoubtedly the elimination of pseudo problems and a clear understanding of what is the real and limited task of present town-planning: we have thus arrived at a kind of rehabilitation of functionalism but on less naïve grounds, getting rid of the humanistic rationalizations. Besides we have been able to formulate the major problem of urbanization of underdeveloped countries in constructive terms which show the scale of the issues involved, the kind and amount of knowledge necessary for the creation of any solution—and the necessity of using special, transitional spatial systems.

But apart from consciousness, does the semiological approach lead anywhere else? Does it open any field of action or any prospects for the so-called 'post-industrial' times? Is the liberation from physical environment really acceptable? Isn't there, at the bottom of the human heart, an eternal, recurring longing for grounding, for roots, for the old and close involvement in space? If that is so, it seems that a clear understanding of the built-up agglomerations as a system of meaning may lead us to the construction of conscious new systems, dealing with new sets of meanings. The theory of games and models of simulation would then help us formulate what would eventually prove also a kind of game. But not a game in the sense of gratuitous aesthetics. A game in the sense that man *en miettes* might use the new framework, the new meaningful patterns, and mime a pretended, recovered unity.

◄ FRAMPTON: However paradigmatic or metaphoric, it can be argued that certain of the 'progressivist' urbanists (Tony Garnier and Le Corbusier) were well aware of the problem. Their frameworks may have been neutral but the intrinsic organisation of their propositions were hierarchical. Devoid of all authoritarian structure, Garnier's *Cité Industrielle* nonetheless has a 'house of assembly' in which the Saint-Simonian beliefs of society are embodied.

◄ FRAMPTON: This is exactly the predicament so precisely outlined both by Fromm (see Norberg-Schulz article) and by Hannah Arendt.

BAIRD: Françoise Choay's idea of applying semiological concepts to urbanism is an excellent one, and her application here seems to me widely illuminating. Still, I have to admit to a disappointment at the implacable determinism underlying her argument. It would seem on her view, that the progression from 'pure' to 'mixed' systems, the advent of hyposignificance and of semantic reduction, were all utterly inevitable, and allow therefore, of no regret whatsoever. If that really were true (and I don't think that it is), then a semiological approach really could lead nowhere other than to a 'heightened consciousness'. About the 'eternal, recurring longing', no
◄ initiative could realistically be undertaken.

This article has been rewritten by the author; the original from which this stems is in *L'Architecture d'aujourdhui*, June-July 1967.

[1] F. de Saussure, the founder of structural linguistics, coined the concept of 'semiology' (from the Greek semeion = sign): 'a science which studies the life of signs in the middle of social life'. For him *la langue* as a 'system of signs expressing ideas . . . and thus comparable to writing, to the deaf and dumb's alphabet, symbolical rites, forms of politeness . . . is nothing but the most important among these various systems'. But this 'particular system' is a kind of ideal-type, from the study of which research in other fields of symbolic activity may be stimulated and developed. Saussure foresaw that 'linguistics might become the general model of any semiology'. And such was, after him, the point of linguists like E. Benvéniste or R. Jakobson. Some non-verbal semiological systems have been studied in such a light by C. Lévi-Strauss and R. Barthes. In his *Elements of Semiology* the latter indicates that 'the aim of semiological research is to restore the functioning of systems of meaning, other than language.' (See F. de Saussure, *Cours de linguistique générale*, Payot, R. Jakobson, *Essais de linguistique générale*, Paris: Editions de Minuit, R. Barthes *Elements of Semiology* and *Writing Degree Zero*, London, Cape, 1967.

[2] *Tristes Tropiques*, Plon, pp. 223–256. *Anthropologie Structurale*, Plon, ch. VII & VIII. (Both available in English language editions.)

[3] *Tristes Tropiques*, p. 229.

[4] Ibid., p. 241.

[5] See R. Martin *L'Urbanisme dans la Grèce antique*, Picard, and *Recherches sur L'Agora grecque*. For the interpretation of archaeological evidence see J. P. Vernant *Les origines de la pensée grecque*, P.U.F. and *Mythes et pensée chez les Grecs*, Maspero, as well as P. Leveque et P. Vidal-Naquet *Clisthène l'Athénien*, Les Belles Lettres.

[6] P. Vernant, *Mythes et Pensée*, pp. 161–2.

[7] Ibid., p. 169.

[8] Ibid., p. 167.

[9] The word has been borrowed from the linguists who, following Saussure, have differentiated two fundamental kinds of relations between linguistic elements: i.e. spatial contiguity and similarity (which schematically correspond to two forms of mental activity conjunction and association). Syntagm corresponds to the relationship of contiguity, paradigm to the relationship of similarity. 'To implicitly speak of the selection of certain linguistic entities and their combination in linguistic units of a much greater complexity . . . the concurrence of simultaneous entities and the concatenation of successive entities are the two modes according to which we, speaking subjects, combine the linguistic constituents', says R. Jakobson in his *Essais*. From this double process, which one finds in all semiological systems, this author has taken (in borrowing from the field of rhetoric) the concepts of 'metaphore' and 'metonymie' which he uses to characterize the styles in the aesthetic systems (literature, music and painting). Regarding my own use of the word syntagmatic (I could have used metonymic) if 'placed in a syntagm, a term acquires its value only in opposition to preceeding or following terms, or both'.

[10] The first stage of such an approach has been given for the Gothic architectural system by E. Panofsky in his *Gothic Architecture and Scholasticism*, in which he brilliantly displays the homology between the two different structures: architecture and philosophical thought.

[11] First stages of this progress: the numbering of houses and the naming of streets with special signs.

[12] In *La formation de l'esprit scientifique* and also *La Philosophie du Non*, P.U.F.

[13] Henri Coing, *Rénovation urbaine et changement social*, Ed. Ouvrières, Paris, 1966. Compare with Alvin L. Schorr, *Slums and Social Insecurity*, U.S. Gov. Printing Office, 1963.

[14] *Le Destin de l'Occident*, vol. II, p. 91.

[15] Excerpts from an unpublished letter from the French sociologist J. F. Clément. For some interesting comments regarding the connections between space structures and cultural behaviour (language, work, family structure) in Moslem North African countries see also: P. Bourdieu *Le déracinement*, Paris: Ed. Minuit 1965 (dealing with Algerian southern villages).

[16] Rousseau was among the first writers to use the word urban in the sense of 'belonging to the town or city' in opposition to 'belonging to the country'. In his *Confessions*, in particular, he evokes the 'urban crowd' from which he escaped to a rustic retreat.

[17] F. Choay, *L'Urbanisme Utopies et Réalités*, Le Seuil, Paris 1966. Not only has the invasion of verbal languages in urban matters to be studied under its systematic, theoretical aspect, as I did in the latter book, but also an analysis remains to be made of the transformations which urban terms have undergone in the West since the 19th century. As far as Latin languages are concerned, we see the progressive obsolescence of concrete words coupled with the growth of a taxonomy full of neologisms (see CERDA, a fascinating book in this respect) and the whole development of an abstract vocabulary. Most striking, for instance, is the case of the French *espace-vert* (a legacy from the times of Napoleon, popularized by Corbusier and the CIAM), now the most common French word in daily vocabulary. It has taken the place of the former *jardin*. Its very composition *espace-vert*, shows the meaninglessness of the areas to which it is attached.

[18] With a single meaning (opposed to polysemic).

Structuralism & Semiology in Architecture

Gillo Dorfles

In recent years there has been a surprisingly rapid spread in the application of linguistic schemes derived from different structuralist schools, and from a certain point of view this is pure gain. The application of linguistics to literature was not only an advantage but a necessity: because of the relationship between the analytical instrument and the analysed medium. It is quite otherwise with the other artistic languages. I am convinced that we should regard linguistics as a branch of semiotics, and not semiology as a branch of linguistics, as certain French authors are inclined to do. The fundamental reason for this is that semiotics, the theory of signs, can be applied to any system of signs such as Morse Code or street signs no less than to artistic activity; but a strictly verbal semiology can only be applied to works which are expressed in the 'speech' of the verbal language. And we can define the 'speech' used in literature and poetry as 'poetics' in Jakobson's sense.[1] I am not here concerned with poetics or verbal linguistics but only with a tentative architectural semiotics; and for this, I must lay down certain premisses.

Already in an essay of mine published in 1959,[2] and in my book *Simbolo, Comunicazione, Consumo*,[3] I had suggested that even architecture could, with advantage, be considered as a *sign-system*: one of its tasks being to 'communicate a particular message, namely the architectural message'. In my book,[4] I maintained, among other things, that:

'The problems of architecture, if considered in the same way as the other arts, as a "language", are the basis for a whole new current of thought, which allows it to be treated in terms of information and communication theory; and that the meaning can be treated as a process which connects objects, events and beings with "signs", which evoke just these very objects, events and beings. The cognitive process lies in our ability to assign a meaning to the things around us, and this is possible because the "signs" are links between our own consciousness and the phenomenological world. So signs are the first and immediate tools of every communication. I am sure of one thing: architecture, like every other art, must be considered as an organic whole and, to a certain extent, institutionalized ensemble of signs, which can be partially identified with other linguistic structures'.

Some of these early observations of mine were taken up for study by architects at the Florence School (Gamberini, Koenig),[5] who put forward schemes. Gamberini's scheme tended to identify the *elements* of architecture with the words of the architectural language. He reached the paradoxical situation of admitting a relationship between architectural *signs* (such as diverse forms of construction) and their *designata*, which according to him should be the individuals (persons) using them. Koenig attempted to describe the language of architecture on the basis of Charles Morris's semiotics. Koenig emphasized the impact of the architectural *sign* on the inhabitant's behaviour, and concluded that architecture is made up of sign-vehicles which promote certain types of behaviour. Building a school for example, Koenig said the '*denotata*' of this sign-complex are the children studying there; and the significatum is the fact that the children go to school. The *denotata* of a house are the members of the family who live there, etc., etc.

Obviously, the imposition of such a behaviouristic scheme opens the door to rather confused interpretations, limited to situations liable to be extensively changed in the space of a few years with the changing of sign-interpretation. I wanted to mention these two examples in Italy of a semiological interpretation of architecture, but I cannot dwell on the many other attempts which have appeared in recent years, among which I should like to recall those of Norberg-Schulz,[6] Umberto Eco,[7] besides those of Max Bense,[8] Alsleben,[9] A. Moles,[10] and many others. Relinquishing the field of other scholars' researches, I should like to concentrate a little more deeply on my own vision of a Semiotics of Architecture. First, however, I must warn you that I shall always speak of 'language' in the broadest sense, as a means of communication as valid for the transmission of scientific as of artistic messages; whereas by the term 'tongue' I mean only that particular language based on speaking. I have no intention of ever reducing the languages of the other arts to the language of speech.

Moreover, I do *not* intend to avail myself of de Saussure's well-known distinction between *langue* and *parole*; I consider the two terms are usually convergent in architecture. One of the immediate purposes of architecture is to be *langue*, and the possible presence of elements belonging to *parole* does not deserve consideration in this context.

The reason why I find the division of *langue* and *parole* unsuitable in architecture is due to the fact that, unlike other arts, it is irrevocably geared to practical and utilitarian functions. These limit the possibilities of expression, or give it a direction which is communal and intended for public enjoyment rather than private. For this reason, so far as architecture is concerned, the distinction between *langue* and *parole* can in this case be surmounted.

Neither would I consider it an advantage if we could carry out for architecture and the other visual arts the same systematization of its semiotic material as applies to verbal language. The subdivision of the verbal language into its parts (already called Stoicheia by Aristotle), and phonemes, morphemes and syntagms, today cannot be duplicated in the visual arts. In other words, even if we can admit the presence of an architectural code in large part institutionalized, and able to communicate to its users in a sufficiently precise way, this code cannot be reduced to discrete units, identifiable with those of the common spoken language.

Besides it ought to be clear that I consider absurd the idea of the constant presence of a 'double articulation' in every sign system, as has been elsewhere pointed out.[11] Evidently one cannot talk of a division into phonemes and morphemes, even if one can, analogically or metaphorically, discuss 'architectural syntagms' as the conjunction and sum of various architectural 'signs' among themselves. Anyone is entitled to call a stairway leading to a *piazza*, or a lift leading to a roof-terrace, or the aluminium panel of a curtain wall, an architectural 'syntagm', but only in a metaphoric way. No-one is entitled to treat windows as 'syntagms' or bricks as 'phonemes'. I have already had to warn some Italian scholars on this point.[12]

I maintain on the contrary (and this point seems to me fundamental, though most recent researchers contradict it), that there is often if not always a '*quid-formale*'—which we could define as a 'gestalteme'—which communicates exclusively on a formal and configurational basis.

This is for reasons partly analogous to those which incline me to accept principles wholly opposed to those maintained by most recent linguists, about the conventionality of the connection between verbal sign and its referent. I do not need to remind you here of the importance of some illuminating intuitions of Giambattista Vico, taken up by Schelling and Cassirer, in order to explain the reasons for the meaning of some words (of some morphemes) and of some mythical elements strictly bound to linguistic and etymological factors. Indeed in many vocabularies the relation between the morphological and the phonetic element is just as important (and it is no mere convention) as is that between the 'meaning' of certain architectural forms and their primitive functions.

There exists a semantic element implied in the very phonetic structure of the word. (I shall go on affirming this principle even if most recent linguists contradict it or limit it to solely onomatopoeic expressions.)

Can we say as much for architecture? Can we, that is, allow that certain architectural signifiers, which do not necessarily have to correspond with precise institutionalized typologies, correspond to definite 'signifieds' and their associated functions? It is a question which is asked from time to time, and which recalls certain ancient theories aired by Wölfflin, by Schmarsow, by the Empathists, and by more recent theories of Schilder bound up with the body-image.

For my part, I do not doubt the existence of some *isomorphic analogies* between building or object form and bodily structure. We can thus visualize a neat connection between architectural or urbanistic signifier and its 'signified'. This

BROADBENT: Nevertheless, there are vast differences of expression in the work of different architects. This was certainly the case in the 19th Century, when an architect could choose a *style* – Greek, Gothic, Hindoo and so on, and having chosen, say, Greek Ionic as the most suitable *langue*, the *parole* of individual architects varies greatly (see my paper for comparison of Smirke and Schinkel). But it is true even of systems building today, from the same kit of parts as *langue*, the *parole* of two architects working on adjacent drawing boards can be remarkably different.

BAIRD: I cannot disagree more with Dorfles on this point. The distinction between *langue* and *parole* seems to me the most important part of Saussurean semiology – even for architecture. The question whether or not 'practical and utilitarian functions . . . limit the possibilities of expression' strikes me as a red herring. (See the discussion of utilitarianism and art-for-art's-sake in my own article in this collection.) Moreover, as an aspect of the collective/individual sense of *langue* and *parole*, the public/private distinction in architecture cannot very usefully be discussed in a semiological context, once those terms have been dismissed.

JENCKS: Fortunately one does not have to claim that 'bricks are phonemes' in order to claim that architectural meaning is partially conveyed through units analogous to phonemes and morphemes (see my discussion of the sign situation). Linguists no longer make the kind of mistake that Dorfles fears and there is no reason for him to curtail future development on the mistakes of the past. The point is that in any sign situation (such as architecture) there *has to be* a percept, a concept and a representation (this is the most fundamental truth of semiology), so naturally these can be broken down into their basic atomic units according to the context (as he argues later).

is so, whether one is invoking the ancient Vitruvian anthropomorphic concept, or referring to more recent assertions about the expressiveness of certain forms, which have been confirmed by the canons of *Gestalt* psychology (cf. Arnheim[13]).

That is to say, the architectural sign (the relation between signifier and signified) will most probably be of a symbolic, non-conceptual, non-rational order, even if the whole execution and operation of this art seems to presuppose reason and logic.

BAIRD: This dispute, in which Dorfles ▶ seems to feel obliged to take sides, is surely *resolved* in Jencks' discussion (in 'Semiology in Architecture') of intrinsic and extrinsic explanations of meaning.

Some examples given recently by Kenzo Tange[14] confirm the above:
'How the architectural and urban space . . . need a symbolic approach . . . in order to secure humanity, human meaning or human value in architecture. . . . In my work *Ise, Prototype of Japanese Architecture* I mentioned how Japanese people created a symbole: Ise-shrine. . . . The architecture is composed partly of column-beam structure, partly of wall-type structure. In this sense the extension of rafter Tigi and Katuogi have no effect on the structural strength of the building and the building would not incline if Munamochi-bashira (central posts at both sides) should be taken away. They are not ornamental but . . . essential elements of the building . . . they lost their functional significance but acquired a *symbolic value* . . .'

This demonstrates that an element without static and functional value can be visually necessary to achieve its symbolic duty even if one ignores its conceptual value.

This particular factor, which is trans-conceptual, and is normally ascribed (by Cassirer[15]) to the will or the feeling and not to the intellect, comes immediately into play in many cases of architectural semantics.

In architecture we are confronted with an expressive form whose initial purpose has been that of signifying something, and not just with a simple functional commodity. It is obvious that the first savages building their dwellings in caves or on piles probably had no intention of expressing anything. But as soon as it was possible for them to construct not only for reasons of protection and defence, their tendency was certainly to turn the forms used for shelter into forms expressing something.

BROADBENT: Weren't they expressing ▶ 'protection' from the hostile environment? And isn't that what all building is still about, bearing in mind hostility may be a function of wild animals, enemies, climate – or the visual disorder around us.

It is at this point that architectural semiotics begins. Why did the Greek temple, the minaret, the pyramid, the *nurago* of Sardinia and the dolmen have just those forms? These well-known architectural forms announce firstly their symbolic sacral sexual function. In the course of centuries, architecture has perpetuated the existence of symbolic forms. Among all those made by man these have been the ones which could best rank as potent, expressive signs. The system of signs in architecture is always being renewed, but is also always being repeated.

Another type of distinction seems at this point necessary. One must distinguish within architectural semiology that which has a *semantic intention* and that which does not; or it may be accidentally and without genuine intentionality and consciousness on the part of the architect. The importance of this distinction gives noticeable results even to the aims of a successive interpretation of individual architectural monuments.

Let us see how this can be verified. We know that in the pre-romanesque basilica, many of the structural elements refer directly to sacramental motifs.[16] Among these, the stones of the church are identified with the faithful 'cemented together with the mortar of charity'; the columns represent the Apostles; the sacristy represents the Virgin's womb where Christ donned human flesh as the priest dons sacramental vestments (*Sacrarium in quo sacerdos vestes induit, uterum sacratissimae Mariae significat in quo Christus se veste carnis induit*); and we even know that the inclined axes of certain mediaeval churches have been explained by the inclination of the head of the crucified Christ. Such examples can be multiplied and applied to many religious constructions at all times. Still keeping to Christian symbolism, we can recall certain architectural reflections of well-known numerical symbolisms: the three doors in the façade and the three-sided apse invoke the Trinity. Octagonal baptisteries recall the figure 8, the

*Gubbio. Recent marketplace in the fore-
ground, Palazzo Communale in the mid-
ground and Cathedral and Etruscan wall in
the background.*

number of birth and increase; twelve columns recall the twelve Apostles and so on.

Now in this case the architect builds on a basis of institutionalized and pre-established meanings based on a precise iconological code so that the building has precise referents for most, if not all, of its parts.

Do we in this case speak of 'double articulation'? Or do we say that besides having the normal functional meaning (columns carrying, doors opening, etc.) these elements have another, transferred, allegorical and metaphorical one? We can accept this, and even invoke a 'second articulation', provided we do not reduce this double articulation to the verbal one of spoken language, as Barthes and other French semiologists have done.

In the other case, the building and its parts will only occasionally be semantic, and will not correspond to the precise intentions of the builder.

Is the first type of semanticity still possible? Almost all the attempts in our own day to subject architecture to the first type of semanticity have proved spurious and insincere. It is thoroughly inartistic to incorporate into buildings sacral and religious and initiatory components which are no longer valid, and numerical relationships which have lost their magic and their mystery.

As regards the second type of semanticity, we can divide it into two sub-orders: the one based on the 'distributive character' of a building, and the other on its typological peculiarities. We can still take account of them, even if they seem to be condemned in present-day architectural teaching.

We must distinguish between the presence of a symbolic-iconological aspect, which was justified in the sacred buildings of antiquity, and a typological-iconological aspect, which is still present in many recent buildings, especially when these clothe particular 'semantic' requirements. Both these aspects will have to form the starting-point for any final linguistic analysis. In other words, there is no point in analysing a building with semiological apparatus without first deciding what was the iconological task, whether symbolic or typological, which the building had to perform. In the case of a modern air terminal, such a task is exactly decipherable, whereas in the case of an ancient building whose real function is unknown, we can only presume it. What is still important is that the building shall have a presence, provided with just those formal and formative aspects which guarantee it an autonomous and unambiguous expression.

Moreover, we must be cautious in insisting on the connotative evaluation of a given building, to the detriment of the denotative. The connotative aspect is obvious in many cases, for instance in Saarinen's American Embassy in London. Besides denoting an important public building in vaguely neo-Georgian style, it also connotes the power and wealth of the United States, the neo-capitalist super-power, with its gilded eagle and its metal windows. Such connotations may be true and authentic, whether or not they proceed from the architect's intentions. Nevertheless connotative and denotative aspects are almost always mingled in architecture, and it is neither possible nor convenient to distinguish them, as we can often do in the case of verbal communications. Actually we can assert that certain 'symbolic' functions, especially in ancient architecture, survive the oblivion of their actual connotative and denotative functions. For this reason, I consider that we can speak of the ability of architectural forms to communicate across ages; or of the possibility of deciphering them, not on the basis of a lost code, but on the basis of a type of symbolic message which transcends the passage of time, being a synchronic one as happens in many forms of ritual and myth, and in symbolic and metaphorical expressions in general.

I had occasion to dwell on this already in my book *The Oscillations of Taste*,[17] and I believe that applying even more subtle linguistic analyses than I had then attempted, such a hypothesis might prove acceptable. Unless we are archaeologists, it is not very important whether we regard the megaliths of Stonehenge as ancient initiatory sanctuaries or, as I recently read in a book of science fiction, as a landing and launching pad for intergalactic space-ships. That its original denotation is now lost, or that its connotations are no longer the original ones, will detract very little from the architectural value of a building, which we

BAIRD: As I understand it, Dorfles is using 'iconological' exactly where Panofsky would use 'iconographical'. It seems to me that Panofsky's terminology is more apt.
◄ JENCKS: But having granted two articulations, why not grant a third: form. Then having triple articulation we could, through a series of commutation tests, find out
◄ what constituted the communicating units in a given instance: i.e. what the particular formemes, funcemes and techemes were.
BAIRD: Dorfles speaks here of 'occasional semanticity', and of 'intentions', yet it
◄ seems to me that no discussion of the relation between intention and semanticity can proceed outside the context of *langue* and *parole*, because of the fact that the intention lying behind a design act can only appear semantically as the design act is a gesture-in-a-social-context.
◄ BROADBENT: But isn't the conspicuous display of a de Stijl based on 'functional' aesthetic just as sacral, religious and initiatory as anything in a pre-Romanesque basilica? It is absurd to justify such an aesthetic on technological grounds – there are no reasons apart from aesthetic ones why steel and concrete should be built in rectilinear frames – by analogy with timber construction.

BAIRD: Dorfles here takes his conclusion to an extreme that forces me to dissent. He is right to deplore an exclusive preoccupation with the 'real' meaning, or the 'original' meaning of any architectural phenomenon, but that doesn't justify the extreme relativism for which he opts in consequence.

venerate for its aesthetic, psychological, historical and anthropological effectiveness.

At this point I should like to introduce a practical example of what I have been trying theoretically to say up to now, by instancing the elementary analysis of a mediaeval monument in a township in central Italy. This seems to me to evidence many of the principles which I have already mentioned. Here is how a fragment of this 'architectural narrative' might sound:

'I mount the low curved ramp, which shelters the flank of the imposing Gothic Palazzo Comunale. On my left, the lateral wall is very high, and is interrupted only by two or three irregularly placed windows. Higher up the bell-tower of the romanesque cathedral stands out against the olives of the hillside; and still higher up, the girdle of the Etruscan walls surrounds the whole of the ancient city'.

From such a description, freed from technical detail, we can extract enough to give us an idea of the relationship of the individual buildings and their surroundings. (1) Above all the value of the curved ramp, which serves to raise the traveller from the level of the palace façade to the level of its flank and rear parts; a ramp which like the rest of the city accommodates the rising hillside. (2) The asymmetrical disposition of the side windows of the palace, which do not have, like the regularly alternating front windows, a representational function, and so create an unusual condition. (3) The distribution of the townscape, which is all ramped. The cathedral has already been described as being higher up than the palace, and the surrounding boundary wall is higher up still.

Certain evident 'signifieds' result from this, which cannot be separated from the description of the relationship between the various buildings. This shows (if necessary) how dangerous and inappropriate it is to reduce architectural semantics to single discrete 'signs'. It is almost always necessary to refer to an ensemble of many 'signs' united among themselves. We can call these 'syntagms', but only if we mean this metaphorically and not as a literal transposition of the meaning the word has in the analysis of the spoken language.

We can now look at the other 'signifieds':

(1) The great palace is pre-eminent over the rest of the city: the palace as the seat of power is typical of the period of the communes.

(2) The cathedral (11th century), which is historically earlier than the palace, is noteworthy but its importance is relative. Although it is in an elevated position on the hillside, it has been deliberately eclipsed by the bulk of the palace, built at a period when the power of the Church was evidently on the wane and that of the commune in the ascendant.

(3) The spiral ramp which was inserted in the baroque period adds a new spatial dimension to the rigid and closed stereometry of the palace and to the static 'everlastingness' of the Etruscan walls.

(4) The boundary walls, partly Etruscan in origin, reveal the presence of human settlement even in pre-romanesque times, and explain the primitive circular arrangement of the city. Later periods conserved this wall for defence and protection against enemies; and our period obviously retains them as 'picturesque ruins'.

(5) The palace flank is asymmetrical. We can interpret this as follows: the builder was indifferent to the aspect of this part of the palace, since it was not intended to be seen and admired. The baroque ramp was built later and has brought to light this aspect of the building, which the original designer had not considered. The extraordinary effectiveness of the juxtaposition must be ascribed to the sensibility of our own day for the asymmetrical. This is one of the most typical examples of an element which our predecessors would have considered as crude and defective, but which we regard as attractive and original. The same thing has occurred with the rediscovery and performance in our own day of certain pieces of mediaeval music which we experience as new and original because of their unexpected character in comparison with more recent music which we are used to.

I meant to choose these few elementary suggestions for a possible interpretation of an architectural description by restricting myself to a semiotic-structuralist key and deliberately eschewing technicalities. In this way I hoped to show how each one of the elements described corresponds to quite precise and non-arbitrary characteristics, which would not be legible if they referred only to single elements such as 'window', 'ramp', 'bell-tower', but are so owing to the presence of their reciprocal relationship.

We are thus faced, as we anticipated, with a syntactic aspect of architectural language which in my opinion is much more important than the merely semantic aspect of the individual elements.

Meanwhile, what is meant by 'architectural sign'? A step, a staircase, an entire façade, or the whole complex? Where does the subdivision end? Evidently the architectural sign varies according to the case and the context it is found in; and evidently a single 'Gothic' window has a very different 'signified' as part of a gothic building than inserted in a building from an earlier period.

JENCKS: This is all incontestible but in ▶ a sense it misses the point, because linguists do not call simple elements (words) phonemes or morphemes either: they divide words into more basic elements according to their context (as the next sentence indicates).

In short, we must determine our architecturally significant units *after* the analysis and with respect to the particular context. Otherwise we will isolate false units which reflect our own categories and not the specific, comprehensive situation. The problem is similar to that found in linguistics where the context determines the significant units and not just some traditional concept.

47

I must touch on a final problem in order to point out the principal problems of architectural semiotics, so far as notation by means of drawing is concerned. An architectural object (or a piece of industrial design) can be rendered visually by means of a sketch, drawing, or model.

Architecture (like music in a different way), can communicate directly by itself, and indirectly by means of a drawing and other symbolic renderings of the object. This immediately confers a double kind of semioticity on this art.

Indeed, the graphic renderings, the orthogonal projection, the plan, the model, the cross-section, or the working drawings of a piece of industrial design or architecture are not the 'flesh and blood' object: they are an equivalent to it, on which we can conduct those semiological operations which we usually conduct on authentic works.

In the case of printed music, the reading of the score, although it is informative and even complete in a very precise way for certain pieces of music, is a non-musical reading according to the opinion of numerous musicians and musicologists (for example, Castaldi, Stockhausen, etc.). The authentic enjoyment of a musical work can only take place through the organ of hearing, whereas a reading of it by means of well codified signs exists only in a virtual manner. Indeed, Stockhausen maintains that the type of enjoyment afforded by the rapid perusal of a score, in which one can skip and invert at will, is of quite another order than listening to the same piece.[18]

I mentioned music, because in architecture we are in a similar situation. It is certainly true that a working drawing informs us pretty adequately about a building or object, but, neglecting the pictorial value of the drawing, the project or model can never give us the particular perceptual quality which the fact of entering, traversing and inhabiting a particular building allows us. Thus the spatial relationship between man and the world, between man and the inside and the outside of a building, is almost entirely lost. (This has been studied, for instance, in Edward Hall's *The Hidden Dimension*.)

So we can assert that the type of communication and information transmitted to us by architectural language, or, if we wish, the type of semiosis contained in the architectural message, is strictly bound to our stereometric spatial perception, or, to be more precise, to our stereognosis. I include in this our sensation of depth and other forms of deep sensibility which are indispensable for an exact enjoyment of the architectural object in its completeness. Thus the architectural message differs from the verbal one, which is usually non-spatial except in a few restricted cases of 'concrete' poetry, from the pictorial one, which is almost always two-dimensional, and from the musical one, which is mainly temporal, as it is constantly based on a complex spatio-temporal dimension. Only in this sense can its 'code' be deciphered.

So if we want to systematize architectural analysis from a semiological standpoint, we shall have to say that there is the possibility of a twofold semiological distinction: one kind of semiographic analysis based on the elements of notation and of symbolic transcription of its language (in a certain way similar to certain primitive ideographic writings) and another kind linked to the work itself and to its constitutive elements (spaces, rhythms, volumes). These last elements can undergo an analysis according to the linguistic patterns we tried to define, but cannot by any means, be reduced to schemes typical only for the verbal language.

This article was translated by Mary and Thomas Stevens.

[1] Roman Jakobson. *Essais de Linguistique Générale*, Paris, 1963. (Part four: Poetics.)

[2] *Valori semantici degli 'elementi di architettura' e dei 'caratteri distributivi'* in 'Domus', no. 360, 1959.

[3] *Simbolo Comunicazione Consumo*. Einaudi, Turin. 1962.

[4] Op. cit. Chapter V. 'Valori comunicativi e simbolici nell'architettura, nel disegno industriale e nella pubblicità.' p. 180.

[5] See especially the essay of Italo Gamberini at the beginning of my book, the first to be devoted to the problem in Italy: *Introduzione al primo corso di elementi di architettura*, '*Gli elementi dell'architettura come "parole" del linguaggio architettonico*'. Coppini, Florence, 1959, to which my article in 'Domus' refers. Giovanni Klaus Koenig: *Lezioni di Plastica*, Florence, 1961, and by the same author: '*L'invecchiamento dell'architettura moderna*'. Florence, 1963.

[6] Christian Norberg-Schulz: *Intentions in Architecture*. Oslo, 1963.

[7] Umberto Eco: *Appunti per una semiologia delle comunicazioni visive*. Bompiani, Milan; 1967.

[8] Max Bense: *Aesthetica IV*. Agis Verlag. Baden-Baden, 1965.

[9] Kurt Alsleben: *Aesthetische Redundanz*. Schnelle, Hamburg, 1962.

[10] Abraham Moles: *Théorie de l'Information et Perception esthétique*. Flammarion, Paris, 1958.

[11] A. Martinet: *Eléments de Linguistique générale*. Colin, Paris, 1964 (IV).

[12] Art. cit. in 'Domus' sub. 2.

[13] Rudolf Arnheim: *The Dynamic of Shape* in 'Design Quarterly 64'. Minneapolis, Walker Art Center, 1966.

[14] Kenzo Tange, in 'Chiesa e Quartiere'. December, 1967. no. 44.

[15] Ernst Cassirer: *The Philosophy of Symbolic Forms*. Vol. II, Mythical Thought. Oxford, 1923.

[16] Cf. my '*L'estetica del mito*'. Milan, 1967. Chap. IV. 'Possibilità d'un'ermeneutica dell'arte non figurativa medio-evale', p. 74, where such examples of architectural hermeneutics are provided.

[17] Cf. '*Le oscillazioni del gusto*'. Lerici, Milan, 1958. (2nd Ed. 1967).

[18] Karlheinz Stockhausen: *Texte zur elektronischen und instrumentalen Musik*. Du Mont Schauberg, Cologne, 1963. pp. 178 and 183: 'This form of contact with music is fundamentally different from the hearing of it'.

Meaning into Architecture

Geoffrey Broadbent

It was a good idea of Saussure's to divide the whole of verbal communication into two parts—*language* and *speech*[1]; and it was certainly ingenious of George Baird to draw parallels from this into architecture [2] But I am not sure that he drew the right parallels, and in a little while, I hope to show why. First of all, though, I should like to make my own reading of Saussure clear. It seems to me that, like so many other people in the philosophy of communications, he and his successors were fascinated by the whole business because personally they could not do it very well. One might paraphrase Shaw: 'He who can, communicates, he who cannot, writes a theory about it'. Worst of all, they have found it necessary to invent private languages. It is perfectly possible to penetrate the fog which surrounds a sentence like this one from Roland Barthes: 'The aim of semiological research is to reconstitute the functioning of the systems of significations other than language in accordance with the process typical of any structuralist activity, which is to build a *simulacrum* of the objects under observation'.[3] But why should you have to make the effort? For the author to leave it in that state is mere self-indulgence and one suspects that if his own thoughts were clearer, he would express them better.

So let us quarry out from Saussure and his disciples some of the things which seem relevant to the argument. Language, for Saussure, is a social contract, an agreement implicit between people as a whole that each word should have a particular meaning, and also that words should be used in certain ways. There is a direct parallel to this in architecture, which used to be called *style*. Style, too, was a social contract between people, who agreed that certain elements of architecture should mean certain things, and like language it also comprised a set of rules for the use of those elements in certain ways. The Greek Ionic order, for instance, consists of certain features such as columns, an entablature, steps, which must be put together in a particular way. It would be unthinkable, to a Classical stylist, that he should use a Doric capital with an order which, otherwise, was entirely Ionic. So the order is a social contract in precisely the way that Saussure's language is a social contract; no individual can alter it at whim, it embodies certain agreed values, and it must be learned in detail by the user before he can manipulate it.

Saussure's *speech* represents an individual's choice of words from the *language*, and his personal way of putting them together. This is paralleled in architectural style too, within which the individual has considerable freedom of manoeuvre; Schinkel's Altes Museum in Berlin, and Smirke's British Museum were built almost simultaneously, they are both Ionic—they share a common architectural *language*, but the speech of each is different. And when examples of this kind spring so readily to mind, it is not surprising that, having drawn parallels between linguistics and architecture, Baird should be castigated, and notably by Banham, for advocating monumentality in architecture again.

The criticism is inevitable, and just, where the words of language are equated with the physical parts of architecture. Certainly Saussure and his disciples tempt us to draw such parallels. Saussure himself draws analogies with a classical order when he describes the ways in which words relate to each other. These relationships, briefly, take two forms, which Saussure describes as 'syntagmatic' and 'associacive' respectively. His successors have chosen to rename the second of these 'systematic', which is confusing because a complete language 'system' includes 'systematic' relationships. Naturally this gives rise to ambiguities, which I shall attempt to resolve by always using italics for the second meaning of 'systematic', which is concerned with word relationships. The 'syntagmatic' relationship is concerned with the ways in which words occur together, frequently, in ordinary language, as 'spoken chains'. A phrase such as 'How are you?' forms such a chain, so does 'It's been a nice day'. In each case, the 'syntagm' satisfies Saussure's rule that it is composed of two or more consecutive units. The *systematic* relationship, by contrast, can take many forms. Words are linked 'in the mind' according to similarities in sound, meaning or even because they rhyme. Roland Barthes gives examples of each kind: 'Education can be associated, through its meaning, to "upbringing" or "training" and

BAIRD: Broadbent condescends to ▶ Saussure and his disciples too quickly, for his reading of them isn't really satisfactory. Generally speaking, he underrates semiology because he trivializes the basic concepts of *langue* and *parole*, and of signifier and signified. Throughout his argument, as I will suggest in subsequent comments, that trivialization leads him to unwarranted criticisms and conclusions.

BROADBENT: I'm sorry Baird thinks my usage of language and speech, signifier and signified, 'trivializes' the words. I don't know what that means, but my paper was checked by the very able linguistics staff of my own College, as distinct from architects playing at semiology. The linguists found that the only term I misused was *morpheme* and their correction has been incorporated into my paper. The only reason anyway for the rather tedious description of semiology which forms the first part of this paper is that neither Baird, nor Jencks, nor any of the other contributors offered an intelligible description of the subject. I commend Janet Daley's remarks to them from the Portsmouth Symposium of 1967 (see Arena/Interbuild, February 1968 for report): 'disciplines which encourage, thrive on, or revel in, incestuous private languages should always arouse suspicion. Coherence and clarity are not simply aesthetic attributes; they are the most reliable and consistent indicators of the integrity and intelligibility of a discipline'. On this basis, semiology seems to me highly suspect but let us agree, that she (and I) should have said private *speech*.

through its sound to "educate, educator," or to "application, vindication".' The 'systematic' relationships can often be tabulated—one could take all the cases of an adjective, or the declension of a verb; such a table is called a 'paradigm'. So given a 'spoken chain' of words, each of which suggests other words by similarities of sound, meaning and so on, the possibilities of these two relationships—'systematic' and 'syntagmatic' are endless. They relate to each other much as the column relates to other parts of the Classical order: 'On the one hand', says Saussure, 'the column has a certain relationship to the architrave that it supports; the arrangement of the two units in space suggests the 'syntagmatic' relationship. On the other hand, if the column is Doric, it suggests a mental comparison of this style with others (Ionic, Corinthian, etc.) although none of these elements is present in space; the relationship is 'associative'— which his followers now call *systematic*.

But let us leave this analysis of language for the moment, and consider its application in other fields. Barthes and Lévi-Strauss both insist on the parallels between language and the organization of physical things. Barthes takes various systems—the garment system, the food system, the car system and the furniture system—and defines which parts of them represent language and which parts represent speech. When fashion writers report on haute couture, for instance, there is practically no speech. The social contract between them is so strong, the rules of fashion so systematized, that they use almost pure language. But when an individual chooses clothes to wear, both parts of the system come into operation. The language of fashion is set by social contract; men, after all, rarely wear skirts, but within the limits set by this social contract, each of us is free to choose individual garments in terms of size, shape, colour and so on. Barthes takes this analysis further in pointing the differences between 'syntagm' and 'system'. The 'syntagms' of the garment consist of the ways in which different elements, such as a particular skirt, a blouse and a jacket always put together as a 'garment chain'. The garment *system* on the other hand is concerned with the variety of forms which a particular kind of garment may take. On the head, for instance, one may wear a hat, a cap, a toque, bonnet, hood and so on. These all serve the purpose of head-covering, but only one of them can be worn at one time.

Similarly, in analyzing the language of food, Barthes is concerned with the various rules by which, say, certain foods are never eaten together; by which certain flavours, such as sweet and savoury, are contrasted; by which different flavours are combined in the same dish, or follow one another at the level of the menu, and by which the preparation, serving and eating of food is hedged by certain rituals. Alimentary speech, on the other hand, comprises variations within this language of food, which may be at personal, family or national level. A menu is concocted with reference to the overall structure, but even with individual users it will vary from day to day. Unlike the garment system, and in spite of the women's magazines, the food system lacks the direction of an effective deciding group. An actual meal, of course, will consist of a real sequence of dishes chosen from those available, and Barthes calls this the 'syntagm' of the food system. He also calls it the 'menu', but in English terminology the menu is actually a food *system*, a list showing the various categories into which foods are grouped. And within each category—*hors d'oeuvres*, soups, fish and so on— the various foods will be associated by their common 'meaning', in relation to the menu as a whole, but there will be essential differences between them, which will form the basis of choice. So, as Barthes says, the horizontal reading in a restaurant menu, of one category—soups, for instance—represents the *system*, whereas a vertical reading, taking elements from each category, represents the 'syntagm'. It is not surprising, therefore, that in his analysis of the architectural system, Barthes identifies the 'syntagm' as the 'sequence of details at the level of the whole building', whilst the *system* is a matter of 'variations in style of a single element in a building, various types of roof, balcony, hall, etc.' So again, he provides a direct analogy with style, in the most traditional sense.

But structural analysis is one thing, and 'meaning' quite another. At the simplest level, a word 'stands for' something else—it refers to another thing, and we may call this its *referential* meaning. The relationship between words and the thing they stand for was first investigated systematically by the American philosopher, Charles Sanders Peirce (1838–1914) who published a series of papers devoted to this topic in the 1860's.[4] He called this science of signs 'semiotic' and it is typical of the confusion in this field that the Saussureans now call it 'semiology'. A 'sign', in Peirce's sense is simply something which makes thought possible and as he developed it, his 'semiotic' became a comprehensive study of signs, of sign-processes, of sign-mediation and of all the other complex transactions which take place when people exchange real objects with one another or, which is more important from our point of view, when they exchange *thoughts* about objects.

The important components of a sign, from this point of view, are two: that which acts as the sign itself, and the other thing to which the sign refers. The most sophisticated analysis of signs which has yet been produced is the work of another American philosopher, Charles Morris,[5] but it will fog the issue even further if we use this terminology in addition to Saussure's. The Saussureans call that which acts as a sign the 'signifier' and that to which the sign refers the 'signified'. But there is further ambiguity here, because on the whole they think of the 'signified' as the mental representation of an object, rather than the object itself. But one of the most important points in the whole of Saussure's argument is that the 'sign' (which consists of 'signifier' and 'signified' considered together) is entirely arbitrary. There was no particular reason, in the first place, why the signifier 'ox' should be associated with the particular animal which it now signifies. In French, the equivalent signifier is *boeuf* and in German it is *Ochs*; but when the animal was being named, any other pattern of speech-sounds would have done just as well. That is why Saussure prefers the word 'sign' to the word 'symbol'; because a symbol is not arbitrary. The pair of scales which acts as a symbol for justice relates by analogy to what it represents. It has a particular significance in that context and it could not be replaced by, say, a chariot. But the arbitrary nature of signs does not imply that the choice of a signifier can be left to the individual speaker. There are times when we use different words for the same things, and we then find it difficult to understand each other. Once the relationship between a signifier and its signified has become established in the language, it cannot be changed at will. It is part of that social contract which is essential to the definition of language. But the initial choice of a sign *is* arbitrary, and a sound could stand for anything —until the social contract has been agreed which attaches particular signifiers to particular signifieds.

There is another difficulty too, when words are chained together into syntagms. The syntagm itself becomes a multiple signifier of some complex signified. All the signifiers added together, in fact, become a 'plane of expression', whilst the signifieds become a 'plane of content'. The problem then, is to break these planes, simultaneously, into basic units of 'meaning'. One could start with the individual speech-sounds—*hard*, *short*, *pink* and so on, which are known as 'phonemes'. Phonemes can be classified in various ways, according to whether they are voiced or unvoiced, nasal or oral; Jakobson identifies twelve such characteristics, or binary oppositions, against which the various phonemes can be plotted.[6] Given such a binary opposition, the phoneme is marked with a plus sign if it agrees with the first term and a minus sign if it agrees with the second. If we take for instance, the 'b' in 'bill' and the 't' in 'till', and plot them against two of these oppositions—grave/acute and tense/lax, the 'b' scores + on the first and − on the second, whereas 't' scores − and + respectively. But that is the only difference, their sounds are similar and their marks are identical against each of the other ten oppositions.

If we took three of these binary oppositions, we could plot them within a cube, as dimensions of length, breadth and height. Any phoneme then could be located within this cube and Jakobson's twelve oppositions allow them to be plotted within a twelve-dimensional space, which allows for very fine shades of difference to be indicated. The technique, then, is a valuable one, but at the level of phonemes, it is of no use whatsoever in helping us to identify referential 'meaning'. A phoneme, by definition, has no meaning of its own; it is merely a speech sound. Phonemes are the raw material out of which words are made and, as we have seen, a word itself means nothing until a meaning is agreed for it by social contract.

So the analysis of referential meaning, after all, has to be carried out at the level of 'morphemes', the roots, prefixes and suffixes of words. And the difficulty still is to split up the continuous stream of referential 'meaning' into separate units. Suppose, for instance, that we were trying to find the individual units of meaning in a spectrum. Traditionally, the spectrum is divided into seven colours, yet for some purposes, the number might just as well have been three, or thirteen. But seven, at one time, was considered to be a magic number, and it serves the purpose of breaking down, or *articulating* the spectrum well enough. At the plane of expression, the spectrum consists of a 'syntagm' formed from the names of seven colours; at the plane of content it is a continuously varying transition from red to violet. So how do we know that the signifier 'red' actually represents a unit of meaning? The answer is to exchange or commute two of the signifiers, within the plane of expression, and to see if this results in a corresponding commutation of two signifieds on the plane of content. If we were to commute the signifiers 'red' and 'violet' a corresponding change would apparently take place in the equivalent signifieds, and in the 'meaning' of the spectrum itself. Where such commutation makes this kind of difference, we know that our initial chain of words was indeed a 'syntagm' and we have therefore isolated a 'syntagmatic unit'. A building is a 'syntagm' in this sense, as we shall soon find if we try to commute an actual roof and wall, or window and ceiling. The individual members of a 'syntagm' which can be isolated in this way, are called 'significant units', and each operates at the level of both signifier and signified.

We have seen from Saussure's analogy with the classical column, each 'significant unit' is related to others in two ways—'syntagmatically', because it is part of a chain, and *systematically*, because it is associated with others by ideas of meaning, rhyme and so on. Again, these relationships have been analysed, and as we might expect, the analysis is in terms of binary oppositions. Catineau indicated six such oppositions, of which the commonest is 'privative'.[7] In private opposition, a signifier may, or may not be 'marked' in a particular way. The French word *mange* for instance, is unmarked because it indicates neither person nor number, whereas *mangeons* is marked because it indicates first person plural. Some linguists take the unmarked term to represent the general case. It is the most frequent form, the standard case, and therefore it may include all the possible exceptional cases.

This method of binary analysis has been carried into anthropology by Claude Lévi-Strauss; class/clan, group/unit, marriage prescribed/marriage prohibited, are typical of these binary oppositions, and a particular society may be marked, or unmarked, for any of them.[8] Of course it would be easy to work out similar kinds of binary analysis for architecture: mass/frame, flat/pitched, and so on, but there may be better ways of finding out what architecture means than by recording whether it is marked or not for particular structural elements.

So far, then, we have seen that Saussure's 'language' and 'speech' can be applied at the level of whole buildings, to define the relationship between a pervading style and a particular example, which shows the architect's use of that style. Not only that, but style itself most certainly has meaning, in the sense that it is a social contract, a system of values which has to be learned before it can be manipulated. But in this case, 'meaning' is not a matter of 'standing for' something else, as it was in the case of referential meaning. We are concerned here with a second-order meaning, 'parasitic' according to Barthes, which we may call connotative. The Gothic style, for instance, does not 'stand for' a ◀ church, but for most people it still 'connotes' church, just as Modern Architecture 'connotes' the International Style and Contemporary 'connotes'

JENCKS: Throughout this essay Broadbent uses 'meaning' in inverted commas to mean connotational meaning. As such it plays a key role because it is the kind of meaning which will be built 'into architecture' as his title states. In semiology, connotational meaning is the same as 'signified, associational, or systematic' meaning, but unfortunately this is not made clear by Broadbent with the result that connotational meaning becomes too arbitrary and personal while at the same time the very generation of new 'Meaning into Architecture'.

BROADBENT: See my reply to Baird 1. The hair-splitting definitions which Ogden, Richards and others apply to the word 'meaning' simply reinforce the point about incestuous private speech, and few modern linguists would support them.

JENCKS: Like so many pessimists about semiology, Broadbent concludes that because there is not an absolute social contract to connotational meaning, therefore there is none. But of course, semiology posits a relative, changing social contract so that, for instance, yellow has all those connotations he mentions and not implausible ones. Three paragraphs later, he argues for a possible inherent connotative meaning which in fact would give a relative plausibility to the social contract idea of meaning.

BROADBENT: My point, specifically, is that the social contract is complete and binding where it involves direct, physiological, sensory response – as in the child's reaction to the visual cliff. (See below). But where *signs* of any kind are involved, the social contract itself is a sum of arbitrary relationships between signifiers and signifieds.

BAIRD: Broadbent's expectations don't necessarily follow at all. Here, he has trivialized and atomized what Jencks in his article describes as 'intrinsic' meaning. 'Vastness' and 'height' need in no way 'on the whole' guarantee an 'awe-inspired' response. The response will be determined by the overall set of the space's characteristics, and by the cultural milieu of the observer in question.

BROADBENT: Oh but they do! Baird concentrates on visual and verbal matters and thus misses the importance of perception by other modes. The need to look up and around, which 'vastness' and 'height' imply, engages the kinaesthetic sense; a 'crick in the back of the neck' is an essential part of such an experience, which is quite independent of the 'overall set of the space's characteristics' (whatever that may mean) and the observer's cultural milieu. 'We' in this context meant me, and those who share my cultural milieu who, by social contract, have agreed to call this experience 'awe-inspiring'. Clearly people in different social milieus are going to attach different names to it, but the physiological effect, on all of us, is the same – see my reply to Jencks.

Festival of Britain. These are matters of social contract, and they do point to relevant parallels between linguistics and architecture, even though such parallels invite Banham's charge of encouraging monumentality. We have found too that 'system' and 'syntagm' can be applied where significant units are at the level of large building elements, such as floors, walls, roofs and so on. And indeed, connotational meaning sometimes applies at this level too. One remembers Ruskin's comparison of a cottage 'with a thatched slope, in which the little upper windows are buried deep, as in a nest of straw' to its equivalent with a flat roof 'making it look like a large packing-case with windows in it'.[9] The social contract still attaches these Ruskinian meanings to the two forms of roof, although professional architects and students tend to opt out of this particular social contract; our opinions are determined instead by decision-making groups, rather like those in Barthes' garment system, who may advocate anything from Systems Building to Brutalism.

But it seems fruitless to pursue the idea of connotational meaning in architecture to any greater degree of detail. In linguistics, no meaning attaches to the individual phonemes of which words are constructed, the smallest unit of meaning is the word itself, the morpheme, and in many ways, the structural elements of building correspond to the morphemes of linguistics, so they too represent the smallest units which are capable of carrying meaning. It is clear, in fact, that because meaning is a function of the social contract, architecture can signify in other ways also, through the medium of style. If we eliminate style, we find ourselves concerned with abstraction, and it is clear that in terms of the social contract, abstraction has no meaning. There have, of course, been many attempts to attach meaning to abstract concepts such as form, colour, texture and so on. Klee, Kandinsky and other members of the Bauhaus had a great deal to say about the meaning of individual colours. Here, for instance, is Kandinsky: 'yellow has a disturbing influence; it pricks, upsets people . . . the sour-tasting lemon and the shrill singing canary are both yellow . . . it might be said to represent not the depressive, but the manic aspects of madness'[24]. But equally, yellow might be described as the colour of sunlight, of a sandy beach, or of ripening corn—in other words, there is no social contract as to the meaning of yellow.

As Saussure said, the relationship between signifier and signified is arbitrary *until* it is agreed by social contract. No such contract has ever been agreed for the elements of abstract form, although contracts have been agreed on the basis of *style*. To suppose that we can generate architectural forms which do *not* subscribe to style, and still expect people to know instinctively what they 'mean', is to flout Saussure's ruling on the arbitrary nature of signs. It is possible, of course, to suppose the existence of certain fundamental characteristics which all men recognize in architecture because they are human. It might be sensible to look for these at an atavistic level, to analyse the kinds of spaces which people find cosy and to compare them with those which they find awe-inspiring. We should expect, on the whole, that vast, high spaces would be awe-inspiring, and small, low-ceilinged ones would be cosy. We might also find that cave-like buildings, constructed of mass-masonry, with small windows, would 'mean' protection for their inhabitants, whilst cage-like structures—steel-framed curtain-walled buildings—would 'mean' exposure and discomfort.

But at this level, the problems are so complex that only tentative conclusions can be drawn. So let us take two related fields in which adequate research *has* been done, and which have considerable bearing on how people *see* buildings, and how they feel comfortable in them. Until the advent of Cubism, it was axiomatic in Western European art and architectural design that people saw things in perspective. Renaissance painting, and axial planning, both building and town planning scales relied on the fact that at an infinite distance from the observer, in line with his eye, there was a vanishing point towards which all lines diminishing into the distance converged. Yet it has been known for some time that this particular way of seeing is not inherent in the mechanism of visual perception, but has to be learned. One of the clearest tests as to whether it has been learned is to present the observer with the Muller-Lyer illusion—two parallel lines, of equal length, with arrows at the ends. In one case the arrows point inwards, in the other, they point outwards and invariably people brought up in a Western culture 'see' the line with the inward pointing arrows as longer than the other. Gregory explains the rather complex reasons for this, which are concerned in part with our experience of seeing the internal corners of rooms, and the external corners of rectilinear buildings.[11] But Segall, Campbell and Herskovits have shown this, and other illusions, to a wide range of 'primitive' peoples who do not live in rectilinear buildings. Zulus, for instance, live in circular huts and they cannot 'see' the difference, but they can 'see' other things which depend on their sensitivity to vertical forms—men, trees and so on—against the horizon; in this case, it is the 'cultured' Westerners who cannot 'see' them.[12]

This suggests that one of the fundamental precepts of Western design—that people see things three-dimensionally in perspective—is not by any means inherent in human perception. Yet some things are inherent. Eleanor Gibson has described her experiments with the 'visual cliff'—a board laid over a glass sheet, about three feet above the ground. A sheet of squared material is placed directly below the glass to one side of the board, and another sheet of the same material at floor level to the other side of the board, connected to the underside of the glass by a three-foot 'cliff', also covered with the same material. Infants, as soon as they are able, can be persuaded to crawl across the 'bridge' and even over the glass, on the high side. But they cannot be persuaded to crawl off the 'edge' and over the 'deep' side, even with their mothers' reassurance.[13] So this instinct for self-preservation at least seems to be inherent, and it may be that if any other connotative 'meaning' is to be found at the roots of architecture, it will have to be at this level.

But it seems to me that in trying to attach meaning to architecture in this way we are begging the question anyway. There is no doubt that, as in language, the sign or unit of architectural meaning is composed of a signifier and a signified. But in linguistics there is an ambiguity between what is 'real' and what is 'unreal'. In speech, for instance, the signifier consists of a *pattern* of phonemes, or physical sounds, which may signify anything, from an abstract concept to a simple, solid object. In writing, the signifier itself is essentially physical in form. It consists of words, written in ink on paper, and again they may signify anything from an abstract mental concept to a simple, solid object. But we have assumed that in drawing analogies between linguistics and architecture, the signifier is the building—a simple, solid object—and the signified is some abstract concept or 'meaning'. It may be that this is an over-simplification.

It could also be the other way round. Suppose, for instance, that the signifier were an abstract concept, and the building itself were the signified. There is no doubt that throughout history, buildings have been designed in this way, as the embodiment of abstract concepts and at many levels, from Suger's mystical embodiment of light at St Denis[14] to Pugin's[15] embodiment of a sentimental, mediaeval ideal in, say, St Augustine's. This reversal of roles between signifier and signified removes, at one stroke, the greatest obstacle to translating Saussurean linguistics into architectural terms, for style is no longer relevant. Language no longer refers to the physical entities of the building; it is translated from the plane of content to the plane of expression, which is where it should be.

Let us take a simple example of significance in architecture, at this level. It is well known from Giedion that there is *some* relationship between relativity, cubism and the villas which Le Corbusier built in the 1920's.[16] In many ways, Giedion fogs the issue, because his examples are not well chosen. He mentions the Theory of Relativity, with Einstein's careful definition of simultaneity, and relates this to Cubist simultaneity in which an object is depicted on the same canvas from several points of view. This description is supported by plates of collages by Picasso and Braque, a Mondrian, a de Stijl villa and a photograph of the Bauhaus, which are not particularly relevant to the case, so it is not surprising that, altogether, Giedion has left many people unconvinced. But he

JENCKS: This is the main point of Broadbent's article 'Meaning into Architecture', that connotational meaning precedes and gets built into architectural meaning. But as semiology makes clear, this is just one possible course and not the pre-eminent one at that. Think for instance of the consistent attempts to read Gothic ribbed vaults as a forest of Bavarian pine trees tied together at their tips. Since this connotation was read in *after* the form was constructed and quite consistently again and again, it shows exactly the kind of thing which Broadbent's theory would seem to deny: i.e. that 'meaning' can be *a posteriori* and a relative social contract.

BROADBENT: Certainly I described only one possible course. That is why I said 'It *could* also be the other way round!' And how does Jencks *know* that the Gothic ribbed vault was not derived, by analogy, from the forest?

could have pointed out that towards the end of the 19th century, many people in many spheres were concerned with the relationship between space and time. H. G. Wells, for instance, published *The Time Machine* in 1895, and over the next thirty years or so, interest grew in the idea that time is merely another dimension, additional to the other three—length, breadth and height. Certainly Einstein found this concept valuable, so, for that matter, did Minkowski, who had elaborated a four-dimensional geometry by 1915. And the whole philosophical tendency culminated in Samuel Alexander's *Space, Time and Deity* of 1920.

There is not the slightest doubt that in his post-Cubist canvas, the *Nude descending a staircase* (1911), Marcel Duchamp did indeed try to represent on a two-dimensional canvas the movement of a three-dimensional human body through the fourth dimension of time. He did it by close analogy with Marey's *chronophotographs*, multiple exposures showing people and animals in successive stages of frozen movement.[17]

So physics provided the signifier in this case, the philosophical concept of time as a fourth dimension, and it is signified on Duchamp's canvas by the various planes of colour, which represent the various parts of the body in successive stages of movement. And furthermore, this same signifier is signified, in appropriate terms, by artists in other fields. Arnold Schoenberg, for instance, describes his *Method of composing with twelve notes related only to one another* as a device for achieving an equivalent unity between the various dimensions of music.[18]

Maison La Roche, plan of first floor.

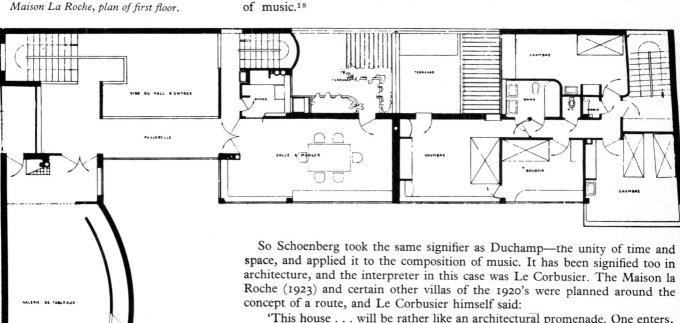

So Schoenberg took the same signifier as Duchamp—the unity of time and space, and applied it to the composition of music. It has been signified too in architecture, and the interpreter in this case was Le Corbusier. The Maison la Roche (1923) and certain other villas of the 1920's were planned around the concept of a route, and Le Corbusier himself said:

'This house . . . will be rather like an architectural promenade. One enters, and the architectural vista presents itself immediately to view; one follows a set route, and a great variety of perspectives present themselves: there is a play of light, highlighting the walls or casting shadows. Bays open onto perspectives of the exterior, and one rediscovers architectural unity'.[19]

In other words, Le Corbusier too is talking about the unity of time and space. The villa is planned in such a way that one must follow the route prescribed by the architect with absolute precision. It is impossible to move through the sequence of reception spaces in any other way; one must enter by the front door, cross the hall, climb the stairs to a first floor landing, cross it, walk the full length of the projecting picture gallery, turn through 180 degrees, move up the ramp which is built against the curving outer wall of the gallery, to finish up in the library, which takes the form of a balcony, opening out over the hall, and the door through which one first entered. The Maison la Roche, therefore, represents a very close analogy indeed, in architectural terms, with the space-time continuum of Duchamp's *Nude*, and even with Einstein's Relativity.

Maison La Roche, hall. Le Corbusier, 1923.

In some ways, the analogy is too convenient. It takes time, after all, to move through the spaces of any large building, landscape or town planning scheme. One treads the nave of some vast cathedral, and new vistas constantly open to view. Humphrey Repton knew one essential difference between painting and landscape architecture was that, with the former, the observer's eye point was fixed, whereas as one moves around the landscape, it is constantly changing.[20] There is one essential difference, however, between these and Le Corbusier's routes. However ordered and symmetrical a cathedral, a garden, or a city square may be, the observer is free to choose which route he will eventually take; but in Le Corbusier's case, the route is absolutely fixed. It is a prescribed series of spaces through which one must move in an ordered sequence of time.

One vital aspect of 20th century art is the search for complete abstraction. Haftman identifies its origins in the curlicues of Art Nouveau woodcuts[21] and traces its development through Kubin's attempts to paint what he saw under the microscope to Kandinsky's final inspiration in one of his own canvases, lying in his studio at dusk, on its side so that no actual object was recognizable. Kandinsky himself admits the enormous difficulties he met. Firstly he felt it blasphemous to paint anything which had not been invented, in the first place, by the Creator; and secondly, once these religious scruples had been subdued, he found it difficult to paint nothing at all, because that meant there was nothing to paint. So he copied the colours which had swirled together on the interior of his pallette and once their forms and relationships were enlarged onto canvas, they seemed non-representational enough, at least to other people.[22]

Other artists found other ways of representing nothing; but one of the most promising lines of enquiry seemed to be the use of pure mathematical abstraction. Vantongerloo, for instance, made sculptures determined by formulae such as $y = ax^2 + bx + c$.[23] Too bad for him that this particular one, as he interpreted it, generated a symbol with the most potent meaning of all, the Christian cross. Gabo, Max Bill and others pursued similar lines of enquiry; Bill's *Unendliche Schleife* is a Mobius strip, whilst Gabo's *Construction* (1936) is a development of a cubic ellipse.[24] In many cases the sculptor is not content with the 'pure' mathematical model. He finds it necessary to 'bend' it slightly, to introduce some personal quirk, which destroys its abstract perfection. Several British sculptors, led by Antony Caro, have tried very hard indeed to remove all human 'meaning' from their work by using intractable materials—sheet metal and plastics—in ways which have no reference whatsoever to the body, or even to landscape. But even using rolled steel joists and wire mesh Caro finds it extraordinarily difficult to remove every trace of 'meaning'. A vertical joist inevitably suggests a standing figure, whilst a horizontal one will insist on looking like a bridge. Only a diagonally placed joist seems to avoid both these references.[25]

But none of these artists has pursued the search for true abstraction with the unremitting zeal that François Morellet has brought to the task. Many of his paintings are based on grids and nets; typical of them is *Doubles trames traits minces* $0° - 22°5 - 45° - 67°5$ which consists simply of fine black lines, ruled at these angles, on a smooth white board.[26] But, as Morellet and many others have found, even this will not lead to complete abstraction, for grids and nets of this kind tend to set up curious optical effects, or moirés, and in this particular painting one reads shifting patterns of interlocking circles which, presumably, were never intended initially by the painter.[27]

The pursuit of true abstraction has found its way into music too. Key works in these developments are Stockhausen's *Kontra-Punkte*[28] (1952), *Zeitmasse*[29] and the *Structures* of Pierre Boulez.[30] The *Structure* for two pianos, which takes some $3\frac{1}{2}$ minutes to play, has been analysed in 26 closely reasoned pages by Georgy Ligeti.[31] Boulez started with a Schoenberg-like 12-note row and concerned himself not so much with notes themselves as with the intervals between them. He then tabulated these intervals in the 48 forms permitted by 12-note theory and used these tables to determine the various strands of 'melody'. He also used them to determine the duration of individual notes: twelve values are arranged in a simple arithmetic series, from the shortest possible note —a demi-hemi-semiquaver—to the longest he actually used, a dotted minim. The tables were used also to determine the relative intensities of notes, from *pppp* to *ffff*, although in practice, these had to be adjusted to allow for relative intensities in performance. Boulez had a similar problem with modes of attack —the ways in which a note is actually struck, within the limits defined by *legato* (very smoothly) to *staccatissimo* (very sharply). It was not possible, in performance, to distinguish twelve modes of attack, and Boulez limited himself to ten. Finally the tables were used to determine how the whole work would be put together, to define, for instance, the number of strands of 'melody' which would be going on at any one time, and the implications for these of the other physical parameters by which the music is composed—note qualities, time-durations, intensities and modes of attack.

In essence, then, Boulez' method of composing was as follows. He decided, firstly, on a set of rules against which all decisions were to be made. Schoenberg's method anyway would determine the nature of the note row, and Boulez devised ways of ensuring that this determined also the four ways in which an individual note could be played. It also determined the overall structure of the composition. Once the rules had been decided, and the note-row itself set up, the second phase of composition was entirely automatic. The system generated the music,

Screen Painting, 0° — 22 5 — 45° — 67°5, *François Morellet, 1958.*

or, as Ligeti puts it: 'Elements and operations, once elected, are . . . fed into a machine, to be woven into structures automatically, on the bases of relationships chosen'. This stage, as it happens, was not effected by computer, but it could well have been, and certainly it would have been a more rational use of the machine than the attempts to recreate Mozart, or to write pop songs, for which composing computers so far have been used.

But once this computation stage was over, the music was by no means complete. Certain parts were literally unplayable, the performers' fingers simply could not negotiate them. So Boulez submitted them to close scrutiny as a practising musician, and made a further series of decisions as to how the mechanically derived pattern of notes should be altered to make them suitable for performance. In other words, the characteristic man-machine relationship was set up. Man makes a series of decisions, the machine operates on the basis of those decisions, and man then takes over again to use his judgement on what the machine has thrown up, and to reduce it to practicability.

Curiously enough, attempts to design architecture by computer have resulted in precisely the same sequence. The most sophisticated attempts so far have been undertaken by Gill, Phillips and others of Bristol University, who seek, eventually, to devise a series of *algorithms*—sequences of precise, mathematical instruction, by which the whole of architecture can be determined. So far computation has proved itself suitable for only a few rather simple areas of architectural design, such as the calculation of structures, heating systems and, most particularly, circulation. The best known 'computerized design', probably, is the work of Whitehead and Elders, of Liverpool University, on circulation patterns in single storey buildings.[32] A published example shows the derivation of a plan for an operating theatre suite which is based, in the first place, on the careful analysis of an existing plan. Whitehead and Elders observed a series of operations in action, and noted carefully the routes which people took into, and through, the various rooms. This information was recorded by means of a 'string-diagram' in which increasingly thick bundles of strings are built up on well traversed routes. Eventually, the same information was reduced to the form of an interaction chart, on which each room was listed, numbered and allocated its number of journeys 'to' and 'from'. The chart also recorded the actual number of journeys between every pair of rooms in the suite and, on the assumption that an efficient plan would reduce the number and distance of journeys, this information was fed into the computer. The computer's task, then, was to plot a plan-arrangement which would minimize the journeys in this way. To facilitate this, the room areas were reduced to a system of squares; an operating theatre, for instance, might consist of six squares, whilst a surgeon's scrub-up consisted of one. Each of these squares was numbered, and the computer's function then was to locate them within a ten by ten grid. Its print-out, in fact, was simply a list of these squares with an appropriate grid reference for each. In many ways it worked very well, the individual squares forming, say, one of the operating theatres, were in fact plotted together as one rectangular room and all the rooms were plotted in relationships to each other which would, in theory, lead to quite short journeys. But there were snags. The initial decisions themselves had been suspect. The problem with operating theatres is not so much to reduce journeys as to prevent cross-infection, and the plan as presented, in any case, was quite unworkable. There was no way into the main circulation area without crossing one of the important rooms; some rooms could be entered without crossing others, and certain of them were plotted in very awkward shapes. So as Boulez found with his music, it was necessary in the case of the plan also to go through a phase of reduction to practice, based on man-made decisions and judgement. So the situation is identical: man makes a series of decisions, the machine operates on the basis of these decisions and man then takes over again to use his judgement on what the machine has thrown up.

It is significant that in all three fields—painting, music and architecture—the human operator should always find it necessary, eventually, to modify what the machine has generated. It is probably inherent in the man/machinery relationship and, as we shall see shortly, it is a matter of cybernetics. But at the moment, what interests us is the desire on the part of the human operator to leave as much decision-making as possible to the machine. In one sense, this is inevitable—especially since the invention of the computer. The fact that the machine is available means that some people will feel constrained to use it. The quest for absolute abstraction is a real and valid one. Like the quest for absolute zero, the four minute mile, the top of Everest, it is inherent in human nature that it should be pursued. But, let us be quite clear, it is an ideal, the pursuit of abstract perfection, and as such it is an *aesthetic* ideal. There is nothing inherently rational in it and eventually the fruits of such abstraction are going to be perceived by people using their senses in traditional ways. Morellet's painting

BAIRD: Having shifted the discussion from intrinsic meaning to abstraction, Broadbent has now moved on to a consideration of design procedure. In a semiological perspective however, it is clear that design procedure can only be discussed simultaneously with user response, Broadbent has apparently failed to grasp the basic point that designing an object and perceiving that object are both gestures in a social context, gestures that is, which are interdependent in terms of *langue* and *parole*.

BROADBENT: Of course designing an object and perceiving that object are both gestures within a social context, but so are writing snide comments, peeling a banana, or driving a car. It would be nice to think that the interdependence of the first two was a strong one, but the two acts often, not to say usually, take place in quite different social contexts.

is fascinating, not for its abstract perfection, but because it stimulates the sense of sight by the optical illusions which it generates. Boulez' *Structures* hardly bear listening to by anyone who is not familiar with the philosophical arguments behind them. And there is no reason to suppose that architecture will be any different. So let us be quite clear that the pursuit of fully computerized architecture is not a rational aim, but an intuitive one, and as such no better, and no worse, than any other attempt to translate some philosophical meaning into architecture.

As we might expect, this pursuit of painting, music and architecture which is fully determined by mathematical rules has precipitated an equal, and opposite reaction from those who wish to escape the effects of such determinism.

John Weeks, for instance, has described a hospital planned on open-ended 'streets' so that when expansion is necessary, these streets can simply be extended. Not only that, but in order to allow free floor space within the building, all loads are supported at the external wall by structural mullions, and these mullions are spaced, not equally or in accordance with some proportional system, but in clusters whose position is determined entirely by structural needs. [33]

Northwick Park Hospital, John Weeks of Llewelyn-Davies, Weeks, Forestier-Walker and Bor.

It is an extremely interesting prospect, but it seems to me to confuse two issues, simply because the wrong word, 'indeterminacy', has been used to describe two quite different phenomena. Indeterminacy, of course, refers to Heisenberg's Uncertainty Principle (1927), which is concerned with behaviour of matter at the smallest scale, the individual particle. Heisenberg speculated as to what would happen if a microscope were made powerful enough to allow an individual particle to be observed in motion. To observe it, of course, one would have to bombard it with photons of light and the photon is thought to exist in some ambiguous state, something between a wave of energy and an actual particle. Whichever form it took, it would change the position of the particle under observation. As Heisenberg says:

'It was discovered that it was impossible to describe simultaneously both the position and the velocity of an atomic particle with any prescribed degree of accuracy. We can either measure the position very accurately—when the action of the instrument used for the observation obscures our knowledge of the velocity, or we can make accurate measurements of the velocity and forego knowledge of the position'. [34]

And while Heisenberg's principle undermined once and for all the idea of certainty in physics, it seems to me to offer spurious analogies with what has been called indeterminate architecture.

In Weeks' case, two principles seem to be at work. The position of the mullions is very determinate indeed—statically determinate, in fact, although the *visual* effect may be random. Chance is an honoured device anyway in the generation of visual form—Leonardo da Vinci advised the young painter to look at a stained wall, and to use the random forms and colours which it displayed as the basis for painted compositions.[35] Duchamp used many kinds of chance in his famous large glass *The Bride Stripped Bare by her Bachelors Even*.[36] Hans Arp found that the pieces of coloured paper he was trying to make into a collage would not arrange themselves to his satisfaction, so he tore them up, and dropped them on the floor. Sometime later, he looked down and saw that they had arranged themselves into a pattern which pleased him, so he picked them up, very carefully, and pasted them onto a background.[37] In these and other cases, the chance event on its own was not enough; it was selected by a prepared mind. In Weeks' case too, the mullions arrange themselves in a way which visually is random, and confronted with this, he judges by eye where to 'grade the mullion intervals after the basic interval density has been established to avoid jumps, lacunae or clusters which look as if they were reflecting a local situation where this is not in fact present'.[33]

But the future expansion of the hospital will be by no means random. It will result from pressures and decisions made as the result of human needs and the informed interpretation of those needs. In other words, the hospital will be built, it will be observed in use, and decisions will be made as to how it should be changed. This, of course, is the classic cybernetic situation, and we remember that Norbert Wiener derived the term itself from the Greek *kybernetes* or 'steersman'. In his first book *Cybernetics* (1949) he traces a history of feed-back mechanisms from an article on the governors of steam engines, which was published by Clerk Maxwell in 1869, to his own interest in the subject of communication and control systems which dates from the middle 1940's. The term 'cybernetics' itself was coined in 1947.[38]

The painterly expression of cybernetics is to be found in *action painting*. In this case, there is no question of direct influence from communications engineering to painting, for Pollock was developing his technique over precisely those years in which Wiener was formulating his theories. Like Kandinsky, and many other 20th century artists before him, Pollock had been struggling for some time towards a kind of painting which aspired to the condition of music; in other words, it would be freely 'abstract', and certainly it would represent nothing in nature. Certain techniques were available to him. Hans Hofmann, a refugee from Nazi Germany, had been experimenting with drip-painting in New York during the war years. Matta, Robert Motherwell and others had been fascinated by the Surrealists' idea that painting should well up from the unconscious as a kind of automatic writing. Pollock was aware of these things, and from 1943 onwards, his working methods became increasingly frenzied—he applied paint with sticks, with worn out brushes, or squeezed it directly on to the canvas from the tube. And finally, in 1947, he found the technique which suited his purpose, which was to drip paint from a wet brush, or from a tin with holes in it, to form a dense filigree of lines over the whole canvas. Two paintings of 1947 mark the transition: *Full fathom five* is drip-painted but using oils, while *Cathedral* is also drip-painted, but in Duco, a synthetic, and aluminium paint.[39]

Pollock was filmed in action, and it is quite clear that the entire painting is made up of a vast number of cybernetic actions. He makes a mark, looks at it, assesses the effect it has had on the canvas and then makes a rapid decision as to where, and what, the next mark should be. The whole process, of course, is less conscious than such a description would suggest; as Pollock says:

'When I am in my painting, I am not aware of what I am doing. It is only after a sort of 'get acquainted' period that I see what I have been about. I have no fears about making changes, destroying the image, etc. because the painting has a life of its own. I try to let it come through. It is only when I lose contact with the painting that the result is a mess. Otherwise there is pure harmony, an easy give and take, and the painting comes out well'.[21]

The clue here is 'contact with the painting', for Pollock proceeds with consummate control, each flick of the wrist, each swirl of the paint can, has the precision of a master-stroke in tennis. Then one remembers Wiener's description of kinaesthetic sensation. A kitten is flicking at a swinging spool:

'. . . messages of a very complicated nature are both sent and received within the kitten's own nervous system through certain nerve end bodies in its joints, muscles, and tendons; and by means of nervous messages sent by these organs, the animal is aware of the actual position and tensions of its tissues; it is only through these organs that anything like a manual skill is possible.'[40]

There is, of course, an aural equivalent of this, and, in a sense, it is the essence of improvisation. Jazz groups for years have played together on the understanding that what one musician did would inspire another to even greater heights. But there is a preconceived structure to jazz. The musicians agree beforehand what melodies they shall play, what harmonic structure they will use, who will take the lead in successive choruses. The whole scheme is clear and simple, though none the worse for that, but certain experiments in (disparately) serious music come closer to signifying the cybernetic principle. Again there is confusion here because John Cage, in particular, speaks and writes about 'indeterminacy' in connection with his and other musicians' work.[41]

A great deal of this new musical theory derives from the great *Livre* which the French poet Mallarmé was writing towards the end of his life,[42] on the pattern of the ancient Chinese divination manual known as the *I Ching*.[43] The *I Ching* consists of sixty-four forecasts, suggesting courses of action; each of which is given a name, and associated with a hexagram, a pattern of six lines. One consults the oracle by throwing a set of sticks, and a particular hexagram is indicated by the way they fall. One's forecast depends entirely on the chance formation which the sticks take up. In Mallarmé's case, the *Livre* was to have taken the form of six boxes placed diagonally on the table, each containing five sections of the book. It was to be read in public and the 'operator' would take a number of sections out of the boxes, according to the number of people in the audience, and each section would be divided into two half-sections of eight pages each. Half-sections would then be interchanged so that the reading, inevitably, would cover a random selection from the vast substance of which the book was composed. Individual pages were set out in such a way that the typography itself had an important contribution to make to the meaning of the poem. As Mallarmé says, the white paper takes on importance—it is not mere silence, as it would be with an ordinary poem but: 'The paper intervenes each time an image, of its own accord, ceases or withdraws, accepting the succession of others . . . it is a question . . . of prismatic subdivisions of the Idea . . . it is in variable positions near to, or far from, the latent conductor wire that the text asserts itself.'[44] This leads in the reading to accelerations and slowings up and the poem takes on the qualities of a musical score to be read aloud. Different type-faces are used to differentiate the predominant motif from secondary ones, whilst the position of a word on the page indicates whether the intonation should rise or fall.

These reading instructions actually apply to a poem, a working example of the *Livre*, which reads *A thrown dice never will abolish chance* but the actual words are set over the eight pages of a half-section, with secondary motifs, in smaller type running through, between and beyond them: 'UN COUP DE DES (3 pages) N'ABOLIRA (4 pages) LE HASARD (2 pages)'. It is also worth noting in this context that Mallarmé tried to work with what he described as 'strings of pearls', 'crystalline structures', 'diamonds' and so on, as elements of an overall *structure*, whose basic elements were to be the 26 phonemes of French speech.

One piece of music at least, has been inspired by Mallarmé's *Livre*, the *Pli selon Pli* ('Fold upon Fold') of Pierre Boulez, which is subtitled *Improvisations sur Mallarmé*.[45] It is a vast concept, in five movements, some of which contain sections which are improvised by members of the orchestra. The overall structure, therefore, is determined by the composer, but individual sections within it are improvised by the performers. Such a procedure is known to composers of the avant-garde Darmstadt school as 'Aleatoric', from the Latin *alea* a dice.[46] This is rather different from Cage's music, although this too is incomplete when it leaves the composer's hand. Stockhausen's *Klavierstück XI* is incomplete in this sense, in that it consists of a large sheet of paper, on which nineteen separate sections of music are placed, each fully composed and complete in itself. In addition to playing them, the performer must decide in what order they should be played—this is a matter of conscious or unconscious whim. But once he has chosen the order, certain conventions operate which govern the tempo and intensity of each section, so a given section is likely to be played differently each time it is performed. A performance ends, in fact, when any one section has been played twice.[47]

In many ways this is unsatisfactory, and in particular, there may be difficulties in performance when, according to the rules, a particular rhythmic structure has to be adapted to an unsuitable tempo. Pierre Boulez tried to overcome this, and other difficulties in his *Third Piano Sonata*.[48] It consists of five pieces of which one named *Constellation* is longer than the others and occupies a central position. The other four may be grouped around it in any symmetrical order, and there are possibilities of choice within individual pieces. As Hodeir says: 'The pianist may invert or omit whole passages, choose between two alternative circuits, switch from one circuit to another at given points or even transpose entire structures (this by means of 'magic squares' and tablatures . . . [49])'. In both these cases, therefore—Stockhausen's *Klavierstück* and Boulez' *Sonata*—the individual details of the composition are worked out very carefully, but the actual *form* of the whole is left to chance, or at least to a sequence of decisions which is made by the performer rather than the composer.

Cage himself has brought a great deal of chance into music but like Duchamp, Arp and even Leonardo da Vinci, he found that the brain is incapable of generating chance events, that it will consistently tend to throw up patterns and structures of various kinds. So, like his illustrious predecessors, he found it necessary to introduce some mechanical device which could be relied upon to throw up random sequences. He might throw a dice, or toss a coin. In *Music of changes* for piano, he used the *I Ching*, tossing coins in threes, and relating the results to a series of charts which control, rather like those of Boulez, the various characteristics of each note. One difference is that in addition to the twelve notes of the musical scale, Cage also indicates that sounds of indefinite pitch (noises) should be used. In this case, all the chance events took place before the music was written down, and the performer is asked to play the actual notes. As Cage says, he is rather like a bricklayer working to the architect's blueprint (sic). It is possible that by this means, a composition might be generated which would satisfy the traditional canons of unity—everything depends on the composer's skill in selecting from the material generated by chance. But in other works of Cage, there is no such possibility; the chance event takes place at the moment of performance. The *Concert* for piano and orchestra (1957–8) consists of eighty-four 'sound aggregates, each of which may be played, or not played, in whole or in part, in any sequence'.[50] Some of them are actually written on musical staves, over which linear or curved forms have been drawn; these define the position of notes. There are similar parts for wind and string instruments and an optional part for voice. The conductor also has a part, which he may or may not use and certainly his function is not to beat time! All this, of course, merely offers clues for improvisation and where some instruction is needed as to how to proceed from one section to another, this may be determined by tossing a coin or noting the imperfections in the music paper. Each player is instructed to play all, any or none of the notes in his part and, as Wilfred Mellers says, it is theoretically possible, if improbable, that a performance could result in complete silence.[51]

So what seemed at first to be simple 'indeterminacy' in music has turned out to be at least three quite different things. One is 'aleatoric' music, in which the structure as a whole is determined by the composer, but within this structure, the performers are encouraged to improvise the details. The *Pli selon Pli* of Boulez is an example of this. In the second of these musical systems, the composer writes structural blocks of music which may be put together in different ways, as in Stockhausen's *Klavierstück*, whilst the third type, which is certainly indeterminate, depends on pure *chance*; John Cage is responsible for much of this. All three have a high *cybernetic* content; the performer inevitably reacts to what he has just done, whether he is asked to do so or not. But from our point of view it will be interesting to draw whatever architectural parallels can be found for these musical systems.

All architecture, to some extent, is aleatoric, in the sense that it is capable of being changed, over the years, to accommodate the changing needs of its inhabitants. Sometimes the changes are slight; in the past century they have amounted often to taking advantage of new servicing systems—electricity, plumbing, central heating and so on. But recently there has been a great deal of discussion on the possibility of buildings which can be changed easily, and drastically, to accommodate new uses. John Weeks' hospital is designed with this in mind—the essential feature of this is that, as with *Pli selon Pli*, the overall structure is determined at the outset, but extensions and alterations can be carried out without materially disturbing it. The most dramatic example of aleatoric architecture, in this sense, is probably the Fun Palace which Cedric Price has designed for Joan Littlewood.[52] Here the essential structure is rather like a shipyard, with steel towers at sixty foot centres, overtopped by an enormous gantry crane. Within this, there are flexible communications and service systems, together with stacks of panels, inflatable structures, staging, seats and so on, from which auditoria can be made. The Fun Palace will offer a wide range of attractions—film shows, wrestling matches, violin recitals, discussions— and each day the manager will check what is to be offered, and issue instructions for the appropriate auditoria to be raised. Next day, of course, a different series of attractions will be on offer, and a different series of spaces will be arranged to house them. In a sense all that Price has done here is to speed up, very dramatically, the process of growth and change which occurs in any building, anyway.

The second musical system, in which composed blocks are put together at random, has very obvious analogies with systems buildings. Their intentions, in fact are identical—to provide a kit of parts from which a structure may be erected which is appropriate for the purpose in hand. Nor need anyone be surprised that what at first sight seems to be an entirely rational approach to architecture should have such deep aesthetic roots. As for the third system— the use of pure chance—we shall not dismiss this lightly when we remember that in many circumstances a chance event has triggered off some discovery of enormous importance. The clue to this, of course, is that the action of chance must be observed by a prepared mind. So when everything else fails, we might emulate Hans Arp by tearing up a recalcitrant plan, and throwing it on the floor. It might just conceivably arrange itself in the kind of order which previously had eluded us. So again a profound philosophical concept—in this case cybernetics—has acted as a pervading signifier, which has then been signified in painting, in music and in architecture.

The fourth major field I wish to consider, in which philosophical principles have been applied to the arts, can best be described as 'perceptual enquiry'. It is concerned with the psychology of perception and its application to painting and music; so far, it has had little impact on architectural design, but if my thesis is correct, then it will inevitably have a very profound effect before long. As Morellet found, certain mathematically generated paintings threw up optical illusions, and, even in the 1920's, experiments at the Bauhaus and elsewhere in form, colour, texture and so on, had demonstrated this. There is for instance, the well known *Construction 99* by El Lissitski in which an equilateral triangle is formed by a grid of interlocking lines, radiating from the two equal angles to the two opposite sides.[53] All the lines are straight, but a curious moiré effect takes over to produce the effect of curved lines overlaying them. And many other artists who have been concerned with optical painting have suggested that their first intentions were to produce completely abstract pictures, with no reference whatsoever to forms in nature, that to do so they worked systematically

Vibration III, J. R. Soto.

with grids and progressions, and that the optical effects appeared as an unforeseen by-product.

Victor Vasarely started to exploit the effects of optical illusion in painting during the late 1940's,[54] and it is not surprising that other artists were attracted to Paris, where he was working, in the early 1950's. One of these was the Venezuelan Jesus-Rafael Soto, who, like Vasarely, was interested in the possibility of simulating the effect of movement on a flat canvas (as distinct from Duchamp's *record* of movement), an interest which stemmed from his first sight of Mondrian's last works, such as the *Broadway Boogie Woogie*, in which the lines themselves are made from alternating dashes of red, yellow and blue. This seemed to Soto to be very near an image which actually moved optically; and he experimented further along the same lines with the repetition of forms such as squares, or later dots, arranged in accordance with some musical series. These were only partially successful in producing the illusion of movement, and the effect was enhanced immeasurably when, in 1952, Soto superimposed two or more such patterns on sheets of plexiglass. In the last of these, *Spiral* (1956), two broken spirals are superimposed in this way and the effect of movement, as one walks past, is very impressive indeed. Before long Soto discovered that if he ruled a background of fine black and white lines, the edges of almost anything suspended in front of it would appear to dissolve because of the intense moiré effect. Wire shapes in particular lost all their apparent substance. As Soto says:

> 'What has always interested me has been the *transformation* of elements, the dematerialization of solid matter. To some extent this has always interested artists, but I wanted to incorporate the *process* of transformation in the work itself. Thus, as you watch, the pure line is transformed by optical illusion into pure vibration, the material into energy.'[55]

The most impressive thing is that Soto's works have precisely this effect. Solid wire seems to turn to glass, or to liquify in front of one's eyes. It raises a great many questions about the 'reality' of matter and one cannot in the least be sure just what the relationships are between Soto's ruled picture plane, the space behind his dissolving wires, and the space in which one is standing. Clearly this has strong implications, on a large scale, for the reality of architectural space.

The field of perceptual enquiry seems to be following the usual sequence. It started in painting, and before long it had found its way into music. As early as 1955, Karlheinz Stockhausen was raising a great many questions about the nature of aural perception. Suppose, for instance, that we generate a signal covering say, a bandwidth of 20 cycles per second between 980 and 1000 cycles per second. We shall hear a clear, medium-pitched note. But suppose now we start to change the frequency of our fixed note, reducing it towards zero. We shall, of course, hear a gliding tone which becomes lower and lower in pitch until eventually, it will cease to be an audible note. At a certain, critical point, it will turn into a series of beats, a rhythm. Stockhausen suggests that this turnover point occurs at around 20 cycles per second; we can hear up to twenty separate notes in one second, and the lowest pitch we can hear approaches 20 cycles per second from the other direction.[56]

A great deal of this sensory investigation in music depended on the availability of electronic devices, and by 1956 the first acknowledged piece of electronic music, Stockhausen's *Gesang der Jünglinge*, had been 'performed' on Cologne Radio.[57] Yet there are intriguing things about the chronology of perceptual enquiry, and its signification in the arts. Op Art and electronic music were available in the middle 1950's, yet they failed to make much impact then, and there is no real sign, yet, of their equivalents in architecture. Indeed the Sunday Colour Supplements have been telling us for some time now that Op is dead, killed at its first major showing—the Responsive Eye Exhibition at the Museum of Modern Art, New York, in 1965.[58] Two London galleries, Indica and Signals, which were devoted to it, have both had to close their doors; the indications are that, valid as it was philosophically, the world was not ready for Op.

Recently, however, there has been a tremendous upsurge of interest in the senses, and in the nature of perception. Drug-taking is one aspect of this, so are psychedelic experiences of other kinds. Richard Gregory's introduction to the psychology of seeing, entitled *Eye and Brain*, has sold consistently well since its publication in 1966, and more recently still, Stockhausen has become something of a cult-hero. The indications, therefore, are that the world is ready for perceptual enquiry now and there is not the slightest doubt that before long it will find its way into architecture.

The key to this is the social contract which determines what phenomena will be important as signifiers at any given time. To make the point, let us look at the rather sad story of an architect who ignored it, and built meaning into his work which was so far in advance of the social contract that it was misunderstood at the time, and has been ever since. Rietveld's little house for Mrs Schröder in Utrecht has been described in many ways.[69] The Smithsons distinguish it as one of three Canonic buildings in 20th century architecture because, like Duiker's Cinéac and Le Corbusier's villa at Garches, it possesses a 'completely consistent and unified plastic system'.[60] In other words, they are concerned with its *formal* properties, and so is everyone else who has commented on the house. It is easy to look at it as a three-dimensional (just) habitable version of a Mondrian painting; but hardly anyone has commented on it as a *house*. Banham says of it: 'Tiny, structurally timid, badly sited, undistinguished in plan, it may have had compelling logical and private virtues for its inhabitants that are now difficult to make convincing to outsiders, but what assures its place in the world is its exterior'.[61] The house, in other words, is a machine for looking at. But Mrs Schröder, who has the most compelling of private reasons—she has lived there for over forty years—for understanding the house and its faults and virtues,

Schröder House at Utrecht, G. Rietveld, 1923.

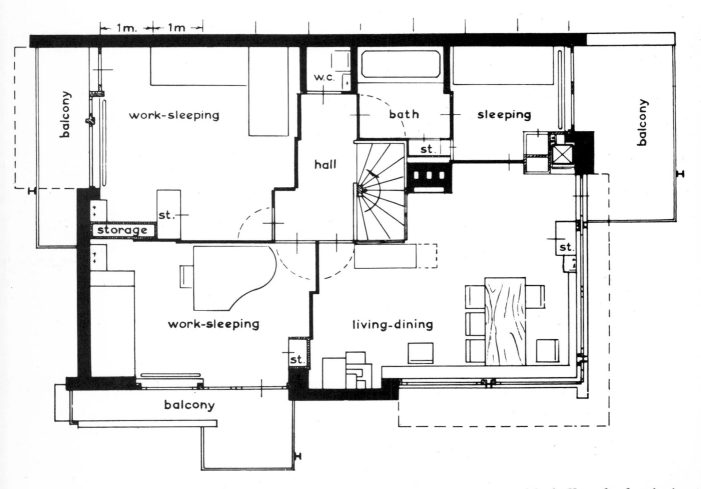

← 1m. → ← 1m →

balcony

work-sleeping

w.c.

bath

sleeping

balcony

hall

st.

storage

st.

work-sleeping

living-dining

st.

st.

balcony

SOUTH EAST

Schröder House, first floor closed.

Schröder House, sliding partitions between work-sleeping area and living-dining area.

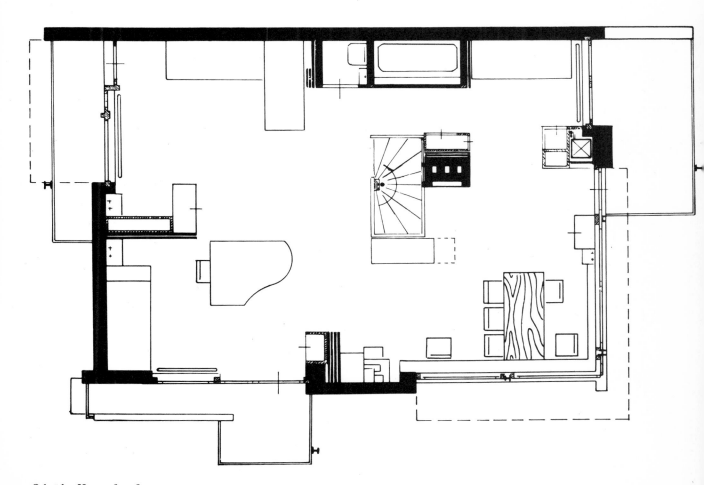

Schröder House, first floor open.

is quite clear that for her particular family, it was, and is, a perfect house for living in.[62] She points to a dozen details which were designed around the specific needs of particular members of her family—form following function very closely. There is a window seat outside a son's study, on which passing friends could sit, chatting for a while without disturbing his studies too seriously. There is a two-way cupboard for parcels delivery at the entrance, neatly concealed but easily convenient storage units, and many other highly practical devices; yet Banham calls the plan 'undistinguished'. And the most remarkable feature of all, which went unremarked in the 1920's and has hardly been noticed since, is in fact the first floor plan. Like any good architect of his time, Rietveld was concerned with infinite space, the relationship of interior to exterior and so on. He took this to such lengths, in fact, that all the windows open exactly at right angles, for only in this way can the pure geometry of spatial relationships be preserved. But as a practical housewife, Mrs. Schröder wanted a series of individual rooms for her sons, so she and Rietveld compromised—it was a true dialogue between architect and client—to the extent that he designed, and made, a series of sliding, folding partitions. The upper floor can be opened into one clear space, closed into five individual rooms, or left in a variety of states in between. It is, in fact, the first cybernetic house plan to be built in Western Europe, and there is not the slightest doubt that if it had been built in 1964 instead of in 1924, it would be recognized as such.

But cybernetics had not been invented in 1924, nor, for that matter, had Heisenberg discovered his Uncertainty Principle. So, philosophically, the world was not ready for a changeable house; those who saw it—and they included a range of distinguished critics, not to mention Gropius and Le Corbusier—were unable to perceive the importance of this quality in it. They were totally unprepared to find this particular meaning in architecture.

In other words, Rietveld ignored Saussure's social contract, he opted out and spoke a private language. This exception, then, reinforces the rule that when we speak of 'meaning' in architecture, we are concerned with 'language' in Saussure's sense, as the social contract to which, at a particular point in history, a significant number of people subscribe. But this only begins to hint at the complexity of the relationship between architecture and linguistics. In many ways, for instance, Peirce has much more to offer than Saussure. His treatment of signs was more profound and, as extended by Morris, it is concerned not just with signs themselves, but with their relationship to the interpreter and his disposition (the interpretant). We ought to consider also Wittgenstein's cryptic statements on the absolute limits of language,[63] not to mention Ogden and

◀ MRS. T. SCHRÄDER-SCHRÖDER: As a matter of principle I would like to refer to your statement of 'form following function very closely'. As to the design of the interior of the house I would rather say that we were inclined to let form prevail over function, though ultimately we always consciously tried to balance the importance of form and function.

◀ MRS. T. SCHRÄDER-SCHRÖDER: The design of the house was conceived in close collaboration between Rietveld, the architect, and myself as interior designer. It was not the result of a summing up of requirements by a housewife–client but rather one of mutual discussions on planning and development based on new philosophies of life and living.

In this light you will understand that no part of the interior can be regarded as an isolated suggestion by any one member of the team. The idea of the sliding walls was rather a synthesis than a compromise.

◀ BAIRD: Here is the core of Broadbent's misconception of *langue* and *parole*. As Jencks has already said, Broadbent takes the absence of an absolute social contract vis-à-vis the meaning of 'yellow' to imply that there is no social contract at all, in that respect. Here, he inverts the situation, and speaks of a 'private language', which in terms of *langue* and *parole*, is a contradiction in terms. What the social contract really amounts to, is a spectrum of possibility from absolute predictability to minimal predictability, always of course, within a given context.

BROADBENT: See my reply to Baird 1. I'm amazed that neither Jencks nor Baird criticise my choice and description of abstract signifiers which for me are the vital content of the paper.

Richards' contention that words themselves may form an actual barrier to understanding.[64] We ought to be aware of the violent opposition to structural linguistics which is led by Noam Chomsky; the point at issue, fundamentally, is how man actually learns to use language in the first place.[65] As we have seen, the Structuralists claim that he learns by listening to other people, and then by imitating them. But for Chomsky that is not enough, because it tells us nothing useful about meaning, nor does it help us much with the correct usages of grammar. But every day, each of us generates dozens of sentences, most of which have never been heard before, yet on the whole, they are 'correct' in grammatical terms. So Chomsky believes that listening only triggers off an understanding of language which is inherent in man anyway; the study of language should start with sentences, the ways in which they are constructed, and by which they convey their meanings. Clearly there are parallels here with architectural design; sentence construction may be very like the act of designing, and the building itself may carry meanings in the way that sentences do.

Once we have raised the implications of all this for architecture, we might analyse the product, as Birkhoff did, by measuring aesthetic standards against degrees of order and complexity,[66] and we might look at the ways in which Moles applies information theory to aesthetic perception.[67] We might even try, with Osgood and his colleagues, to actually measure connotational meaning.[68] After all this, we may find that Saussurean linguistics merely helps us to scratch the surface of the problem, and might encourage us to attach such special meanings to words that no one else can understand us. But it will have served a valuable purpose if it helps us to realize that architecture is not only the signifier of some abstract meaning, but is itself the signified of some pervading philosophy. This pervading philosophy is often called the *Zeitgeist*, for want of a proper English term, but Saussure at least has given us a concept against which the idea of *Zeitgeist* may be understood. My interpretation of it will be very easy to test. We merely have to set up a series of privative oppositions, of the kind that Lévi-Strauss uses in anthropology, and use them to mark the key works of 20th century painting, music and architecture. We might try some of the following oppositions (I have indicated the first term in each case and we shall also need the

Schröder House, first floor in different states; cybernetic architecture before its time.

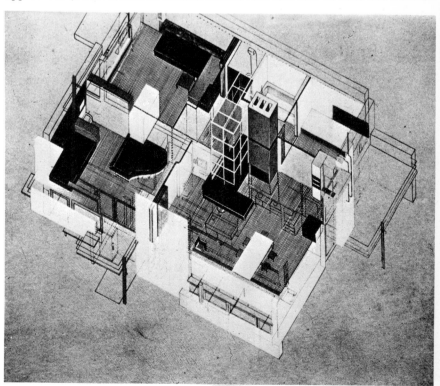

73

second one): simultaneity, time as a fourth dimension, abstraction, machine forms, urban, chance, cybernetic, aleatoric, sensory stimulus, impermanent, disposable, pop.

There will be others—like Hjelmslev and Lévi-Strauss, we might find that they total twelve. And there is a chronology about these oppositions too: what seemed important in the 1920's is not quite so relevant now. We should expect to find that the signifiers of the 'twenties were concerned with 'simultaneity', 'time as a fourth dimension' and 'machine-like'; if a work of the 'sixties signified only these, we should think it an anachronism. I leave the formation of further oppositions, and their testing, to you. It seems to me that, anyway within the limits of the social contract, the most important meaning in architecture is the meaning it has for you.

[1] de Saussure, Ferdinand: *Course in general linguistics* trans. Wade Baskin. London. Peter Owen, 1960.
[2] Baird, George: 'La dimension amoureuse' *in architecture* in Arena, vol. 83, no. 913. June 1967.
[3] Barthes, Roland: *Elements of semiology*, trans Lavers, Annette and Colin Smith. London, Jonathan Cape, 1967.
[4] Harthorne, Charles and Weiss, Paul: *Collected papers of Charles Sanders Peirce* (6 volumes) especially volume 2. Cambridge, Mass., Harvard U.P., 1931–35.
[5] Morris, Charles: *Foundations of the theory of signs.* International Encyclopaedia of Unified Science. Chicago U.P. 1938 and *Signs, Language and Behaviour.* New York, Prentice Hall, 1946.
[6] Jakobson, R.: *Sound and Meaning*, quoted in Cherry, Colin: *On human communication.* New York, John Wiley, 1961.
[7] Catineau quoted Barthes, Roland: p. cit.
[8] Lévi-Strauss, Claude: *Structural Anthropology*, trans. Claire Jacobson and Brooke Grundfest Schoepf. London, Allen Lane the Penguin Press, 1968.
[9] Ruskin, John: *Lectures on architecture and painting* (The Edinburgh Lectures). London, George Allen, 1905.
[10] Kandinsky, Wassily: *Concerning the spiritual in art*, trans. Sadleir and others, New York, George Wittenborn 1947, reprinted 1964.
[11] Gregory, Richard L.: *Distortion of visual space as inappropriate constancy scaling* in Nature, vol. 119. London, 1963.
[12] Segall, H. H., Campbell, T. D. and Herskovitz, M. J.: *Cultural differences in the perception of geometrical illusions* in Science 139, 22 February, 1963.
[13] Gibson, Eleanor and Walk, Richard D.: *The 'Visual Cliff'* in Scientific American, April, 1960.
[14] von Simson, Otto: *The Gothic Cathedral.* New York, Bollingen Foundation, 1956. 2nd edition, 1962.
[15] Clark, Sir Kenneth: *The Gothic Revival.* London, Constable 1928. New edition Harmondsworth, Penguin Books, 1962.
[16] Giedon, Sigfried: *Space, Time and Architecture.* Cambridge, Mass. Harvard U.P., 1941. New edition London, Oxford U.P., 1962.
[17] Lebel, Robert: *Marcel Duchamp*, trans. G. H. Hamilton, London. Trianon Press, 1959.
[18] Schoenberg, Arnold: *Style and idea.* London, Williams and Norgate, 1950.
[19] Le Corbusier: *Oeuvres complètes vol.* 1, 1910–1929 p. 60. Zurich, Boesiger, 1929. Reprinted London, Thames and Hudson, 1966.
[20] Repton, Humphrey: *The art of landscape gardening*, edited J. Nolen. Boston, Houghton, 1907.
[21] Haftmann, Werner: *Painting in the twentieth century*, vol. 1, trans. Ralph Manheim. London, Lund Humphries, 1960.
[22] Kandinsky, Wassily: *Reminiscences* (1913) in Herbert, Robert L.: *Modern artists on art.* Englewood Cliffs, Prentice Hall, 1964.

23 Vantongerloo, Georges: *Paintings, sculptures, reflections*—Problems of contemporary art . . . number 5. New York, Wittenborn, Schultz, 1948.
24 Hill, Anthony: *Constructivism—the European phenomenon* in Studio International, vol. 171, no. 876, April, 1966.
25 Caro, Anthony interviewed by Andrew Forge in Studio International, vol. 171, no. 873, January, 1966.
26 Morellet, François: Exhibition catalogue. Paris, Gallerie Denise René, 1967.
27 Steele, Jeffrey: private communication.
28 Stockhausen, Karlheinz: *Kontra-punkte* for 10 instruments (1952). London, Vienna, Zurich, Milan, Mainz: Universal Edition recorded on Vega C-30-A-278, ensemble conducted by Pierre Boulez, and on Victrola 1239 (stereo), ensemble conducted by Bruno Maderna.
29 Stockhausen, Karlheinz: *Zeitmasse* for woodwind quintet. London etc. Universal Edition. Recorded on Phillips A 01488, ensemble conducted by Robert Craft.
30 Boulez, Pierre: *Structures* for two pianos, book 1 (1951–52) London etc. Universal Edition. Recorded under the supervision of the composer on Vega C-30-A-278, by Alfons and Zloys Kontarsky.
31 Ligeti, Gyorgy: *Pierre Boulez* in Die Riehe, vol. 4. Bryn Mawr. Penn. Theodore Presser Co. 1961, in association with Universal Edition, London, Vienna, Zurich, Milan and Mainz.
32 Whitehead, B. and Elders, M. Z.: *Approach to the optimum layout of single-storey buildings* in Architects' Journal, 17 June, 1964.
33 Weeks, John: *Indeterminate architecture* in Transactions of the Bartlett Society vol. 2, 1963–64. London, Bartlett School of Architecture, 1965.
34 Heisenberg, Werner: *The physicist's conception of nature.* London, Scientific Book Guild, 1962.
35 Leonardo da Vinci: *A way to stimulate and arouse the mind to various inventions* in *The notebooks of Leonardo da Vinci,* trans. E. McCurdy, vol. 2. London, Jonathan Cape, 1938.
36 Duchamp, Marcel: *The bride stripped bare by her bachelors, even.* A typographic version of The Green Box by Richard Hamilton, translated by G. H. Hamilton. London, Lund Humphries, 1960.
37 Richter, Hans: *Dada, art and anti-art.* London, Thames and Hudson, 1965.
38 Wiener, Norbert: *Cybernetics.* New York, John Wiley, 1948.
39 Robertson, Brian: *Jackson Pollock.* London, Thames and Hudson.
40 Wiener, Norbert: *The human use of human beings.* New York, Anchor Books, 1954.
41 Cage, John: *Silence.* Middleton, Connecticut, Wesleyan U.P., 1961—*Lecture on indeterminacy*—new aspects of form in instrumental and electronic music. Recorded on Folkways FT 3704 (2 records), 1959.
42 Zeller, Hans Rudolf: *Mallarmé and serialist thought* in Die Riehe, vol. 6 (1964).
43 Sacred books of China: *The I Ching,* trans. James Legge. Reprinted New York, Dover, 1963.
44 Mallarmé, Stéphane: Preface to *Un coup de dés* in *Mallarmé,* edited with an introduction and prose translation by Anthony Hartley. Harmondsworth, Penguin Books, 1965.
45 Boulez, Pierre: *Improvisations sur Mallarmé I* (1958) and *II* (1958)—the only published parts so far of a larger work in progress, *Pli selon pli.* London etc. Universal Edition.
46 Metzger, Hans-Klaus: *Abortive concepts in the theory of musical criticism* in Die Riehe, vol. 5 (1962).
47 Stockhausen, Karlheinz: *Klavierstück XI* (1956). London etc. Universal Edition.
48 Boulez, Pierre: *Third sonata for piano* (1961, 1963). London etc. Universal Edition.
49 Hodeir, André: *Since Debussy,* trans. Noel Birch. London, Secker and Warburg, 1961.
50 Tomkins, Calvin: *The bride and the bachelors.* London, Weidenfeld and Nicolson, 1965. Republished as *Ahead of the game.* Harmondsworth, Penguin Books, 1968.
51 Mellers, Wilfred: *Music in a new found land.* London, Barrie and Rockliff, 1964.
52 Price, Cedric and others: *First giant space mobile in the world.* London, Fun Palace Trust, 1965.
53 Moholy-Nagy, L.: *Vision in motion.* Chicago, Paul Theobald, 1965.
54 Vasarely, Victor: *Victor Vasarely,* translated by H. Chevalier and with an introduction by M. Joray. Neuchatel, Editions du Griffon, 1965.
55 Soto, J.-R. and Guy Brett: Dialogue in Signals, vol. 1, no. 10.
56 Stockhausen, Karlheinz: *Actualia* in Die Riehe, vol. 1 (1958). (See ref. 45 for publishers.)
57 Stockhausen, Karlheinz: *Gesang der Jünglinge* (1955–56) recorded on DGG LP 16133 (mono) and 138 811 SLPM (stereo).
58 Seitz, William G.: *The responsive eye* (Exhibition catalogue) New York, Museum of Modern Art, 1965.
59 Brown, Theodore M.: *The work of G. Rietveld, architect.* Utrecht, Bruna and Zoon, 1958.
60 Smithson, Alison and Peter: *The heroic period in modern architecture* in Architectural Design vol. XXXV no. 12 December, 1965.
61 Banham, Reyner: *Guide to modern architecture.* London, Architectural Press, 1962.
62 Schröder-Schrader, Truus: private communication.
63 Wittgenstein, Ludwig B.: *Tractatus Logico-Philosophicus,* trans. D. F. Pears and B. F. McGuinness. London, Routledge, 1961.
64 Odgen, C. K. and Richards I. A.: *The meaning of meaning.* London, Routledge, 1949
65 Chomsky, Noam: *Syntactic structures.* The Hague, Mouton, 1965.
66 Birkhoff, G. D.: *Aesthetic measure.* Cambridge, Mass. Harvard U.P., 1933.
67 Moles, Abraham: *Information theory and aesthetic perception,* trans. J. E. Cohen. Urbana, Illinois U.P., 1966.
68 Osgood, C. E., Suci, G. E. and Tannenbaum, P. H.: *The measurement of meaning.* Urbana, Illinois U.P., 1957.

Part 2
Public and Private

'La Dimension Amoureuse' in Architecture [I]

George Baird

'. . . la rhétorique, qui n'est rien d'autre que la technique de l'information exacte, est liée non seulement à toute littérature, mais encore à toute communication, dès lors qu'elle veut faire entendre à l'autre que nous le reconnaissons; la rhétorique est la dimension amoureuse de l'écriture.'[2]

It is not unprecedented to suggest that architecture occupies its place in human experience through some kind of communication. By the mid-18th century, Germain Boffrand had already speculated that 'the profiles of mouldings and the other parts which compose a building are to architecture what words are to speech'.[3]

Nowadays we know all too well that Eero Saarinen's TWA terminal at Kennedy Airport symbolizes 'flight'; we have heard him say that the 'beauty' of his CBS building 'will be, I believe, that it will be the simplest skyscraper statement in New York'.[4] In fact, even discussions of 'symbolism' and 'statement' provoke vigorous protest today. The young English architect, Cedric Price, for instance, recently criticized architects' preoccupation with 'the role of architecture as a provider of visually recognizable symbols of identity, place and activity'. Call it a fix or the 'image of a city', said Price, 'such overt self-consciousness is embarrassing only to a few—in general, it is both incomprehensible and irrelevant.'[5] Familiar as it may be, then, the issue is a contentious one.

Now Saarinen's and Price's importance for this paper does not only lie in their having made their positions as clear as that. As Saarinen was, so Price is a designer of facility and sophistication. As one might expect, then, both of them have produced designs which aptly reflect their respective views. This means that it is possible to see even more clearly in their work than in their remarks, just how fundamentally they have both misconceived the question which presently concerns me; the question of just how it is that architecture occupies its place in human experience. The designs I mean to discuss are Saarinen's CBS building,[6] and Price's 'Potteries Thinkbelt' project for a technical university in the English Midlands (Figs. 1 and 2).[7] There is no doubt that CBS, the prominent seat of a prestigious American corporation, is a definitive example of what Robert Venturi calls 'establishment Modern architecture';[8] it is well-known that the Thinkbelt, conceived in terms of minimum cost and maximum efficiency, has been proposed as the antithesis of a building like CBS. Yet the designs' similarities are really more extensive and more important than their differences. That CBS and the Thinkbelt are thought of as antithetical seems to me only to show the shallowness of the controversy they represent; the depth of their designers' misconception of architecture's place in human experience.

This misconception is neatly summed up in the respective approaches of the two designs to the detailed organization of human occupation of space. In the Thinkbelt project, the designer stops well short of offering the occupant, say, an ash-tray (on the grounds that there is no guarantee that the designer and the occupant have the same cultural values), while at CBS, the designers only *allow* him one approved by Florence Knoll (since there is no guarantee that the designers and the occupant have the same cultural values). But this is just an ironic illustration of my point. To grasp the full scale of the misconception involved requires examination of these designs' historical context. After all, the concept of 'total design'[9] underlying CBS (Fig. 2a), following Gropius' 'total theatre' and 'total architecture', is nothing more nor less than a Wagnerian *Gesamtkunstwerk*. And Price's idea of architecture as 'life-conditioning'[10] rests on essentially the same view of human experience as Jeremy Bentham's *Panopticon*. Both designs' conceptual premises then, lie deep in the intellectual history of the 19th century. What we ought eventually to understand, is how CBS and the Thinkbelt, as manifestations of *Gesamtkunstwerk* and 'life-conditioning', show the bizarre consequences which even today follow from that century's loss of faith in rhetoric.

The first of those consequences is that modern designers, especially those like Saarinen and Price, become caught up in partly conscious, partly unconscious attempts to assume privileged positions with respect to the groups of people who will occupy the environments they design. The architectural *Gesamtkünstler* assumes a stance towards those groups analogous to that of Wagner *vis-à-vis* his audiences. He takes quite for granted his capacity to enhance the lives of the occupants of his buildings; he believes that enhancement ultimately depends upon the occupants' conscious experience of their environment being dramatically heightened; he is thus committed to a 'total' pre-determination of their experience of the environment, from every conceivable point of view. In short, were he successful, he would occupy a privileged position in the sense that he would stand utterly *over and above* his fellows' experience of the environment he had designed.

The 'life-conditioner', on the other hand, is not paternalistic, but scientistic. He assumes a stance towards his fellows analogous to that of a 19th century natural scientist towards an experiment he is conducting. He is anxious to take nothing for granted, to sustain an absolute neutrality with respect to the experience the occupants have of the environment he has designed. He believes his neutrality precludes his taking any account of their experience of it and he thus resorts to a designed anonymity, the purpose of which is a 'total' non-determination of the occupants' experience of that environment. Were the 'life-conditioner' successful, he would occupy a privileged position in the sense that he would stand utterly *outside* his fellows' experience of the environment he had designed. To sum up, the *Gesamtkünstler* treats his fellows as children; the 'life-conditioner' treats them as objects.

Now I introduced this matter of the attempt to assume a privileged position, as one of the bizarre consequences of the 19th century's loss of faith in rhetoric. What I should really in the first instance say is that the *Gesamtkünstler* and the life-conditioner forget—or else take completely for granted—just how ines-

COLQUHOUN: Of course the designer's position is 'privileged'; society offers him this position in the expectation that it can enhance its experience. Judgement as to whether this privilege is being abused remains in the province of the 'privileged' critic.

BAIRD: 'A palpable hit', I admit. But I think my argument is more obscure than wrong. For what I have done is indiscriminately to have used 'privileged' to describe a position, the assumption of which makes Colquhoun's 'judgement' of potential 'abuse' more difficult.

BANHAM: Price's contemptuous refusal to reply to these strictures is more than justified by the author's insistence on treating him as an 'object' – i.e., a finite series of magazine articles – rather than a living human being whose evolving

intentions could easily have been discovered by Baird through personal conversation during the years he was in London. As I have come to understand Cedric's view of the architect's function, over the ten years I have known him, what he intends by 'life-conditioning' is little different (except less mechanistic) from what is generally understood by 'life-support'. Baird's un-informed sarcasm and much of his argument therefore falls to the ground (but was well worth publishing as a clinical example of the Pavlovian response of certain academics to anything they suspect of Pavlovian or Behaviourist tendencies). Far from treating the occupants of building as 'objects', Price pays them the compliment of treating them as independent-minded adults capable of ordering their own environments.
BAIRD: I don't understand these remarks. Are Price's 'intentions' supposed somehow not to be manifest in his magazine articles? I took it that they were, and I accepted them at face-value having no reason to suspect them. What I criticize here is not his intentions at all, but rather his 'misconception' of architecture, as represented by the Thinkbelt project.

capably the design act is always a gesture in a social context. Their oversight can be seen to have been part of a loss of faith in rhetoric only in the light of the current revival of interest in the ancient subject, which surrounds the work of men such as Roland Barthes, Ernst Gombrich, Claude Lévi-Strauss, and Marshall McLuhan.[11] This revival is due, of course, to the fact that all of these men have attempted to analyze and understand various kinds of gesture-in-a-social-context, by means of either the traditional categories of rhetoric, or the concepts of modern communication theory.

In criticizing Saarinen's and Price's misconceptions, in discussing how it is that architecture occupies its place in human experience, I shall rely most heavily upon the ideas of Lévi-Strauss. The reason is that he has staked the most audacious, yet most intellectually tenable claim of the four, proposing anthropology as the intellectual discipline of most comprehensive human relevance, and doing so in an expansive fashion which appears to accommodate many of the others' most impressive ideas. Lévi-Strauss has explained his claim for anthropology, by calling it the 'bona-fide' occupant of the domain of *semiology*. This, the comprehensive theory of communications, the linguist Ferdinand de Saussure introduced half a century ago as the study of the life of signs at the heart of social life.[12] Taking its cue from Lévi-Strauss' 'structural' anthropology, modern semiology looks on *all* social phenomena as communication systems; not just the obvious ones such as literature and films, but also kinship systems, culinary customs, clothing habits, and, of course, architecture.

The part of semiological theory which bears most directly on the problem of modern designers' attempts to assume privileged positions, is the part Saussure described by means of the *langue/parole* distinction. For semiology, any social phenomenon is made up of both a *langue* and a *parole*. In the first of three senses, the *langue* is the collective aspect of the phenomenon, and the *parole* the individual aspect. Thus, semiology incorporates the fundamental sociological insight that human experience, in so far as it is social, is simultaneously collective and individual.

In the second of the three senses, semiology sees the *langue* as the unconscious aspect of a social phenomenon, and the *parole* as the conscious aspect. In this way, it incorporates one of the most obvious insights of post-19th century psychology, and posits that any conscious gesture in a social context always involves an unconscious component. With respect to these two senses of the *langue/parole* distinction in language, Barthes has said: 'The *langue* is both a social institution and a system of values. As a social institution, it is never an act; it utterly eludes premeditation; it is the social part of language; the individual can, by himself, neither create it, nor modify it; it is essentially a collective contract, which, if one wishes to communicate, one must accept in its entirety. What is more, this social product is autonomous, like a game which has rules one must know before one can play it . . . As opposed to the *langue*, institution and system, the *parole* is essentially an individual act of selection and actualization . . .'[13]

In the most modern sense of the distinction, the *langue* of a social phenomenon is considered to be its 'code', and the *parole* its 'message'. In some respects, this new sense of the distinction is the most interesting, because it introduces into semiology a number of precise mathematical techniques of analysis, commonly grouped under the name 'information theory'. In terms parallel to the collective/individual and unconscious/conscious senses of the distinction, we may say that the particular 'message' which any gesture in a social context constitutes, necessarily involves the use of the 'code' which that context entails.

Of course, information theory goes even further than that nowadays, viewing communication systems as dynamic. While the *relation holding between* the *langue* and the *parole* is necessarily constant, the system as a whole is in a continuous process of development. More specifically, 'information' occurs as a function of 'surprise' within a matrix of 'expectancy'. In order to register, a message must be somewhat surprising, yet not utterly unexpected. If it is too predictable, the message won't register at all. It is in this sense that 'background noise' tends to slip below the threshold of awareness, and that we speak of clichés as not having enough 'information value'. Conversely, if the message is too unpredictable, the result is the same. As Paul McCartney has said, '. . . if music . . . is just going to jump about five miles ahead, then everyone's going to be left standing with this gap of five miles that they've got to all cross before they can even see what scene these people are on . . .'[14][15]

We can now, I think, begin to see how the *Gesamtkünstler* and the life-conditioner become involved in their attempts to assume privileged positions. If, for example, we examine their stances in the light of the collective/individual sense of the *langue/parole* distinction, the following becomes apparent. In undertaking 'total design', the *Gesamtkünstler* presumes *ipso facto*, either individually, or as part of a small élite, to take over comprehensive responsibility for the *langue* of architecture, and to do so, moreover, in a fashion which leaves the *langue*'s collective validity unimpaired. In other words, 'total design' amounts to an attempt to shift the impact of the individual design act from the level of *parole* to that of *langue*. On the other hand, in making his individual design gesture, the life-conditioner pretends to act altogether independently of the *langue* of architecture. But of course, since he, like the *Gesamtkünstler*, is only an individual acting in a social context, his pretence really amounts to a single-handed attempt at a radical modification *of* the *langue*. And that is just another way of saying that he too attempts to shift the impact of the individual design act from the level of *parole* to that of *langue*.

Then, too, the unconscious/conscious sense of the *langue/parole* distinction throws further light on their attempts at privileged positions. As I have said above, the *Gesamtkünstler* makes his attempt for the purpose of dramatically heightening the occupants' conscious experience of the environment he has designed. The life-conditioner, on the other hand, makes *his* for exactly the opposite purpose. But what they both do, in this respect, is to take for granted

82

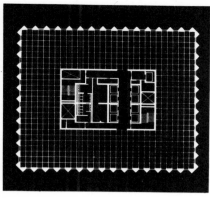

Typical floor plan of Eero Saarinen's CBS Building. 'I think I now have a really good scheme for CBS. The design is the simplest conceivable rectanglar free-standing sheer tower. The verticality of the tower is emphasized by the relief made by the triangular piers between the windows. These start at the pavement and soar up 491 feet. Its beauty will be, I believe, that it will be the simplest skyscraper statement in New York' (to the client, March 31, 1961). Quoted from Eero Saarinen on his Work, New York 1965, p. 16.

their own capacity for consciously manipulating their fellows' *threshold of awareness* of the environment in question.

An examination of such designers' attitudes in terms of code and message only confirms the picture now emerging. Neither sees fit to modulate his design gesture in terms of either its 'surprise' or its 'expectancy'. Indeed, were it not the case of architecture under consideration, I would say that the emphatic manner in which the CBS environment has been imposed upon its occupants would no doubt result in its being sensed only as 'background noise', while Price's look-no-hands gesture would leave the Thinkbelt's occupants with their own gap of five miles to cross before they could make any sense of the environment in which they found themselves. But alas, it *is* the case of architecture under consideration, and analogies from music don't apply perfectly straightforwardly. Unlike music, architecture is inescapably operative in human experience. When music becomes 'background noise', its unconscious impact is incidental; when architecture becomes 'background noise', its unconscious impact is still far from incidental.

The illumination provided by the *langue/parole* distinction is also capable of graphic representation. Extracting from it two of its particular senses, unconscious/conscious, and code/message, one can portray the *field of meaning* of any social phenomenon, as shown in the following diagram.

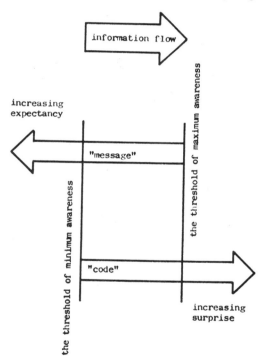

The line across the top of the diagram represents increasing expectancy, and that across the bottom, increasing surprise. In terms of the capacity for registering messages which I described above, the extent of the overlap between the line indicating the threshold of minimum awareness, and that indicating maximum awareness, defines the field of meaning. The length of the bottom line then, from the one threshold to the other, represents the scope of articulation of the social phenomenon in question.

In the language of information theory, the *langue* of architecture is the gamut of conceivable perceptible articulations, while the *parole* comprises the possibility of selective combination across that gamut. But that is only the abstract formulation of the relation. Since, as Barthes says, the *langue* is a 'social institution and a system of values', one can say much more. Take as examples those very concepts 'house', 'overcoat', 'commuter service', and 'shop', whose

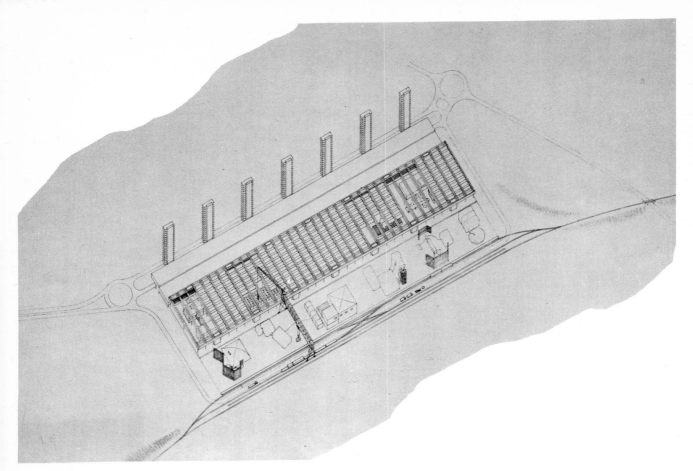

Axonometric view of the Madeley Transfer Area, a part of Cedric Price's 'Thinkbelt' project.

'existing definitions' Price deprecated in his introduction to the Thinkbelt.[16] We can consider the *langue* as the gamut of articulation defined in such complex environmental concepts as those. The *parole*, then, comprises the selective possibility of variation implicit in that gamut. To suggest that the *langue* comprises such a gamut is not to imply that there is anything inherently significant or stable about those particular, or any particular concepts. For the *langue* lies in the gamut of articulation, and not in any primary functional category those concepts might be thought to represent. To suggest that there were such categories would be to fall into the historicism and/or the functional Platonism which, one presumes, have provoked Price's objections.

On the other hand, to suggest that the *langue* comprises such a gamut is very much to claim that the place as 'social institution', which such albeit non-primary concepts hold, can be ignored only at the risk of diminishing the scope of articulation of the whole of the environment. In short, as *langue*, such concepts establish the fixes which allow the corresponding variability of *parole*. The greater the scope of the *langue*, the greater the possible variation of *parole*.

In fact, Price's attack on the 'ephemerality' of those definitions is most noteworthy in the way it recalls the linguistic crusade which was launched in immediately post-revolutionary Russia, and which has been described by Roman Jakobson.[17] In that case, a number of theorists argued that phrases such as 'the sun is setting' ought to be expunged from Communist speech, on the grounds that they were obsolete remnants of a non-scientific mentality. Obviously, a success in either of these cases would have as its chief result simply an impoverishment of the existing cultural situation.

Up to this point, I have concerned myself with modern designers' attempts to assume privileged positions. But that is only the first of the consequences of the 19th century's loss of faith in rhetoric. For the premises underlying the

Interior view of a secretarial area in CBS Building.

Gesamtkunstwerk and life-conditioning also involve such designers in a belief that their designs embody what we might call an *absolute perceptual transparency*; a belief that they can take for granted their fellows' capacity to see each design 'as it in itself really is'.[18] And, of course, the corollaries of that belief, typical of both the *Gesamtkunstwerk* and life-conditioning, are an aversion to ambiguity, and an incapacity for ever sustaining irony.

Consider again Saarinen's conviction concerning the CBS building. 'Its beauty will be', he said, 'that it will be the simplest skyscraper statement in New York'. Later on, he continued, 'when you look at this building, you will know exactly what is going on. It is a very direct and simple structure'.[19] What Saarinen has done, it seems to me, is to take the 'objectivist' aesthetic of orthodox modernism in its most literally expressionist sense, and then to assume that his design was capable, through its transparent 'simplicity', of rendering directly accessible to his fellows an ultimate, universal, even metaphysical reality.

Price, for his part, looks on all such concerns with considerable contempt. He prefers, like his Utilitarian predecessors, to affect a matter-of-fact pragmatism with respect to all aspects of human experience. Nevertheless, his pragmatism rests on an assumption of architecture's perceptual transparency which is just as absolute as Saarinen's. For he takes for granted the capacity of a configuration of built form as elaborate as the Thinkbelt, to unfold *itself* in his fellows' experience as nothing more nor less than a 'servicing mechanism', that is to say, as unambiguously and unobtrusively as, say, a coffee-vending machine.

If however, we take seriously the proposition put above, that there is nothing *inherently* significant, or stable, about any particular environmental concepts, then we must at the same time recognize the impossibility of taking it for granted that architecture can be perceptually transparent, or that people can *a priori* perceive any environment 'as it in itself really is'. Indeed, it has been one of the preoccupations of modern philosophers to indicate that we do not even possess any criteria for deciding *in advance* how to measure our fellows' estimates of reality 'as it in itself really is'. To use Merleau-Ponty's words, 'the phenomenological world is not pure being (as Saarinen and Price assume), but rather the sense which is revealed where the paths of my various experiences intersect, and also where my own and other people's intersect and engage each other like gears'.[20]

Semiology takes account of these matters in defining the *langue* of a social phenomenon as a set of signs, each of which comprises a *signifier* and a *signified*. That is to say, each signifier *is* something, which *stands for* something else. It is because social phenomena are coded as such sets of signs, that the reality of human experience is socially representable. In the most general perspective, one can say that the ultimate *signifier* is the social phenomenon's set of signs *itself*, and the ultimate *signified* is the 'reality' which that set of signs discloses, and which is accessible to us only through those signs. In other words, for semiology, there is no 'getting to the bottom of' any social phenomenon.

JENCKS: I find this obscure, and where not obscure, wrong, just for the reasons which I. A. Richards criticized Saussure in

86

CBS Building: the urban office building as symbolic object.

1923: i.e. one must make a triple distinction between signifiers, signifieds and *things* (Baird here conflates the last two as did Saussure).

BAIRD: I see the point of this distinction; and as I state elsewhere in this margin, I admire the elegant explanation offered by the 'semiological triangle'. The danger in Jencks' formulation is, of course, that it may inadvertently encourage lazy followers to assume they have the option of dealing with Richards' 'things' directly, 'as in themselves they really are'.

◁ *Interior view of a corridor in the CBS Building. Refinement of detail, in the name of an objectivist aesthetic, approaches an approximate present-day limit, and any perception of such a space, which is not absolute and ultimate, in metaphysical terms, is probably either blunted or ridiculous.*

Plan showing Madeley Transfer Area, a part of Cedric Price's 'Thinkbelt'.

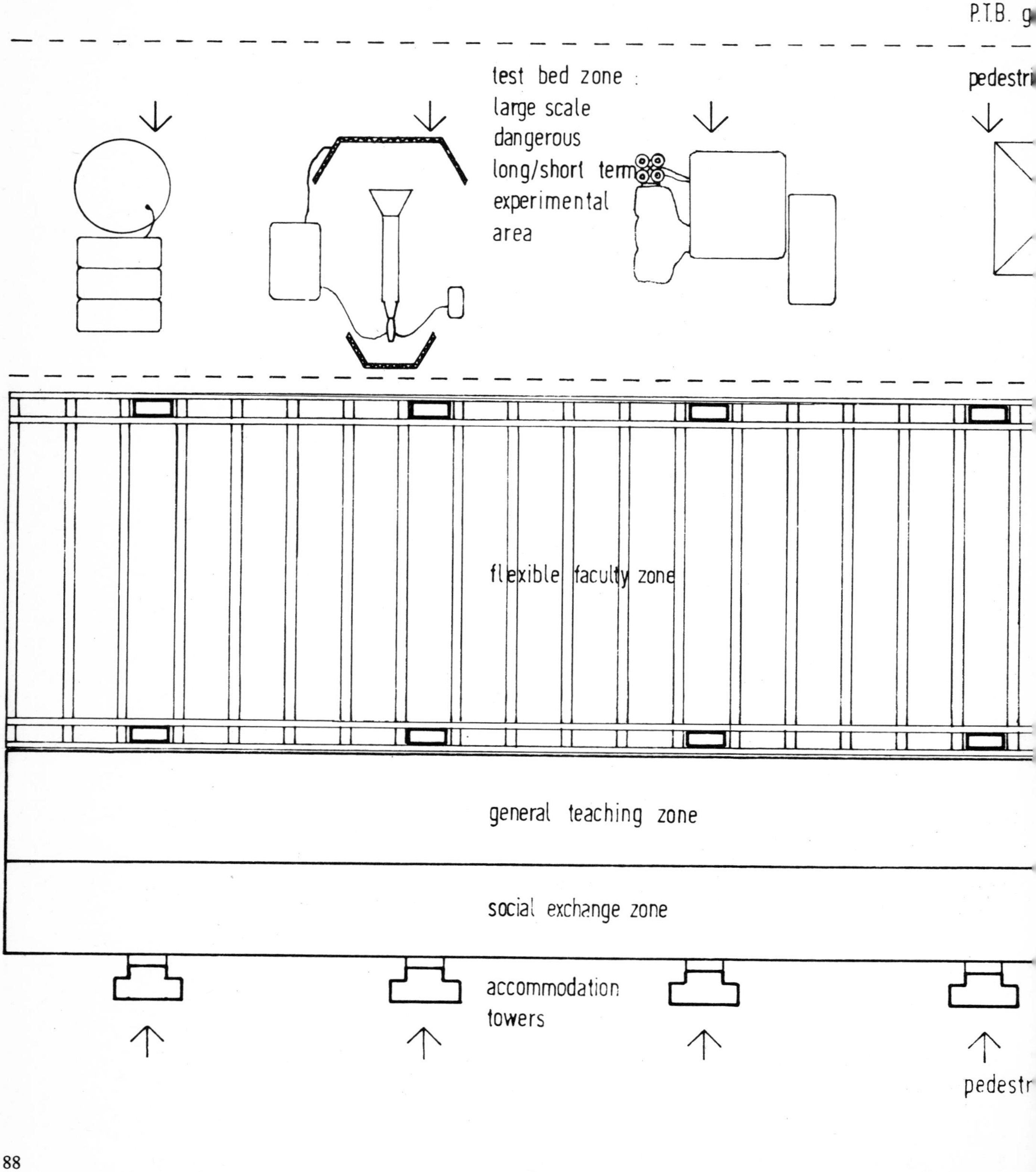

test bed zone :
large scale
dangerous
long/short term
experimental
area

P.T.B. g

pedestr

flexible faculty zone

general teaching zone

social exchange zone

accommodation
towers

pedestr

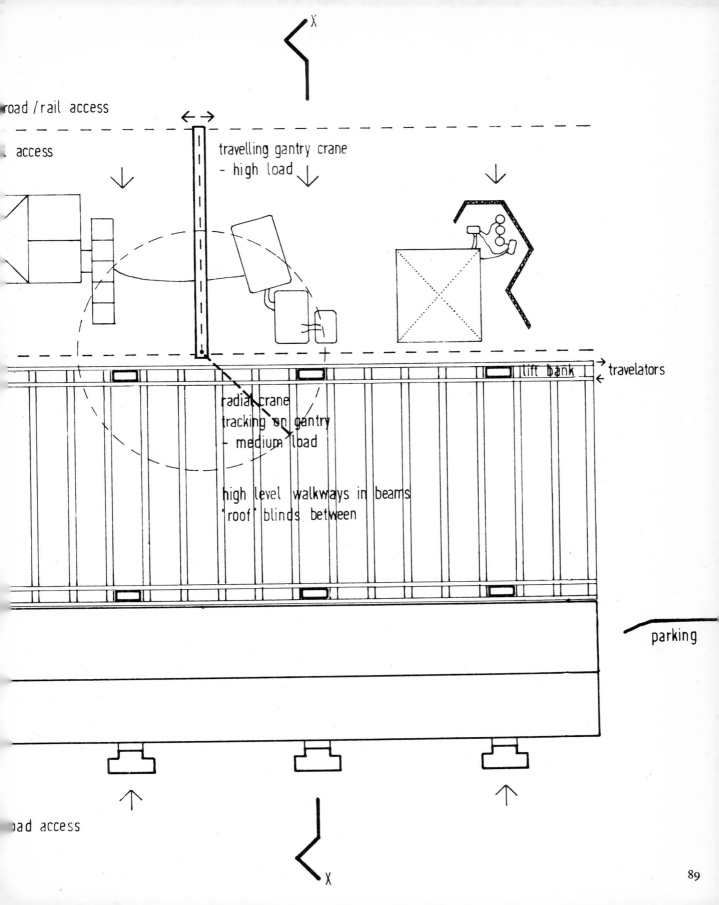

road / rail access

access

X

travelling gantry crane
- high load

radial crane
tracking on gantry
- medium load

high level walkways in beams
'roof' blinds between

lift bank

travelators

parking

road access

X

89

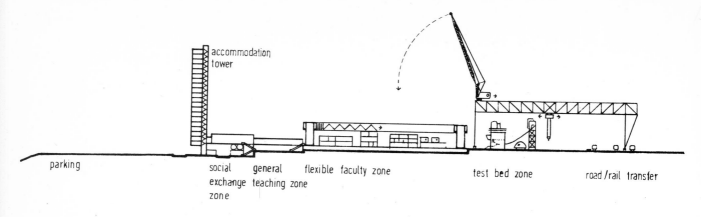

accommodation tower

parking

social exchange zone

general teaching zone

flexible faculty zone

test bed zone

road/rail transfer

SECTION X-X

Section through the Madeley Transfer Area in Cedric Price's 'Thinkbelt' project showing the particular organizational principle assumed. Lateral layering of areas occupied by specific functional activities, including a 'zone' for 'social exchange'.

Furthermore, semiology looks on the relations holding between *signifiers* and *signifieds*, as having been established arbitrarily, or non-isomorphically. For instance, it is not necessary for the purposes of communication, that the signifier 'tree' be the most 'tree-like' signifier to describe the phenomenon 'tree'. So long as once a tree is called a 'tree', everyone involved agrees to call it that (or at least to call it that sufficiently frequently that occasional ironic, or humorous exceptions will still make sense). Alternatively, it is this same non-isomorphism that accounts for the simultaneous precision and flexibility of a signifier such as 'spring', which can, depending on its context, have as its signified either 'the season of the year following winter', 'a natural source of fresh water', or 'a mechanical device for providing flexible support for weight'. In short, semiological theory holds that the relations of signifiers and signifieds depend on both a conceptual arbitrariness and an operative non-arbitrariness. And that means, of course, that it is exactly the extent to which signs are capable of misinterpretation, that they are also capable of re-interpretation. To return to the case of architecture, it is just this fact that enables Aldo van Eyck to say that 'it is not merely what a space sets out to define in human terms that gives it place-value, but what it is able to gather and transmit'.[21]

We can now see why the beliefs underlying the *Gesamtkunstwerk* and life-conditioning both entail such an aversion to ambiguity, such an incapacity for ever sustaining irony. In so far as either conception still allows any appreciation of the fact that the environment consists of a set of signs, it involves designers in an attempt to cut through all that, to 'get to the bottom of the situation' in exactly the fashion I have just described as impossible.

Take the case of Saarinen. In assuming that the 'ultimate reality' which he intended his design to reveal depended so completely upon its 'directness' and 'simplicity', he would obviously feel that he could not afford to leave any part of the detail of that design 'unsimplified', that is to say unclear or less than utterly straightforward. On the other hand, in taking for granted the capacity of the Thinkbelt to unfold *itself* in human experience 'as it in itself really is', Price would obviously see no reason to concern himself with such 'ephemeral' matters. The life-conditioner, like the *Gesamtkünstler*, always sees ambiguity as compromise, and irony as hypocrisy.

The irony of ironies is that there is no ambiguity less controlled, no irony less sustained, than that which follows from these naivetés. But to show that requires two further tenets of semiological theory. I have already quoted Merleau-Ponty to the effect that *what we perceive* is 'the sense which is revealed where the paths of my various experiences intersect, and also where my own and other people's intersect and engage each other like gears'. In other words, not only are we able to perceive only in terms of a past and present context, but we inevitably do perceive in such a context, if we perceive at all. Semiology takes account of this by positing that the signs which make up the *langue* of a social phenomenon carry meaning through the fact of their *total mutual inter-relatedness*. It is in this sense that Colin Cherry said: 'signals do not convey information as railway trucks carry coal'.[22] That is, any individual sign in a code has a particular meaning by virtue of its distinctiveness from every other sign in that code. To understand a sign means in this sense to be aware of the set of alternative possible signs from the code that could conceivably take that sign's place. This dimension of meaning Saussure characterized as 'the relationship of substitution' between the signs in the code.

However, the distinctiveness of all the signs in the code—one from another—needn't be absolute. For a sign, or to be more precise, a signifier, can stand for, or substitute for, a range of signifieds, the precise reference to be established through the actual context of the sign in question. (Recall again the example 'spring' discussed above.) To understand a sign in this sense means to be aware of the extent to which the signs surrounding a particular sign qualify its particular significance. This dimension of meaning Saussure characterized as 'the relationship of contiguity' between the signs assembled in any particular message.

Saussure illustrated this distinction by an actual architectural analogy himself, saying: 'Each linguistic unit is like a column of an antique temple: this column is in a real relation of contiguity with other parts of the building, the architrave for example; but if this column is Doric, it reminds us of the other architectural orders, Ionic or Corinthian; and this is a relation of substitution'.[23]

Jakobson has subsequently argued that Saussure's distinction between contiguity and substitution is capable of further elucidation.[24] While, in Saussure's sense of the distinction, any message would necessarily be defined in terms of both contiguity and substitution, Jakobson thought that at the level of 'style', one could point to a possibility of emphasis on one or other of the two poles. He claimed that certain works of art were characterized primarily through relations of substitution (metaphor, in his terminology) while others were characterized more through relations of contiguity (metonymy, in that terminology). Thus, he saw romanticist and symbolist poetry, and Chaplin's films, as emphasizing the pole of metaphor, and realist literature and Griffith's films as emphasizing metonymy. In architecture, one can point to a work like Mies' Farnsworth house as emphasizing the pole of metaphor, not only because of the reductive substitution from the norm 'house' which that design involves, but also because each element which remains is thereby super-charged with metaphorical significance. On the other hand, works like Carlo Scarpa's renovation of the mediaeval palace of Verona, or an interior by Alexander Girard, emphasize the role of metonymy, since they do not substitute reductively from their norms, nor powerfully metaphorize their individual elements, but rather build up their significance out of the assembly of relatively diverse parts.

When however, in this perspective, we get to designs like CBS and the Thinkbelt, we encounter what can only be described as a radical polarization between metaphor and metonymy. The Thinkbelt makes a radical substitution, both reductive (through the complete elimination of anticipated academic elements), and non-reductive (through a major shift from academic to industrial iconography), from the norm 'university'. CBS on the other hand, undertakes a radical intensification of the assembly of all its diverse elements (from the details of the window wall right down to the relations of the already-mentioned ash trays and potted plants).

It is this radical polarization which results first in the uncontrolled ambiguity and unsustained irony and eventually in the impoverishment of the existing cultural situation, which I referred to above. The first result occurs because polarization has the effect of eroding the occupants' capacity for detecting *in the particular design itself* any very helpful evidence of its relation to the historic and present context in which it has taken its place. Thus, the occupants are obliged all by themselves to bring to their experience of the environment that awareness of alternative possible environments on which that particular environment's whole distinctiveness rests. Far from being perceptually transparent

FRAMPTON: It is difficult to see how the CBS building could not also be regarded as ▶ an act of reduction from the pre-existing norm of the skyscraper. However, the paucity of metaphorical content is all too evident. Saarinen's simplicity is empty and perverse. Man goes 'down' and not 'up' into a building imbued with a falsely honorific aura. The total suppression of the act of entry, Eliade's 'rite of passage' can only be regarded under the circumstances as an anthropomorphic denial, reminiscent of the extremes of utilitarianism.

then, CBS and the Thinkbelt are in fact highly opaque; they tend to confront their occupants in the first instance as uncontrollably ambiguous, except in so far as those occupants' previous experience lends any stability to the situation. Subsequently, of course, when that previous experience is no longer so effectively operative, the second result of polarization occurs. The precarious ambiguity and irony of the first stage collapse altogether, and the occupants are no longer even able to *conceive of* those alternative possible environments. And that, effectively, amounts to an impoverishment of the existing cultural situation.

Of course, in discussing the results of this polarization, I have moved on a stage in my general argument, from a consideration of the consequences of the 19th century's loss of faith in rhetoric, to a consideration in turn, of those consequences' own effects. Let me briefly go back over my argument so far, so that I may try to indicate, in the light of semiological theory, just what *those* effects might be.

My first conclusion in these terms was that both the *Gesamtkünstler* and the life-conditioner both attempt to shift the impact of the individual design gesture from the level of *parole* to that of *langue*. Just what that involves is neatly illustrated in the now-so-fashionable quotations from *Through the Looking-Glass.*

'When I use a word,' Humpty Dumpty said in a rather scornful tone, 'I mean just what I choose it to mean, neither more nor less.' 'The question is,' said Alice, 'whether you can make words mean so many different things.' 'The question is,' said Humpty Dumpty, 'who is to be master.'[25]

Now, short of establishing a dictatorship which is either ruled or managed by designers, neither the *Gesamtkünstler* nor the life-conditioner is likely to have much success on this front. Nor would it seem that their failure in this respect would have any serious consequences. But there is the assumption that they are in a position to consciously manipulate their fellows' threshold of conscious awareness. In this case, it seems to me, the situation is more complicated. After all, it *is* possible to manipulate others' thresholds of awareness, at least to some extent. And not only that. An attempt at such manipulation which fails has consequences almost as serious as one which succeeds.

Take the case of CBS. To the extent that its designers fail to heighten the occupants' conscious awareness of their environment, the occupants will end up in the position described above, their capacity to conceive of, let alone to respond to alternative possible environments having been correspondingly reduced. On the other hand, to the extent that the designers succeed, they beg the question as to what those occupants will be so dramatically conscious of. After all, the chief part of their extraordinary effort at intensification has been devoted to making the building a ruthlessly simplified symbolic 'object' as a whole, and a highly formalized continuum in its minutest details. No effort of equivalent power has been devoted to a reconsideration of peoples' experience of the environment at the crucially important level intermediate between those extremes, the level of work a day experience of an 'office-building' in central Manhattan. At the same time, as I indicated above, the designers' extraordinary effort (at the levels where it has been made) erodes the occupants' capacity for detecting in the building itself any evidence of its relation to its context. In other words, it erodes that evidence at every level but the workaday one. This combination of circumstances will guarantee that any heightened awareness of the environment of CBS will reveal not an 'ultimate reality' at all, but rather just a monumentalization of the already familiar phenomenon of mass bureaucracy.

In the case of the Thinkbelt, the situation is slightly different. If Price were to fail to leave the Thinkbelt's occupants unconscious of their environment, those occupants would become consciously aware of their environment. The question then arises, what would they perceive? Well, they would perceive a configuration of built form which, in the terms of both the historic and the present kinds of context we have discussed, would demonstrate a quite particular and identifiable set of characteristics. Among those characteristics, as I see it, would be the following: first, a fundamental organizational scheme in terms of a mechanical flow pattern; second, a pattern of human occupation of built form, which is itself articulated mechanistically; third, the restriction upon the potential psychological intensity of any particular space to a maximum level of a 'zone'; fourth, a construction technique which formalizes the actual temporariness of the built form involved. In short, although Price claims to have succeeded in devising an environment which stands for no particular 'values' at all, what he has in fact done is simply to exchange one set of values for another. What the occupants of the Thinkbelt would consciously perceive would, in my view, be the most concrete symbolization there has yet been of bureaucracy's academic equivalent, the 'education-factory'.

On the other hand, what of the consequences if Price were to succeed, to some extent, in leaving those occupants unconscious of their environment? The environment would correspond to 'background noise', in the sense I discussed above. But of course, as I said at that point, when architecture becomes 'background noise', its unconscious impact is still far from incidental. To cite one of the most apt recent McLuhanisms, 'the most successful television commercial is the one you are least aware of'. So if Price were successful the Thinkbelt's occupants would be *processed* without realizing that was what was happening to them. Faced with an 'educational service' which made no claims on their values, the students would be unable to make any claim on that education's values. They would, in short, have become part of the 'servicing mechanism'.

It seems unnecessary, in conclusion, to do more than repeat: the *Gesamt-künstler* treats his fellows as children; the life-conditioner (and we can see now ▶ with what unwitting aptness Price chose that term) treats them as objects.

FRAMPTON: The predicament of a falsely 'valued' monumentality on the one hand, as against a hypothetical 'value-free' utilitarianism on the other. Saarinen's CBS is a 'monumentalized' office building, a giant megalith devoid of reference to human form. Perversely enough, its organization is in no way hierarchic.

Part Two

The question that now arises is why, in the mid-twentieth century, there should arise two such strikingly distinctive architectural schemes, which both betray a conception of architecture's place in human experience, and which do so in terms I have described as the bizarre consequences of the nineteenth century's loss of faith in rhetoric. To answer that question, or at least to try to answer a part of it, will require an even larger historical context than that I have used so far. But here as before, the precepts of semiological theory offer illumination.

The issues at stake really began to be unmanageable two centuries before the concepts of *Gesamtkunstwerk* and life-conditioning gained their definitive, 19th century formulations. It was at that particular time in European history when, to use Pascal's terms, the relation of 'nature' and 'custom' in human experience was first seen as such an urgent philosophical question. In 1683, Claude Perrault's *Treatise on the Five Orders* was published, a work which outlined the particularly architectural implications of that question, with astonishing clarity and foresight.

Perrault was convinced that the twin tenets of traditional architectural theory, the authority of classical precedent, and the assumption that 'beauty' was a kind of Platonic absolute, were too seriously discredited to guide contemporary practice any longer. Regarding the traditionally acknowledged authority of ancient precedent, he said: 'we cannot find, either in the remains of the Buildings of the Ancients, or among the great Number of Architects that have treated of the Proportions of the Orders, that any two Buildings, or any two Authors, agree, and have followed the same rules.'[26]

So much then, for classical precedent. As for the assumption of 'beauty' as a Platonic absolute, Perrault was so unconvinced of that as to speculate 'whether that which renders the proportions of a building agreeable be not the same thing as that which makes a modish Habit please on account of its Proportions, which nevertheless have nothing positively beautiful, and that ought to be loved for itself; since when Custom, and other reasons not positive, which induc'd this Love, come to change, we affect them no longer, tho' they remain the same.'[27]

Perrault's controversial suggestion, based on that argument, was: 'To judge rightly in this case suppose two sorts of Beauties in Architecture, namely those which are founded on solid convincing Reasons (positive beauties, in that terminology, corresponding to nature in Pascal) 'and those that depend only on Prepossession and Prejudice (arbitrary beauties for Perrault, corresponding to custom in Pascal).'[28]

It is this argument in terms of a relationship between 'positive' and 'arbitrary' beauty, which can instructively be set alongside Saussure's distinction of *langue* and *parole*, where the *langue* is the 'invariant' and the *parole* the 'variant' aspect of a communication system. I have said that in information theory, 'information' is a function of 'surprise' within a matrix of 'expectancy'. Or, to return to Perrault's terminology: 'architecture has no Proportions true in themselves; it remains to be seen whether we can establish those that are probable and likely ('vraysemblable', in the original French text), founded upon convincing Reason, without departing too far from the Proportions usually received.'[29]

As well-known as Perrault's argument is the extraordinary theoretical dispute that followed it. For over a century after its publication, Perrault's treatise dominated French architectural writing. Each successive writer from Blondel to Boullée established his own position primarily with respect to the concepts of 'positive' and 'arbitrary' beauty as originally discussed by Perrault. However, no influential contributor to that dispute attempted to sustain his concern for 'those [proportions] that are probable and likely'. Rather, each laid a particular emphasis on either 'positive' or 'arbitrary' beauty.

Although, as I have said, Perrault's argument and the ensuing dispute are well-known, the consequences of the split emphasis laid by his important successors are not, as far as I can see, well-known at all. If they were, I do not think we should be faced with such designs as CBS and the Thinkbelt. Generally speaking, we seem to be as yet too much a product of that split to recognize the extent of its influence upon our thinking. All the same, I would suggest that all subsequent architectural theory lies in the shadow of this distinction.

Consider the school of thought which, upon following Perrault, chose to assert the primacy of 'positive' beauty.[30] Their commitment involved them in a moral obligation to 'get to the bottom of' architecture, an effort whose modern guises I have already discussed in Part One. In the three centuries since Perrault, there have of course been numerous proposals put forward, purporting to reveal what that solid 'bottom' was, among them Laugier's ethnological primitivism, Choisy's technological determinism, Guadet's elemental geometry, and Hannes Meyer's dialectical materialism. However, as Perrault knew quite well, it is not possible to lay such an exclusive emphasis upon the 'positive' aspects of architecture, to the exclusion of the 'arbitrary'. Indeed, for those who wished to see, the persistent quest for a solid bottom for architecture was shown to be pointless before the eighteenth century was half over. The philosophical experience of David Hume demonstrated that such sceptical rationalism as the advocates of a solid bottom to reality were required to exercise towards the whole of *apparent* reality would end up leaving indubitable virtually no aspect of human experience whatsoever.[31]

Alternatively, consider the school of thought which chose to assert the primacy of 'arbitrary' beauty. Their commitment involved them in resolutely sticking close to the diverse surface of architecture as they saw it in all its forms. Once again, three centuries have produced various approaches to the 'arbitrary', ranging through early versions of cultural relativism, such as Fischer von Erlach's, Louden's and Schinkel's calculated eclecticism, Gilbert Scott's uncalculated eclecticism, and Philip Johnson's 'Camp'. But of course, here again, by the mid-18th century, the theoretical premises of the position were already (albeit inadvertently) demolished in Hume's claim that 'beauty is no quality in things

JENCKS: Quite apart from one's agreement or not with George Baird's particular assessments, I think they do demonstrate very well the possibilities and quandaries of 'the amorous dimension'. For what else is this dimension but a relative, moving thing with no 'solid bottom' or fixed standards? No doubt one of the implications of this realisation is that one has responsibility for expanding the 'dimensions' rather than 'impoverishing it by radical polarisation', but another is that whenever one agrees or disagrees with anything, one is really putting his own thresholds on display rather than referring to ultimates as his tone suggests. This seems to me to have enormous implications because it suggests a new tone and sensibility quite different from the pervasive authoritarian one.

94

themselves: it exists merely in the mind which contemplates them, and each mind sees a different beauty'.[32]

With that celebrated remark, Hume both out-flanked and superceded the advocates of arbitrary beauty. For were he correct—and all he did was to take the argument for 'arbitrary' beauty to its radically subjective conclusion—then the result was not just that there was no such thing as 'positive' beauty, but that there was no such thing about which one could generalize at all. From the time of Hume, until that of Marcel Duchamp and John Cage, the unqualified commitment to the 'arbitrary' has always ended in utter silence.

Now semiology does not only offer us a simulacrum of the relation of 'positive' and 'arbitrary' beauty, in terms of *langue* and *parole*. It also suggests a means of correlating the approaches of the various theorists that succeeded Perrault. I have discussed the semiological poles of metaphor (the relationship of substitution) and metonymy (the relationship of contiguity). In the light of those concepts, I think we can see that the three-centuries-old drive to 'get to the bottom of' architecture, has been characterized by a continual, radically reductive pattern of substitution for the given architecture at any particular time; while the corresponding effort to stick close to the given architecture's diverse surface has been equally characterized by a pattern of radically inclusive correlation of the forms of that given architecture.

Consider again the first tradition. As each successive proposal of a truly solid 'bottom' for architecture was made, the very force of exclusion of some factor previously taken for granted was what imbued the new proposal with a certain plausibility, not to say moral authority. Thus, Laugier proposed to substitute for the accepted architecture of his day a new one which excluded arches, niches, and applied pilasters. And the force of that exclusion lent his argument sufficient plausibility to dominate the development of architecture (especially in France) for several years. In his turn, Choisy proposed to substitute for the history of architecture which was accepted in his day a new one which excluded legitimate formal intention, and that exclusion lent his argument its conviction. And, of course, Hannes Meyer proposed to substitute for architecture in his day simply 'building', deriving his moral authority from the exclusion of 'architecture' altogether. Thus, the quest for the solid 'bottom' has proceeded. In every case, only the passage of time revealed that the particular reductive substitution involved was insufficient to guarantee the indubitability of the new proposal.

As for the second tradition, the defenders of 'arbitrary' beauty have taken the opposite tack. Instead of effecting reductive substitutions for the given architecture at a particular time, they have always attempted to correlate all that architecture's forms to the greatest extent possible. Both Louden and Schinkel, for example, devised theoretical systems in which the various stylistic motifs used in their period were carefully correlated, so that each would have a particular programme significance (Gothic style for churches, Greek style for public buildings, etc.).[33] For that matter, Saarinen's well-known effort to find the 'style for the job' is only another version of the Louden-Schinkel approach. But this school of thought has never established any real authority, since, in the face of its adversaries' reductive scepticism, it has continually failed to demonstrate any conclusive 'authenticity' for its elaborate sets of stylistic distinctions.

Now, what I suggest, in the face of designs such as the CBS building and the Thinkbelt, is that we regard both of those traditions as bankrupt. The attempt to 'get to the bottom' of architecture has now clearly shown that there is no such 'bottom'. In this respect, it is only appropriate that Price, who has in the Thinkbelt taken radical reduction to one of its extremes, should *himself* have been publicly chastised by Reyner Banham, for his unwarranted presumption in taking it for granted that he could even describe himself as 'in the enclosure business'.[34] In its latest stages, 'getting to the bottom of' architecture has turned into a game of nihilist oneupmanship. At the same time, the parallel struggle to stick close to architecture's diverse surface would seem to have shown itself as finally self-defeating. When the commitment to the 'arbitrary' has been serious, it has always fallen into the trap of making 'comprehensibility' an end in itself. In seeking 'the style for the job', and in undertaking a *Gesamtkunstwerk* such as CBS, Saarinen has in just this way promoted a kind of petrification of architecture's communicativeness. On the other hand, frivolous commitment to the 'arbitrary' has always tended to dissolve that communicativeness. To see this, one has only to think of any modern hotel interior, with its Bali Hai Room, its Charles Dickens Pub, its Old West Saloon, etc., etc. As William Burroughs puts it: 'Nothing is true; everything is permitted'.[35]

The bankruptcy of both those traditions, and the illumination cast upon them by semiological theory, suggest to me that there would be good reason to look again at Perrault's long-forgotten query as to 'whether we can establish those [proportions in architecture] that are probable and likely, without departing too far from the proportions usually received'. If Perrault's tone seems cautious, it is no more so than Paul McCartney's. The point is simply the abstract one made by Norbert Wiener: 'The essence of an effective rule for a game . . . is that it be statable in advance, and that it apply to more than one case. . . . In the simplest case, it is a property which is invariant to a set of transformations to which the system is subject.'[36]

The possibilities for architecture which open up in the perspective of semiological theory are numerous and even exhilarating. Consider again the diagram which I used above to illustrate the 'field of meaning' of a social phenomenon. As I said at that point, one dimension of that field can be considered to represent the 'scope of articulation' of architecture. Then too, in terms of the overall 'social context' of which I spoke, that 'scope of articulation' is co-extensive with our society's total social awareness of architecture, both historically and geographically.

Take the case of our relation to architecture which is distant in time, yet clearly within our own cultural tradition. A semiological perspective reveals how it is that so long as we take the trouble to observe the buildings of the past, they will assume a greater and greater distinctiveness, simply by virtue of the 'perceptual distance' as it were, which separates us from, yet connects us to them. In other words, semiology provides a kind of theoretical apparatus to back up T. S. Eliot's famous remark: 'what happens when a new work of art is created is something that happens simultaneously to all the works that preceded it'.[37] We may even conclude that there is a sense in which Wiener's 'effective rule' applies to history. Like the human unconscious, it is inexhaustible, since present action perpetually transforms it. At the same time, an acknowledgement that the distinctiveness of our architectural heritage is so largely a function of 'perceptual distance', has an important reverse implication. For example, once we recognize that the 'visual coherence' which we admire in mediaeval towns is so much due to our own historical perceptual position, then we can see that attempts to reproduce that coherence are really attempts to seize hold of our own shadows.

On the other hand, if we take the case of our relation to an exotic architecture which is remote geographically, and therefore completely incommensurable with our own historically, such as that of a 'primitive' society, then the implications are even more interesting. As Lévi-Strauss has said; 'the paradox is irresoluble; the less one culture communicates with another, the less likely they are to be corrupted one by the other; but, on the other hand, the less likely it is, in such conditions, that the respective emissaries of these cultures will be able to seize the richness and significance of their diversity'.[38] In other words, if it is the case that there exists no overlap at all between the architectural 'fields of meaning' of our own society, and those of the 'primitive' society in question, then what we can say that we *perceive* in their architecture will be nothing but a shallow (if diverting) reflection of our own. If, on the other hand (the more likely possibility nowadays), there is a partial overlay between the two 'fields of meaning', then what we perceive of their architecture may indeed bear some relation to that society's own perception of it. However, in such circumstances, our threshold of conscious awareness of that architecture still does not coincide with that society's threshold. There will be a large area of meaning of which the society is conscious, but which we can only take for granted; there will be another area, which we will consciously perceive, but which they will take for granted. It is exactly this discrepancy which, in my view, prompts certain observers, such as Bernard Rudofsky, to extol the formal precocity of primitive architecture,[39] and others, such as Christopher Alexander, to savour its 'well-adaptedness' and 'unselfconsciousness'.[40] One hopes the realization that both of these characteristics are so largely a function of our own position as observers, that it will indicate how condescending it is of Alexander to attribute such 'well-adaptedness' to an 'unself-conscious design process'.[41]

For that matter, while it is not possible here to examine Alexander's views in a general way, it is, I think, important to point out that semiological theory sees virtually all current versions of functionalism, whether 'organicist' like Alexander's, or not, as inadequate to explain or generate *any* social phenomenon. Since those social phenomena are socially representable structures of reality, they obviously 'go far beyond any possible considerations of utility'.[42] Indeed, although semiology nowhere yet includes a full-scale refutation of functionalism, it does very strongly imply the kind of critique which Hannah Arendt has formulated. 'The perplexity of utilitarianism', according to Arendt, 'is that it gets caught in the unending chain of means and ends without ever arriving at some principle which could justify the category of means and ends, that is, of utility itself. The "in order to" has become the content of the "for the sake of"; in other words, utility established as meaning generates meaninglessness'.[43]

Arendt's point is particularly important in my present context, for in continuing her argument, she then charged that utilitarian ideas had become so pervasive in the late 18th century as to affect even the thinking of Kant. His characterization of the only objects that are not 'for use', namely works of art, cannot, in her view, deny its origins in utilitarian thinking, since he described them as objects in which we take 'pleasure without any interest'. That charge has the most remarkable implications for architecture, for in the perspective of the subsequent century, it shows that the attitudes of 'arts for art's sake', and 'utilitarianism' are really two sides of the same coin. In the light of that revelation, we could conclude that the *Gesamtkünstler* and the life-conditioner do not only follow parallel paths, but in fact derive their design attitudes from the same philosophical premises.

But we must not be *too* surprised at this revelation. After all, to have understood that, we need not have turned to anthropology, communication theory and social philosophy. All we need to have done is to remember the eloquent statement (well within the normal scope of our discipline) by this century's greatest interpreter of 'meaning in architecture', in defence of the ideas of Marsilio Ficino and Pico della Mirandola. What concerned Erwin Panofsky was their 'conviction of the dignity of man, based on both the insistence on human values (rationality and freedom) and the acceptance of human limitations (fallibility and frailty); from this,' argued Panofsky, 'two postulates result—responsibility and tolerance. Small wonder,' he continued, 'that this attitude has been attacked from two opposite camps whose common aversion to the ideas of responsibility and tolerance has recently aligned them in a common front. Entrenched in one of these camps are those who deny human values: the determinists . . . the authoritarians. . . . In the other camp are those who deny human limitations in favour of some sort of intellectual or political libertinism . . . .'[44]

Responsibility and tolerance. At the intersection of those two postulates lies the role of the architect who attempts to take the measure of '*la dimension amoureuse*'. In assuming that role, in designing *in* his fellows' experience, rather than above it, or outside it, such an architect will devise forms analogous to those of Lévi-Strauss' projected anthropology; forms, that is, which 'correspond to a permanent possibility of man'.[45] In short, that architect will *offer*, with neither the arrogance of the *Gesamtkünstler*, nor the indifference of the life-conditioner, 'ideal' images of human existence, 'ideal' frames for human action.

PAWLEY: The weakness of Baird's part two lies in the absolute symmetry of this conclusion. Who is this once and future architect who will design *within* user experience with neither arrogance nor indifference? He swims, priest, analyst, folksinger, into the mind's eye like some little known outside lecturer at the A.A. Preaching a practice shorn of objects, contracts, functions and decisions he treads a narrow tightrope, arrogance on the one hand, indifference on the other . . . If Baird catches him with the stuff on him he's done for.

COLQUHOUN: It must seem tendentious to criticise such a closely argued thesis at particular points, but is difficult to accept Baird's wholesale rejection of reductivism and of the *Gesamtkunstwerk*. He does not explain how we can distinguish between good and bad *Gesamtkunstwerk* e.g. between Wright and Saarinen. Nor does he explain how work that can be shown in some sense to be reductive, for example a cubist painting or a painting by Mondrian, can appear rich in content.

BAIRD: I don't think my rejection of reductivism is 'wholesale'; in fact I distinguish in my text between reduction (the Farnsworth house) and radical reduction (the Thinkbelt). As for *Gesamtkunstwerk*, I reject it *only as I characterize it at the beginning of my text*. And although the counter-example of Wright is challenging, I would have to be convinced that my characterization of Gesamtkunstwerk damns him — or at least that it damns his most admirable work.

[1] This is an extensively revised version of a paper which originally appeared in the June 1967 issue of *Arena: the Journal of the Architectural Association*, in London.
[2] Roland Barthes: *Essais critiques*, Editions du Seuil, Paris, 1964, p. 14.
[3] Germain Boffrand, quoted in Peter Collins: *Changing Ideals in Modern Architecture*, Faber & Faber, London, 1965, p. 174.
[4] *Eero Saarinen on his Work*, Yale University Press, New Haven and London, 1962, p. 16.
[5] Cedric Price: 'Life-conditioning', in *Architectural Design*, October, 1966, p. 483.
[6] Eero Saarinen, op. cit. See also, *Progressive Architecture*, July, 1965, pp. 187–192.
[7] Cedric Price: 'Potteries Thinkbelt', in *Architectural Design*, October 1966, pp. 484–497.
[8] Robert Venturi: *Complexity and Contradiction in Architecture*, Museum of Modern Art, New York, 1966, p. 103.
[9] Life Magazine, April 29, 1966, pp. 50–58, and Chris Welles: 'How does it feel to live in total design'. pp. 59–60a.
[10] Cedric Price: 'Life-conditioning', op. cit.
[11] Roland Barthes: op. cit. See also: *Elements of Semiology*, Jonathan Cape, London, 1967; Ernst Gombrich: *Art and Illusion*, Phaidon Press, London, 1962, and *Meditations on a Hobby Horse*, Phaidon Press, London, 1963; Claude Lévi-Strauss: *A World on the Wane*, Hutchinson, London, 1961; *La Pensée Sauvage*, Plon, Paris, 1962; *Structural Anthropology*, Basic Books, New York, 1963; Marshall McLuhan: *Understanding Media*, McGraw-Hill Paperbacks, New York, 1966; Barthes is the best short introduction to the thought of Lévi-Strauss, *and* that of Peter Caws: 'What is Structuralism', in *Partisan Review*, Winter 1968, pp. 75–91.
[12] Lévi-Strauss: *The Scope of Anthropology*, p. 16.
[13] Barthes: *Eléments de sémiologie*, p. 93.
[14] Paul McCartney, quoted in the *International Times*, London, January 29, 1967.
[15] Readers of Gombrich's *Art and Illusion* and *Meditations on a Hobby Horse*, may have noticed the striking conceptual similarity between semiology's use of *langue* and *parole*, and Gombrich's use of *schema* and *correction*, which he has derived from perception psychology. Then too, of course, Professor Gombrich has been influenced as much as the semiologists by the precepts of information theory.
Readers of Christian Norberg-Schulz' *Intentions in Architecture*, Allen & Unwin, London, 1963, will also recognize how the semiologists' use of information theory is similar to his own use of it, as well as of perception psychology.
[16] Price: 'Life-conditioning', op. cit.
[17] Roman Jakobson: 'Aspects linguistique de la traduction', in *Essais de linguistique générale*, Editions de Minuit, Paris, 1963, p. 81.
[18] The phrase comes, of course, from Matthew Arnold's 'The Function of Criticism at the Present Time', of 1864, but it is characteristic of a whole 19th century tradition. Compare, for example, Ranke's description of the proper scope of historical studies, 'to show only what really happened'.
[19] *Eero Saarinen on his Work*, p. 16.
[20] Maurice Merleau-Ponty: *The Phenomenology of Perception*, Routledge and Kegan Paul, London, 1962, p. 00.

[21] Aldo van Eyck quoted in *Team 10 Primer*, edited by Alison Smithson, Standard Catalogue Co., London, p. 40.

[22] Colin Cherry, quoted by Gombrich in *Meditations on a Hobby Horse*, p. 61.

[23] Saussure, quoted by Barthes, in Communications No. 4, p. 115.

[24] Jakobson: 'Deux aspects du langage et deux types d'aphasie', in op. cit., pp. 43–67.

[25] Lewis Carroll: *Alice in Wonderland*, and *Through the Looking-Glass*, New American Library, New York, 1960, p. 186.

[26] Claude Perrault: *A Treatise on the Five Orders*, translated by John James, London, 1722, p. ii.

[27] Perrault: op. cit. p. v.

[28] Perrault: op. cit. p. vi.

[29] Perrault: op. cit. p. xi.

[30] Admittedly, not all members of this school have talked in terms of 'beauty'. But they have all taken a consistent attitude to what architecture 'ought' to be, as opposed to what it 'is', at any particular point in time (using 'is' as 'ought' in the manner of modern sociology).

[31] *Enlightenment*, Beacon Press, Boston, 1960, p. 307.

[32] David Hume: *A Treatise of Human Nature*.

[33] My information regarding Louden's efforts I owe to George L. Hersey, of the Department of Art at Yale University; that regarding Schinkel's, to Professor Christian Norberg-Schulz, of the State School of Architecture, Oslo, Norway.

[34] The incident is described by Robin Middleton, in *Architectural Design*, July 1966, p. 322.

[35] William Burroughs: *Dead Fingers Talk*, Tandem Books, London, 1966, p. 197.

[36] Norbert Wiener: *Cybernetics*, M.I.T. Press, Boston, 1965, p. 50.

[37] T. S. Eliot: *The Sacred Wood*, Methuen, London, 1964, p. 49.

[38] Lévi-Strauss: *A World on the Wane*, p. 45.

[39] Bernard Rudofsky: *Architecture without Architects*, Museum of Modern Art, New York, 1965.

[40] Christopher Alexander: *Notes on the Synthesis of Form*, Harvard University Press, 1964. See especially chapter 3.

[41] Alexander: op. cit., p. 32 ff.

[42] Caws: op. cit., p. 80.

[43] Hannah Arendt: *The Human Condition*, Doubleday Anchor Books, Garden City, New York, 1959, p. 135.

[44] Erwin Panofsky: 'The History of Art as a Humanistic Discipline', in *Meaning in the Visual Arts*, Doubleday Anchor Books, Garden City, New York, 1955, p. 2.

[45] Lévi-Strauss: *The Scope of Anthropology*, p. 49.

The Architecture of Wampanoag

Reyner Banham

A magazine article topical enough to be worth publishing must be dead mutton by the time the next issue appears—no matter what spark of eternal truth the author vaingloriously believes to glimmer within it. Re-publication can only be justified by some change in external circumstance which revalidates (and thus subtly falsifies) the original premises, argument or conclusion—and I do not exclude the possibility that the circumstances may have been changed by the content (or, more likely, the reputation) of the article itself.

No such inflated claim need be made for the two pieces reprinted below—however much any form of re-printing goes against my deeply felt preference for letting sleeping articles lie. One has the pseudo-topicality of referring to an article by another hand which is also re-published in this volume, though the original reference was highly co-incidental. That is to say, *Flatscape* was not written as a refutation of George Baird; it was undertaken as an attempt to extend (modestly) the range of architectural discourse by including the visual and other values of the so-called 'container revolution', and looking round for an explicit reference to typify the timidity and conservatism of the architectural profession, I found Baird's piece neatly and topically to hand (it had appeared in print only two months before).

I realize that I may be accused of intellectual coarseness in deliberately misinterpreting the word 'structuralism' in a sense which, if not Lévi-Straussical, is nevertheless highly probable in an architectural context, (but I had, apparently, made a correct intuitive estimate of the trend of his argument). In the worst (i.e., most time-honoured) academic tradition, Baird had adopted a defensive position based on the traditional monumental 'values' of architecture as we have known it. In this, the only original contribution seems to me to be the use of Lévi-Strauss as an external buttress to the academic/traditionalist position, instead of one of the earlier instant gurus who were conscripted for this duty; older readers may remember how, five or six years ago, Karl Popper was employed by Stanford Anderson as a bulwark of the 'Tradition that is not Trad, Dad'.

JENCKS: In spite of all the polemical fireworks, I don't think the positions of Banham and Baird are as different as would appear. As I pointed out in answering *Flatscape* before, Baird is not defending monumentality (he attacks Saarinen for unsuccessful monumentality – Banham's intuitive estimate is wrong) and furthermore both Baird and Banham argue against fixed, Platonic values and realize their changing nature in a pluralist situation. In fact, both of them seek to enlarge that situation by pointing out new relevancies to architecture – either semiology or responsive and homeostatic structures. The only substantial difference in their positions is that Baird might accept monumentality with equanimity whereas Banham would send it up and out of the house (to have it sneak back in through the electronic spaghetti).

There seem to me to be two key objections to all argumentation of the sort advanced by Baird. Firstly that they are undemocratic and restrictive, requiring the inhabitants of, say, a university to accept at second-hand the values of the architectural tradition, still heavily contaminated with the fall-out of that Tradition's past as the creature of Baroque despotism, rather than being permitted to discover and impose their own values on their buildings. Secondly, and more damagingly, all such academic constructions are retrospective and/or (since pop anthropology set in) exotic, whereas any body of theory which offers to instruct architects on how they should proceed needs to be both predictive and local, since all but a minute fraction of architectural activity is concerned with propositions about the environmental future of particular pieces of land. (*Archigramtype* visionaries may regret, and justifiably combat, the fixity of buildings, but their uniqueness of location seems likely to be with us for a long time to come.)

Baird is therefore right to identify Cedric Price as his enemy—the Thinkbelt project offers its future inhabitants freedom from other people's values left over from the past. In the same way the buildings of the Hochschule für Gestaltung at Ulm, in spite of Max Bill's bloody-mindedness and the retrospective (if politically admirable) reasons for their commissioning, have always possessed the inestimable virtue of being so nearly value-free and self effacing that they left their occupants in peace to go about their business. The absence of 'values' identifiable by historical or philological techniques does not in fact produce a value-free architecture; the absence of those academic values can in itself be a 'value' if it frees the environment from cultural clutter.

PAWLEY: 'Cultural clutter' begins the day you find yesterday's newspaper in today's node – or see an old movie on television.

It was for this reason that I wrote, in *Flatscape*, of '*almost* value-free buildings', and a design like the Thinkbelt would always retain the paradoxical and residual value of being free of gratuitous values. The evident reluctance of Baird and his apologists to perceive this as anything but a prospective evil is a classic example of what we shall doubtless learn to identify as the 'Wampanoag Effect', following the exposition set out in *New Scientist* (February 22, 1968). Briefly, the

USS Wampanoag was withdrawn from service in the 1870's, after a year of exemplary performance, simply because senior US naval officers were so culture-bound to more primitive navigational and propulsive techniques that they could not admit the virtues of the Wampanoag's more advanced technology.

Most striking, in view of Baird's arguments, was the objection of senior brass that service on vessels like the Wampanoag'would not produce the sort of sailor the American navy had hitherto reared'. This kind of response is known on our side of the Atlantic as the 'price of Admiralty' and Baird seems prepared to exact it from architecture because, realizing that the kind of student who would emerge from a non-institution like the Thinkbelt might be different from the ivy-mouldering product of value-littered campuses, he can only fearfully reject them, in advance and without evidence, as 'contemptuous . . . bureaucratic . . .' and all the rest of it.

The prevalence of this fear of an environment devoid of preformed values but capable of generating new values symbiotically with its inhabitants is one of my reasons for agreeing to the reprinting of *A Home is not a House*. Since it first appeared in 1965 this article has acquired some sort of legendary status which is obviously due to the quality and architectural appeal of François Dallegret's marvellous illustrations. I think, however, that some aspects of the text will bear a second reading, because the intention of the piece was indeed predictive; it was intended to be about the sort of things that could happen after the architectural profession has found 'ways of by-passing such intellectual dead ends' as are created by successive generations of Bairds (to quote the penultimate paragraph of *Flatscape*), and because there are some veiled discordances between the text and the illustrations that will bear looking at.

On the predictive point; the aim was to discuss non-rigid, and thus non-monumental architecture. Since the spring of 1965 an increasing amount of that kind of architecture (mostly inflatables) has come within the experience and creative capacity of a whole generation of students and younger architects, but the argument, it will be observed, is conducted on the basis of technological probabilities and the questioning of entrenched mental schemata. This was largely because I had too little experience at that time of non-rigid enclosures to offer any very informed comments on them as environmental situations. Since then, the situation (of myself and of any potential readership) has changed radically.

What we know, since that change, is that while non-rigid structures are—for better or worse—devoid of the 'values' of rigid monumental buildings, they are not value-free. Rather, they offer the prospect of alternative value-patterns based not upon the monumental and the static, but upon the responsive and the homeostatic—an inflatable structure does not just stand inflexibly there and deteriorate, like a building of stone or steel, but constantly, visibly, audibly, reassuringly and suggestively moves and adjusts to accommodate changing internal and external circumstances. Changes in a rigid structure are irreversible, short of surgical repair, but an inflatable, by the application of power, can resume a former shape and thus appear to play old harry with entropy. And the splendours and miseries of this agile and homeostatic architecture are something for which no amount of history or Lévistrology has prepared us.

This, however, does not mean that the old historical and monumental 'values' cannot get back into the act. Dallegret's drawings evoke those values so effectively that it is clear that any fetishist of the *Dimension Amoureuse* who wants to keep up that particular ritual has room to do so in at least the static equipment, if not the enclosing membranes, of inflatable architecture. But the cultivation of such rituals is in no way essential or integral to the quality of that environment. The sketches of the equipment which I made for my own illumination while writing the technical specification from which Dallegret prepared his drawings look like the productions of a different culture—which they are, since I was trained as an engineer, and mechanical engineering has its own amorous dimensions, expressed in the time scarred phrase 'If it looks right, it is right'.

PAWLEY: Elting Morison, the original source for the New Scientist article, used the *Wampanoag* story to illustrate a diametrically opposed and far subtler point: that human beings react against advanced technology when it constitutes a violent and comprehensive attack on their ambitions, beliefs, obligations, purposes and feelings.

The Officers of the 1869 naval board investigating the *Wampanoag* 'perceived that a machine, any machine, if left to itself, tends to establish its own conditions, to create its own environment and draw men into it. Since any machine is designed to do only a part of what a whole man can do, it tends to wear down those parts of a man that are not included in the design'.

The real point is not that stupid naval officers block advanced technology, or that George Baird is a card-carrying reactionary; but that *identity and meaning* are more likely to be threatened by 'advanced technology' in this context than by 'secondhand values'.

I say 'time-scarred' because every major innovation in mechanical engineering has 'looked wrong' to the higher punditry of the profession—it is just another sanctified Wampanoag Effect. In other words, both the architect's Amorous Dimension and the engineer's Right Look, are simply habitual modes of styling up the facts of the matter in hand, and the function of that styling is, equally simply, reassurance, the fortification of the entrenched prejudices of closed corporations, and there is nothing to choose between them—except that mechanical engineers make fewer claims than do the professionals of humane learning to be in touch with fundamental values or eternal verities.

Flatscape with Containers

It's amazing how many educated minds' eyes still visualize docks in the imagery of, say, Quentin Hughes' *Seaport*—tall craggy warehouses, masts, cranes and funnels silhouetted against the sky, picturesque Trotskyites in silk mufflers toting that box, lifting that bale, getting a little drunk and landing in the Tower magistrates' court. But this is now an iconography of death, all the standard images of rich clutter belong to a world that has had it.

The wealth of nations no longer piles up storeys high, tight under the crutch of Thames. Docks, growing inexorably bigger, slip down round the ankles of estuaries. Thus, Mersey operations no longer pack snugly into Jesse Hartley's Albert Dock, but have slipped down the whole length of the Dock Road and are about to fetch up in a new giant installation in front of the pretty marine terraces of Crosby. The Port of London is growing like crazy down at Tilbury, but Telford's St Katherine Dock is now no more than a candidate for the Michael Young playport.

And when you get to Tilbury, for instance, you see little to recall the typical imagery of ports. What you see, more than anything else, is acreage of flat tarmac, or concrete. Literally acreage; single areas of ten acres, hardly broken by a lamp post or sign, are chicken feed in the new world of freight handling that includes not only ports, but also railway freight-liner yards, and even parcels depots. It's all part of the 'container revolution' about which we are getting so much PRO-chat, but it is important to realize that the container bit is not an extraordinary and unprecedented event, but simply the most recent stage in a revolutionary process that has been going on since about the time Telford and Hartley built their masterdocks.

Their monumental warehouses stood tall at the water's edge, with cranes bracketed off their façades for a very good reason. If you had winched up a bale from the bottom of a ship's hold to deck level, you might as well go on moving it vertically to the umpteenth floor, rather than put it down and start moving it about horizontally, because that was a good deal more difficult before railways and mechanical power. But by the time these heroic schemes were completing, the railway age was already beginning; horizontal movement on land was becoming handy and economical; and the next full generation of docks, like the Royals on the Thames, ceased to look like any part of civil architecture. They started to slip down the estuary, the buildings began to shrink in height and pretension, and were moved back from the waterside to accommodate rail tracks and travelling cranes.

Old Albert and Katherine were thus the first victims of what now appears to be an inexorable law of design for transportation—that by the time you have finally found an architecturally acceptable format for any type of transport, it's obsolete. Bert and Kate finally found the canonical form for a dying mediaeval concept of goods handling; St Pancras Station became obsolete on the day it opened; Idlewild, the perfected propeller-driven airport, is overrun with jets.

And now that the rubber-tyred vehicle can rush about horizontally in all directions without benefit of railway lines, the railway age dock of two-storey warehouses and luffing cranes has had it too. The most conspicuous, because

Fork-lift truck at Tilbury.

At Tilbury or Rotterdam, or the BR freightliner terminals, buildings are of little consequence, look temporary, survive on sufferance at the margins of the action. And for a very good reason; in so far as buildings existed to keep the weather off the merchandise, they aren't much needed now. The essence of both container-isation and roll-on-roll-off techniques is not only that the goods reach the terminal in neat packages, but that the packages provide as much of the right kind of weather protection as the goods need—pork in refrigerated containers, stout in tanks, timber in steel-strapped parcels.

But if the buildings are not needed the one thing that the trailers, straddle cranes and fork-lift trucks must have is vast areas of more or less ideal flat surface on which to roll around. When No. 34 berth at Tilbury was (rather hurriedly) converted to handle packaged timber, its shed had a 72 foot clearance punched through the middle of it, to connect the dockside with 11½ acres of tarmac hard-standing behind it. This can be used indiscriminately as a surface on which to stack, or a kind of omni-directional roadway on which the fork-lift trucks can whizz around with the packages of timber.

And that is the scale of the new dockscape, dictated by the rubber-tyred vehicle. The same rubber-tyrant fixes the wide flat form of practically everything else around. A roll-on-roll-off terminal, for instance, is effectively a motorway intersection, from which two or more of the roads run straight into large holes in the sterns of ships. Or, at the York Way freightliner terminal behind King's Cross station the thing which strikes the eye is that, in spite of the fact that this is a railway facility, the Drott Travelift (no, I didn't make that up) cranes run up

p 104-105

Tilbury docks extension. Conventional berths with warehouse and crane, bottom right; roll-on/roll-off berth, bottom left; and newest container berths under construction, above.

Tilbury Berth 43. Straddle-crane and straddle-carrier.

and down the 1,000 foot interchange on large diameter road-wheels, not rail-way tracks.

At the Stratford terminal the effect is really spectacular. The given landscape is wide, raw, flat and sandy under the expanse of sky that would make poets rave if it wasn't the southern end of Hackney marshes. Nothing stands more than a truck's height, except where containers have been stacked two deep along the side of the terminal, and beside them the outlines of the two big Morris straddle-cranes dominate the sky. In the first week of August, one was still a bare four-legged skeleton, orange-red in its lead-oxide underpaint; the other fully equipped with its lifting tackle and control cab, in its final livery of yellow, with men busy painting diagonal black fright stripes on its lower extremities. (Query: in a scene where nearly every visible thing is covered in yellow and black fright-stripes, how do you know which one to beware of next?)

It's one of the great sights of London (and a pity it's not open to the public, though you get a fair view of it after the kink in Temple Mill Lane). But what are architects going to do with situations like this? As a profession they claim the right and duty to design 'the complete human environment,' but one thing they cannot bear to contemplate is large flat areas of anything at all; they whimper in their campari-soda about airports, supermarkets, 'prairie planning in the new towns' and—above all—car parks. Hence the constant attempts to sweep parked cars up into monumental multistorey heaps, even where there is no great need. At Cumbernauld, Geoffrey Copcutt, tried to make cars disappear by tucking them up under the skirts of his town-centre megastructure, above ground-level.

But they have fallen out again, and are beginning to spread over the surrounding ground. And the logic of transportation seems to say yes. The logic of airport operation says bus the passengers straight to the plane on the tarmac, and scrap the buildings, and the logic of freight handling—logical enough to compete with Europort/Rotterdam, that is—says acres of hard standing with nothing on it that can't be moved out of the way.

This logic is already beginning to make a transitional kind of sense, visually. Where buildings—roofed volumes with side enclosures—persist, they seem to grow naturally as lightweight shells unencumbered by massive masonry or cultural pretensions. In a portscape where corrugated asbestos and ribbed aluminium sheet are not cheap substitutes but the very stuff of building, a brick looks as pompous as rusticated masonry does elsewhere (the passenger hall at Tilbury, with its coats of arms and barrel vaults, would look pompous anywhere, and attains a positively nightmare quality there). And these shed shells, stiff tents almost, can be perfectly adequately designed by engineers without any interference from architects, and usually are.

Architects, at the moment, probably don't mind too much about this, because it doesn't impinge on their chosen scene, the city. No, that's not true—thanks to an unforeseeable series of crossed directives from various higher echelons, the goods-handling aesthetic of horizontal spread and aluminium cladding gets one very good showing, within a few minutes of the British Museum and Regent's Park. After the freeze on office building in central London, Euston station was deprived of sundry architect-designed superstructures, and the upper deck of the surviving rump of the scheme is just a huge parcels-depot shed, single-storey and covering most of the extent of the station below. It's very good, too, especially the long, aluminium-clad side elevation on to Cardington Street.

Curiously enough, credit or blame for this intrusion of the goods-handling aesthetic into central London lies partly with architects. Some of the design decisions affecting its shape and arrangement can be traced back to Theo Crosby's Euston design team at Taylor-Woodrow's, and are all that remain of their original grandiose project. But then, that was a rather remarkable set-up, since it was where the Archigram visionaries met one another for the first time.

And the Archigram vision, as I have indicated here before, is something that many thinking members of the profession don't wish to know about. Personally, I doubt if even Archigram could do the real Tilbury stuff with any enthusiasm. The only architect who might, in fact, is Cedric Price, who applied container technology, near enough, to university teaching in his Thinkbelt project (*New Society*, 2 June, 1966). For this he has recently been attacked, not by some doddering old architectural knight, but by one of the profession's most esteemed younger intellectuals, George Baird, arch-priest of the cult of 'values' (rather than human service) in architecture. According to Baird, the Thinkbelt's avoidance of showy monumentality (for which 'structuralism' is the current flip synonym) will lead to practically every fashionable evil in the book, from contemptuousness to bureaucracy (though the passage in which he made these accusations seems to have disappeared astutely enough, since it exposes Baird to obvious ridicule—in the version of his article that appears in the present publication).

The working profession will find ways of by-passing such intellectual dead-ends—it has to, or it would go out of business—and architects will eventually compose themselves into a frame of mind where they can design a few almost value-free buildings for almost building-free sites, and the architectural magazines will find ways of making the photographs look suitably handsome, and will bring out special issues on 'The Architecture of Megasurface', or some such.

But by then, of course, hovercraft will have made even the *water* in docks obsolete, if multi-function pipelines haven't made hovercraft obsolete, and architects (to make a suitably J. M. Richards-type joke) will have missed the boat again.

A Home is not a House

When your house contains such a complex of piping, flues, ducts, wires, lights, inlets, outlets, ovens, sinks, refuse disposers, hi-fi reverberators, antennae, conduits, freezers, heaters—when it contains so many services that the hardware could stand up by itself without any assistance from the house, why have a house to hold it up? When the cost of all this tackle is half of the total outlay (or more, as it often is) what is the house doing except concealing your mechanical pudenda from the stares of folks on the sidewalk? Once or twice recently there have been buildings where the public was genuinely confused about what was mechanical services, what was structure—many visitors to Philadelphia take quite a time to work out that the floors of Louis Kahn's laboratory towers are not supported by the flanking brick duct boxes, and when they have worked it out, they are inclined to wonder if it was worth all the trouble of giving them an independent supporting structure.

No doubt about it, a great deal of the attention captured by those labs derives from Kahn's attempt to put the drama of mechanical services on show—and if, in the end, it fails to do that convincingly, the psychological importance of the gesture remains, at least in the eyes of his fellow architects. Services are a topic on which architectural practice has alternated capriciously between the brazen and the coy—there was the grand old Let-it-dangle period, when every ceiling was a mess of gaily painted entrails, as in the council chambers of the UN building, and there have been fits of pudicity when even the most innocent anatomical details have been hurriedly veiled with a suspended ceiling.

Basically, there are two reasons for all this blowing hot and cold (if you will excuse the air conditioning industry's oldest-working pun). The first is that mechanical services are too new to have been absorbed into the proverbial wisdom of the profession: none of the great slogans—Form Follows Function, *accusez la structure*, Firmness Commodity and Delight, Truth to Materials, *Wenig ist Mehr*—is much use in coping with the mechanical invasion. The nearest thing, in a significantly negative way, is Le Corbusier's *Pour Ledoux, c'était facile—pas de tubes*, which seems to be gaining proverbial-type currency as the expression of a profound nostalgia for the golden age before piping set in.

The second reason is that the mechanical invasion is a fact, and architects—especially American architects—sense that it is a cultural threat to their position in the world. American architects are certainly right to feel this, because their professional speciality, the art of creating monumental spaces, has never been securely established on this continent. It remains a transplant from an older culture and architects in America are constantly harking back to that culture. The generation of Stanford White and Louis Sullivan were prone to behave like *émigrés* from France, Frank Lloyd Wright was apt to take cover behind sentimental Teutonicisms like *Lieber Meister*, the big boys of the Thirties and Forties came from Aachen and Berlin anyhow, the pacemakers of the Fifties and Sixties are men of international culture like Charles Eames and Philip Johnson, and so too, in many ways, are the coming men of today, like Myron Goldsmith.

Left to their own devices, Americans do not monumentalize or make architecture. From the Cape Cod cottage, through the balloon frame to the perfection of permanently pleated aluminium siding with embossed wood-graining, they have tended to build a brick chimney and lean a collection of shacks against it. When Groff Conklin wrote (in 'The Weather-Conditioned House') that 'a house is nothing but a hollow shell . . . a shell is all a house or any structure in which human beings live and work, really is. And most shells in nature are extraordinarily inefficient barriers to cold and heat . . .' he was expressing an extremely American view, backed by a long-established grass-roots tradition.

And since that tradition agrees with him that the American hollow shell is such an inefficient heat barrier, Americans have always been prepared to pump more heat, light and power into their shelters than have other peoples. America's monumental space is, I suppose, the great outdoors—the porch, the terrace, Whitman's rail-traced plains, Kerouac's infinite road, and now, the Great Up There. Even within the house, Americans rapidly learned to dispense with the

Illustrated by François Dallegret

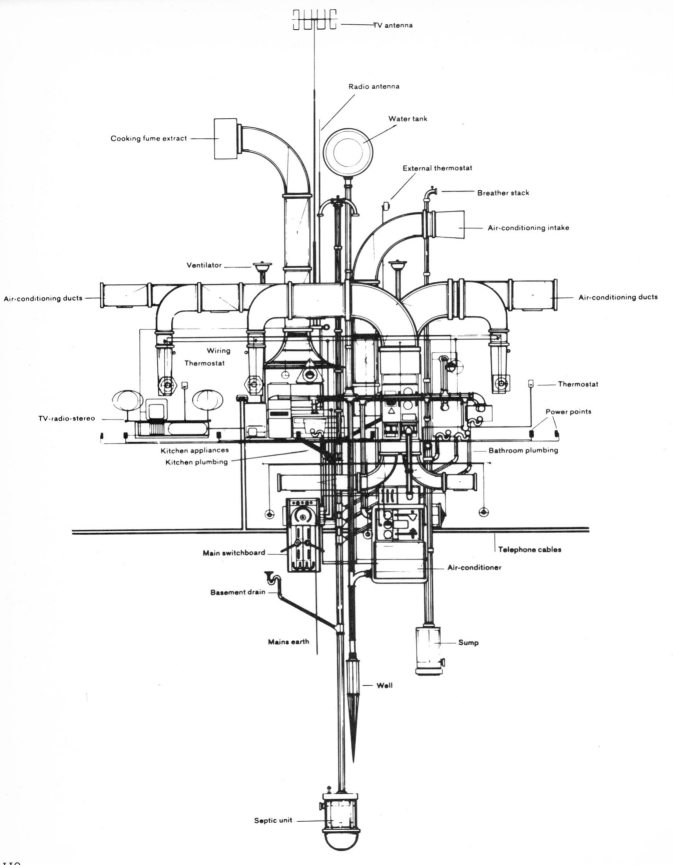

TV antenna

Radio antenna

Water tank

Cooking fume extract

External thermostat

Breather stack

Air-conditioning intake

Ventilator

Air-conditioning ducts

Air-conditioning ducts

Wiring

Thermostat

Thermostat

TV-radio-stereo

Power points

Kitchen appliances

Bathroom plumbing

Kitchen plumbing

Telephone cables

Main switchboard

Air-conditioner

Basement drain

Mains earth

Sump

Well

Septic unit

partitions that Europeans need to keep space architectural and within bounds, and long before Wright began blundering through the walls that subdivided polite architecture into living room, games room, card room, gun room, etc., humbler Americans had been slipping into a way of life adapted to informally planned interiors that were, effectively, large single spaces.

Now, large single volumes wrapped in flimsy shells have to be lighted and heated in a manner quite different and more generous then the cubicular interiors of the European tradition around which the concept of domestic architecture first crystallized. Right from the start, from the Franklin stove and the kerosene lamp, the American interior has had to be better serviced if it was to support a civilized culture, and this is one of the reasons that the U.S. has been the forcing ground of mechanical services in buildings—so if services are to be felt anywhere as a threat to architecture, it should be in America.

'The plumber is the quartermaster of American culture', wrote Adolf Loos, father of all European platitudes about the superiority of U.S. plumbing. He knew what he was talking about; his brief visit to the States in the Nineties convinced him that the outstanding virtues of the American way of life were its informality (no need to wear a top hat to call on local officials) and its cleanliness—which was bound to be noticed by a Viennese with as highly developed a set of Freudian compulsions as he had. That obsession with clean (which can become one of the higher absurdities of America's lysol-breathing Kleenex-culture) was another psychological motive that drove the nation toward mechanical services. The early justification of air-conditioning was not just that people had to breathe: Konrad Meier ('Reflections on Heating and Ventilating', 1904) wrote fastidiously of '. . . excessive amounts of water vapour, sickly odours from respiratory organs, unclean teeth, perspiration, untidy clothing, the presence of microbes due to various conditions, stuffy air from dusty carpets and draperies . . . cause greater discomfort and greater ill health.'

(Have a wash, and come back for the next paragraph.)

Most pioneer air-conditioning men seem to have been nose-obsessed in this way: best friends could just about force themselves to tell America of her national B.O.—and then, compulsive salesmen to a man, promptly prescribed their own patent improved panacea for ventilating the hell out of her. Somewhere among these clustering concepts—cleanliness, the lightweight shell, the mechanical services, the informality and indifference to monumental architectural values, the passion for the outdoors—there always seemed to me to lurk some elusive master concept that would never quite come into focus. It finally became clear and legible to me in June 1964, in the most highly appropriate and symptomatic circumstances.

I was standing up to my chest-hair in water, making home movies (I get that NASA kick from taking expensive hardware into hostile environments) at the campus beach at Southern Illinois. This beach combines the outdoor and the clean in a highly American manner—scenically it is the old swimmin' hole of Huckleberry Finn tradition, but it is properly policed (by sophomore lifeguards sitting on Eames chairs on poles in the water) and it's *chlorinated* too. From where I stood, I could see not only immensely elaborate family barbecues and picnics in progress on the sterilized sand, but also, through and above the trees, the basketry interlaces of one of Buckminster Fuller's experimental domes. And it hit me then, that if dirty old Nature could be kept under the proper degree of control (sex left in, streptococci taken out) by other means, the United States would be happy to dispense with architecture and buildings altogether.

Bucky Fuller, of course, is very big on this proposition: his famous non-rhetorical question, 'Madam, do you know what your house weighs?' articulates a subversive suspicion of the monumental. This suspicion is inarticulately shared by the untold thousands of Americans who have already shed the dead-weight of domestic architecture and live in mobile homes which, though they may never actually be moved, still deliver rather better performance as shelter than do ground-anchored structures costing at least three times as much and weighing ten times more. If someone could devise a package that would effectively

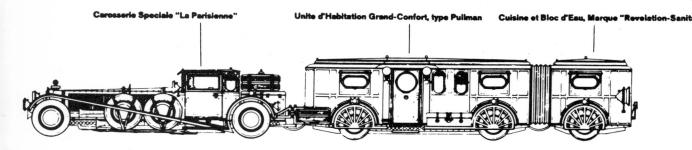

Carosserie Speciale "La Parisienne"   Unité d'Habitation Grand-Confort, type Pullman   Cuisine et Bloc d'Eau, Marque "Revelation-Sanitaire"

disconnect the mobile home from the dangling wires of the town electricity supply, the bottled gas containers insecurely perched on a packing case and the semi-unspeakable sanitary arrangements that stem from not being connected to the main sewer—then we should really see some changes. It may not be so far away either; defence cutbacks may send aerospace spin-off spinning in some new directions quite soon, and that kind of miniaturization-talent applied to a genuinely self-contained and regenerative standard-of-living package that could be towed behind a trailer home or clipped to it, could produce a sort of U-haul unit that might be picked up or dropped off at depots across the face of the nation. Avis might still become the first in U-Tility, even if they have to go on being a trying second in car hire.

Out of this might come a domestic revolution beside which modern architecture would look like Kiddibrix, because you might be able to dispense with the trailer home as well. A standard-of-living package (the phrase and the concept are both Bucky Fuller's) that really worked might, like so many sophisticated inventions, return Man nearer to a natural state in spite of his complex culture (much as the supersession of the Morse telegraph by the Bell Telephone restored his power of speech nationwide). Man started with two basic ways of controlling environment: one by avoiding the issue and hiding under a rock, tree, tent or roof (this led ultimately to architecture as we know it) and the other by actually interfering with the local meteorology, usually by means of a camp-fire, which, in a more polished form, might lead to the kind of situation now under discussion. Unlike the living space trapped with our forebears under a rock or roof, the space around a camp-fire has many unique qualities which architecture cannot hope to equal, above all, its freedom and variability.

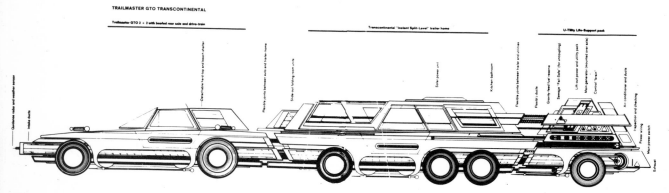

TRAILMASTER GTO TRANSCONTINENTAL

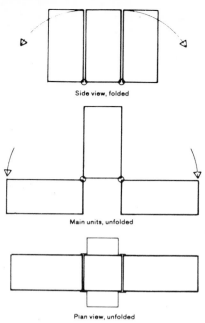

Side view, folded

Main units, unfolded

Plan view, unfolded

The direction and strength of the wind will decide the main shape and dimensions of that space, stretching the area of tolerable warmth into a long oval, but the output of light will not be affected by the wind, and the area of tolerable illumination will be a circle overlapping the oval of warmth. There will thus be a variety of environmental choices balancing light against warmth according to need and interest. If you want to do close work, like shrinking a human head, you sit in one place, but if you want to sleep you curl up somewhere different; the floating knuckle-bones game would come to rest somewhere quite different from the environment that suited the meeting of the initiation-rites steering committee . . . and all this would be jim dandy if camp-fires were not so perishing inefficient, unreliable, smoky and the rest of it.

But a properly set-up standard-of-living package, breathing out warm air along the ground (instead of sucking in cold along the ground like a campfire), radiating soft light and Dionne Warwick in heart-warming stereo, with well-aged protein turning in an infra-red glow in the rotisserie, and the ice-maker discreetly coughing cubes into glasses on the swing-out bar—this could do something for a woodland glade or creek-side rock that Playboy could never do for its penthouse. But how are you going to manhandle this hunk of technology down to the creek? It doesn't have to be that massive; aerospace needs, for instance, have

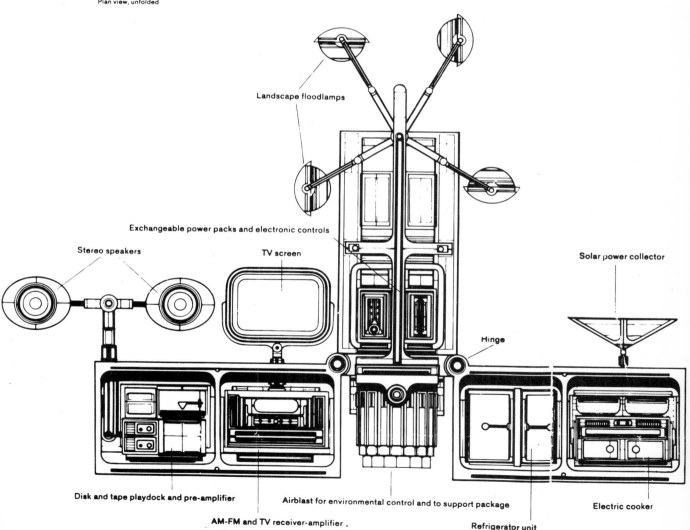

Landscape floodlamps

Exchangeable power packs and electronic controls

Stereo speakers

TV screen

Solar power collector

Hinge

Disk and tape playdock and pre-amplifier

AM-FM and TV receiver-amplifier .

Airblast for environmental control and to support package

Refrigerator unit

Electric cooker

done wild things to solid-state technology, producing even tiny refrigerating transistors. They don't as yet mop up any great quantity of heat, but what are you going to do in this glade anyhow; put a whole steer in deep-freeze? Nor do you have to manhandle it—it could ride on a cushion of air (its own air-conditioning output, for instance) like a hovercraft or domestic vacuum cleaner.

All this will eat up quite a lot of power, transistors notwithstanding. But one should remember that few Americans are ever far from a source of between 100 and 400 horsepower—the automobile. Beefed-up car batteries and a self-reeling cable drum could probably get this package breathing warm bourbon fumes o'er Eden long before microwave power transmission or miniaturized atomic power plants come in. The car is already one of the strongest arms in America's environmental weaponry, and an essential component in one non-architectural anti-building that is already familiar to most of the nation—the drive-in movie house. Only, the word *house* is a manifest misnomer—just a flat piece of ground where the operating company provides visual images and piped sound, and the rest of the situation comes on wheels. You bring your own seat, heat and shelter as part of the car. You also bring Coke, cookies, Kleenex, Chesterfields, spare clothes, shoes, the Pill and god-wot else they don't provide at Radio City.

The car, in short, is already doing quite a lot of the standard-of-living package's job—the smoochy couple dancing to the music of the radio in their parked convertible have created a ballroom in the wilderness (dance floor by courtesy of the Highway Dept. of course) and all this is paradisal till it starts to rain. Even then, you're not licked—it takes very little air pressure to inflate a transparent Mylar airdome, the conditioned-air output of your mobile package might be able to do it, with or without a little boosting, and the dome itself, folded into a parachute pack, might be part of the package. From within your thirty-foot hemisphere of warm dry *Lebensraum* you could have spectacular ringside views of the wind felling trees, snow swirling through the glade, the forest fire coming over the hill or Constance Chatterley running swiftly to you know who through the downpour.

But . . . surely, this is not a home, you can't bring up a family in a polythene bag? This can never replace the time-honoured ranch-style tri-level standing proudly in a landscape of five defeated shrubs, flanked on one side by a ranch-style tri-level with six shrubs and on the other by a ranch-style tri-level with four small boys and a private dust bowl. If the countless Americans who are successfully raising nice children in trailers will excuse me for a moment, I have a few suggestions to make to the even more countless Americans who are so insecure that they have to hide inside fake monuments of Permastone and instant roofing. There are, admittedly, very sound day-to-day advantages to having warm broadloom on a firm floor underfoot, rather than pine needles and poison ivy. America's pioneer house builders recognized this by commonly building their brick chimneys on a brick floor slab. A transparent airdome could be anchored to such a slab just as easily as could a balloon frame, and the standard-of-living-package could hover busily in a sort of glorified barbecue pit in the middle of the slab. But an airdome is not the sort of thing that the kids, or a distracted Pumpkin-eater could run in and out of when the fit took them—believe me, fighting your way out of an airdome can be worse than trying to get out of a collapsed rain-soaked tent if you make the wrong first move.

But the relationship of the services-kit to the floor slab could be re-arranged to get over this difficulty; all the standard-of-living tackle (or most of it) could be re-deployed on the upper side of a sheltering membrane floating above the floor, radiating heat, light and what-not downwards and leaving the whole perimeter wide-open for random egress—and equally casual ingress, too, I guess. That crazy modern-movement dream of the interpenetration of indoors and outdoors could become real at last by abolishing the doors. Technically, of course, it would be just about possible to make the power-membrane literally float, hover-craft style. Anyone who has had to stand in the ground-effect of a helicopter will know that this solution has little to recommend it apart from the instant disposal of waste paper. The noise, power consumption and physical dis-

PAWLEY: It is not an accident that 'almost value-free' Reyner Banham visualises his un-house in the eye of a hurricane of natural phenomena. Parked in Harlow or in the shadow of Salisbury Cathedral (which is metaphorically where it always would be) the inhabitants would need their memory banks erased every night. With 'ordinary people' (no, I didn't make that up) the 'values' booted out through the airlock would simply pour back in through the media with which the pad is so well endowed. A 15 second commercial can do it – ('I always give my best dinner parties in the country').

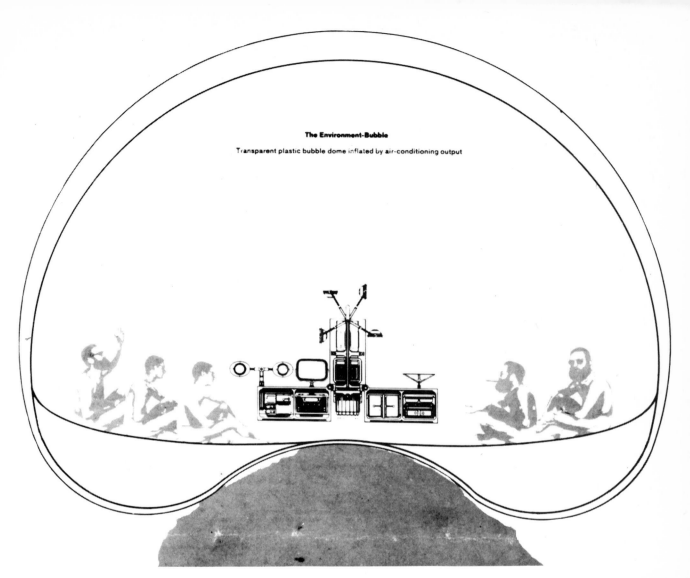

The Environment-Bubble

Transparent plastic bubble dome inflated by air-conditioning output

comfort would be really something wild. But if the power membrane could be carried on a column or two, here and there, or even on a brick-built bathroom unit, then we are almost in sight of what might be technically possible before the Great Society is much older.

The basic proposition is simply that the power membrane should blow down a curtain of warmed/cooled/conditioned air around the perimeter of the windward side of the un-house, and leave the surrounding weather to waft it through the living space, whose relationship in plan to the membrane above need not be a one-to-one relationship. The membrane would probably have to go beyond the limits of the floor slab, anyhow, in order to prevent rain blow-in, though the air-curtain will be active on precisely the side on which the rain is blowing and, being conditioned, will tend to mop up the moisture as it falls. The distribution of the air-curtain will be governed by various electronic light and weather sensors, and by that radical new invention, the weathervane. For really foul weather automatic storm shutters would be required, but in all but the most wildly inconstant climates, it should be possible to design the conditioning kit to deal with most of the weather most of the time, without the power consumption becoming ridiculously greater than for an ordinary inefficient monumental type house.

Obviously, it would still be appreciably greater, but this whole argument hinges on the observation that it is the American Way to spend money on services and upkeep rather than on permanent structure as do the peasant cultures of the Old World. In any case, we don't know where we shall be with things like solar power in the next decade, and to anyone who wants to entertain an almost-possible vision of air-conditioning for absolutely free, let me recommend *Short-stack* (another smart trick with a polythene tube) in the December 1964 issue of Analog. In fact, quite a number of the obvious common sense objections to the un-house may prove to be self-evaporating: for instance, noise may be no problem because there would be no surrounding wall to reflect it back into the living space, and, in any case, the constant whisper of the air-curtain would provide a fair threshold of loudness that sounds would have to beat before they began to be comprehensible and therefore disturbing. Bugs? Wild life? In summer they should be no worse than with the doors and windows of an ordinary house open; in winter all right-thinking creatures either migrate or hibernate; but, in any case, why not encourage the normal processes of Darwinian competition to tidy up the situation for you? All that is needed is to trigger the process by means of a general purpose lure; this would radiate mating calls and sexy scents and thus attract all sorts of mutually incompatible predators and prey into a compact pool of unspeakable carnage. A closed-circuit television camera could relay the state of play to a screen inside the dwelling and provide a twenty-four-hour program that would make the ratings for Bonanza look like chicken feed.

And privacy? This seems to be such a nominal concept in American life as factually lived that it is difficult to believe that anyone is seriously worried. The answer, under the suburban conditions that this whole argument implies, is the same as for the glass houses architects were designing so busily a decade ago—more sophisticated landscaping. This, after all, is the homeland of the bull-dozer and the transplantation of grown trees—why let the Parks Commissioner have all the fun?

As was said above, this argument implies suburbia which, for better or worse, is where America wants to live. It has nothing to say about the city, which, like architecture, is an insecure foreign growth on the continent. What is under

SILVER: Banham's articles make welcome propaganda for the good fight against gratuitous architectural monuments. But I can't help worrying about his tacit proposition, a familiar one in some circles, that architects should *ipso facto* be spearheading progressives. It will take, for example, years of cultural doublethink before the possession-minded middle classes are satisfied with a home which protects against 'most of the weather most of the time'. Indeed it will be a new dawn in the suburbs on the day the hurricane blows through households indifferent to their birch veneer furniture or Kodachromes of last year's vacation. Architects – the most hopelessly culture-compromised of technologists – have to play safe, and we goad them towards hasty innovation at our peril. Remembering the fate of those who rushed to use a few sealants and new finishes prematurely, I think their conservatism makes things safer for all. Of course not every client wants to play safe. But I'm less impressed with the spearhead of technology than I am with forgotten runes waiting to be read on the shaft – the technology of compressed air, for instance, which, from a central home compressor and tank, could operate every appliance in the house (except heat-producing ones), each appliance thereby becoming cheap, quiet, easier to maintain, and shock-free. Let's by all means needle architects for not using such familiar things better.

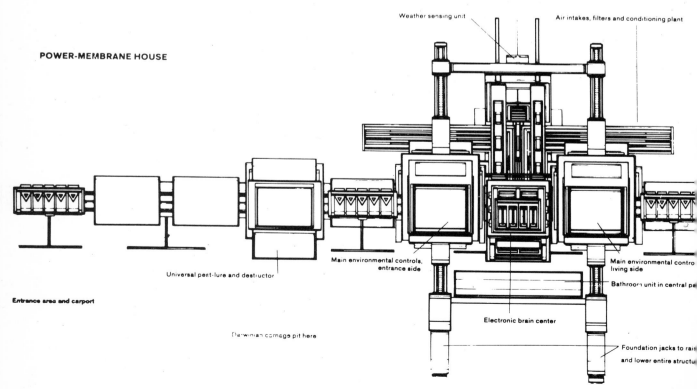

POWER-MEMBRANE HOUSE

Weather sensing unit

Air intakes, filters and conditioning plant

Universal pest-lure and destructor

Main environmental controls, entrance side

Main environmental contro living side

Bathroom unit in central pa

Entrance area and carport

Darwinian carnage pit here

Electronic brain center

Foundation jacks to rais and lower entire structu

PAWLEY: The dream of *starting again* underlies the un-house idea, just as it underlies most consumer psychology ('brand new job, brand new breath – every day'). Unfortunately 'second hand values' are like food particles lingering in the interstices of the teeth – they are by-products of an essential process. For the un-house or the thinkbelt to be really 'value-free' we need more than tooth paste – we need to stop eating.

discussion here is an extension of the Jeffersonian dream beyond the agrarian sentimentality of Frank Lloyd Wright's Usonian Broadacre version—the dream of the good life in the clean countryside, power-point homesteading in a paradise garden of appliances. This dream of the un-house may sound very anti-architectural but it is so only in degree, and architecture deprived of its European roots but trying to strike new ones in an alien soil has come close to the anti-house once or twice already. Wright was not joking when he talked of the 'destruction of the box', even though the spatial promise of the phrase is rarely realized to the full in the all-too-solid fact. Grass-roots architects of the plains like Bruce Goff and Herb Greene have produced houses whose supposed monumental form is clearly of little consequence to the functional business of living in and around them.

But it is in one building that seems at first sight nothing but monumental form that the threat or promise of the un-house has been most clearly demonstrated—the Johnson House at New Canaan. So much has been misleadingly said (by Philip Johnson himself, as well as others) to prove this a work of architecture in the European tradition, that its many intensely American aspects are usually missed. Yet when you have dug through all the erudition about Ledoux and Malevitsch and Palladio and stuff that has been published, one very suggestive source or prototype remains less easily explained away—the admitted persistence in Johnson's mind of the visual image of a burned-out New England township, the insubstantial shells of the houses consumed by the fire, leaving the brick floor slabs and standing chimneys. The New Canaan glass-house consists essentially of just these two elements, a heated brick floor slab, and a standing unit which is a chimney/fireplace on one side and a bathroom on the other.

Around this has been draped precisely the kind of insubstantial shell that Conklin was discussing, only even less substantial than that. The roof, certainly, is solid, but psychologically it is dominated by the absence of visual enclosure all around. As many pilgrims to this site have noticed, the house does not stop at the glass, and the terrace, and even the trees beyond, are visually part of the living space in winter, physically and operationally so in summer when the four doors are open. The 'house' is little more than a service core set in infinite space, or alternatively, a detached porch looking out in all directions at the Great Out There. In summer, indeed, the glass would be a bit of a nonsense if the trees did not shade it, and in the recent scorching fall, the sun reaching in through the bare trees created such a greenhouse effect that parts of the interior were acutely uncomfortable—the house would have been better off without its glass walls.

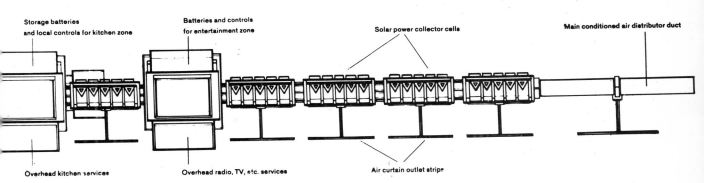

Storage batteries and local controls for kitchen zone

Batteries and controls for entertainment zone

Solar power collector cells

Main conditioned air distributor duct

Overhead kitchen services

Overhead radio, TV, etc. services

Air curtain outlet strips

Kitchen-eating area overlapping into main living space which extends as far as necessary into surrounding landscape

When Philip Johnson says that the place is not a controlled environment, however, it is not these aspects of undisciplined glazing he has in mind, but that 'when it gets cold I have to move toward the fire, and when it gets too hot I just move away'. In fact, he is simply exploiting the campfire phenomenon (he is also pretending that the floor-heating does not make the whole area habitable, which it does) and in any case, what does he mean by a controlled environment? It is not the same thing as a uniform environment, it is simply an environment suited to what you are going to do next, and whether you build a stone monument, move away from the fire or turn on the air-conditioning, it is the same basic human gesture you are making.

Only, the monument is such a ponderous solution that it astounds me that Americans are still prepared to employ it, except out of some profound sense of insecurity, a persistent inability to rid themselves of those habits of mind they left Europe to escape. In the open-fronted society, with its social and personal mobility, its interchangeability of components and personnel, its gadgetry and almost universal expendability, the persistence of architecture-as-monumental-space must appear as evidence of the sentimentality of the tough.

BAIRD: Banham claims that he advocates 'an environment capable of generating new values symbiotically with its inhabitants'; yet there is a great discrepancy between that commitment and the examples he discusses in these articles. Whether one sides with Banham or with Pawley (see his comment on Banham) over the Wampanoag incident it seems to me quite impossible to think of the relation of the ship to its inhabitants as symbiotic.

In the case of the home that is not a house, the discrepancy is greater still. How can Banham describe it as symbiotic when there exist 'countless Americans' (his estimate) who are too 'insecure' to want to live in it? For that matter, why does he even propose it as symbiotic to Americans, when they 'astound' him by their 'profound insecurity', their 'persistent inability to rid themselves of those habits of mind they left Europe to escape?'

When he is no longer quite so astounded, Banham should look again at that 'insecurity', for until he comes to terms with it, he will fail to grasp the full implications of environmental symbiosis.

BANHAM: I reply to Baird and Pawley thus: food particles do not linger in the interstices of every mouthful of teeth, because some people don't eat that kind of food, or have different eating habits, or better spaced teeth, or have had them fixed. In other words, the human race is variable: there are the astoundingly insecure who need the perennial structural props Baird and Pawley advocate; and there are others of us who don't. Neither Baird nor Pawley seems psychologically secure enough to admit this human variability, both claim to be in possession of 'the real point' or of 'the full implications of environmental symbiosis'. But there will be no chance of the kind of environmental symbiosis that interests people of my psychological type and cultural background if the world is cluttered with Baird's values cast in irremovable concrete or Pawley's old bedroom furniture. Our values, being piped through the media, can be switched off if they prove privately or publicly deleterious, but how do you switch off a mahogany wardrobe? This is not a debating point (like Baird trying to pretend I had offered the Wampanoag as an example of symbiosis) because the over-permanence of our built environment could become as much a form of pollution as the over-permanence of polythene and other non-degradable rubbish. Or the overpermanence of exclusive value-systems; what I find admirable about advanced technology is the number of embalmed 'meanings and identities' that it threatens. Responses to that threat show very clearly which admirals are stupid and which architectural theorists are card-carrying reactionaries.

THE TIME HO...

OR ARGUMENT FOR AN EXISTENTIA...

DWELLING **Martin Pawley**

In a celebrated attack on the traditional concept of history as 'the last refuge of the transcendental humanist', Claude Lévi-Strauss wrote that the only way the historian could evade the choice between history which taught more and explained less, and history which explained more and taught less, was to get out of history 'either by the bottom, if the pursuit of information leads him from the consideration of groups to that of individuals and then to their motivations which depend on their personal history and temperament . . . or by the top, if the need to understand incites him to put history back into prehistory and the latter into the general evolution of organized beings'.[1]

This predicament seems to me to parallel closely that of the environmental designer. Out of the wreckage of the old creative mode there seem to be two distinct paths: one leads into an infra-structural domain in the realms of psychology, physiology and anthropometrics—the man/object interface. The other leads into a world of super-structural systems in the realms of mathematics, geometry and logistics—the 'second, organized surface of the earth'.[2]

My concern is with the former of these two alternatives, for I perceive at the man/object interface an externalization of that ambiguity which is a condition of human consciousness. Simone de Beauvoir terms this the 'tragic ambivalence' which man knows and thinks but animals and plants merely undergo.[3] Man, she believes, escapes from his natural condition without freeing himself from it. He is still a part of the world of which he is conscious. This means that his subjectivity can be vulnerable while his body and objects are preserved, and vice versa.

The closer design moves to the interface, the more essential it is that the designer recognize this ambiguity, which is often quite clearly expressed, but tends for some reason to be discounted as a mistake or atavism. This is clearly illustrated by attitudes to styles of clothing: many critics stress the objective functions of clothing, to keep warm, dry, etc., at the expense of the extravagances of fashion, which they regard as in some way superfluous or secondary in importance. The truth is of course that fashion, in terms of decoration, exaggeration and distortion, pre-dated any 'functional' concept of clothing and is an equally fundamental expression of consciousness.

Designers often believe, in quite good faith, that they can produce designs from which subjective factors have been totally excised. In the case of automobiles for instance, where it is not uncommon for over a million identical units to be produced, it could be assumed that the combination of a ruthlessly objective brief with strictly limited conditions of use would provide a wholly functional product sterilized against subjective infection. The result is very far from the case: within a week of purchase the vast majority of automobiles are personalized by one means or another. A vast accessory industry exists for just this purpose, with innumerable permutations of gadgetry to differentiate individual means of transport.

No matter how ruthlessly the designer rationalizes his product, no matter how drastically the number of models is reduced, this intimate identification of individual with object continues. Even in a relentlessly limiting design system, like the adjustment mechanism for the driving seat, in which it is practically impossible for the driver to 'go beyond' the range of adjustments open to him (and thus inform the system with greater significance than it originally contained), subjective association can be expressed through fantasy—by painting on the red triangle of an ejection seat—or simply covering it with simulated leopard skin. The automobile world, with its 'Cooper S' titled minivans, 'GT's' and bat-mobiles is the graveyard of objective design theory.[4] No sooner is function crowned than myth, image and fantasy usurp the throne. At the man/object

121

The Subjectivisation of the Object.
a) Primitive distortion and decoration of the body. A Suk tribesman of North West Kenya.
b) Sophisticated distortion and decoration of the body. 'Top Art' in San Francisco.

interface the confrontation between subject and object is inescapable. If the designer cannot express *his* subjectivity the lack is made good by the user: if neither knows how to associate with the object, the seller or advertiser finds a way.

Even in the academic field the conviction is growing that design is meaningless without appraisal: that creation is helpless without feedback: that feedback is design in reverse. Designer and user are on opposite sides of the created object, but their relation to it is identical. The middle aged man fixing plastic imitation-magnesium racing wheels to his family saloon is a designer, perhaps as much as the man who designed the car. The same is true of the motorcyclist with a skull and crossbones on the back of his leather jacket; for *design is the arrangement and metamorphosis of objects to correspond to the ambiguous demands of human consciousness.*

An old-age pensioner sits in a squalid room; all around him his furniture is arranged: Edwardian veneered cabinets, tortuously carved tables, high-backed chairs. Amongst the furniture is further bric-à-brac in the form of vases, prints and photographs in frames. All these possessions represent the 'object evidence' of the pensioner's life, for his relations are all dead and he is alone, using the collection as a barricade against the increasingly cold and hostile world without.

The Subjectivisation of the Object.
c) *Contemporary animism: Guynemer's aero-plane exhibited in Paris after 19 victories, 1917.*
d) *Personalising the impersonal: the Hot Car Champion Boy Racer.*
e) *Conquest of the Image: a defaced poster in the Underground.*

His mementos are living proof of the reality of his former life, evidence that he once existed beyond his present fate.

Not far away, in a contract furnished office, sits a development architect. He is studying some drawings: on one of the drawings the very house in which the pensioner huddles is ringed in red. The architect is planning the erection of a multi-storey office building on a site of which a part is at present occupied by the pensioner's tenement. He summons his secretary . . .

Here is one designer, equipped with technical, legal and economic expertise and a brief drawn from the uncompromising facts of commercial life, marshalling his resources to carry out a clear and ruthless plan. Opposite him is a desperate individual in a shrinking world, staking the very meaning of his existence on the effort of externalization which has transformed mere furniture into the contents of life. Neither of these characters would acknowledge that they were at opposite ends of a single scale. One would see the other as a threat, the other, if he acknowledged his presence at all, would see his counterpart as a nuisance. They do not see themselves—or each other—as exponents of the binary condition of consciousness, for in effect they are the same person.

Because of this blindness, today's environmental designers are committed for the most part to the obliteration of their subjectivities in becoming the agents of an authoritarian, organizational technology that refuses responsibility for the violence done to human consciousness by its mechanisms. In this they are Utopians in the tradition of More, Fourier and Verne.[5]

This utopianism is exactly what separates designer object from the designer subject—the development architect from the pensioner. The designer's idea of the dwelling is a *mélange* of functional fabrications; the more closely he looks into it, the larger the mirror image he sees. Until he can move beyond this convention into a deeper acceptance of the experience of environment, he must remain incapable of moving the act of dwelling back from the realm of configuration where it now rests, into the realms of action and meaning where it really belongs. The conception of the meaning and purpose of environment in the minds of most contemporary designers is a convention unrelated to their experience of it: a convention which enables them to *see* the world in a different way from the way in which they feel it.

'The smiling credit manager you spoke to this morning is a piece of company apparatus like the filing cabinet from which he extracts the card that is you; his human appearance is a disguise and his real name isn't Brown but Agent F-362.'

In these terms Harold Rosenberg[6] summarises the Jeremiads of contemporary prophets of the American social scene. Their fears of dehumanization, role absorption and 'other-directed' behaviour, which are by now part of the intellectual currency of the Western World, are closely related to reification—the objectivization of living things—and thus to the man/object interface where both fact and fantasy begin.

In this connection, the contemporary designer occupies a curious position: he is the mixer of traditional prejudice with untested theory. The environments which are his creation were born of the marriage between the undigested, unintegrated body of experience that is the presence of the past, and the organizational concepts of production and distribution which are the presence of the future. The outcome of this marriage is an environment in which the roles of function, action and consciousness are hopelessly confused.

This is because contemporary designers do not know how to integrate the vast museum of stone, iron and yellowed paper into a world whose meanings must all be expressed functionally, in the applied scientific sense of tending towards the optimization of technique in some field or other.

For this reason we still build houses with room for servants when our real servants are electronic mechanisms. We call rooms after functions which once produced sweat but now rarely occasion a broken finger nail. In industry men serve and circle round assembly-line monsters that will shortly operate far better without them. In this sense operators, with their human demands, have become an embarrassment to production.

Along with them most of the environmental spaces in our man-made world have become temples to the dynamism of functions long since reduced to anachronistic double talk. Libraries have become microfilm, cinemas have become television; corridors, telephones; travel, arrival and departure with a shortening limbo between. All the functions of a house have imploded into a service core the diameter of a telegraph pole. Even the physical space required by its human occupants has been miniaturized to the point where the 'essential' capsule could be sunk to the bottom of the sea or shot to the moon.

A surprisingly large number of design-theorists are prepared to follow this kind of logic to its bitter conclusion. The architectural avant-garde prepare to live in ergonomically designed plastic 'living pods', shifted periodically by crane from megastructure to megastructure, while futures-oriented writers like Reyner Banham actually portray naked figures hunkering round television sets in small, collapsible plastic domes.[7] These latter day nomads have long since abandoned the 'cultural wardrobe', and as their sun-bronzed fingers twitch from channel to channel their possible reflections on the monumental architectural environment from which they sprang are summarized for them in advance. 'It was', says Banham, 'a cultural solution to the problem of enclosure—apart from that it became obsolete.'[8]

The fantastic notion underlying this attitude—that electronic media are in some way interchangeable with history—springs from two basic origins. First, that as a result of the Industrial Revolution, nuclear weapons, antibiotics and technology, the historical continuum is broken and consequently man in 1968 is utterly different from man in 1868 or man in 1768. Second, that man is no greater than his role—which today is the satisfaction of his physical needs and desires by collaboration in the productive organization of his society.

FRAMPTON: As Arendt would say 'the victory of the animal laborans who labors and mixes with his product'. ▶

The image of humanity which results from a ruthless application of these two determinants can be clearly seen every week on television. The puppet characters of Thunderbirds, Fireball XL5 and Captain Scarlet are all perfect prototypes for the role-imprisoned futurists eagerly awaiting Banham's command to leap from the highest peaks of the present into the bottomless

future—without their cultural parachutes. Curiously such delusory flights from place and history often end in the Portobello Road or the antique supermarket.

THE LIMITATIONS OF FUNCTION

Functionalism was originally a morality for environment in that it sought to establish *correct conditions for use* rather than usefulness itself. In doing so it had the effect of reducing action to configuration and consciousness to objective physical presence.

The manner in which this arcane doctrine—a relic of the positivism which in science crumbled long before the Second World War, and in philosophy collapsed shortly after it—has maintained itself in the face of daily proof of its inadequacy is little short of miraculous. Faced with the constant modification of structures whose 'immutable' function changed overnight, the functional theorist was obliged to don an ill-fitting suit of clothes called flexibility. Every functional environment today is obliged to be able to become anything else— or nothing—instantly. Otherwise it is useless.

Despite this implicit acknowledgement of the relatively short life of any functional organization pattern, the method is still the basic tool used for shaping our environment.

In the organization world—in office blocks, industrial facilities, military and scientific complexes, the presence of individuals is acknowledged only by reference to their functional roles. They are incorporated as elements in planning according to their administrative or productive place in the organization. They are provided with desks, chairs, typewriters, telephones, paper and pencils—

BANHAM: If this is a 'not too unfair' appraisal of the concepts examined in my article all I can say is that the mind boggles. Readers who enjoy a good boggle should turn at once to 'A Home is not a House', read it, and then look at this paragraph again. On a point of art-historical information, the nude figures, like the casework of the complex and multi-functional device which Pawley takes for a TV set, were the invention of François Dallegret, who was allowed full freedom to illustrate as appeared fit to him – as long as the technical specifications that I wrote were completely fulfilled.

The *real* 'fantastic notion' underlying this article, as sharp readers will observe, is not that 'electronic media are . . . inter-changeable with history' (let's all have another jolly boggle) but that the development of electronic and other technologies is a continuation of the living process of history, while the deification of monumental form is a panicky attempt to freeze that process.

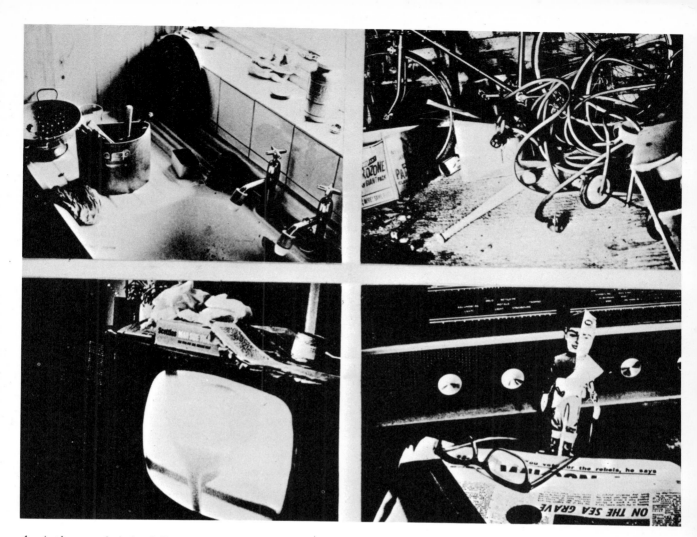

A simple, speculatively built bungalow, viewed and criticised as a design – left, and as a lived entity – right. The designer cannot bear to think that the anonymity of the exterior merely masks a seething particularisation of objects within.

a mass of impersonal, objective equipment within which they can only express their subjectivity by stealth and fantasy—by keeping novels in their desk drawers, or making personal calls in the lunch hour.

Functions at basis are objectivizations of human needs, and because human beings are more than object-entities, these objectivizations are at best simplifications, at worst distortions of the possibilities of real men. The environmental designer's recognition of function or role instead of *consciousness* as the basis for such 'human engineering' as he attempts, is a contributory cause of the anxiety of meaninglessness which is a well-documented neurosis of our time.

It is in the realm of the dwelling that functionalism becomes pernicious in the extreme. Primarily because it is impossible to functionally define the *act of dwelling*, which is a continuously evolving drama, not a pattern established once and retained forever.

A man can 'function' in a certain sense six hundred feet beneath the surface of the sea in total blackness. He can 'survive' in a prison cell six feet square, an underground train, a space capsule or a pot hole—but he cannot *live* there—not unless he drastically truncates the possibilities of action and thought that consciousness confers upon him. To 'live' in such situations a man must accept the status of an object, as though the world were always in a state of warfare, famine or pestilence, as though life were a job.

Sociological techniques can never indicate more than that human beings survive in a relatively sociable form in certain environments. The outer limits of those environments must be determined by the sometimes 'unfunctional' demands of action and consciousness—demands which the functional mode is committed to either castrate or ignore.

A measure of our loss of awareness of the importance of these demands is our endless obsession with the *kind* of environment we construct, instead of with the act of environmental creation itself. It is the *creative act*, whether carried out with pick and shovel or a highly sensitive electronic system, which is of overriding importance.

The pleasure felt from observed alterations in the external world brought about by the will of the individual[9] is extremely wide-ranging, covering

The 'unfunctional' past.

BAIRD: It seems to me that Pawley has in common with those he (not unreasonably) criticises, a tendency to talk in terms of a too-simple polarity – functional/unfunctional. This leads me to suspect that one could say of his argument what Arendt says of Kant's view of works of art; namely, that it cannot 'deny its origin in utilitarian thinking'.

FRAMPTON: This suggests that 'means', i.e. the act of creation and destruction itself is all important, not the end result; a therapeutic emphasis on process and not upon the 'world' as separate from process.

everything from growing vegetables to blowing up bridges; but it is a fundamental expression of consciousness wherein a simultaneous expression of the essential ambiguity becomes unavoidable.

The ruthless development architect of earlier pages, holding no truck with subjectivity, may well deny that in implementing his redevelopment plan he is exercising his *subjective* will, personalizing an impersonal process, subjectivizing for his own purposes the applied energy and expertise of others—but his denial is philosophically untenable.

The claim to objective impartiality advanced from time to time by environmental designers can best be brought into perspective by considering the fate of an analogous claim delivered hypothetically in The House of Commons by a Minister of Transport who had just awarded a huge motorway contract to a firm in which he was both a shareholder and a member of the board.

Once we remove the mystique of function and objectivity from the process of design we see an interpersonal struggle for ego domination indistinguishable from that to be found in any other sphere of human endeavour. For this reason it is hardly possible for the designer to speak of the 'objectivity' with which he conceived his own design. He is already compromised—as much as if he stood to gain financially by what he had done. His consciousness is an inescapable master.

BAIRD: In spite of my sympathy for the ▶ argument. I object to Pawley's subjective/ objective polarization here. For me, the fascination of architecture lies, in this respect, in its evident inter-subjectivity. That is what Saussure's *langue/parole* distinction is meant to elucidate.

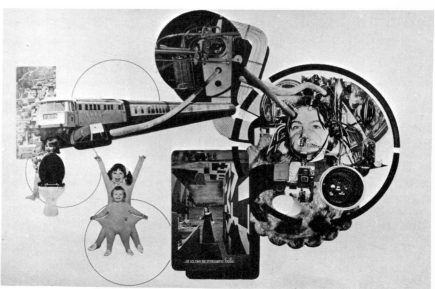

The individual as a functional element.

Faced with the bankrupt sensibilities of the functional approach, we are committed to finding some other means of defining an area of subjective presence in the man-made environment. A possible line of approach suggests itself through the process of miniaturization, which Buckminster-Fuller has identified as one of the laws of technological development. For him the ever-increasing capacity of design science to extract greater energy from smaller resources is a revolutionary concept in itself,[10] but the long term effect of this trend on the distribution of available space is perhaps of greater interest.

For instance, if we tentatively divide the man-made environment into two basic area concepts, Functional space and Human space, we can enunciate the following definitions:

Functional space = Space required for life-sustaining systems. (All existing service and environmental control systems in buildings fall into this category, as do most media installations, movement systems and contemporary notions of human circulation requirements.)

Human space = Space voluntarily occupied by individuals beyond the influence of external duties or controls.

Assuming that human space need only connect with functional space at the input and output terminals of the life-sustaining systems, we are left with the possibility that, as miniaturization contracts the volume of the life-sustaining systems (LSS), the volume of human space (HS) can increase *irrespective of any contraction of overall volume resulting from population increase.*

This relationship can be expressed in a formula and applied to earlier states of civilization as well as our own. Overall volume = LSS + HS. It is important to note in the application of this formula that LSS is not a constant for all levels of civilization, but fluctuates in relation to living standards. To an Australian aboriginal tribe LSS might mean witchety grubs and water, to a Southern Californian, air conditioning and two cars per person. At all events it is essential that LSS be identified as *configurational* and HS as *active*. In this way we can be sure that no *function* for any part of human space is of greater importance than the existential possibilities created by its users in their act of *dwelling* in it.

The formula we have constructed is remarkable only for the separation of HS from LSS, and its recognition as a separate *quality* as well as quantity. The absence of this distinction has consequences which can be clearly seen in any of the institutional environments mentioned earlier.

FORM FOLLOWS CONFLICT

Territoriality can today be considered as a primary instinctual drive, alongside sexual desire or the will to power. Recent research in the behavioural sciences suggests in fact that individual distance and private territory are invariably present in all societies of living things, ensuring that internecine strife never overcomes the basic cohesion of any group.

The Best-Rubinstein experiment with planarian worms,[11] which are among the most primitive forms of life still extant in the world, indicates that psychological characteristics normally associated only with higher animals and humans are already present in a highly developed form demanding the identity, stimulation and security which proceed from the ownership of territory. While on the same theme, from an anthropological standpoint T. G. H. Strehlow describes the fanatical devotion of the Aranda people of the Australian interior to their birthplace and ancestral home-site: 'Mountains and creeks and springs and waterholes are, to him (the native) not merely interesting or beautiful scenic features . . . they are the handiwork of ancestors from whom he himself has descended. He sees recorded in the surrounding landscape the ancient story of the lives and deeds of the immortal beings whom he reveres . . .' The Aranda people assemble visual evidence of the past in Iconic terms as do civilized peoples; their *churinga* are carved pieces of stone or wood representing the presence of individual ancestors. They 'prove' the existence of past time and confirm the duration of identification with place.[12] Territoriality is thus a significant element in the relation between being and environment from the bottom of the evolutionary scale to the top.

Robert Ardrey has endeavoured to formalize a relationship between environment and behaviour in a manner which is indirectly relevant to the contemporary designer's predicament. The sum of amity (A) he claims is equal in any society to the aggregate of enmity (E) and hazard (h). This formula, expressed as $A = E + h$, suggests that the progressive reduction in natural hazard, which has been a characteristic of civilization, should have been accompanied by a parallel development of enmity (E) to balance the question.[13] Ardrey himself sees this equilibrium achieved through the development of destructive and sophisticated weaponry and concludes that an artificially stimulated feedback or friction from the environment might be essential to maintain a reasonable level of co-operation. Following Lorenz he foresees an increase in ritualized violence as the best means of bringing this about.

The weakness of this conclusion lies in its assumption that the modern world is drained of environmental hazard: a view which seems to me only tenable in the context of a comparison between the stochastic survival processes of animals and the systematic survival mechanisms which sustain Western individuals. This comparison inevitably leads to a concept of hazard as limited to fang, claw and natural disaster, and a corresponding ignorance of that contemporary form of environmental hazard which is capable of retreating from the object world into the world of fantasy even as the individual in his alienation retreats into it also. This form of hazard is both more generalized, less concrete, and is reflected in a fear of madness and institutionalization rather than death. It expresses itself in a full conflict of imagery between the external manifestations of individuality and its essence: between the projection of the self that can be *seen* and the subjectivity which is *felt*. I have termed this psychic variant of environmental hazard 'cereconflict' because it associates the characteristics of conflict with those of cerebration.

Cereconflict can be identified in many of the situations discussed earlier, particularly in the large, impersonal office, where evidence of the presence of individuals is generalized and functional rather than active and particular. To the individual this kind of context can represent a devaluation of the personality by its failure to portray any part of his subjectivity. At the same time this conflict in imagery, while causing much unhappiness, can also generate energy which in the end is purposeful in terms of survival. This last factor is important in relation to motivation for change, which is closely connected to the human capacity to resist dehumanization in any context. Cereconflict plays a part in this resistance by generating in desperation some of the energy required to arrange and metamorphose either the 'devaluing' context or the self into a less distressing relationship.

Thus cereconflict functions in the same way as Ardrey's hazard, except that it generates creative energy which is not always co-operative. That this creative energy is socially necessary is self evident, and can in any case be deduced from the conclusion that the polarisation of person and projection, being an externalisation of the duality inherent in consciousness itself, must be an inexhaustible commodity. It is born and dies with the individual, even if the environment external to the body seems of minor significance. Women, for instance, express a particular and sometimes beautiful cereconflict when they make radical alterations in their appearance by means of cosmetics and fashion.

Cereconflict is to the modern individual as natural hazard was to primitive man, in that its *meaning* is to be found in the changes which it brings about. Primitives developed speech and tool-making not to obliterate natural hazard but to conform to the behavioural demands it made on them. Similarly the processes of inner and outer change which result from cereconflict do not find their purpose in the eventual exhaustion of conflict, but in the simulation, or acting out in projection, of the inner antimony of consciousness itself.

Psychology and animal physiology together supply impressive proof of the significance of context in the interpretation of action, particularly in those areas of study where mental and behavioural disturbance can be related to deprivation.

One particular scientific *idée fixe*, which greatly influenced Sigmund Freud, was that primates were obsessed with sex and that it was this sexual attraction which held troops together. This conclusion was drawn entirely from extended observation of captive specimens and it was not until the field studies of the late 1930's that it could be conclusively proved that the role of sexuality had been greatly exaggerated by unnatural living conditions.

In human terms Goffman has shown that in the context of the mental hospital deprivation of meaningful context can make rational, though desperate human behaviour seem to confirm insanity, when in reality it merely confirms deprivation.[14]

Searles[15] cites many examples of schizophrenics whose loss of orientation stems in their own eyes from excessive movement and loss of personal possessions: the movement of the family from one town to another, the movement of the individual from one room to another in the family house, even the re-allocation of desks at a school or the seizure of a favourite chair. In all these cases Searles affirms that '. . . for such patients . . . the loss of various elements of the non-human environment, elements which have become part of the person's body image, may be experienced as a mutilation of the physical body itself'.

The entire body of this scientific and clinical evidence suggests that in animals as well as humans, behaviour can only be understood in the context of the environment in which it takes place. This is because environment confers its own movements, contortions and vistas on to those who use it, becoming in the process effectively a part of the personality.

The social implications of this contention are readily visible in the stratification of *status* in terms of possessions, type and location of dwellings, and personal appearance. Also in the more intangible benefits which the long genealogy of an aristocratic family confers upon its descendants. The family home, in the case of many aristocratic families in Europe occupied for two or three hundred years by successive generations, offers a unique basis of stability as well as evidence of experience which is ordered in space and time. The human need for this sense of identification is illustrated most pathetically by institutional recidivism: the tendency for long hospitalised or imprisoned persons to be unable to establish themselves in the outside world and instead to seek re-entry to the cell or bed they know, despite the rigours of the concomitant life.

The deep-seated nature of the contextual impression and its presence as a major motivation in contemporary resistance to change and the rejection of 'consumer product' housing, has not been specifically recognized in architectural circles. Burnham Kelly points out that 'the largest marketing problem is found in the fact that houses are not mere consumer goods, to be used and thrown

The imitation of permanence.

away when they fall apart. They are the focus of the basic unit in our society.'[16] This he explains by a discussion of current systems of house finance, all of which require the dwelling to be an asset whose durability is supposed at least to match, if not exceed the term of the loan with which it is purchased. This explanation only partially touches on the true value of the dwelling as 'the focus of the basic unit of our society'. Apart from its viability as a product, which is attested by its steadily appreciating value and potentially infinite life span, the traditional house represents territory in a way that its wheeled or prefabricated counterpart can never do. The language alone in which these rival concepts of dwelling are discussed leaves little doubt as to their relative value in this regard. The house is 'a castle', 'security',[17] 'a home of our own'. The caravan or prefabricated dwelling is 'accommodation', 'emergency housing', 'temporary' or 'mobile'. The key factor in this comparison is the permanent status accorded a house in its relation to the ownership of land, and the non-status accorded the owner of a caravan who buys something to live in but nowhere to live.

This desire for permanence underlies the general hostility to redevelopment plans exhibited by the inhabitants of the areas to which they refer, the relatively large numbers of persons implacably opposed to even the surface appearance of the newer forms of environment, the plethora of organizations devoted to the preservation and reclamation of historic buildings and towns, and the large numbers of technologically aware individuals who prefer to live in the rehabilitated dwellings of a century or more ago. To these persons redevelopment is as destructive as it is creative. The old environments blotted out by the bulldozers are the physical context of human experience. What replaces them is generally pure form, unrelated to persons or to history.

The hostility that the public exhibits to consumer housing is thus as rationally based as its hostility to demolition and redevelopment. Neither of these concepts recognizes the importance of identification with place or known objects, and neither comprehends the significance of the kind of behavioural history that accompanies and stabilizes successive generational occupations of the same dwelling.

In a relatively little known book published in 1961, N. J. Habraken outlined these defects in both the redevelopment programme and the short-life dwelling. He also clearly enunciated the principle stated earlier—that it is in the action of changing and creating it that the individual confers meaning on his environment. Habraken saw the redevelopment process not only destroy existing environments to replace them with memoryless novelties, but also remove individual responsibility for the ordering of environmental space by rigidly establishing identical equipment and layout for hundreds of thousands of dwellings at a time. He denounced the entire process as an emergency measure which in practice continually created emergencies by replacing the evolutionary process of accumulation and modification with the strophe and catastrophe of creation and destruction. He saw the industrialization of the housing project as a direct impediment to the industrialization of housing itself.[18]

Unlike the majority of the architectural avant-garde, Habraken is not at heart a futurist.[19] His concept of separation between megastructure and dwelling unit is based on a logical division between heavy, long life support structures and light, short life dwellings whose design and construction would be a matter of choice for their occupants. The restraint and humanity of this concept places it in a different class from those for example of Yona Friedman which would facilitate yet more drastic and continuous redevelopment.[20]

The overriding factor with Habraken is an acute consciousness of continuity in time and place, which he attempts to achieve by means of support structures with a useful life of the order of bridges or dams; thus guaranteeing an unchanging overall environmental pattern in spite of changes in dwelling units.

Because he does not examine any means of retaining the evidence of the past within the dwelling unit itself, Habraken is committed to achieving continuity in the public realm—the realm of life-sustaining systems. Consequently his

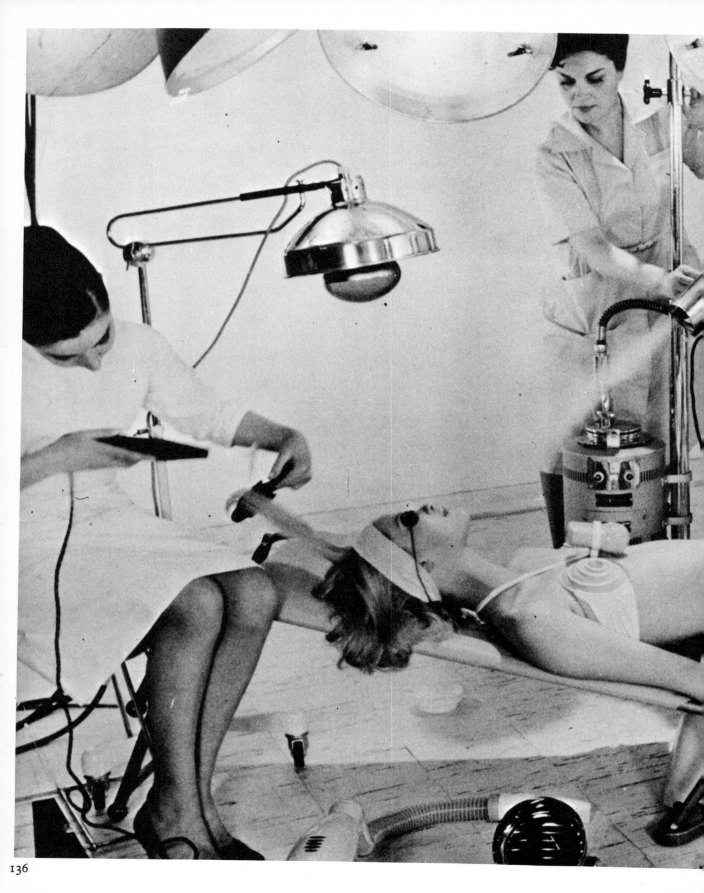

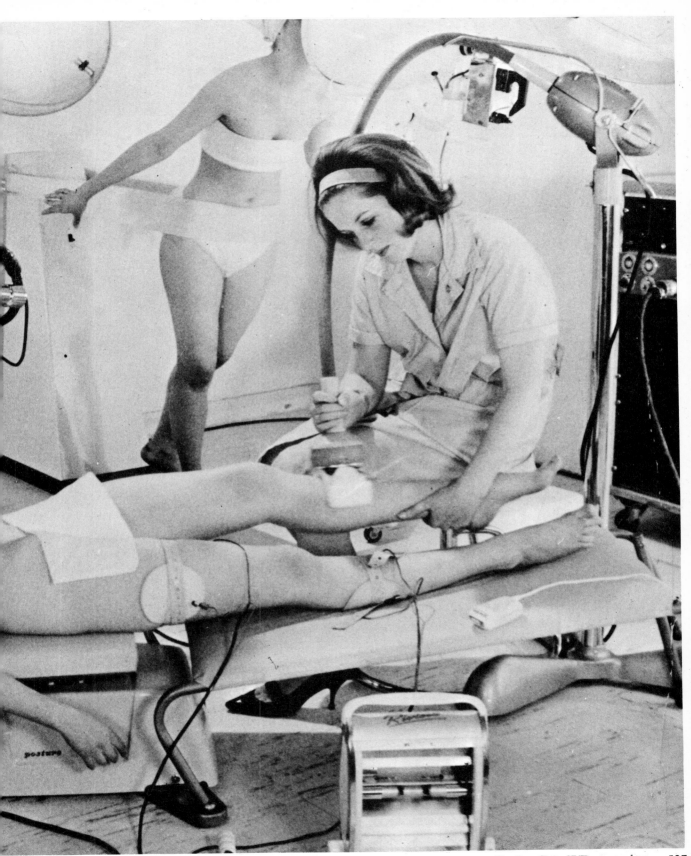

Cereconflict in action: the beauty parlour. 137

major arguments are directed against the massive increase in bureaucratic environmental control that has taken place in this century under the guise of planning, for it is from this direction that the greatest threat to formal stability comes.

For some reason Habraken does not see any hope of a solution to this creeping paralysis of the creative will in the process of privatization with which the mass populations of Western societies have greeted it. For him, just as the problems of efficient communication, distribution of resources and maintenance of public order have called forth a massive volume of environmental legislation, so has the political progress of this century—towards equal distribution of wealth, higher living standards, social security and administrative populism—worked against the freedom of individuals to express their subjectivity in the outside world. The result has been an ingrowing privatization, facilitated by media and overpopulation, whereby individuals withdraw into their homes as a refuge from the dangerous exposure of public life.

This process, variously castigated as 'apathy', 'lack of initiative' and 'ignorance', is in fact a perfectly rational response to the confusing and destructive demands of an uncomprehending and largely unsuccessful environmental administration.

Habraken's efforts to stabilize the rapidly evolving world of life-sustaining systems are doomed before they begin. In this context change cannot be arrested —though this is the desperate dream of preservationists. All that can be done is to equip human space with mechanisms capable of absorbing the evidence of time and change in order to mitigate the horror of change itself. By incorporating into each successive configuration the elements of all its predecessors, change could be separated from destruction and loss and a continuum achieved in the private realm ·which is still to some extent legally and economically protected.

The technical achievement of this goal, which is the concretization of the evidence of human association with place within the dwelling itself, would correspond to the division between life-sustaining systems and human space described earlier, and take us one step nearer to the concept of the Time House.

BEHAVIOUR, OBJECTS AND TIME

'Just been listening to an old year, passages at random. I did not check in the book, but it must be at least ten or twelve years ago. At that time I was still living on and off with Bianca in Kedar Street. Well out of that, Jesus yes! Hopeless business. (pause) Not much about her, apart from a tribute to her eyes. Very warm. I suddenly saw them again. (pause) Incomparable! (pause) Ah well . . . (pause) These old P.M.s are gruesome, but I often find them—(Krapp switches off, broods, switches on)—a help . . . .'

Krapp's Last Tape.
Samuel Beckett. 1958.

The individual's attitude to the part of his environment that he establishes more or less on his own terms is a function of the differentiation of the ego. That process, by which the human being in childhood and youth determines what he is, is one of elimination. Piaget in *The Construction of Reality in the Child*[21] traced four stages in this process. At the first stage life is characterized by all activity in general; at the second (6–8 years), life is indicated only by movement; at the third (8–10 years), life is denoted only by spontaneous movement; at the fourth (10–12 years), life is finally restricted to animals and plants. Many mental disturbances in later life, as well as many well-known psychopathological symptoms such as projection, introjection and transference have their origins in the imperfect development of the ego differentiation process. Under relatively normal conditions it can range from the complete self-absorption of the child (who sees himself as the centre of all life and sensation), to the utter self-rejection of the recluse who avoids seeing himself at all by shunning contact with the

BAIRD: Here, I fear Pawley is slipping into a too-easy existentialist cant. In her paper, Françoise Choay asks whether a semiological approach can lead anywhere other than simply to a 'heightened consciousness'. Pawley's approach, I think, is surely incapable of leading anywhere else.

FRAMPTON: In many ways this seems to me to be the key to Pawley's whole thesis. The public realm previously bonded man into the past and the future; the eternal return and reappearance in this realm transcending the tragedy and futility of individual life. An episodic record of each individual life would to my mind take man out of time, but only loose him in the infinite corridors of change as nebulous as the mirror world of human dreams.

The environments blotted out by the bull-dozers are the physical context of human experience: the evidence of being.

matrix of civilization and the ubiquitous threat of other persons.

Another influential factor in the individual's conception of his own context is the amount of direct control that he can assume over it. Human interaction with environment has been historically a matter of movement and transformation, construction and destruction. Consequently the individual tends to limit his conscious response to the sphere of his conscious responsibility, in that he blocks out conscious reaction to those parts of his environment that are painful to him, or which operate without concern for his wishes. This is a primary human defence mechanism, essential for the retention of any conviction of autonomy in a collectively organized world.

In the same way as he erases consciousness of the unpleasant aspects of his life and environment, the individual magnifies his consciousness of those parts of time and space that are completely under his control. We can see this in the apparently disproportionate importance given to weekends, holidays, even evenings, by persons who are capable of forgetting utterly the immeasurably longer periods of time they spend in less self-regulated occupations. The individual dwells on, and as far as possible in, those parts of his life which yield him, in Geoffrey Gorer's phrase 'The pleasure felt from observed modifications on the external world produced by the will of the observer'.[22] He likes to become what he has made, whether this be a thing, an idea or a fantasy.

This tendency to grow in upon what best protects and projects him is the reason why the dwelling is unique in Western societies in the possibilities for expression it affords the individual. In addition to converting his home situation into a guardian of those hours of his life spent in fruitless travel or travail, the individual uses it as a kind of incorruptible model of his personality at its best. A tool to convince him repeatedly that his personality has a status going far beyond the unfulfilling imperatives of his daytime occupation.

Identification of the home as the big arena of human situation is only occasionally misleading; but the varying stages of ego differentiation, as well as the myriad permutations of interpersonal, economic and social pressures, can create instances where an individual's office, car or public house becomes his true situation. His flat or room, if he possesses one, can be as anonymous as a hotel bedroom, while his car is a wonderland of quasi useless technology, a collection of servo-mechanisms multiplying the power impulses of his weakened personality.[23] These cases however must be regarded as the exception rather than the rule. The substitute is generally more fragile, less legally reinforced, less universally recognized than the home—which excels as a territorially stabilised arena.

Substitute situations become even more tenuous when they exist in nooks and crannies in the institutional world. In such environments monstrously unbalanced cere conflict is often the underlying cause of the many seemingly trivial squabbles about positions in a room, ownership of box files, upper or lower bunks, best or largest cups, that plague the smooth running of all institutions. Lipman for instance, recounts conflicts over chair ownership between the occupants of old persons homes as being accompanied by verbal invective and physical attacks, ostracism and prolonged endurance of physical discomfort before surrender.[24]

It is interesting to speculate on the possibility of using a kind of portable personality machine in such a context. This role is of course already performed to some extent by the contents of pockets, wallets and handbags, but the idea of combining such reified identity information with the audible establishment of territory which birds achieve might be worth pursuing.

The presence of such a mechanism might have a curious effect upon cere conflict; portable radios and tape recorders already create mixed responses in work and leisure places, ostensibly as a result of increased noise levels, but perhaps also because the perpetrator is projecting an image of himself altogether too assertive and individual for such collective occasions. Tom Wolfe wrote that teenagers used transistor radios 'as a background, the aural prop for whatever kind of life they want to imagine they're leading',[25] and it is true that in very few non-industrial work situations is such a 'background' permitted. Where it is, in boutiques and photographic studios for example, the intention is clearly to break down any institutional or even functional atmosphere so that the activities which take place within the space seem, or actually are, things one does voluntarily.

THE ARRANGEMENT OF OBJECTS

An individual populates his own dwelling with objects and information, some of iconic value, some purely functional, some sharing the characteristics of both. No outside observer could ever estimate the subjective value of these objects and messages according to an external scale of values, although in the least inventive and most conventional surroundings he might roughly approximate them. The *subjective* value of these objects resides not in themselves but in their interrelation, their sequence and their significance as extensions of the personality of their owner. In other words they are not really isolated objects but connected molecules in the atomic structure of the individual's own consciousness. This factor alone is sufficient to demonstrate the absurdity of the separation between user and designer, and designer-object and designer-subject, that we observe today. It has been calculated that although a very high percentage of the perceived urban or suburban environment is man made, only about 5% is planned in terms of its juxtapositions and sequences. The rest is a confusion of object-disorder, conforming to either random or subjective patterns.

The ideas and images of his own life that the individual entertains are for the most part expressed in this latter world of subjective 'content', where the value system which links the object-evidence of these ideas and images is locked inside the sequential code of behaviour that first gave them meaning. This circuit is unbreakable, it can only be *simulated* by media, for in the human situation *ideas and images derive from and create content—even when external considerations totally determine form.* Thus value systems as well as ideas and images are expressed in the object world.

Our approach to the area of the individual-in-context must be to treat it as a *Gestalt* or unity, whose parts are fused and made interdependent by the juxtaposition in which they are perceived. To study this *Gestalt* or 'situation' from the standpoint of its totality, which is the unifying element of human perception, we must try with our technology to perceive what the individual perceives through his own cerebral and sensory mechanisms. We must try to construct as accurate a picture of nuclear behaviour as the sensitivity of our mechanisms will allow.

Though repetitive and cyclic in configuration, the individual's interaction with his 'situation' is a linear experience. The creation of the 'situation' itself is not an instantaneous process, starting the moment a person takes possession of a new house. For practical as well as psychological reasons the assembly of dwelling 'content' is a function of maturity. The possession of objects older than oneself or invested with meaning by connection with the deceased is not merely an implicit acknowledgement of the passage of time, but objective evidence of the human continuum. Similarly the particular patterns of behaviour conferred on an individual by the formal idiosyncrasies of his dwelling are only 'learnt' or absorbed into the consciousness over a period of time.

Recognition of the violence done to the concept of a continuous tradition of human identification with place by contemporary notions of mobility and obsolescence is vital to the idea of context as a part of personality which was developed earlier. George Kubler, in *The Shape of Time*,[26] a book which revolutionized my conception of the real meaning of changes in the configuration of objects, suggests that to treat the dwelling as a finite object, subject to obsolescence, corresponds to a lifelong sequence of violent and discontinuous changes in time: alternate destruction and creation so complete as to resemble conditions reigning under bombardment, evacuation or earthquake.

Historical evidence seems to indicate that the design, use and retention of objects is an accumulative process like learning or growth. The design doctrine of functionalism on the other hand implies that it is a selective process, whereby different conditions demand successive and radically different personality orientations.

Figuratively speaking the functional doctrine requires that the individual be prepared periodically to shed his skin like a snake; whereas the theory of continuity suggests that he carry out a continuous process of digestion, converting the evidence of his experiences into subjectively informed objects, or 'memories' contained in the 'content' of his dwelling. This in fact is what, in a non-systematic fashion, already occurs and has done for many centuries: which serves to indicate, not the redundancy of the concept, but the acute importance of the phenomenon of object association within the human situation today as much as at any time in history.

THE PERCEPTION OF CHANGE

The problem of representation and simulation posed by the continuous nature of human perception and experience is analogous to the mystery posed for many hundreds of years by the true configuration of the legs of a galloping horse. Before Eadweard Muybridge's successful use of multiple cameras the problem seemed insoluble because the legs moved too fast for the naked eye. In the case of human experience and perception the position is reversed. The changes in physiology, musculature, attitude and posture, which are the critical 'movements', happen too slowly; and the change in objects, their entropy trend, is an irreversible process of a duration which cannot easily be measured. The slowness and repetitiveness of formal change is such that any human observer will 'change' either faster, as in the case of objects, or at the same speed, as in the case of humans, as the object of his study. It is as if Muybridge had himself been a running horse, obliged to find some method of stopping himself before he could decipher the identical performance of his subject. The only possible method of coming to terms with a synchronized record of behaviour in this sense would be to achieve a system of classification, or speeded up perception, which could only be termed consciousness expansion. The very existence of such a record would bring this about—just as other behavioural demands of this century have brought about skills and perceptions unimaginable years ago.

In a sense, each individual lives in the same world as his fellows only by virtue of his, and their, relationships with the same objects. Either through their universality, as in the case of a cup of tea, or through their uniqueness, as in the case of their own bodies. Proof of this can be seen in any war situation when questions of identification and allegiance are settled by interrogation on matters of national or provincial shibboleth; or in art or entertainment where success often depends on the close observation and reproduction of key associations which link the performer to his or her audience. The 'situation' of these relationships, destined to be forever insoluble to the objective designer, is centred in the fate of the individual to feel and to observe simultaneously. His 'situation' is the relationship between the experience of being and the evidence of being; the relationship between behaviour, objects and time. It is here that Kubler's theory of replication is of vital importance. In the forementioned work he demonstrates that our understanding of behaviour can only be understood as experience if it is repetitive, and only varied repetitions can create a consciousness of time and change. Without change there is no history, without regularity there is no time.[26]

By treating the dwelling, which is legally, economically and socially the only uncompromised space left in any technologised western society, as the repository and analyst of the repeated actions that constitute human experience, the user-designer might productively rationalize the capacity that the changing but continuous dwelling has maintained throughout recorded history—the capacity to comprehend time.

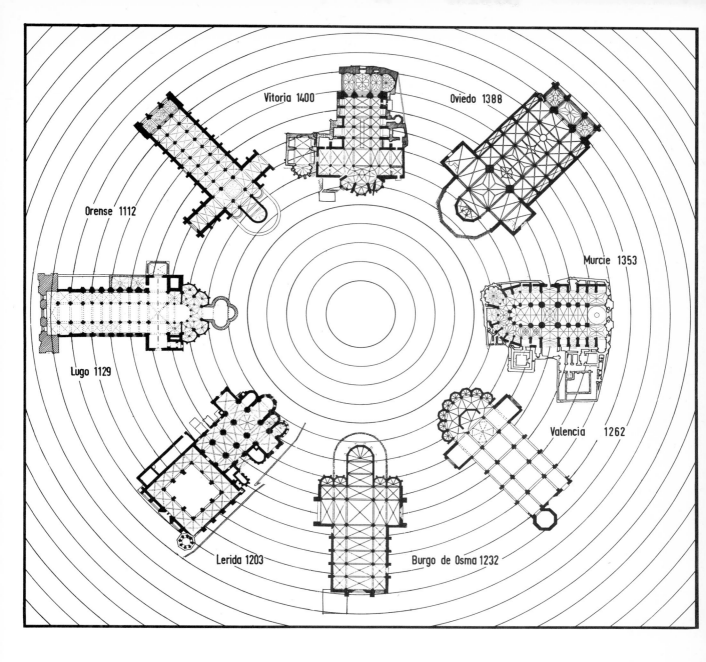

Vitoria 1400

Oviedo 1388

Orense 1112

Murcie 1353

Lugo 1129

Valencia 1262

Lerida 1203

Burgo de Osma 1232

'The whole of human experience consists of replicas, gradually changing by minute alterations more than by abrupt leaps of invention, George Kubler.

THE TIME HOUSE

Five basic axioms underlie the previous text:

(1) That today the public realm is doomed to inauthenticity through its inability to acknowledge the simultaneous presence of subject and object in the individual—even though this is a condition of his consciousness.

(2) That subjective and individual aspects of the design process can only be expressed in the authentic world of individual experience, never in the factitious world of collective enterprise.

(3) That in the process of dwelling the individual authenticates his environment, so that the private realm, which is the realm of dwelling, must be the realm of authentic experience.

(4) That places and objects are the proof of individual experience; so much so that their destruction involves the destruction of the evidence of being.

143

(5) That a continuous record of individual object relations could not only clarify the significance of place and object, but also enable the individual to come to terms with such environmental change as is a condition of his existence in a technological society.

The Time House itself is intended to absorb the object-evidence of experience: to listen, see, smell, touch remember and replay. It is to be a neutral memory to externalize the crucial area of the man/object interface, a cybernetically controlled instant recall system with a storage capacity measured in centuries. Its mechanisms are intended to work automatically, unobtrusively and comprehensively. Nothing will escape its notice, everything will await recall.

In many ways Jean Paul Sartre anticipated the behavioural effects of such a record when he wrote: 'Giving names to objects consists in moving immediate, unreflected, perhaps ignored events on to the plane of reflection and of the objective mind.'[27] The example he gives is of the oppression of the Negroes, which is nothing until someone says, 'Negroes are oppressed'. Until then nobody realizes it, perhaps not even the Negroes themselves.

This is currently the case with the study of human behaviour. Much of the unanalysed activity of the individual is the unconscious manifestation of inner tendencies which are only realized or spoken of at a much later stage in their evolution, when they become more or less intelligible social behaviour. The formerly popular 'retirement with a headache', or any of the obvious manifestations of shyness are cases in point. Much 'inexplicable' social behaviour is inexplicable solely because it is but the socially visible tip of an immense subjective iceberg. The key to the understanding of the social behaviour of persons is locked away in the strongroom of their private existence. People do not 'name' their subjective activity to themselves, let alone to anyone else. The social game they play is to create an 'intelligible' surface motivational system to explain their *observed* behaviour.

It is the capacity to penetrate this barrier of superficial explanation that is the unique value of an analytical dwelling, for the real importance of the Time House as a concept derives from its immunity to the scrutiny of other persons. The

◀ BAIRD: In this breathlessness, in this unqualified acceptance of a 'technologistic society', Pawley leaves me thinking that the Time House is really a Trojan Horse. Positivist utilitarianism, which we had expected the Time House to vanquish, would have triumphed from within after all and *memory*, to paraphrase Marx, would have become the opium of the people.

THE TIME HOUSE

A proposed Time House structure. The heavy concrete installation is built for introspection and defence, like a bunker. It consists of a circular basement for mechanisms; pre-cast concrete floor and fin units (6) with motorised aluminium blinds (7) between, enclosing the living area, and a central pylon (8). Under the optically black aluminium/polyurethane sandwich dome (10) a silently rotating boom (3) carries a camera, microphone and sensor complex (1) which responds to impulses received from ammonia sensors installed throughout the house and continuously recording the behaviour of the occupants. The video/audio recording, together with synchronised recordings of other environmental data are transferred to computer tape and stored in the basement memory to await recall in the replay room. The boom control mechanism (4) automatically adjusts the elevation, depression pan and tilt mechanisms (2) and compensates via the counterweight (5).

sensations of those whose behaviour is observed and recorded for public performance are not the same as the sensations which result from observation in the domestic context. The revelation of subjective behaviour and motivation which the Time House mechanisms can make available is no more related to the pitiless exposure of public life than is the act of looking into a mirror to the experience of seeing oneself on television. Its quality lies in the absence of interference by other persons, for the mechanism will remain throughout totally under the control of the individual, who can have as much or as little of himself as he wishes.

This very process must before long give the occupant a new perspective on his existence, for the neutral objectivity of the recording mechanisms which surround him will provide an image totally different from the partial insights of any human observer. The messages he elects to receive will be discrete from his own recollections or those of other individuals. A good analogy is with the two channels of a stereophonic record player: the pure objectivity of the non-human recording mechanism combined with subjective recollection creates a third dimension in the *portrayal of experience*. I have termed this process 'existential stereophony': a method of triangulating self-perception in relation to two signal sources separated in space and, in a sense, in time. The result of this experience will be as illuminating as the sudden depth which stereoscopic photography gives to landscape.

In response to this sudden access of continuous information the individual's image of himself will change from the fragmented distorting mirror of others, the reflections in shop windows, the statistical evidence of his presence on the files of the bureaucracy, to a comprehensive, perhaps frightening image, for the first time communicable: a named, identified record of his being, his character, his personality.

Such a 'picture' is only just technically feasible today: the immense difficulties at a purely practical level—audio filtering to prevent blurring and distortion during conversations, camera movements and positions which are both concealed and still provide meaningful, recognizable images—all these still

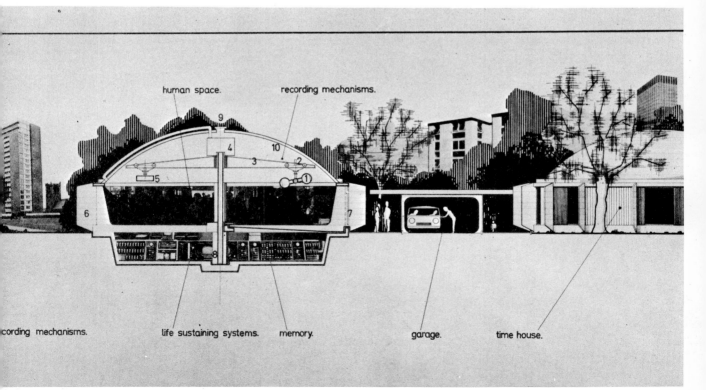

human space.   recording mechanisms.

cording mechanisms.   life sustaining systems.   memory.   garage.   time house.

require considerable research and expertise, not all of which is readily available. All that can be certain is that from many and disparate fields of research, from space technology, weapon development, cybernetics, micro-data storage, time lapse photography, physiology and anthropology, methods and mechanisms have been developed which, if integrated and modified, could provide the entire technical matrix for the Time House.

The desideratum is in fact a 'cool' medium, requiring less and less personal involvement and more and more detachment from the observer. In the stereo analogy, the two consciousnesses, one reflective, one objective, must be statically and dynamically separated. There must be as little crosstalk as possible. The less the individual has to piece together with his empathy the gaps and blurs in the record of his consciousness, the more he can use it as a beacon to triangulate his own position. A terminal situation must arise where the subject can relive his experience to the extent that its pure externality forces him to say 'That is not me. It is my-self'.

This means that initial moves towards the concept of the Time House, though tending toward the complete object, will in fact create an image of consciousness that is very much less than the real thing. A truncated distorted image of the self that is only a little better than the eyeless, emotionless image that emerges in Bank statements or Manikins. The imperfect mosaic of the face of humanity, that is seen in the design of its artefacts, will be brought only a little closer to completion by the objectification and externalization of some aspects of the behaviour of its individuals.

This objection, or warning, is not trivial. The fragmented evidence of the presence of a person left when they die is very seldom enough to give pleasure, let alone recognition. A few photographs, some letters, empty clothes, even a home movie of a baby on a sunny lawn. Incomplete information constitutes a 'hot' medium. . . . Hot with tears and the receding and distorting effort of the empathetic pursuit of fugitive images. The act of completion is an act of distortion. We end up filling the gaps in the object evidence of the past with the energy of the present. And this is true of the memories of our own actions as well as those of the dead.

The partial Time House will be painful. More painful than its totality.

FORM AND CONTENT

The mechanism of the Time House could of itself dictate a dwelling form, or it could be inserted, like central heating or air conditioning, into the matrix of an existing dwelling. The first alternative involves a curious and perhaps productive mixture of existential and functional design. Each of the various mechanisms that the several processes of the simulation of consciousness dictate, has its own set of functional requirements and conditions for optimum performance. At the same time the 'functionless', or 'existential' nature of the space into which they must fit demands that these considerations do not dominate the spatial patterns that individual interaction with the new context will bring about.

The second alternative does seem to offer the opportunity for the insertion of the mechanism into existing forms and spaces without great visible disturbance of their previous arrangement. The choice at this stage seems invidious, between living in a film studio and bugging one's own house. Only a restatement of the goal can resolve both the dilemma and the reluctance to accept either choice.

The purpose of the Time House is to make behaviour intelligible. This requires that such behaviour as takes place within it must be recordable without interference, distortion or danger of interruption. One way to achieve this would be to regulate behaviour by means of the form of the dwelling so that it took place at a specified distance from camera and sensors. From here it is but a short step to chalk marks on the floor, scripts and set hours for 'drama'. The real choice is between an environmental separation of the elements of behaviour for the purpose of intelligibility, or a ritualized form of behaviour ('acting'). This last

◀ BAIRD: With a naivete I find astonishing, in view of the subtlety of the argument thus far, Pawley concludes by assuming the possibility of comprehensive technical encapsulation of reality 'as in itself it really is'. A discussion which began in the nuance of existential phenomenology, reverts in the end to a banal millenialism.

◀ JENCKS: In so far as technical means have the potential to modify our sensibility and way of life, the Time House opens up possible liberating routes to the future. Perhaps the new technical means of storing and conveying information signal a shift in culture as great as that when writing was systematized in Egypt to create the first large cities (and bureaucracies). In any case they offer fantastic potential just waiting the kind of imaginative use that Martin Pawley makes of them. My only objection is that, for philosophical reasons, he confines their use to the private realm – and confined too much in the private realm one might deserve the ancient Greek definition of the word 'idiot' ('given over to private interests'). But there is no logical reason why these techniques couldn't be applied to the public realm as well and we could have a 'Time City' that would make the palimpsest Rome look like a Tabula Rasa.

would not of course invalidate the concept of the Time House any more than the action of a play invalidates its subject matter. As Searles has pointed out, stylized patterns of behaviour can still express the realities of cereconflict and the patterns of consciousness; they are part of the response to observation that recording and replay make devastatingly clear. However, experience with restricted environments such as submarines, seems to indicate that individuals can adjust themselves more readily to specialized environments than they can to special occasions for self revelation. The productive choice for the occupant is not between, for example, a tutor and a teaching machine, but between himself as subject—in recollection—and himself as object—in replay. The aim of the Time House is that he should at length synchronize the two images so that he can see on a reflective plane, as well as feel, that he is both.

The disintegration of the traditional 'functional' determinants of human space, which was discussed in the first part, left the form of the 'subjective environment' open to the individual. If he should choose to determine it with the objects and evidence of his being, which has been his historic choice, it would seem logical that in the pursuit of this aim he might be prepared to accept an overall formal definition directly dependent on the needs of mechanisms designed to enable him to look more closely at himself. If this is his purpose, the Time House is his logical answer. In making this choice he is not surrendering himself to formal anonymity. The mechanisms that record his behaviour may be neutral, but the evidence they project is most certainly partisan.

From the total neutrality of formal definition by mechanism can arise the total personality of a 'content' that becomes an image of consciousness as endless and fragile as the lineage of a royal house: a presence that can survive change as the whale survived in the sea—by designing itself into a new mode of being.

[1] Claude Lévi-Strauss. *The Savage Mind*, Weidenfeld and Nicholson, 1966 (originally published in French as *La Pensée Sauvage*, Plon, 1962) Chapter 9: History and Dialectic.
[2] The evocative phrase used by Yona Friedman at The Folkestone Conference of Experimental Architecture. June 1966.
[3] Simone de Beauvoir. *The Ethics of Ambiguity*. Citadel, 1961. Translated from the French by Bernard Frechtman.
[4] Stephen Black. *Man and Motorcars: an Ergonomic Study*, Secker and Warburg, 1964. Black maintains, as a result of numerous experiments on drivers involving hypnosis and hallucinogenic drugs, that the elements of fantasy and wish fulfilment lie at the very foundation of automania.
[5] This parallel was developed by Robert Boguslaw into a book entitled *The New*

Utopians. A Study of system design and social change (Prentice-Hall, 1965). Boguslaw states that whilst writing a textbook on the design of contemporary large scale computer-based command and control systems he 'became more and more impressed with the similarity between the intellectual underpinnings of the modern material (he) was using and the formulations of social theorists in the utopian tradition who analysed existing social systems and designed new ones. (He) saw that modern system designers were unconsciously treading well worn paths—that they were embracing the most fundamental errors of earlier efforts and were incorporating them into the fabric of even the most sophisticated of push button systems.'

He claimed that 'The current preoccupation with computer-based systems and automation (had) left the contemporary social scientist, together with the overwhelming majority of our population, occupying the role of bystander. His characteristic involvement in system design is *ex post facto*, and this greatly circumscribes the range of his possible influence on the design of these crucially significant frames for social behaviour.'

[6] Harold Rosenberg. *The Tradition of the New*, McGraw-Hill, 1965. Chapter 19, 'The Orgamerican Phantasy'.

[7] This does not seem too unfair a description of the concept Banham originated in his 'A Home is not a House', Art in America, April 1965, which is reprinted here.

[8] Reyner Banham. Folkestone Conference of Experimental Architecture. June 1966.

[9] A paraphrase of Geoffrey Gorer's surprising definition of sadism, quoted in *The Life and Ideas of the Marquis de Sade*, Peter Owen, 1953.

[10] Buckminster-Fuller wrote in the pamphlet 'Utopia or Oblivion' (1965), 'Despite the constant increase in human population and constant decrease in metals per person, between 1900 and 1965 the number of people attaining physical regeneration success by full participation in the highest standard of living progressively developed by world industrialization . . . rose steadily from less than 1% to 40% of all living humanity. The 40% of humanity surprisingly grown successful, despite constantly diminishing physical resources, *per capita*, can only be explained by the doing-more-with-less invention revolution.'

[11] The celebrated experiments with planarian worms carried out between 1958 and 1961 by J. B. Best and I. Rubinstein in Washington, were first publicized in the magazine 'Science' in 1962. Robert Ardrey, in *The Territorial Imperative*, quotes from Best's report as follows:—'. . . Planarian behaviour resembles behaviour that in higher animals one calls boredom, interest, conflict, decision, frustration, rebellion, anxiety, learning and cognitive awareness. . . . The apparent similarity between the protopsychological patterns of Planarians and the psychological patterns of rats and men turns out to be more than superficial. This would indicate that psychological characteristics are more ancient and widespread than the neurophysiological structures from which they are thought to have arisen. Two possibilities suggest themselves. Such patterns may stem from some primordial properties of living matter, arising from some cellular or sub-cellular level of organization rather than nerve circuitry. An alternative possibility is that . . . the psychology of animals may evolve in response to compelling considerations of optimal design in the same way that whales and other cetacean animals have assumed a fishlike shape.'

[12] Strehlow, T. G. H. *Aranda traditions*, Melbourne 1947. Quoted in *The Savage Mind*.

[13] Ardrey, Robert. *The Territorial Imperative*, London. Collins 1967.

[14] 'Persons who are lodged in "bad" wards find that very little equipment of any kind is given them—clothes may be taken away from them each night, recreational materials may be withheld, and only heavy wooden chairs and benches provided for furniture. . . . When a patient finds himself in isolation, naked and without visible means of expression, he may have to rely on tearing up his mattress, if he can, or writing with faeces on the wall—actions authority takes to be in keeping with the kind of person who warrants confinement.' Goffman, Erving. *Asylums. Essays on the Social Situation of Mental Patients and Other Inmates*. New York. Doubleday Anchor, 1961.

[15] Searles, Harold F. *The Nonhuman Environment*. New York. International Universities Press, 1960.

[16] Burnham Kelly. *The Prefabrication of Houses*. London. Chapman & Hall, 1951.

[17] The deep seated desire to achieve this form of 'security' is indicated by the zeal of the new council house purchasers of Birmingham, who spoke of 'A lifelong desire. An opportunity we had been waiting for all our lives'. And described their purchases as 'Their last chance'. Conservative Party Political broadcast on the sale of council houses to tenants. March 1967.

[18] Habraken, N. J. *The Supports and the People*. Scheltema and Holkema Ltd. Amsterdam, 1961.

[19] (Ibid) Habraken speaks of environments which can be 'old without being outdated, which can incorporate the latest techniques and yet retain their history.'

[20] Friedman proposed to use space grids for slum redevelopment by building aerial structures over the stricken area, inserting new dwelling units, raising the occupants of the condemned areas vertically into the new environment and then demolishing their old beuildings before their eyes. Folkestone Conference of Experimental Architecture. June, 1966.

[21] Piaget, J. *The Construction of Reality in the Child*. New York. Basic Books, 1954.

[22] Gorer, Geoffrey. *The Life and Ideas of the Marquis de Sade*. London. Peter Owen, 1953.

[23] Black, Stephen. *Man and Motorcars*. London. Secker and Warburg, 1964.

[24] Lipman, A. 'Building Design and Social Interaction.' A preliminary study in three old people's homes. The Architects' Journal. 3 January, 1968.

[25] Wolfe, Tom. *The Kandy Kolored Tangerine Flake Streamline Baby*. London. Jonathan Cape, 1966.

[26] Kubler, George. *The Shape of Time*. New York. Yale University Press, 1962.

[27] Sartre, Jean-Paul. 'The Responsibility of the Writer'. Translated by Betty Askwith in *Reflections of our Age*. New York. Columbia University Press, 1948.

Labour Work & Architecture[I]

Kenneth Frampton

'You show us, Rome was glorious, not profuse,
And pompous buildings once were things of use,
Yet shall my lord, your just and noble rules
Fill half the land with imitating fools
Who random drawings from your sheets shall take,
And of one beauty, many blunders make;
Load some vain church with old Theatric State,
Turn Arcs of triumph to a Gardon-gate; . . .'

Alexander Pope.
Epistle to the Rt Hon. Richard Earl of Burlington,1731.

In her book 'The Human Condition,' appropriately subtitled, 'A Study of the Central Dilemmas facing Modern Man', Hannah Arendt designated three activities, 'labor', 'work' and 'action', as being fundamental to the 'vita-activa' or to human life in the public realm. She properly establishes at the very beginning of her thesis, the particular meaning that she assigns to each of these three terms.[2] Of *labor* she writes: 'Labor is the activity which corresponds to the biological process of the human body, whose spontaneous growth, metabolism and eventual decay are bound to the vital necessities produced and fed into the life process by labor. The human condition is life itself.' Whereas of *work* she writes: 'Work is the activity which corresponds to the unnaturalness of human existence, which is not imbedded in, and whose mortality is not compensated by, the "species" ever recurring life circle. Work provides an "artificial" world of things, distinctly different from all natural surroundings. Within its borders each individual life is housed while this world itself is meant to outlast and transcend them all. The human condition of work is worldliness'. Her definition of *action*— as pertaining to transactions occurring between men without the intervention of things, and as corresponding essentially to plurality and to the fact that men and not man inhabit the earth—in itself specifies the existential preliminary of every building act.

SILVER: I would argue that a most essential aspect of architecture falls within the category of what Arendt calls 'action' (and I do so argue in my own essay).

In her discussion of the public and private realms of the 'vita-activa', Arendt amplifies her definitions of 'labor and work'. She argues firstly that 'labor' by virtue of being a constantly changing process of survival is inherently *private* and *impermanent*, whereas, conversely, the very act of human public appearance depends upon 'work' as the sole agency through which the relative permanence of the human world, testifying to human continuity, may be established. Thus she determines 'labor' as 'impermanent' and synonymous with the 'private' realm and work as 'permanent' and synonymous with the 'public' realm.

As Arendt admits, it is unusual to designate the constituents of 'vita-activa' through proposing this particular distinction between 'labor' and 'work'. In our current usage, these two terms have become synonymous and we are by no means accustomed to distinguish between them. Nevertheless, an etymological basis for such a distinction exists according to Arendt in almost every European language both ancient and modern and under certain circumstances our usage persists in maintaining this distinction. We continue for instance, to refer to the 'work' as opposed to the 'labor' of a creative artist or thinker.

It is, of course, equally unusual that concepts such as these should be used to predicate an essay on architecture and planning, although building as an act appears to possess an inherently public character. A construction, as opposed to a work of fine art, is almost invariably erected to serve or house a function of the society, hence it is of essence in some respect public, save on those increasingly numerous occasions when it comprises the single family unit or isolated private house. Although the repetition of this unit inexorably determines today large tracts of our 'public' environment, the unit in itself remains essentially ephemeral and private, dedicated as it inevitably is to the process of biological survival. In our repetition of this unit, as an almost infinite aggregate of isolated cells dispersed over vast areas of land, we act in confirmation of Arendt's main thesis, that the processes of labor, the processes of biological survival do at present largely dominate and determine our human environment.

If one postulates that 'architecture' is 'work', through its predisposition to be permanent, public, and to predicate life; and if one acknowledges that our present life is largely dominated by the processes of 'labor', then it follows that the socio-cultural validity of any building act depends upon a discrete determination at the outset of the inherent cultural context, within which this particular act is to be realized. The determination of such a context demands that we, as architects and planners, must initially attempt to answer two questions before proceeding further; firstly, what do we mean by the term architecture; and secondly, how do we relate our understanding of this term to the concepts of 'labor' and 'work' as defined by Hannah Arendt?

One traditional definition of architecture in the West is found in Wotton's famous dictum, derived from Vitruvius: 'Fine building hath three things, commodity, firmness and delight'. It is obvious that this dictum depends ultimately upon the dictates of current taste, in order to serve at all as a definition of architecture as opposed to the process of building. As a definition it only remains apposite in a situation where a method and a formal syntax of building have been firmly established and continue to be understood and developed by a relatively stable society. It is an inadequate definition, in a highly pluralistic epoch such as ours, which possesses no cultured minority who are equipped with the necessary capacity, inclination, and power to determine a ruling taste. The Wotton of the Renaissance, one supposes, had little reason to imagine that a suitable context for fine building would one day become a critical issue in itself. His classic definition born out of Rome is relatively inapplicable to our present situation.[3] The very concept of 'fine' building does not assist us. We are all witness to a great deal of building, yet whether it is fine or not, in the sense of being 're-fined' although pertinent to a particular quality, remains irrelevant to our general cultural predicament. An adequate theory of architecture and more particularly of the realm of architecture continues to elude us. As yet no contemporary theory even attempts to discriminate between the word-concepts 'architecture' and 'building'. Yet the dictionary[4] continues to proffer two significantly different definitions for the word architecture, which suggests that men have for a long time subconsciously nurtured the idea that there are in essence two distinct levels at which the 'building act' may take place. The word 'architecture', from the Greek word 'architecton' meaning constructor, is defined firstly as 'the art or science of constructing edifices for human use' and secondly as the 'action and process of building'. These two definitions, at once suggest themselves as parallels to the distinction that Hannah Arendt draws between 'work' and 'labor'. The phrase 'for human use' imports a specifically human or anthropomorphic connotation to the whole of the first definition, alluding to the creation of the 'human world'. Conversely, it may be argued that, in the second definition, the use of the words 'action' and 'process' in the phrase 'the action and process of building' clearly implies a continuous act of building, forever incomplete, comparable to the continual process of biological labor. The additional fact that, according to the dictionary, the word 'edifice' may strictly be used only to refer to 'a large and stately building such as a church, a palace, or a fortress', (i.e. the houses of the priest and the prince) serves only to support the connotation 'work' in the first definition, as in developed human society these building types have always been considered to be typically both permanent and public. Furthermore, the word 'edifice' relates directly to the verb 'to edify', which not only carries with it the meaning 'to build' but also the meanings 'to educate', 'to establish', 'to strengthen' and 'to instruct'. Again the Latin root of this verb: *aedificare*, from *aedes*, a building, or, originally, a hearth, and *ficare*, meaning to make, has latent in it the intention of work being made 'public'; for although the hearth is only to be found today in a private domestic realm, it was not always so and even now it still embodies a public aspect. No place is more public as a forum in a private home than its 'hearth' or its successor the television set, which as an encapsulated public substitute tends to inhibit the ritual emergence of an 'actual' public aspect in private life, i.e. conversation. As Le Corbusier has pointed out the size of

BAIRD: It makes me nervous when the discussion moves this far so quickly; I find it difficult to imagine, in terms consistent with Arendt's position, just what an 'encapsulated public substitute' might be.

a village was once measured by the number of fires it contained, the fire being the public source of heat, food and human contact.[5]

Architecture then, according to its dictionary definition, appears to have always been open to at least two distinct levels of interpretation: the act of edification of stately structures and the process of building. Paradoxically an analysis of the private cell at once reveals the presence of an 'operational' public aspect contained within it. This alone is sufficient to suggest the degree of discretion necessary to correctly determine the cultural context of any particular building act. Furthermore not all building at the 'private' cultural level is dedicated to the dwelling. Indeed it may be more appropriate to speak of the *cultural complex* of such an act and to urge that the conceptualization of a more viable cultural model of the process of building implies that those concerned in the design of the built environment have the responsibility to make and

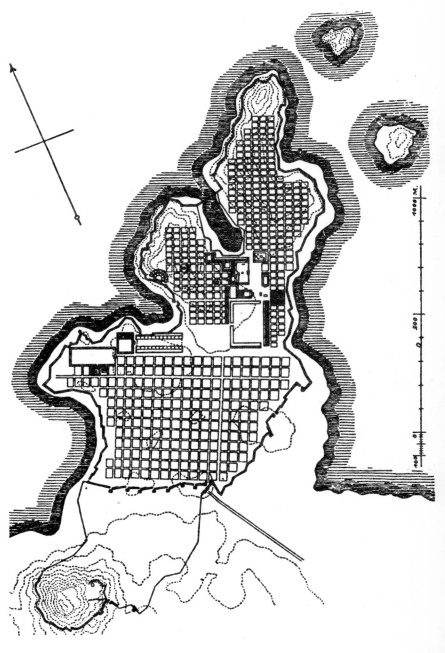

Miletus. Greek Hippodamia, city fifth century B.C. The gradual growth of three sequential public realms or 'agoras' linked to each other by Stoa: the harbour agora, the market agora, and the civic agora. The 'sacred' public realm is removed from this sequence to one side.

express discrete distinctions between labor and work, between private and public, between impermanent and permanent in every particular case.

For Vitruvius in Roman times, the architect was the universal *homo-faber par excellence*. To him Vitruvius assigned not only the art of building but also the making of timepieces and the fabrication of machinery.[6] The elaborate specializations of our complex present had not yet been envisaged. For Hannah Arendt 'fabrication' or the work of the *homo-faber*, consists in 'reification'; that is, in the creation of the 'human world' in the face of nature. The *homo-faber* she states, who 'makes and literally works upon' his material is to be distinguished from the *animal laborans* who 'labors and mixes with his product'. The difference between man the maker and man the laboring animal cannot be better expressed than in Arendt's own words. 'The man-made world of things, the human artifice erected by the *homo-faber* becomes a home for mortal men, whose stability will endure and outlast the ever changing movement of their lives and actions, only insomuch as it transcends both the sheer functionalism of things produced for consumption, and the sheer utility of things produced for use. . . . If the *animal laborans* needs the help of the *homo-faber* to ease his labor and remove his pain, and if mortals need his help to erect a home on earth, acting and speaking men need the help of the *homo-faber* in his highest capacity, that is the help of the artist, of poets, historiographers, of monument builders and writers, because without them the only product of their activity, the story that they enact and tell, would not survive at all.' Arendt regards the *homo-faber* as a figure crucial to the survival of human consciousness. Elsewhere in her study, Arendt demonstrates how the ideals of the *homo-faber*, the very notions of permanence and stability, have today been sacrificed to abundance and to the ideals of the *animal laborans*. 'In our need', she writes, 'for more and more rapid replacement of the wordly things around us, we can no longer afford to use them, to respect and preserve their inherent durability, we must consume, devour, as it were, our houses and furniture and cars as though they were the 'good things' of life which would spoil uselessly if they are not drawn swiftly into the never ending cycle of man's metabolism with nature. It is as though we had forced open the distinguishing boundaries which protected the *world*, the human artifice from *nature*, from the biological processes which surround it, delivering and abandoning to them the always threatened stability of a human world.'

This all too convincing and somewhat bleak analysis of our present circumstances argues that the *homo-faber* in his highest capacity today can only act with integrity in a discrete and differential manner; an act of reification being only capable of completion and fulfilment by the society under appropriate cultural conditions. This in turn implies that a responsibility now devolves upon the architect to determine as precisely as possible the conditions under which he is being asked to act. If one accepts this implication, the present role of the architect in relation to the society becomes problematic. The architect who recognizes this predicament is at once compelled to reformulate his operating image as a functionary within the society. Such a reformulation necessarily involves an attempt at a complete re-assessment of the cultural significance of the full range of building.

Architectural history, as it is traditionally taught in architectural schools, is essentially still a primer course in the masterworks of western architecture. As such it concerns itself with the 'works' of architecture as opposed to those anonymous structures that have always arisen out of the never ending processes of biological 'labor'. As an historical education this necessarily prejudices the young student architect, in favour of an understanding of all building as 'work', as opposed to a recognition of the sober fact that a very large amount of building today comes, as it always has, within the province of 'labor'. Indeed we are hard put today to isolate and secure any building type or act that may be thought of exclusively as work. Only comparatively recently have historians and for that matter architects begun to concern themselves with the anonymous, unconscious and semi-spontaneous building of the *animal laborans* and with its relation to

BAIRD: This seems to me most important. In fact, so far as its specifically architectural implications go, I would prefer to regard Arendt's labour/work distinction as representing the extremes of a spectrum, rather than as a sharp polarization.

BAIRD: This argument throws up a most interesting issue. While the architect must indeed, as a professional man, carefully ponder his 'role . . . in relation to the society', he must at the same time ponder his role as a member of that society. In doing so, should he accept, or should he fight what Arendt calls 'the victory of "animal laborans" '?

BAIRD: Here, it seems to me, Frampton is polarizing the labour/work distinction in an untenable fashion.

the public, defined and durable works of the whole society.[7] Until the early industrial revolution, all human settlements, from those of the fertile crescent onwards, successfully expressed a balance between 'labor' and 'work' both in building and in social organization. In their public buildings and spaces, which were invariably situated at the intersection or convergence of major axes or movement routes these settlements, in various ways, managed always to achieve a clear reification of the 'human world'. In each instance within the interstices of these arterial, radial or graded urban structures there always grew the infinite foliage of biological shelter, forever changing in detail yet always maintaining its essential cellular character, clearly distinguishable from the static isolated public form situated within its midst. From the Greek towns of Miletus and Priene to the Roman towns of Pompeii and Pavia, to the walled cities of mediaeval Europe and of the Renaissance, the pattern holds good in all its forms. In all instances, at least in the West, the basic relationship of public to private remains embodied always in the presence of a public 'form' or 'forum' within the cellular biological urban structure. With the obsolescence of the walled city as an economic necessity, those boundaries separating, as physical actualities, the human from the natural world, the 'civilization' of the city from the 'idiocy' of the countryside, were in a specific sense literally forced open.[8] We may assume, then, that the human conditions of 'labor' and 'work' have always been present since the advent of human civilization. When man first emerged on the face of the earth, his continual struggle for survival, repeated daily throughout the centuries, amounted to a state of unremitting biological toil. Only with the agricultural revolution did man truly begin to establish his first permanent settlements, his first human

Siena. A dramatic example of 'sacred' and 'profane' public realms clearly established in a mediaeval city. Around these reified places is the 'biological process' of the residential structure.

world and its accompanying economic surplus. Only then did he acquire tools and goods other than the weapons and the primitive animism of a nomadic hunter. First his settlement and later the fortified town constituted for man a material realization within which a certain degree of security and continuity was assured, in contrast to the perilous, overgrown or desolate wilderness of nature that otherwise surrounded him.

The foundation of a town in these early times was always a precarious venture. The choice of a new town site in the Roman epoch for instance was subject to augury and the foundation itself entailed a ritualistic ploughing of the earth in order to establish the cosmic ideogram of the town.[9] This ideogram comprised the outline of the public or 'work' elements of the town; that is, the principal axes, the town forum, and the circumference of its walls. After the reification of this ideogram, 'labor' found its appointed place in its subsequent growth, through filling out the interstices of its remaining four quarters, with the physical process of human shelter. Thus public and private aspects found clear expression in the ancient town. A similar balance of work and labor can be found in the most primitive town forums. We have become familiar with the tribal settlements, which frequently comprise a circle of huts enclosing a space in the middle. Except possibly for the chief's hut, all the huts are identical in size and in construction, each one a private unit containing its hearth or family public element. Together they constitute a ring of private units enclosing a public

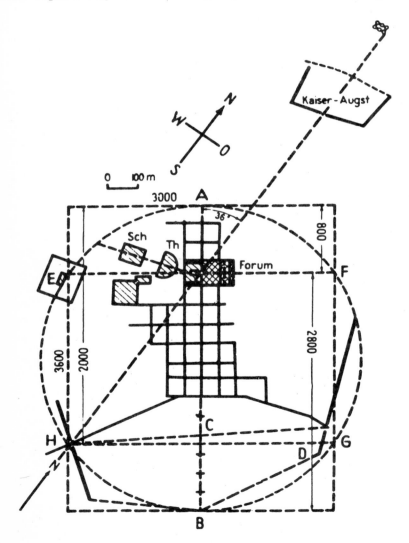

Augusta Raurica 44 B.C. The Roman Ideogram of the town as reflected in the street is rotated through 36° from the cardinal north so that on the summer and winter equinoxes respectively the sun shines down the streets on rising and setting. In contrast, the land division, the sub-urban area surrounding the town was divided to correspond with the cardinal points.

Zulu Kraal. A circular settlement comprising family huts, storehouses, and cattle compounds. The chief's compound is isolated in the centre. Cattle tracks lead out of the compound to grazing areas, past two 'sacred' trees close to the point of entry.

space and are inherently the most simple expression of collective human life, that of the individual and of the community.[10]

Until 50 years ago this simple relationship could be found at the base of almost every human settlement. The energy and population explosions, however, that accompanied the Western industrial revolution and the advent of secularization led to the formation of industrial societies largely dominated by the process of 'labor' and such societies as proliferations of 'labor' could only support with difficulty the continued expression of 'work'. The technical inventions of the 19th century supported by the population explosions essential to the industrial and commercial exploitation of such innovations. The walled city, 'balance of work and labor', hitherto based upon an agrarian trading economy, became predictably difficult to sustain under such radically new conditions. The spontaneous 19th century revolution of imperialistic nationalisms to compliment the newly won industrial power and wealth did not serve as truly adequate and effective 'work' substitutes either culturally or architecturally, for these new 'isms' were to prove even more precarious institutions than the more time proven but by then already obsolete institution of the city state. Yet in spite of the difficulty of giving public expression to secular institutions within industrial settlement of such unprecedented dynamism, size and diversity, a difficulty to which the so-called 19th century battle of styles in architecture may be cited as a testimony, it was not industrialism alone that diminished the capacity of Western society to maintain 'the space of human appearance', to recreate the archetypal *agora* of the ancient *polis*.

For further explanation one must perhaps look to the accompanying disintegration and collapse of traditional Western idealism *per se*. Under the impact of a new concept of man's individual nature and with the growth of atheistic thought and scientific knowledge, the old humanist, classical, part-pagan, part-Christian model of man's relation to the universe began to disintegrate. This progressive philosophical erosion of classical idealism from Rousseau to Marx was accompanied by the parallel decay of established institutions such as the church and the princely city state which had hitherto depended for their authority upon the maintenance of essentially 'classic' ideals. Latterday 19th century aesthetes and social thinkers such as Ruskin, Pugin and Morris were eventually to react against this disintegration, but were only to offer highly romantic and equally inappropriate cultured panaceas as an alternative.

Hegel gave, as did all other Neo-Platonists up to Comte, primacy to idea reality (or ideal reality) over existential reality (or empirical reality): the primacy of thought over being. The Neo-Hegelianism of Feuerbach and Hess, and later Comte's Positivism, simply reversed this relation.[11] It stood the dialectical idealism of Hegel on its head, giving primacy to the existential world over the world of ideas. It was this transposition that led eventually to dialectical materialism and to the denial of idealistic philosophy. Hegel was the last propounder of the neo-platonic humanist ideal and through the re-interpretation and reversal of Hegelianism by later philosophers culminating eventually in the thought of Marx, modern materialism became theoretically established. The progressive emphasis given to the realm of the unique individual and the gradual eclipse of the ancient humanist ideals led eventually to a total devaluation of the *agora* and by this agency to the primacy of private over public and to the progressive rejection of the city as a way of life.

It may be argued that it is this very primacy of being over thought that constitutes the essential secularization of the modern world. The fundamental secular nature of the society of the New World, in spite of its publicly professed theology, may well in the end explain the traditional rejection of the 'city idea' in American life. In this respect one is not surprised to learn that the early American agrarian settlements and settlers had no regard whatsoever for the city, but the persistence of an effective American anti-city tradition through all the vicissitudes of 19th and 20th century industrialization amounts to a more complex phenomenon. As Morton and Lucia White point out in their study 'The intellectual versus the City', the American anti-city consensus is an unbroken tradition of ambivalence towards the city extending from Jefferson to Frank Lloyd Wright and Lewis Mumford.[12]

One may question, as the Whites do, the reasons for such a consistent anti-city tradition and equally fail, as they do, to come up with an entirely satisfactory answer. While it is true to claim that the grass roots romanticism of an Emerson or a Mumford is not the sole basis for the aversion of these writers to the city, and that considerable concrete environmental evaluation is incorporated into their critical reaction, one may nonetheless argue that, given a profound societary respect for the city in the first place as the embodiment of a human ideal, the amorphous agglomeration and deterioration of our modern industrial cities would never have occurred. The unsentimental Romantic ideal of individual primacy, property and privacy has indeed produced, and now continues to proliferate, our present pluralistic society, and one is lead to the conclusion that the American city since Jefferson has always been regarded, with few exceptions, as the expedient, necessary, but uncherished concentration of people, power and machinery from which the material support for an individual 'pastoral' life may be ruthlessly extracted. As Arendt points out, due to enrichment of the private sphere through modern individualism, we no longer attach the connotation of deprivation to the word privacy.

The urbanism of Frank Lloyd Wright, as represented in his Broadacre city, is the apotheosis of such hard-headed but nonetheless Romantic thought, and the Whites justly show the ironic parallel that exists between the thought of Wright and that of Marx. Ebenezer Howard's garden city movement of the late nineties of which Wright was at least ideologically a part, formed, to the later chagrin of certain European intellectuals, one of the very fundamentals of Marx's political program. The garden city principle was in effect written into the Communist Manifesto of 1848 (Françoise Choay's *Pré- urbanisme Sans Modèle*) which advocated: 'the gradual abolition of the distinction between town and country by a more equable distribution of the population over the land'.[13] Wright for his part intended that his Broadacre city should be 'everywhere and nowhere', and he wrote of it in 1932 as 'a city so greatly different from the ancient city or from any city of today that we will probably fail to recognize its coming as the city at all'.[14] In short, to paraphrase Gertrude Stein 'there would be no more there, there'.

This metamorphosis of the city into something physically unrecognizable as the entity 'city', through dispersion and attenuation, inevitably vitiates the 'city' and divests it of all public significance. The secular triumph of modern

◀ BAIRD: I find it interesting to compare this discussion with Jencks' account of the 'semiological triangle'.

materialism is thus made physically manifest, the city is dispersed and evacuated of all 'civilised' public content. It is physically incapable of embodying a collective human idea as it now becomes progressively indistinguishable from 'nature', which it continues to invade without pause. Of all the 20th century form makers Wright was the most culturally integrated and prescient in his prophecy, for his Broadacre City has since arisen spontaneously from the society which certainly nurtured his thought, if it did not consciously heed his advice. With his insistence on the decentralization of all institutions and his emphasis upon the family home as the important *res publica* of the emerging society, 'the fire burning deep in the heart of the prairie', Wright assisted, ideologically at least, in the creation of the so-called regional city of which Los Angeles is now the 'classic' example. Los Angeles, still growing today, now stretches 70 miles from north to south, with a population of 3 million people occupying an area of nearly 5,000 square miles. To such conurbations Jean Gottman has already given the ironic name 'megalopoli'.[15]

American grass roots philosophy and the English post palæotechnic preoccupation with the garden city, together with Marxist doctrinal polemics against capital cities, comprise a constellation of opinion that was not to be shared in exactly the same way by the 19th century Utopian Socialist Charles Fourier. Fourier sought to reconstitute humanist form as the physical environment for his new concept of social order, and surprisingly enough we are to find in his work the baroque palace pressed almost subversively into service, as the architectural format of his commune or *phalanstère*. This transposition of the palace model from a seat of autocratic power to the built domain of the 'liberated' socialised man of Fourier's 'phalange', constitutes a unique fusion of public and private realms into a single collective entity.[16] Fourier's idea of a city seems to have been equally 'humanist' inasmuch as from his vague description it was evidently centralized and concentric. His model thus serves as a link between Ledoux's Ideal City of 1804 and Tony Garnier's Cité Industrielle of 1904.

Garnier's Cité Industrielle was the conscious embodiment of certain cultural ideas which may now be seen as critical to the ontology of 20th century architecture. These ideas today bring up the whole problem of the content of architecture and of the valid mode for its expression, in an age dominated by industrial process that is, by the 'labouring' cycle of production and consumption.

In Garnier's city an attempt is made to fuse the Elysian city of antiquity with the promise of radical social concepts and a greatly increased industrial and technological capacity. The institutions responsible for the alienation of man in the thought of Feuerbach and Hess are absent from the city. The age-old repressive forces are to be withheld and therefore their buildings are not represented. There are no law courts, police stations, jails or churches in a project which is otherwise replete with every conceivable building type. When questioned as to their absence Garnier replied that under socialist law there would be no need for repression. Garnier thus deliberately excluded those 'edifices' which are strictly crucial to our first definition of architecture, limiting his concern to the 'palaces' and the *res publica* of the people. (i.e. the railway station, the hydrotherapy, the assembly building, etc.).[17] The Cité Industrielle is a regional city of industrial process. Its various zones can expand independently of each other and are at the same time connected by the typical palæotechnic transport network of railway and tram. Mumford has referred to the necessary 19th century expansion of this network as the means for carrying the process and the products of the mine into everyday life. Amid this plethora of process Garnier consciously seeks to establish the *res publica* of *social* as opposed to *religious* man. Hence the central importance of the large assembly building in the Cité Industrielle and the inscription of this building with texts from Emile Zola's polemical novel 'Travail'. One of the two inscribed passages invokes the Saint Simonian dream of a continental railway infrastructure, extending over the earth, crossing all national boundaries and unifying all men,

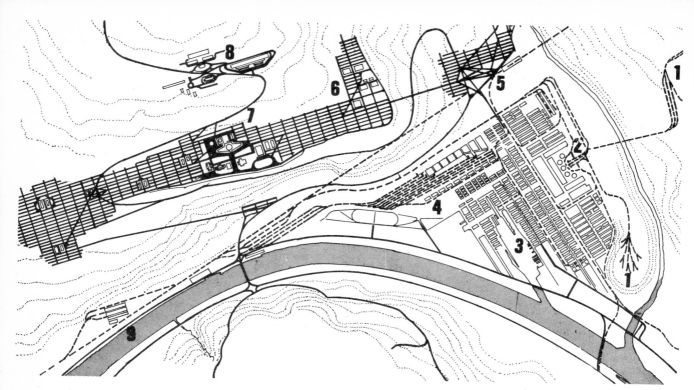

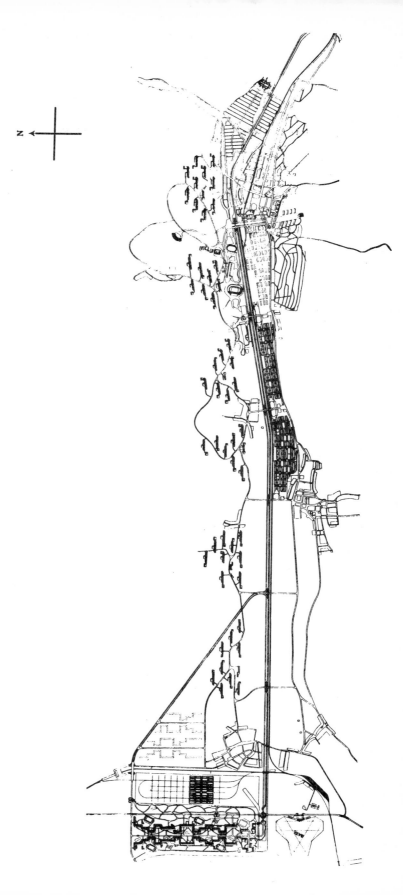

Tony Garnier's Cité Industrielle, 1904. The first twentieth century project of a regional city of 'process'. The city comprises independently expandable sectors, yet maintains a fixed central res publica *and house of assembly. Regional distribution systems, modes of production and consumption are essential features (road is solid, rail is dotted). The mining facilities consume its physical environment as the number key indicates. 1. Mines. 2. Blast furnaces and steel works. 3. Harbour and shipyard. 4. Autoworks. 5. Main stations and express rail. 6. Schools. 7. Centre and house of assembly. 8. Sanatoria. 9. Abattoir.*

Tony Garnier's Cité Industrielle. View of the central assembly building for 3,000 people: Garnier's res publica. *Its façades are inscribed with texts from Zola's novel* Travail, *alluding to the Utopian Socialist union of industry with agriculture (cf.* Communist Manifesto). *The text also refers to the Saint Simonian dream of uniting all the nations of the earth by means of the railway.*

Zlin, Czechoslovakia. Project for Bata in ▶ *1935 by Le Corbusier. This is his second linear city project after Algiers. Significant for the juxtaposition of the blocks* à redent *of the* Ville Radieuse *(e.g.* Fouriers phalanstères*) with the* Unités d'Habitation *used at the same time in his plan for Nemours.*

while the other refers to the fulfilment of man through the fusion of industry and agriculture, city and country, into an harmonious entity. The Cité Industrielle is a city without walls; the antiquity being evoked is thus more Hellenic than it is Roman.

Le Corbusier appears to have inherited from Garnier a similar preoccupation with Utopian Socialism. Hence his work must be seen largely as a direct extension of Garnier's ideas. Le Corbusier's early 'essays' on ideal cities quickly gave way to more regional processal concepts such as we find in his projects for Algiers—or Nemours—while the characteristic 'domino-block' formation of Le Corbusier's Maison Domino projects are a deliberate reflection of the anti-corridor street planning of the Cité Industrielle, as well as being related to the 'set-back' palace format of Fourier's phalanstère. The subsequent development of this domino concept into the *blocks à redent* of the Ville Radieuse, produced a format only suitable for use on flat sites. On heavily contoured ground the *blocks à redent* had to be broken down into their constituent elements from which Le Corbusier evolved almost at once his Unités d'Habitation, a name he evidently borrowed from Fourier's pupil Considérant. Le Corbusier's conscious transposition of the house into the palace after Fourier, was an attempt to restore to the dwelling of biological 'labor', the status of architecture, that is of 'work'.[18]

Tony Garnier and Frank Lloyd Wright, born within two years of each other, gave to the 20th century two diametrically opposed models of the regional city; the one manifestly Utopian Socialist, the other implicitly Anarchic Socialist; the one partially centralized, incorporating a *res publica*; the other totally decentralized, distributing its public elements at random over the earth. Wright's city appears to have been little more than a rationalisation of the land settlement pattern of the American Mid West. As Wright foresaw: '. . . America needs no help to Broadacre City. It will haphazard build itself.'[19] In the subsequent realization of Wright's Utopian vision, two 20th century techniques have made and continue to make their inroads into the public realm and into the public structure of existing cities. These are of course television, which as an electronic public substitute has effectively invaded the public forum of the home (the fire no longer burns deep in the heart of the prairie), and the automobile, which as a mobile extension of the private cell has virtually evacuated the public realm of all humanity and disrupted the center of existing cities, with those vast freeways which are essential for its effective circulation.

Arendt's thesis and the realised Broadacre City of Megalopolis equally suggest that man, having literally obliterated the boundaries which protect the 'world' of human artifice from 'nature', stands before a future where the maintenance of a 'human' environment becomes precarious. If this is our actual cultural predicament and the ancient powers of 'priest' and 'prince' are seen to be disestablished within the society, then it follows that 'architecture', in the strict sense of 'edifice building,' is largely divested of culturally valid institutions for its embodiment and that we must in consequence turn our attention to 'architecture' in the sense of the process of building. This of course parallels Marinetti's view of 1912, that the decay of religion had made completely useless 'the vast permanent and ornate buildings that once used to express royal authority, theocracy and mysticism'.[20] This view was to find its corollary in the futurist assertion that each generation would have to rebuild its own city anew. As yet, however, this assertion remains largely unfulfilled by our economic capacity to renew our environment and in our design of the environment, which still depend to some extent upon its extant fabric and upon models drawn from the past. Nonetheless a discrepancy now exists between a past which is largely sacred and the desacralized era in which we live.[21] In consequence difficulty is experienced, at every level, in adapting 'past' models to our present ever accelerating rate of growth and change. To simply adopt, as an alternative course, the empirical methods of descriptive science and to base all future action upon the dictates of present statistical extrapolations is to embrace in blind faith the so-called autonomous 'feedback' process and to perpetuate all

◄ BAIRD: I have to say I find this discussion oversimplified. Following the lead of Norris Kelly Smith (Man's Environment? Arena, Journal of the Architectural Association, June 1967), I find an architectural conception named 'Unite d'Habitation' heavily influenced by the precepts of 'animal laborans'.

◄ BAIRD: Here again, I think I find this an over-hasty, over-extended employment of the general principles being discussed. And Wright's role in all this must surely be seen as a profoundly ambiguous one, especially if one takes seriously Kelly Smith's interpretation of his ideas (Frank Lloyd Wright: A Study in Architectural Content, Prentice Hall, 1966). So far as his preoccupation with organicism is concerned, Wright certainly fits within the frame Frampton has here drawn for him; yet Kelly Smith would strenuously, and surely with cause, insist that Wright was equally as committed as Garnier – or any other great architect in the past century – to the reification of a 'public realm'. His objections to the modern city were as often as not, objections to the *de facto* urban ascendancy of 'animal laborans' and his concern for the autonomy of the individual is really a concern for the importance, in Arendt's terms, of 'action' as opposed to 'labour'. In fact, it just now occurs to me how interesting it would be to compare Kelly Smith's view of Wright with Arendt's view of the Jeffersonian tradition (On Revolution, Viking Press, 1965). We might even discover that the 'traditional rejection of the "city idea" in American life' of which Frampton spoke above, had two *opposite* causes; firstly, 'the fundamental secular nature of the society of the New World' to which he referred, but also, the fact that by the time the 'constitution of American liberty' was established, the 'city' had already been too compromised by the precepts of 'animal laborans' to form an appropriate frame for human 'action'. In that case, the Jefferson-Wright connection, and Wright's ambiguity vis-à-vis 'labour' and 'work' would appear in a more fully developed context.

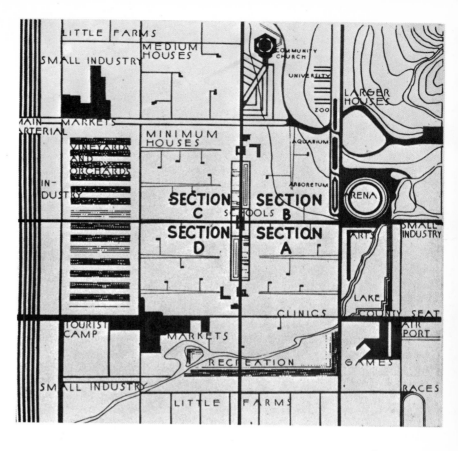

Broadacre City, 1932-35. F. L. Wright's anti-urbanistic thesis based on the automobile and one house per acre. The res publica *is here dispersed into stadium, theatre etc; the vision is based on the socio-economic theories of Henry George.*

BAIRD: It is perhaps worth noting here that according to Arendt, not even 'homo-faber' is capable of reaching conclusions about 'ultimate values and goals'. (See her remarks on the 'perplexity of utilitarianism' and the defeat of 'homo-faber', in 'The Human Condition').

present processes to the risk of excluding from the human condition all considerations of ultimate values and goals. To make such reservations about the efficacy of technological determinism is not to make a total rejection of 'scientific method'.

If, on the other hand, from a desperate lack of a viable model of the process of architecture and planning, we simply impose on each and every building task arbitrary plastic forms, derived directly without question from the past, then the result is the cultural absurdity of much of our recent building. The imposition of monumental symbolic forms or consciously fixed random arrangements on culturally and/or operationally inappropriate situations tends towards absurdity. A culture depends upon the development of a coherent language. In a situation in which process is dominant, an arbitrary individual vocabulary wilfully used is relatively ineffective.

If one is concerned with the creation of a coherent physical environment, and if one believes that such an environment is ultimately crucial to our human consciousness and well being, then it follows that the 'building', the 'city' and the 'region' are critically interdependent and that the tendency for process to expediently diffuse the human artifice across the surface of the earth must be *politically* restrained. This is the *cause conservative* in a sense that Wright may not have acknowledged.[22] A totally diffused environment is not only operationally uneconomic and prejudicial in respect of future action but also beyond perception as a clear environment at all.

If a coherent language of the built environment is ever to evolve, plastic notations in respect of operational performances and states at one environmental scale will still require to be differentially related to corresponding notations, performances and states at another. To hope for such a coherent language in a pluralistic age is no doubt wishful thinking, yet perhaps such a language would begin to 'spontaneously' emerge if only designers would establish and

Ground plan of the restoration project for the Shinjuku district by Maki and Ohtaka. An example of a composition structure of megaforms by the architects built on so-called artificial ground. The mega-forms are not fixed.

express at every public scale discrete distinctions between the public and permanent as opposed to the private and impermanent aspects of our physical environment. The very real design problems posed by indeterminacy have already led to the postulation of such a language, and examples may be cited from Japan and Europe which clearly illustrate the application of this language: such as the elevated ground and collective form projects of Maki and Ohtaka for Tokyo and the studies by Shadrach Woods made for the universities of Bochum and Berlin. In the first instance it is simply the elevated platforms that constitute the prime public element, in the second, it is the matrix or the grid of movement systems. In both instances the old public 'work' element, the *agora* of the ideal city, is largely replaced by permanent 'public' route ordering systems or by permanent public artificial land. In both cases the buildings which feed off the systems or are built on the land may be relatively impermanent, that is to say, like the interstices of the ancient town, they are in 'labor' or in a state of flux. Large-scale permanent and public elements now appear only as totally secular megastructures or infrastructures. In the last two examples we are presented with a curious paradox, in that what was formerly predominantly the movement infrastructure of a Western town, is now seen, potentially at least, as the only element from which to make a viable *res publica*.

University of Bochum by Candilis, Josic and Woods. The architects themselves have since made their initial design intentions for this scheme explicit; that is their intent to distinguish clearly between the public and private realms.

In most current urban projects a single central space can rarely be culturally justified and we find ourselves presented with a new urban model which closely resembles the traditional Oriental city, which, forever lacking the *agora* concept afforded public space only in the 'activity' of the street itself.[23]

If, as Hannah Arendt concludes, the victory of *animal laborans* is complete, then it is necessary for us to continually question what concept architecture

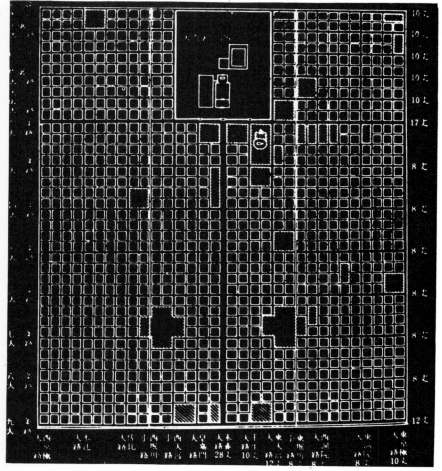

Heianko (Kyoto) A.D. 784. Japanese centralized town after the Chinese 6th century 'model' of Changan. The imperial palace is situated in the auspicious north. Note the 'cardo' activity street centrally located and the corresponding absence of a central agora.

◄ PAWLEY: This argument depends not only on the readers' unqualified acceptance of the parallels drawn between Work and Labour, public and private, architecture and building; but also on his concurrence that the triumph of labour, privacy and building constitutes a major catastrophe. It seems more likely to me that this 'triumph' is a synthetic one in that (as Frampton very nearly says) the public realm (media) has been absorbed *into* the private and consequently the apotheosis of privatisation *necessarily* involves its assumption of the characteristics of 'architecture' as well as those of labour.

◄ BAIRD: As I understand 'The Human Condition', the victory of 'animal laborans' would render 'architecture' utterly obsolete. In that respect, Hannes Meyer was wiser than he knew.

can possibly signify in an age which, although individualistic, in one sense is paradoxically preoccupied with the life process of the species. In doing this, I would submit, we shall need to distinguish carefully both culturally and operationally between acts of 'architecture' and acts of 'building' and to discretely express both 'labor' and 'work' within each building entity irrespective of its scale. Only in this way perhaps can we hope to eventually evolve and impart to the society a coherent structured language of the environment that is both operationally appropriate and a true reflection of our human consciousness.

POSTSCRIPT

Of the four essays of this collection that I have read, namely those by Baird, Choay, Norberg-Schulz and Pawley, two appear to advance points of view closely approaching my own. These are the essays of Françoise Choay and Christian Norberg-Schulz; the one developed from a semiological point of departure, the other from the theoretical schema previously outlined in his book *Intentions in Architecture*.

Both essays ultimately express, in distinctly different ways, anxiety as to our present capacity to create and sustain a significant culture of the built environment. This doubt finds direct expression in the last paragraph of Choay's contribution, while it remains latent in the optimism of Norberg-Schulz's faith in isomorphism as the basis for an ongoing 'collective' symbol system of built form. My own essay expresses similar doubt and faith although I have not chosen to characterise the latter by the term isomorphism.

Under the influence of Hannah Arendt's contentions and 'classical' thesis I have chosen instead to postulate an imperative to express the cultural level or levels of any particular work, invoking the grossly parallel and possibly banal polarities of 'public', 'private', 'permanent', 'impermanent' etc., as the only proper present basis from which to derive a significant culture of environmental form. This is my conception of the necessary architectural 'responsibility and tolerance' finally advocated by George Baird. As such it no doubt seperates me at once from Norberg-Schulz; my essay being initially written as an indirect attack upon the 'new' (and to my mind culturally false—Baird's *Gesamtkünstler*) monumentality as it has manifested itself, over the last ten years, in the USA and elsewhere.

Given Françoise Choay's reference to production and consumption Le Corbusier's dictum that 'the 20th century has built for money and nor for man' is not out of place and we would do well to reflect on the possible ramifications of such a remark. American monumentality has frequently been occasioned in some form or other by money, either by its acquisition or celebration. There is of course precedent for this, but one previously subject to princely or theological authority. In the service of modern philanthropy (i.e. education) it has rarely truly concerned itself with the needs of man. Instead it has perpetuated an architect's architecture, often highly sophisticated but formalistic and symbolically impoverished. An architecture as remote from humanity under neo-capitalism in the West, as Stalinism has been under socialism in the East.

[1] This paper was read at the School of Architecture,Princeton University,on October 19, 1966.
[2] Hannah Arendt: *The Human Condition*, University of Chicago 1958. For definition of terms see Chap. 1. All quotations from Arendt are taken from the above work.
[3] Sir Henry Wotton: *Elements of Architecture*, 1624.
[4] *The Shorter Oxford English Dictionary*. 3rd Edition with Addenda.
[5] Geoffrey Sainsbury: *The Marseille Block* (Translation of *l'Unité d'Habitation Marseille* by Le Corbusier.) p. 41 . . . 'the fire, that is to say the place where we prepare our meals. Of old that word served as a unit and people spoke of a village of twenty fires, etc.
[6] Vitruvius: *De Architectura*. The ten books of architecture translated by Morris Hickey Morgan. Dover. New York 1960. Books IX & X, pp. 251–319.
[7] Bernard Rudofsky: *Architecture Without Architects*,Museum of Modern Art, New York, 1965.
[8] 1850 and 1858 are the historic dates of this disillusion of Boundaries. The beginnings of Haussmannisation in Paris and the corresponding removal of the Parisian *barrières* in 1850; the demolition of the baroque fortifications around Vienna and Copenhagen in 1858.
[9] Joseph Rykwert: *The Idea of a Town*. From Forum No. 3, 1963, published by G. Van Saane. 'Lectura Architectonica', Hilversum.
[10] Rykwert: op. cit. pp. 40 & 41. Also C. Lévi-Strauss, *Tristes Tropiques*, Paris 1955, pp. 227–233.
[11] For a discussion of this reversal in Hegelian thought see *Marx's Religious Drama* by Louis Halle, Encounter, October 1965.
[12] Morton & Lucia White: *The Intellectual Versus the City*, from Thomas Jefferson to Frank Lloyd Wright. Harvard University Press, Cambridge, Mass, 1962.
[13] See the *Manifesto of the Communist Party* by Karl Marx and Frederick Engels, 1848. Progress Publishers, Moscow 1966. Article 9 on page 74 reads: 'combination of agriculture with manufacturing industries; gradual abolition of the distinction between town and country, by a more equable distribution of the population over the country'. The immediate post-revolutionary situation in Russia saw the invention of linear cities, out of a direct response to this article, by architect-planners such as Milutin, Lavrov and Leonidov. A corollary to this invention was the conscious intent to dismantle the existing cities of capital. A paradoxical parallel exists here between Marxist planning on the one hand and Wright's Broadacre City on the other.

[14] Frank Lloyd Wright: *The Disappearing City*, New York, 1932. See also *The Living City*, New York, 1958.

[15] Jean Gottmann: *Megalopis* (A study of the NE seaboard of the United States). New York.

[16] Luigi Benevelo: *The Origins of Modern Town Planning*, London 1967. For the development of Saint Simonian urbanism see section on 19th Century Utopias pp. 55–84 and also section on 1848 and its consequences pp. 105–136.

[17] Françoise Choay: *L'Urbanisme Utopies et Réalités: une anthologie*. Editions du Seuil, 1965. For the complete text of Garnier's Cité Industrielle' see section IV, *l'Urbanisme Progressiste*. pp. 209–219.

[18] Le Corbusier: *Une Maison—Un Palais*. 1928 Collection de l'Esprit Nouveau. Editions G. Gres, Paris. Le Corbusier's intention to elevate the house to the status of architecture i.e. 'work' in the Arendt sense is to be found on page 68. Of the Villa Garches he writes: 'We are strengthened by the past because the past has proven to us that through conditions of clarity and durable equilibruim the house was typified and that when the type was pure it possessed an architectural potential, truly reserved for architecture; it was able to elevate itself to the dignity of a palace'. Later he was to refer to the Unité d'Habitation as an attempt to elevate housing to a similar level.

[19] Frank Lloyd Wright: op. cit.

[20] Reyner Banham: *Theory and Design in the First Machine Age*. London, 1960. p. 124. Extract from F. T. Marinetti's lecture to the Lyceum Club, March 1912.

[21] Mircea Eliade: *The Sacred and the Profane*, 1961. Harper Torchbook T.B. 81. Eliade discusses the modern transposition of *religious* man into *social* man, as well as the non-homogeneity essential to the distinction of 'sacred' from 'profane' space.

[22] Norris Kelly Smith: *Frank Lloyd Wright—A Study in Architectural Content*, Englewood Cliffs N.J. 1966. Chap. 1 is entitled 'The *cause conservative*'. Smith gives an extract in this chapter from Wright's essay entitled 'In the Cause of Architecture' published in the Architectural Record, March 1908 . . . 'the work illustrated here is dedicated to the *cause conservative* in the best sense of the word'. Smith argues that Wright was fully aware that architecture had been in the past and always would be, in essence, the art form of the establishment.

[23] See Günthe Nitschke '*Ma: The Japanese Sense of Place*,' Architectural Design, March 1966. See pp. 124 to 130 for discussion of the traditional Chinese and Japanese concept of the 'activity street'.

The Interior of Time

Aldo van Eyck

As the past is gathered into the present and the gathering body of experience finds a home in the mind, the present acquires temporal depth—loses its acrid instantaneity, its razorblade quality. One might call this the interiorization of time, or time rendered transparent.

It seems to me that past, present, and future must be active in the mind's interior as a continuum. If they are not, the artifacts we make will be without temporal depth or associative perspective. My concern with the ultimate human validity of divergent, often seemingly incompatible, concepts of space and incidental or circumstantial solutions found during past ages in different corners of the world is to be understood in the light of the above. The time has come to reconcile them; to gather together the essential human meaning divided among them.

Man, after all, has been accommodating himself physically in this world for thousands of years. His natural genius has neither increased nor decreased during that time. It is obvious that the full scope of this enormous environmental experience cannot be contained in the present unless we telescope the past, i.e. the entire human effort, into it. This is not historic indulgence in a limited sense, not a question of travelling back, but merely of being aware of what 'exists' in the present—what has travelled into it: the projection of the past into the future via the created present—Anna was, Livia is, Plurabelle's to be[1] (who knows, Anna Livia Plurabelle may yet preside over architecture!).

This, in my opinion, is the only medicine against sentimental historicism, modernism, and utopianism. Also against narrow rationalism, functionalism, and regionalism. A medicine against all the pests combined.

Each culture constitutes a very special case. That surely is a wonderful thing—wonderful in a different way for each different case! To go chasing after historical or anthropological data appertaining to different cultures with the object of propping some preconceived notion is an arbitrary occupation. The issue is not whether it is possible to adventure intellectually into a cultural world not one's own, or whether it is at all possible ultimately to circumscribe successfully the nature of any special case. I merely want to stress the fact that each case *is* a special case and can only be understood in its own terms. It should by now be possible to acknowledge, *sine qua non*, the intrinsic validity and simultaneous justification of all cultural patterns, irrespective of time and place.

Western civilization habitually identifies itself with civilization as such (with what it stands for) on the pontifical assumption that what is not like it is a deviation, less 'advanced', 'primitive', or, at best, exotically interesting—at a safe distance. But Western civilization—what a self-assured jingle—is just one special case in multitude of special cases, each of which carries its own possibilities and deals with them in a way specifically its own. (1962)

Architects nowadays are pathologically addicted to change, regarding it as something one either hinders, runs after, or, at best, keeps up with. This, I suggest, is why they tend to sever the past from the future, with the result that the present is rendered emotionally inaccessible—without temporal dimension. I dislike a sentimental antiquarian attitude towards the past as much as I dislike a sentimental technocratic one towards the future. Both are founded on a static, clockwork notion of time (what antiquarians and technocrats have in common). So let's start with the past for a change and discover the unchanging condition of man in the light of change—i.e. in the light of the changing conditions he himself brings about. If the lasting validity of man's past environmental experience (its contemporaneousness) is acknowledged, the paralyzing conflicts between past, present, and future, between old notions of space, form, and construction, and new ones, between hand production and industrial production, will be mitigated. Why do so many believe they must choose categorically, as though it were impossible to be loyal both ways? I have heard it said that an architect cannot be a prisoner of tradition in a time of change. It seems to me that he cannot be a prisoner of any kind. And at no time can he be a prisoner of change. (1966)

A Miracle of Moderation

Aldo van Eyck

with essays by

Paul Parin &
Fritz Morgenthaler

In memory of Artur Glikson

It cannot have been so very different in Ur 5,000 years ago: the same laboriously fashioned bricks of sandy mud, then as now, the same sun weakly bonding and then harshly disintegrating them; the same spaces around a courtyard; the same enclosure; the same sudden transition from light into darkness; the same coolness after heat; the same starry nights; the same fears perhaps; the same sleep.

I remember with what difficulty I managed to get that paragraph on paper. It accompanied a series of photographs I made in 1951 and 1952 in the central Sahara.[2] One house; several houses; a village; a door; some steps; a place for offerings and a fascinatingly undersized marabout; also a boy smiling at you from the page, then as now. 5,000 years! 15 years! These are long periods indeed.

Meanwhile I still incline towards the immutable. Nor has my affection for those silent desert villages diminished. It is a spleen from which nothing can estrange me; some kind of affinity I have no wish to define, though I do wish something of their gentleness would enter our own sad environments.

At the time, I was unable to get beyond the Hoggar mountain range, 2,500 kilometres south of Algiers. Timbuktu, in any case, was still another 1,500 kilometres or so away—no distance, really, for a fable-city! All the more reason to talk en route, with those travelling with me, about the distant Niger and the cliffs of Bandiagara where the Dogon live.

I had come upon Marcel Griaule's account of the Dogon in *Minotaure* (Mission Dakar-Djibouti 1931–1933) during the war.[3] The illustrations I knew by heart. Thus, for years to come, Ogol was just round the corner.

Later in Paris and elsewhere I searched for more material concerning the houses and villages of the Dogon, but with little success. Although much has been written about these astounding people (they are among the greatest sculptors of the world), too little is devoted to their building activity as a contribution in its own right, whilst the same few photographs are used again and again from publication to publication.

I decided, therefore, to venture out myself and make up for this unfortunate lack. The photographs published here form a selection from the many I took in the winter of 1959 (a more detailed publication in book form is what I have in mind).

When I arrived in Ogol, Dr Parin and Dr Morgenthaler had been there for months probing the Dogon personality structure.[4] Their presence was a great surprise, for without their knowledge and interpretive ability much that occurred would have remained incomprehensible. And a great deal did occur: the funeral rites for the chief hunter, as well as the Dama for the deceased chief of the mask cult, kept us on our feet for days and nights.

Both scholars enjoyed the confidence of the villagers. This helped me to get to know not only the houses and villages I had admired for so long, but their builders also. This I regard as a special privilege. Beyond that, both were so kind as to write essays to augment my own and sustain with relevant data some of my ideas. I was thus able to avoid trespassing into their field further than was strictly necessary. I mean that one cannot respond to built form if one is unable to respond to its users and builders. When this is no longer possible, which it may well be, we know we are dealing with archaeology.

Subsequent discussion and correspondence with Dr Parin and Dr Morgenthaler has clarified many problems that concerned me very much at the time; problems which one is inclined to solve on one's own, thereby often unintentionally misinterpreting data gleaned to support a personal concept. My preoccupation with archaic cultures, however, has made me wary of this.

The kind of awareness the Dogon image wishes to kindle can help us to gather the meaning of certain prerogatives into the scope of our mental orbit again.

It should also enable us to judge them with humility and, if necessary, 'depart' from them consciously. Yet there are perils lurking behind any desire to open the mind to the kind of image chosen here. If we attempt to transfer too directly what we have become aware of again into a construed opinion, thereby freezing the meaning of it through arbitrary influence or ready-made definition, we will not only blunt the acquired awareness but also lame the formative potential this awareness would, without such false exploitation of data, be able to guide. We must, in fact, keep nourishing this awareness; allow it to embrace the dormant meanings it detects, assimilates, and carries with it—apprehended though left significantly undefined. Finally, architect-urbanists must see to it that those meanings which are of lasting human value are silently and unobtrusively contained in what they conceive, and not overemphatically or superficially transferred. The fulfilment of art—hence of architecture also—rests in its potential to perpetuate awareness as such. It does not define or freeze into static form what the artist—or society, for that matter—becomes aware of, it merely represents this as an apprehended or reapprehended aspect of human reality. It perpetuates in time and space 'undefined' meaning, nourishing in turn the awareness which detected it in the first place. Defining dormant meaning through form rather than allowing it to slumber in form is giving the lie to art, molesting the meaning—its repose and continuity. The meaning is gutted and awareness checked.

I am inclined to think that what we perceive is guided by what we conceive. But what we perceive tends to warp what we conceive (and vice versa) if either is grafted too inflexibly on to the other or their coincidence is claimed too ostensibly, so as to leave no play for still hidden meaning slumbering in what is perceived as well as in what is conceived. To force conception and perception (concept and the data found to support it) to coincide completely is to contract rather than to extend the meaning of either. The poetry lies in the persistence of scope—scope for undefined and latent multimeaning. (1967)

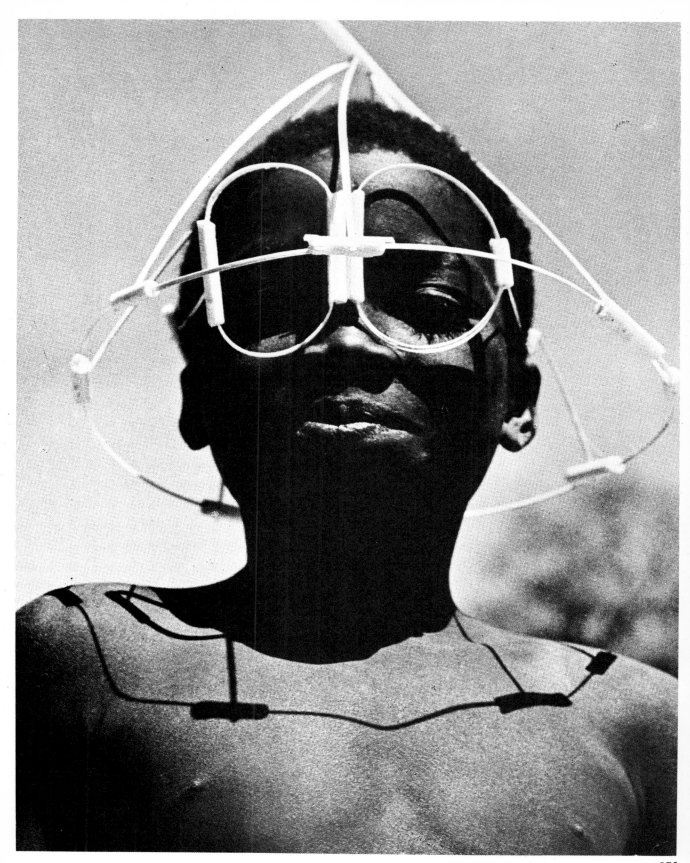

The population of the Dogon today numbers about a quarter of a million. In terms of the natural bases of existence (soil condition, climate, flora, and fauna), in appearance, and in their daily life, the Dogon differ little from their close neighbours, the Peuhl and the Bambara, or even from the Bantu far to the south. Their economy, family structure, political organization, customs, and religion are typical in the Sudan south of the Sahara. Yet it is no contradiction to say that they have developed a way of life which distinguishes them from any other people, in Africa or elsewhere.

They live in the steppe region south-west of the bend in the Niger River at Timbuktu, in some 700 small communities strung along the great falaise of Bandiagara, an escarpment which stretches about 200 kilometres north-east to south-west. The cliffs rise to a rocky plateau 200–300 metres above an arid plain wrinkled with sandy hills. On the irregular surface of the plateau, on ledges and among the rock-strewn slopes at the foot of the cliff, and scattered into the plain lie the compact villages, singly or in small groups. From a distance the houses and granaries appear to be part of the rocky cliff, like greyish-yellow crystal growths, barely distinguishable from the surroundings.

It is not known whether the Dogon came here from 'Mande' in the 10th or in the 14th century, and Mande itself would seem to designate no definite land; the word means 'place where the king lives'. The Dogon came, in flight or in migration, to found their people anew, perhaps after the fall of the kingdom where, one tradition says, they were serfs of the Emperor Keita. Each family and each village still traces its history from one of the four tribal fathers who brought the four original tribes into the region. So sharp is the mythico-historical consciousness of these people that their coming, which we have been unable to pinpoint in time or place, has remained alive in their minds. They have never forgotten the former inhabitants of the land, who fled at their coming and yet whose mythical descendants are still considered the actual owners of the land. They call them the Tellem, a name which they also give to the wooden statuettes and other artifacts left by 'those who were here before us' and found today in caves and in Tellem granaries and shrines that remain. The Dogon ascribe strong magic power to the statuettes, the Europeans high artistic value.

The Dogon God Amma, who created everything living, made first of all the earth, that was then his wife. He slept with her, but the first act of creation failed, because Amma's member hit against his wife's, the clitoris, the termite hill that projected up from the earth. Amma tore out the hill, circumcising his wife, and the earth gave in gently to her master. From the turmoil of this first act of creation arose Yurugu, the desert fox, who brought into the world menstrual blood and incest, and the Promethean theft of the first word of God.

Yurugu came from his mother's womb before his time because of his incestuous wishes, and thus lost his feminine twin Yasigé, who remained in the womb. Yurugu committed incest by stealing his mother's fibre skirt and danced with joy on the roof of the house of heaven; the tracks left by his dancing feet are the first word of God which came to man, the word from dance. Today the diviners consult Yurugu, the first, fallen son of God. They mark off a place near the village, and in the evening scatter food for him. In the morning they read from the tracks in the sand Yurugu's secret wisdom, which he has stolen from God, who alone knows the future.

Soon Amma slept with his wife anew, and the rain, his holy seed, soaked into the earth and made her fruitful. In the second creation she bore the twinpair Nommo, feminine and masculine, the ideal pair, who with the water brought the second word of God to the world. The Nommo have delicate, wavy limbs without joints, like snakes, and a green coat (the plant cover of times to come), and they covered the naked mother with a fibre skirt. Words damp with Nommo's breath became interwoven with the fibres. The fertilization by rain, the quickening of all things by water, continues today when, moist with breath, speech flows from between the teeth of men and rushes into the ear, stimulating; it happens when the thread runs from the shuttle between the threads of the

The Dogon People: 1

Paul Parin

loom, guided by the teeth of the comb. The second act of creation could limit evil, but not wholly remove it from the world. From then on the principle of Yurugu, the restless seeker and thief, has worked in opposition to happiness and harmony with the divine. Yurugu is night, dryness, infertility, and death. Everything that loves is like Yurugu searching for the lost twin Yasige, only in loving union will he find again the happy exchange of the twinpair. Nommo is day, moistness, fertility, and life. For success in an undertaking, a person consults Yurugu through a diviner, and then makes an offering at one of the altars of life, that have their power from Nommo.

Then Amma moved to the third act of creation. This time he formed from clay eight Nommos, four double-beings—the first mythical generation of mankind, the immortal ancestors. In their destinies and in those of their 80 offspring, the five mythical generations, are revealed all of the possibilities of people living today. Each Dogon family therefore includes in principle five generations with 80 individuals.

The seventh of the first mythical generation is the most perfect, because the number seven contains 3 and 4, the masculine principle (penis and testicles) and the feminine (four labia). Over a rainbow to earth God sent the seventh Nommo, who went with a granary—containing all the creatures and stones, all the skills and customs of man—and carried in the snakelike arms an iron hammer. The granary landed hard on the earth, and the arms of the Nommo broke and formed joints, making arms suited for work. Immediately Nommo began hammering on an anvil. The clanging accompanying the first work, ringing from the first smithy, is the third word of God: the present language of the Dogon. The seventh Nommo is called the teaching Nommo for giving man good council and for showing him what to do with the animals and plants and arts that spread from the granary through the world.

The Dogon came to the cliffs without herds, and because of the lack of grazing land they have become planters. They build on bare rock so the dwellings will have good foundations, and so that no arable land will go to waste; new fields can be established only where the bushland is cleared or soil laboriously transported in baskets and surrounded with rows of stones to keep it from being washed away.

In the hot and dry season of the year, from March to June, they patch their houses with a mixture of clay and water so they will be watertight at the coming of the first rains in June, when the entire population celebrates the sowing feast. In October they harvest the eight kinds of staple crops, mostly cereals, which stand between them and starvation and are stored in their mud granaries. The largest and by far the most productive fields are held by each of the Dogon Ginnas. A Dogon, even though he is part of one household, thinks of himself as a member of a larger, patrilocal family composed of many households and founded by one of the original tribal fathers from Mande. Whether this genealogy is biologically accurate is difficult to determine, and not too important. This extended family is called a Ginna, a word which also means 'great house'. This usage is much like ours when referring to the House of Hapsburg or the House of the Medici. Speaking of a Ginna, one may mean both the extended family and the large house in which the Ginna Bana (oldest living member of the family) lives with his wives and children. When the last Bana of one generation dies, the oldest of the generation of sons inherits the position, and after him his next oldest brother. ('Brothers' are not, here, only the sons of one father, but also all cousins within the family.) When a successor moves into the Ginna, the younger members are promoted in the family hierarchy and change dwellings then, too.

In earlier times the fields were taken care of in order, beginning with the land of the oldest member of the family. In many villages today the family works the fields of the Ginna together for four days of the week; the youngest married men, who by tradition still have no claim to land of their own, are given charge of some by the Bana, to be worked as they want. On the fifth day, market day,

The great cliffs of Bandiagara from above and below. Note the ancient Tellem built forms in horizontal recesses of the cliff just above the village of Narni.

which corresponds to our Sunday, the older members of the family may work their own fields, those passed down from father to son and from mother to daughter. The crops from them are stored in personal granaries, of which all Dogon men and women have at least one. And in these fields, after the harvest of the cereals, they plant and tend their second crop, onions which grow in the cool, dry season from October to March.

Most of the onion harvest, in the form of crushed and dried balls, is exported. They are nearly the only (and the most important) product the Dogon can exchange for cash, thus the possession of cash is for the most part individual rather than collective, complementing the cooperative yield of their economic autarky. The production of onion balls probably gained impetus at first from the imposition of a head tax by the French colonial authorities earlier in this century. The Dogon expected from the beginning that each family member would come up with his own tax money. Now the Dogon and their neighbours pay their taxes to the Republic of Mali.

In studying the way of life of these people, or seeing one of the achievements of their culture, their villages or dwellings, we are brought to realize that our Western culture is only a special case among innumerable possibilities that man has developed. Many of their techniques are simpler than ours. For some universal human problems they seem to have found better solutions than we have. Individuals are better adjusted and more content; there is less conflict and hostility among them. Some other problems, such as health care and the production of necessary goods, have been solved less successfully.

The material and spiritual phenomena of Dogon life correspond to each other so well that it is almost impossible to describe them with our words that tend to divide and classify. They see even the most commonplace object

as part of an all-embracing system. The beautiful woven basket which the Dogon woman uses to carry grain and onions on her head, and as a unit of measure, has a square bottom and a round rim; the cosmos is represented by the basket inverted: the sun is round and the heaven above it is square. The heavenly granary in which the Nommo brought to earth all the animals, plants, and kinds of grain has the form of the inverted basket, as do the granaries in which the Dogon store up their food through the long months between harvests. The use of a granary or basket of some other form would disturb the relationship of sun and heaven and affect the annual rains. The granaries would remain empty, and the continuity of the creation with the present generation would be upset. We are accustomed to designating as 'primitive' cultures those in which the material life, such as the economy, and the spiritual, such as religion and the psychological make-up of individuals (formed through traditional upbringing) are in an independent system of manifestations in which they correspond to each other relatively well; we often contrast the symbolic-magical mode of thought with the empiric-logical.[5] The 'correspondences' become more comprehensible as expressions of symbolic thought if one imagines the participative nature of each symbol, which is at the same time the one and the other (for us a flag is as much a piece of cloth as it is also the country).

The efforts of Europeans to achieve greater happiness in life through the accumulation of money, or through good deeds to have a better life in the hereafter, seem just as illogical to the Dogon as their attempts to bring water by magic seem to us.

In the whole steppe-region of Africa, water is scarce and defines the 'being and consciousness' of those who live there. During the part of the year when the

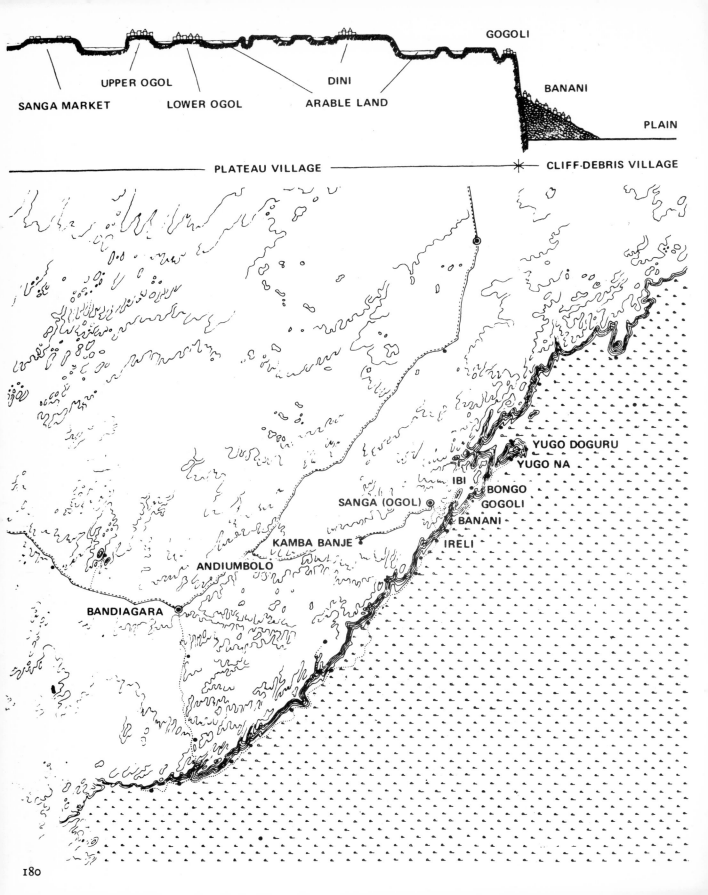

SANGA MARKET

UPPER OGOL

LOWER OGOL

DINI

ARABLE LAND

GOGOLI

BANANI

PLAIN

PLATEAU VILLAGE — CLIFF-DEBRIS VILLAGE

YUGO DOGURU

YUGO NA

IBI

BONGO

SANGA (OGOL)

GOGOLI

BANANI

KAMBA BANJE

IRELI

ANDIUMBOLO

BANDIAGARA

nomads of Mauritania must stay near the water holes with their valued herds, their freedom is limited by an order which permits all to still their thirst. The one-dimensional water hole with the dense pack of animals, usually scattered along the horizon, has given the nomads a system of justice, based on the right to have an animal draw out buckets of water for a certain number of days, and a tribal morality.

Yet in the life of the Dogon, who dip their water from the water holes among the rocks of Bandiagara, the same lukewarm, reddish-yellow and turbid liquid has a meaning different from that it has for other people, even since mythical times. In the flight of migration from Mande, the Dogon ancestors could remain to build houses and found families only where there was water to be found, often hidden in rock crevices or in pools in the low brush. Nangabanu was thirsty, it is said. A crocodile came near him; he followed the animal to the riverlike pool where it lived with others, and there, with that much water, Nangabanu founded Bandiagara—the only large settlement in the land of the Dogon, today their capital. The inhabitants revere the crocodile as a tribal father. Friendship binds them to the animal; none ever harms a Dogon, and no Dogon kills one.

The animal of the water, the life in the water, has remained bound up with the life of the family. In many of the Ginnas the original founder of the family lives on in the form of a turtle. At night when it creeps out of its hiding place, it finds under the family altar its nourishment (as do the spirits of the ancestors, who visit the sacred spot). Millet meal with water is offered—water, which sustains, creates, and binds together. When a wife finally leaves her father's

house after the birth of a second or third child to live with her husband, she is said to have drunk water with him.

At birth and death the family drinks nourishing millet-water together. The elders in council, the men in the market, and all the guests at a feast drink beer, the fermented 'strong' water, which is also taken when people build a house together, begin the planting, or finish the harvest. The water of the Dogon is there so that they can propagate, exercise their skills, drink and speak, take and give. It means the fruition, beginning, and strengthening of the family; it means clothing, understanding, and manners. It is to communicate with God through his seed, and through his breath, which brings the word. Thus everything is due to water. Its use can never be limited by a system of rights; one gives water to strangers as a gesture of hospitality, and all the children of a family have a natural and equal claim to it, just as to life itself, through their ancestors, from God.

With this attitude toward their water may be connected the fact that the Dogon, who otherwise show many technical skills—who can build ingenious houses and weave strong cloth—go about the management of their most important material in a 'primitive' way. Using small gourd shells, they ladle water into large clay pots and take them into the yards of houses, or out to water the fields. Except for this simple way of distributing water, they know none of the other techniques that are found in West Africa. Those who could increase and store up water—the substance closest to God—have, for the Dogon, taken on an aura of superhuman wisdom and power. Professor Griaule, the ethnologist who studied the Dogon for many years, convinced the French authorities to build dams there in some appropriate places. This act raised him to the status of the founding forefathers of the people. When the news that he had died in Paris reached them, his soul was taken up among the spirits of the dead through the ritual of the Dama, so that his life-force or Nyama would benefit the living among 'his' people. The people of Sanga, where Professor Griaule often stayed, built a grave for him near the fields that were 'created'. The French researcher has entered into not only their history but also Dogon myth.

It is in the mask cult and the dance of the masks itself that the most important part of the spiritual and social life of the Dogon people is found. In its dealing with the phenomenon of death, their society has created an institution which draws it together again and again, structures and refreshes it, one in which it finds its most characteristic expression. The death ceremonies, and particularly the Dama, a masked dance for the termination of a period of mourning, distribute the life-force of the deceased among the living, while the soul—liberated from both life and death—is admitted among the immortal ancestors. (In some cases, though, the dead have a harmful force which must be kept away through special ritual.) In a symbolic funeral procession the masks first go to get the deceased from the house where he used to live. They accompany him to the land of the immortal ancestors, to Mande of origin and destination; then they return, winding back through the hills to the village streets. They begin there the dance through which the beneficent Nyama they have brought back is distributed. Thus the strength of their dead renews and protects the living.

Unlike people of other religious convictions, the Dogon expect of the hereafter no compensation through a better life. They find their life not bad, and learn in their well-ordered world that one is immediately rewarded for goodness, and that one soon pays for doing wrong and need not trail it with him after death.

The paradise of the Dogon, where the deceased reside, looks like Dogonland itself. The villages are like those in which the living dwell, the rich are rich, the poor are poor. All live with their families, planting millet and onions as they did on earth. In the dry brush the same trees stand, though the fruits they bear are more beautiful in colour, more lustrous, so that the dead can tell they are in paradise and no longer in the land of the Dogon.

Design Only Grace; Open Norm; Disturb Order Grace- fully; Out- match Need

Aldo van Eyck

There is no limit to what the Dogon basket can hold, for with its circular rim and square base, it is at once basket and granary; at once sun, firmament, and cosmic system; at once millet and the forces which cause millet to grow.

It seems to me that people for whom all things are so much one thing that one thing can also be all things carry this essential unity within themselves. Even Dogon paradise falls within this unity insofar as it resembles the land of the living in everything except the fruits of the baobab tree which are more lustrous so that those in paradise may recognize where they are. Everything prevails—not even the hardships of life on earth are mitigated in Dogon after-life. They too prevail. Nothing is discontinued: in paradise the Dogon is satisfied as he was on earth!

In order to be at home in the universe, man tends to refashion it in his own image, accommodate it to his own dimension. Constructed enclosure was hitherto seldom sufficient. There was always the limitless exterior beyond— the incomprehensible, intangible and unpredictable—harassing man's right composure, shaking whatever 'ground of certainty', to use Joseph Rykwert's phrase, he was able to find. So his cities, villages, and houses—even his baskets—were persuaded by means of symbolic form and complex ritual to contain within their measurable confines that which exists beyond and is im-measurable: to represent it symbolically. The artifact—whether small or large, basket or city, was identified with the universe or the power or deity representing the cosmic order. It thus became a 'habitable' place, comprehensible from corner to corner, familiar and tangible. Mystery was thus rendered at least partly accessible. The transcendental was brought within reach: with the Zuni Pueblos, the great Shilako dance in each house just after completion before it is inhabited—thus, the entire village actually 'becomes' the house of the gods.

Those who agree with Joseph Rykwert[6] that 'the ground of certainty', without which no inner equipoise is possible, must now be discovered within the 'structure and constitution of the human person', i.e. in the interior of the mind and no longer outside it, will probably find it more meaningful to identify the city with the dream than to identify it with the exterior universe. Whilst the latter, I think, is no longer either possible or desirable, the former is singularly suggestive, since it points towards an 'interiorization' of the mind—an 'interior' universe, at once kaleidoscopic, metamorphic, and chaotic, in the way—this is my point—cities are kaleidoscopic, metamorphic, and chaotic—and necessarily so.

The transcendental begins where man leaves his gods behind—this side of the beyond. We no longer need the cardo and the decumanus to feel at home in the universe, but we need to be 'at home' nonetheless. That is why it is no small thing to discover that we are indeed Romans no longer, yet Romans still.[7] Rykwert's suggestion that a town, if it looks like anything physiological at all, looks more like a dream than anything else, is suggestive in many ways. For it is in the nature of dreams that things —all things—escape from the rigid meanings assigned to them, cross their own frontier, merge, and are significantly reshuffled; that absolutes and quantitative antonyms (false polarities)—this concerns me especially—are deflated and rendered meaningless; and, finally, that order and chaos, continuity and discontinuity, the determinate and the indeterminate, are gratifyingly united.

Both the Pueblos and the Dogon tell us, each in a different way, that right-size is not a quantitative matter at all. They reveal once again that what large and small, many and few, far and near, part and whole, unity and diversity, simplicity and complexity, etc., etc., mean in a qualitative and relative sense depends on what they mean in terms of each other, i.e. as a linked sequence of twinpheno-mena. In a valid solution—whether it is a Pueblo or a Dogon village, all these qualities are simultaneously present. Each acquires something of the meaning of the other and is enriched by it—given perspective. This is what I call right-size. It is also what the large house - little city image is meant to suggest. With

Above and next two pages: *These photographs are of the main open space in Upper Ogol. The first was taken in the morning, the others in the afternoon of the same day during an important Dama, the great masked ceremony which terminates a period of mourning, divides the Nyama or life-force of the deceased among the living, and releases the spirit from the life and death so that it can be received by the immortal ancestors.*

Although women and children are forbidden

to watch a Dama – its very essence excludes this – they are seen here standing on the roofs in large numbers doing so! All at once a masked figure dances past the houses bordering the open space with great leaps, emitting fierce noises and throwing gravel up at those watching on the roofs. Screaming, terror stricken, the latter disappear immediately.

The conflict is resolved magnificently at once on both levels, the cosmic and the human. The terrifying figure who scares the women and

children away actually belongs to the Dama and fulfils this particular dance function. The cosmic equipoise is thus quickly restored. But the human one also, for soon the transgressing spectators, having regained the right composure, reappear on the roofs and proceed to watch the Dama below as if nothing had occurred. They are neither forcibly prevented from doing so nor are they punished for it. Instead, in order to safeguard the houses bordering this particular open space from

collapsing under the weight of so many women and children watching what they should not watch, but still 'need' to watch, they are built more firmly than those elsewhere in the village. The extra material this requires is furnished by the village. Just think of it!

The mastery with which the Dogon are able to restore equipoise when it is disturbed is breathtaking. Their sense of reality is such, so it seems, that merely to 'maintain' equipoise becomes insufficiently constructive – a non-inclusive and arbitrary procedure which fails to respond to the reality of the cause of the disturbance and its possible validity, in human terms or otherwise. This creative ability to re-establish equipoise on whatever level (cosmic, social, or psychic) it may have been disturbed, points to a frame of mind both generous, perceptive and functional. Tensions are quickly mitigated and conflicts reasonably resolved. As to the women and children watching the Dama: that the Dogon are con-cerned not only with the consequence of their transgression (disturbance of the cosmic order) but also with the understandable desire of the transgressors to witness the Dama and the mental stress (disturbance of the individual's inner equipoise) which would result were they not to do so – is revealed by the contribution of the extra building material to reinforce the houses bordering the open space.

Upper Ogol.

regard to false physiological analogies, I find the currently quantitative leaf-house or tree-city analogies as meaningless as I find the qualitative leaf-tree or house-city identifications meaningful—i.e. endowed with multimeaning (see note on Christopher Alexander's 'A city is not a tree'). [8]

Whilst in Africa, I discussed the large house-little city image with Dr Parin and Dr Morgenthaler, and was very excited when they told me that the various aspects of the Dogon reality could probably support the image's validity. The essays they wrote show that this supposition was not unjustified. I shall elaborate on the reciprocal identification of house, village, region, and those living there in the last section: Some Comments on a Significant Detour. What comes in between should help the reader to appreciate the implications, since that is the objective.

There are indeed some combined physical and mental problems which the Dogon in particular have managed to solve remarkably well. I am referring in the first place to the way they are able to release from moment to moment inner tensions by means of a mental process which to us, who are wont to accumulate and even nourish grinding remnants left over from former human contact (allowing them to disturb our inner composure and distort our subsequent behaviour), must seem like a miracle.

The Dogon rely on an all-pervading framework which embraces every facet of their existence, material, emotional, and transcendental. Such frameworks are so intricate, complete, and self-contained that they may tend to leave little scope for the individual whose mental structure, though moulded by them to a large extent, nonetheless never coincides fully. Not so with the Dogon, for they include within the intricate, closely knit fabric of their system a gratifying kind of scope (flexibility) which permits circumstantial and incidental modification without transgressing against the system's generative and pro-tective potential, infringing on its essence, or damaging the individual's psychic structure. The Dogon adhere to their system with great accuracy, but never rigidly. This accuracy is due to an astounding responsiveness which enables them to resolve immediately both the conflicts which beset the community at large and the intimate ones which weigh on the individual.

The miraculous vision of paradise to which I have already referred epitomizes the Dogon mind, and also reveals extraordinary mental relaxation. People able to reward a life of great hardship with a vision of afterlife so moderate must in truth be essentially satisfied with the reality they were born into. What measurable grandeur! What sanity!

188

Lower Ogol.

ginna

ginna

Togu Na

+ altaren

Plan of Upper Ogol.
Photos were taken from arrowed positions.

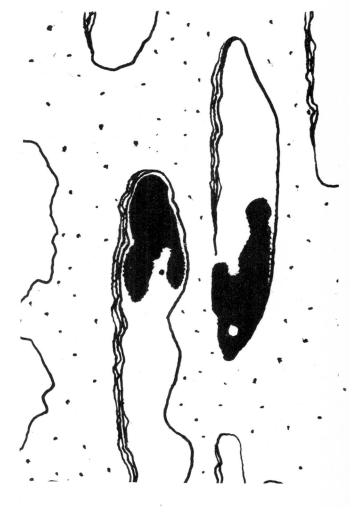

Upper Ogol left, Lower Ogol right.

189

Building both house and village implies inaugurating a microcosm in which life is perpetuated—hence the various rituals which accompany the building process from stage to stage. There is no categorical conflict between those prerogatives which have a physical and those which have a metaphysical basis, since the natural and the supernatural, or the material and the spiritual, do not constitute impregnable or conflicting categories. What is true of the Dogon basket is also true of the Dogon house and the Dogon village; their symbolic meaning is likewise extraordinarily expansive. I am not exaggerating when I say that all the material objects from the smallest to the largest which support daily life are charged with extra meaning and are identified in stages with the totality of creation. A sequential pattern of identification expanding and, finally, corresponding with the universal order. About these stages Marcel Griaule, to use his own words, says that each stage of the process represents the whole, whilst a series of material avatars leads from the world itself to smaller and smaller groupings—district, village, village-section, homestead. He speaks of 'emboitements successifs' progressing from man to cosmos in which every stage contains the whole. His daughter, G. Calame-Griaule, who is also a leading Dogon specialist, affirms that the cosmos projected in a human scale reveals an essential humanism. But let me glean more relevant data concerning symbolic meaning from the two Griaules. I must condense what they say, in places partly in my own words. The house is built in the image of man: the actual place where the cooking is done represents the respiratory organ and is always situated there where a fruit of the nono plant (nono=perpetual) is walled-in during the building process, whilst the kitchen itself is the head. The entrance represents the vulva (the cooking place lies in the axis: kitchen—central living space—entrance). I should like to remind the reader of the Pueblo Indians whom I admire as I do the Dogon and about whom I have written a companion essay.[9] As with the Dogon, marking the plan of a house on the ground calls for complex rituals. Such rituals are continued throughout the entire building process at different stages. Ogotemmeli, the old blind Dogon sage, called this: the imprint of the house's image which commences. It is also the universal arch descended from the heavens to reorganize creation. The four main spaces grouped around the principal one are the four ancestral couples (these together with the animals, plants, minerals, and Nommo constitute the universal arch).

The Ginna or family patriarch's house is Nommo in human form. Also a man lying on his right side procreating. The different heights of the roots over the rooms express the diversity, Griaule says, of the beings which issued from the ejected seed. Each part of the house is thus an original being germinating and growing from its genitor. The whole plan of the house, furthermore, is contained in an oval. It again represents the universal arch from which all space, all living beings, and everything has emerged.

There are definite symbolic proportions for all buildings based on the male number three and the female number four. Thus a normal house is 6 × 8 paces, i.e. twice the male number multiplied by twice the female number. The Ginna is double this. A granary belonging to a man is 6 (i.e. 2 × 3) × 6, a granary belonging to a woman is 4 × 4. The numbers three and four prevail, even in clothing![10]

Now for the villages. Not only are they anthropomorphic like the house, but, to follow Griaule, each part or section of them is a complete or separate entity and, so far as possible, must be laid out on the same pattern as the whole. Thus individual families are fitted into a grouping which itself is a unity. The village, like the house, is the projection of the universe in the form of a man lying on his back in a north-south direction. Smithy and Togu Na are his head; the two menstruation huts standing outside the village precincts are his hands; the main shrines, his feet; whilst the various Ginna situated around the village centre are his chest and stomach.[10]

What excites me especially with respect to the village is the fact that they are generally built in pairs. The same goes for the districts. Since I am deeply concerned with twin-phenomena, the principle of twin-ness—gemelliparite—which

Ogol. Doorway to a yard.

Upper Ogol. The plateau type villages are built to the very edge of flat rock masses.

Ogol. People have always been able to cope with the single house – or a limited multiplicity of houses.

runs right through the entire Dogon cosmology manifesting itself at every scale level can, therefore, hardly fail to excite me! A rare sense of equipoise pervades the life and doings of the Dogon and epitomizes their specific genius. It seems to me that it could well be nourished by this principle of twin-ness, the one sustaining the other reciprocally.

Theoretically, the in-between space formed by such twin villages should be round the way the sky is round—like the rim of the Dogon basket. The Lebe shrine situated there is the sun, whilst the various Binu shrines in the two villages are the stars.[11] The space between an Upper and Lower district is marked by a public meeting place, in the village where the Hogon, the district chief, lives.

What Marcel Griaule says about the villages as seen from above is extremely relevant here. He describes how the roofs shining in the sun and the shadows cast on the ground resemble hillocks of cultivated land casting shadows into the hollows. Moving down in scale, the '80' niches of the Ginna and the checked black-and-white Dogon blanket reveal the same pattern. Thus the settlement where people dwell close together is a representation both of man himself and of the layout of the fields outside the walls; a way of calling to mind the fact that the processes of germination and gestation are of the same kind.

I will conclude with what Griaule has to say about the territorial organization of the Dogon and the Hogon. It accords with the idea that the world developed in the form of a spiral. The fields are laid out in such a way that they represent the world in miniature. In principle they form a rectilinear spiral around three ritual fields, one for each of the basic cults. First, nearest the centre, come the fields belonging to the kin groups. These are followed by those belonging to individuals. Sacrifices are offered in the shrines situated along the spiral starting with the one nearest the centre. The actual process of cultivation and the way the Dogon labour in the fields extends the symbolic meaning of the spiral layout into symbolic action—in accordance with it.

The Hogon priest, the district chief, Griaule says, is the personification of the universe and the regent of Nommo on earth. In consequence, all his material attributes and all the prerogatives attaching to his function represent the qualities and movements of the cosmic mechanism. He controls the cosmic rhythm. Thus his daily life is set against a background which presents the world in miniature and in reference to which his ceremonial acts and movements symbolize the motive power which animates the world.

The daily life of the Dogon is concerned with the gathering of necessary goods. As settled planters, they plan and adjust the course of their labours according to the laws of nature. They naturally expect rain to come at the right time and hope for a good harvest. Their requirements are basic ones, as are the satisfactions they seek from life. They live through their disappointments, gaining from them practical understanding to alleviate their troubles. The work is hard, but the return is generally such that they can live without great hunger—also such that they cannot amass wealth. Yet the Dogon are neither melancholy nor apathetic people; even though they do not expect a better life—or know 'longing', as understood by Western civilization—they are largely content and at their ease.

Psychic tensions arising from contact with fellow men are not of lasting consequence with the Dogon, and so they hardly ever experience the pressure of dammed up feelings that can find expression in hoping and longing. Tension will usually be discharged at the point of its origin and without delay, distributed, and cleared in a common transaction. This can succeed to a high degree, because for each emotion, each disturbance, and all impulses a material or spiritual response lies ready to facilitate abreaction, without disturbing the external or internal order that defines their world.

In the hot hours at noon, by a small river that runs near Andiumbolo, we are resting in the shade of a tree. An old man appears wearing a large straw hat. At a little distance from us he stops and stands for a time—then he comes closer and greets us in his language. It is a long greeting whose rhythm and intonation convey the earnestness of a tradition. At the same time, it holds a cheerful invitation to reply. It is a greeting like a dialogue, or a canon, whose complete structure calls for a matching response. We answer the greeting, but as our answer is without form and spirit, we try to make up for the obvious short-coming with some gestures. The old man smiles. One of us has just finished a mango and throws the stone away. The Dogon comes over quickly, picks it up, and begins a story without words. We will plant the stone, here, and a mango tree will grow up; people will sit in its shade and pick fruits from its branches to eat. With these gestures the man has completed the greeting we failed to carry out properly. He got something from us, the mango stone, and with it has made something whole and appropriate as a response; the tree. Now he stands there laughing, seeing that we have been able to follow him. The greeting that is such comprehensive contact between Dogon is well done with the foreigners too. He drops the stone and goes his way.

That was Bai, the village chief of Andiumbolo. He has gone for people from the village now, so we may come in contact with one another.

In another village I spend quite a while looking for Amba, a young man with whom I have arranged to meet. After many detours, I finally find him in a remote onion garden. We greet each other, and our conversation follows:

'I was told in the village that you were working in a garden on the other side of the hill'.

'That's where my garden is.'

'But you are working here and not in your garden.'

'Today I'm helping my little brother harvest the onions. He is going to help me finish my house.'

'Are you building a house?'

'I was away for four years, and when I came back I married. Now I'm building a house so I can live there with my wife.'

'The people in the village showed me your house, the last one before the rocks.'

'I was there this morning. It's my big brother's house.'

'Do you live there?'

'No, I live with my father.'

'Why did they tell me that your big brother's house is your house?'

'I sleep there with my wife. In the morning she goes back to her father's house.'

Fritz Morgenthaler

'Do you have children yet?'

'No, that wouldn't work. First the house has to be finished. Then my wife will have children, and I will take them in.'

'Most Dogon wives stay with their father until the third child is born. Then they live with their husband in his house.'

'Yes, of course. When a woman bears a child she naturally returns to her father.'

'Even when you have finished your house?'

'Of course. When a child is born, the mother returns to her father.'

'Then why do you have to finish your house before your wife can have a child?'

'You will see the house I'm building now. Then everything will be clear to you.' He looks down at the ground and shakes his head. 'A wife can't have a child as long as the house isn't finished. It just doesn't happen that way.'

'Is the big brother whose place you sleep in with your wife also married?'

'He's married, and his wife has two children. She and the children live with her father.'

'Had he built himself a house before his wife had her first child?'

Amba leans over toward me and taps me on the shoulder. 'Now you understand the Dogon. The big brother's house will be there for the younger brothers when they want to sleep with their wives.'

The substance of our conversation seemed quite simple at first. A young Dogon builds a house, takes in his wife, and starts a family. Then it emerges that the new house is not simply intended for the immediate family, but is placed at the disposal of younger brothers for years to come. Amba thereby gains a new position in the community of the village. He becomes a 'big brother', and that involves his being a mature man with responsible functions. Only then can he too have his own children. The social meaning, still more the whole experience of being a father, is divided into two matching parts in Amba's mind, two parts which are inseparably correlated and yet do not overlap. As big brother, he has the social role of father to all those younger, for whom he becomes an example. As procreator, he secures himself the offspring who will care for him when he is old. For his own children, though, other big brothers will in turn become more important than he. Then just as father and big brother match each other, so do the building of a house and the act of procreation, the house and the child—not symbols of each other, not just comparable parts of a whole, but one and the same, like the square basket with the round opening that is at once basket, granary, and cosmos. In such continuity of psychic experience appears the wholeness of the Dogon culture.

'Would you like to come and see my house?' We get up and go back to the village. Amba's house on the edge of the market place is square and has a small anteroom. There is no roof yet.

'You have a very fine house. There are no windows.'

'White people put windows in their houses. We Dogon don't do that. When the roof is up, the house will be dark inside.'

'Why should it be dark?'

'Anybody who wants light can go outside. In the house it should be dark. It's better that way.'

The wholeness of this culture is also reflected in the words of Dommo, a man of forty from the village of Andiumbolo: 'Everyone here is satisfied. Everyone is content with things as they are.' With a sweep of his hand he indicates the landscape before us. 'When one can work and have a good harvest, there is enough to eat. Then there are holidays, and we go around to the other villages. There is something to drink and a lot of talk with everyone, and then it is time to go home again.'

When I ask Dommo for his opinion about why the white people are not always as content, he can't think of an answer and explains my question to the chief of the village. He considers for a moment, and then Dommo translates his words.

'White people think too much and then do many things, and the more they do, the more they think. And then they earn a lot of money, and when they have a lot they worry that the money could get lost and they would have no more. Then they think more and make still more money, and never have enough. Then they never have any peace again. So it is that they are not happy.'

The ease in this culture is present in the words that Dommo speaks. It is a kind of ease that can forego hoping and longing.

Then comes the day Dommo is with me in the car as we drive by the market place of Andiumbolo. Some children there wave to us. We pass the great rock where the road drops down steeply, and the gentle, hilly landscape gives an impression of distinct loneliness. Far and wide not a village is in sight, as all of them lie hidden to us. We drive on to the great festival of the masks at Kamba

It happens to be the very image of Banani against the cliffs which has been in my mind ever since I saw a photograph in a Minotaure issue during the war. From a distance – see photo of Narni – the villages blend so wonderfully with the environment to which they belong that they are almost invisible. But contrast can be equally wonderful as any Cycladic island village shows. The sister picture on the right shows a man standing next to his huge-small granary.

Banani is a good example of a cliff-debris type village. Each man and each woman possesses one or more personal granaries. Unlike the blacksmith and the weaver, the builder is not a specialised professional. Each man builds his own house assisted by the male members of the large family to which he belongs, and those of his neighbourhood. Building is thus a collective undertaking, though houses are personal property.

Banje, the only village that can be seen from the road, sitting on a rock about 60 metres high. From up there, after a climb, one has a completely different view of the land. What seemed gentle ridges are now terrace-like rock formations with jagged crests of glistening basalt.

Dommo stands there like a king considering the castle grounds. He motions me to look across the wide land into the distance where we see the masks dancing to the village—they come nearer now. On the way to the village open space where the great dance will take place, I stop and, captivated, stand looking into a small yard, over the mud wall where it has been damaged and is low enough for me to see. 'Leave it—come on!'

The tone is severe. But in the way Dommo says it, the Dogon cheer rings through, even more compelling. Immediately I leave behind the strange sight in the yard and follow after him.

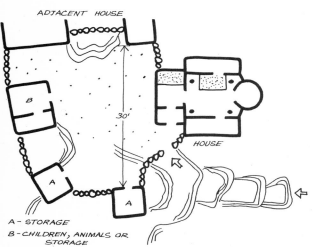

ADJACENT HOUSE

30'

HOUSE

A- STORAGE

B- CHILDREN, ANIMALS OR
STORAGE

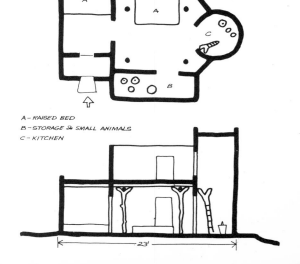

B

A

A

C

A- RAISED BED

B- STORAGE & SMALL ANIMALS

C- KITCHEN

B

23'

◁ *Banani. Granaries around a courtyard.*

Banani-type house.

◁ *Yugo Doguru. Dwelling of the Hogon priest. Note entrance at lower right and ancient (probably Tellem) granaries.*

Yugo Doguru. Cliffs sheltering ancient granaries. ▷
Yugo Doguru. In the background the great ▽
plain of Gondo several hundred feet below.

The small brought about by the large

Yugo Doguru is the Mecca of the Dogon people because the grave of the first ancestral Dogon is situated there. It is the privilege, furthermore, of the male elders of this sacred place to order the advent of the Sigi every 60 years – the great masked celebration which constitutes the renewal of the entire Dogon people. The manner in which the houses, granaries, and yards are adapted and modified owing to the gigantic rocks which lie scattered over the site is revealing. The sacredness of this particular site left no alternative than to build there. As a reward for coping with the difficulties this brought with it, however, many shaded places resulted under and between the rocks and buildings, which are absent in villages elsewhere built, as they are, on more regular and 'suitable' sites.

What this really implies is of crucial importance, since it points towards the old truth that what is just large without embracing what is small at the same time has no right-size in terms of human appreciation and will hence remain inaccessible. Thus right-size is the gratifying reward of magnitude approached as a twinphenomenon. This includes, of course, the interdependence of many and few, far and near; part and whole, simplicity and complexity, unity and diversity, inside and outside, open and closed, change and constancy, movement and rest, and, finally, the individual and the collective – their simultaneous presence as an essential prerequisite if environment is to mean what we wish it to mean. The ingredients we need lie still dormant in what I personally wish to call Labyrinthian Clarity, for in its inclusive ambiguity and scope for multimeaning, it is nourished by and nourishes all twinphenomena together. Labyrinthian Clarity exemplifies a frame of mind as well as what issues from it, a climate in which all false partitions inevitably fall down.

Yugo Doguru. A sacred place.

There is great commotion in the village open space. The dance of the masks begins, and I lose sight of Dommo in the crowd. One may see the masks when they are alive and dancing, but the lifeless masks are taboo. They are put away in caves, to be visited by the initiates in the mask cult only, at night and in secret. I was looking at a dark-red, barrel-shaped mask behind that mud wall. It stood there motionless and enigmatic, one side still faintly lit by the sinking sun. The upper part of the mask tapered like the roof of a cylindrical house, and bore a small head with trunklike finery.

The masked dance nears its climax in the open space. Now moving slowly and deliberately, the barrel-shaped mask appears—and then again from the other side. The dance takes on a particular quality. To the rhythm of the drums the mask moves itself in a circle, rocking up and down. All at once the dancer in it crouches and the 'mask house' is left frozen. The structure, sturdily built, rests on the ground now just as I caught it a short time ago in a forbidden glimpse. But already it has continued its dance.

Dommo says right at my side. 'That's the elephant. He appears only in a few villages, and only once in a while.' The 'elephant' embodies motion and rest together like no other mask. He dances and stays still—then he dances again, and so on. There is no stop, no end of motion without its continuing again immediately. So death too is only a phase. It begins during life, and life still goes on after death. Nothing may ever come completely to an end—something always follows.

Dommo found it hard to bring together his divided feelings toward me in conversation, so one day he took my hand and led me over high rocks up to Andiumbolo. Stopping at the entrance he said, 'This is my village.' He spat, took my hand again, and said, 'I want to show you my house.'

The village is on a rocky hill. From here one sees far into the valley below, to the river, and across the fields to another hill and the twin village of Goloku. Andiumbolo is larger than one would think looking up from the foot of the hill. A few houses stand just at the verge of the rocky slope. They are surrounded by a mud wall, and there are small trees in some of the yards. Further back in the village is a larger open space. Here Dommo points out the shade-roof (Togu Na), under which the old men like to rest, and 'also the young,' as he says. 'I'll show you my house now,' he says again and draws me on. The narrow, winding streets we pass through are shaped by the mud walls that enclose yards. The houses are in these yards, and along the yard walls stand the granaries built up on posts, as if on stilts, and bearing pointed thatched roofs. We meet three men, and Dommo introduces us. They greet me like an old acquaintance—Bai has spread the story about the white people under the tree.

The three men join us. I am no longer sure where we are headed, and Dommo explains. 'We are going to the village chief's house. He's my uncle, my mother's brother.' The house of the village chief is larger than all the others. There are two front doors, and around them 22 rectangular niches have been fashioned in the wall. Various useless items lie in the niches: a broken gourd shell, a few rusty pieces of metal, even two eggs. In a matter-of-fact way Dommo says, 'Birds nest in there.' He shows no awareness of the significance of the niches, that they are supposed to represent the 80 immortal ancestors from the third mythical generation.

After the greeting, and after Bai has offered me some Konjo, I remind Dommo that it is late and I have to go back soon. 'Yes, of course,' he says, 'but let's go to my house.' He chooses a way we haven't taken yet. We come to some houses with small towers, and I stop. Large stones, whitened with a coating of dried millet paste, lie around in the yard. They are altars, at which someone has made an offering. An old crippled man makes his way among the stone blocks. Dommo does not greet him—he pulls me away as if he is afraid I will speak to the old man. 'That is the house of the Hogon priest of Andiumbolo. Come on, we have to hurry. We are going to my house now.'

Again Dommo seems to change direction. He stops before a large mud wall and knocks on the closed gate there. 'This is my uncle's house.' After I ask, surprised, whether we are going to his house or not, I learn that this is the Ginna, the 'big house' of the family, where Dommo's paternal uncle lives, the family elder, or Bana. In the dark vestibule I almost step on the children and women sitting everywhere. Dommo says, 'My father isn't here.' meaning the Bana. His immediate father has been dead for a long time. We continue through the narrow streets and reach once more the open space with the Togu Na.

I turn for home, and Dommo asks, disappointed, 'Don't you want to see my house? I don't live where we just were—when my wife is working in the fields or is sick and can't cook, I eat in the big house. I'm home, here.' So we walk into a yard near the entrance to the village. It is the place where, more than an hour ago, Dommo said he wanted to show me his house.

Dommo's house has two doors. A small mud wall, really an extension of the house, divides the yard, as if in halves. In the yard are three granaries—two near the entrance for Dommo and his first wife, the third in the rear of the yard for his second wife. Standing next to each other are the two women, who greet us. Dommo says, 'My father lived here. He also had two wives. When he died I took over the house. I've been here for fifteen years with my first wife, and for a while my second wife has been living in the other house, that used to be empty.'

Dommo's wish to show me his house took us in turn to the council-place of the elders, to the village chief's place, to the priest's, then to the place of the family elder, and just at last to his own dwelling. To each of these places he is bound by a quite definite part of his sense of 'being home'. So it is in this culture that a house is never sold, for one calls a house the people living there.

A Ginna.

Ogol. Each village has several such houses (Ginna) in which a family patriarch lives with his wives and unmarried sons and daughters. Other members of the family live in small houses of the normal type close around the Ginna. Note the niches (never 80!) which represent the primordial descendants of the four ancestral couples of the Dogon people.

Ogol. A priest's house. Many libations are poured over the façade and shrines from the roof.

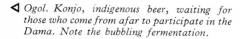

A tree constitutes a shady place – a place also for what the Dogon calls a 'special stone'. Children play a kind of checkers there.

Grinding stones, kept near to jars of water ▷ near the entry to the house. On these stones fresh ears of corn are crushed, yielding a liquid (associated with the male seminal fluid) which is carried to the left of the entry and poured on the shrine of the ancestors.

◁ Ogol. Konjo, indigenous beer, waiting for those who come from afar to participate in the Dama. Note the bubbling fermentation.

A shrine of Ogol.

Some Comments on a Significant Detour

Although it is true that only a particular kind of society conditions the particular kind of emotional place-affinity Dommo has towards the various 'houses' he passed or entered with Dr Morgenthaler before finally entering the house he shares with his first wife and children, it would be wrong to suggest that only an all-encompassing framework can condition the kind of multilocated attachment (web of emotional place-affinity) which is required before one can really say: my house is my village (city), my village (city) is my house, or when I say village (city) I imply the people living there.

The emotional identification of house and village (city) need not of course depend on such collectively conditioned place-attachment, but the idea as such stands out clearly enough. Nor does the emotional indentification of either house or village (city) with the people living there necessarily require an attachment so immediate that a house for example—as is the case with the Dogon—cannot be sold.

If that were so, my desire to conceive of a house as a small city and a city as a large house would be abstract, in the sense that it would be an altogether unattainable objective. I can visualize a culture which is not negatively indeterminate but positively so, because it strives primarily to stimulate the personal self-realization of the individual according to his own personal idea. This in turn would provide the true ingredient that goes to the fulfilment of the multi-coloured entity that society—hence also the city—should be. The house-like city with city like houses (buildings), gratifyingly comprehensible and chaotic; homogeneous and kaleidoscopic at the same time (I call this labyrinthian clarity).

What would have conditioned another man's route through Andiumbolo (with the same object of showing a visitor his house) to differ from Dommo's is not a different kind of emotional attachment, but a similar kind accorded to a different (perhaps partly the same) sequence of houses and places. Their actual location differs from one Dogon to another according to the way he is linked to the community (its total framework). I do not wish to suggest for a moment that Dommo is not emotionally linked to other places, houses, or people for strictly personal reasons—in this, of course, he differs from no man. But they were simply not incorporated in his route, leading from place to place (each of which was his 'own house' in a particular way) until he finally returned to the place from where the detour had started and entered the house he shares with his wife and children (his 'own' in that particular respect).

The fact that the same collectively rooted reasons cause each Dogon to be linked emotionally to a different network of houses and places within his village (so that for each individual within the village community the village is also 'his' house) does not imply that because in the city of today the strictly personal reasons are different from individual to individual, linking each to a network of places (often strangely enough the same), his city cannot be 'his' house also. With the Dogon, the emotional house-village-region relationship constitutes a reality the entire community is aware of, whereas with us such a relationship is a thing each individual is aware of for strictly personal reasons. With the Dogon what is essentially similar becomes emotionally differentiated from person to person. With us what is superficially dissimilar tends to become emotionally stereotyped from person to person. Now, without having to resort to the former it is obvious that the latter is a sad alternative. Surely what is essentially dissimilar can be embraced in what is essentially similar from person to person, establishing the real scope for differentiation.

There are as many Londons as there are Londoners, as many Parises as there are Parisians (as many too as there are Londoners going to Paris!), yet London is not Paris.

A village (town or city) is not just one bunch of places; it is many bunches at the same time, because it is a different bunch for each inhabitant. Consequently there are many Andiumbolos. This means that a village can be identified with each villager individually but also with all the villagers collectively. What implications!

Aldo van Eyck

If and how far an identification similar to that of house and village is tenable for village and region has occupied me a great deal. To illuminate this question adequately in terms of the Dogon, Dr Morgenthaler says, would lead us beyond the scope of this publication. I can, however, quote from what he wrote me on the subject.

'The five-day week of the Dogon is grouped vicariously around the market day of the individual village, the Sunday-market day falling on a different day in each village group. A travelling Dogon could thus, theoretically, experience every day of the week as Sunday-market day. For this is the day when people get together; the day people sense that all Dogon villages belong together. Then there is another thing: that the Dogon feels well and happy only when he is in Dogonland, in the region within which his village lies amongst the other villages. However, it is probably true that his village, within the region and country where it lies, belongs also to the 'entire world order' and that it can be replaced by means of corresponding experiences. He will thus not merely feel himself

Gogoli, and the market place in Ogol. 'The Dogon believes twins are the universal symbol of happiness and perfection. The principle of twinness, inherent in their highest ideas, is present in many everyday affairs. In the marketplace the buyer and seller are "twins", for the things they exchange "match" each other. The market is the most important meeting place. One goes there to drink beer, and over good beer to exchange words of friendship and understanding.'[12]

at home in his village among other villages, in the region and country to which it belongs, but will actually *be* there when he recounts a fable to a fellow Dogon in foreign territory. The difference between the Dogon and us is not that we are unable to remember similar representational images or to transmit them to others in order to feel at home in a foreign land; no, the difference lies somewhere else. With us such images are fantasies. We tend to look at them hoping that they will conjure up what we miss, whereas the Dogon by means of the process referred to above transmits what *is* and not what he misses, because, in fact, he misses nothing.'

Thus the direct emotional affinity to house, village, or region—reciprocally identified—is so complete, reaches so deep psychically that, for the Dogon at least, it includes irrevocably the identification of all three with those who live there (a space is the appreciation of it—a building, that same building entered); this is why a house cannot be sold.

Is it, I ask, in terms of ourselves, still a prerogative that we must rely on place-affinity of a kind thus collectively rooted, in order to really know that when we say house or city we actually imply the people living there, i.e. ourselves; imply that *we* are that city or that house? I would not like to think so. Yet something else will have to persuade us—condition us again—to identify both house and city, in fact environment in general, with the people living there, and to act accordingly.

It is futile to continue freezing abstract notions into poor organized shape, calling this 'human environment' and then just go whistling for 'population'. Environment is for *people*. That is the least obvious thing I could possibly have said.If society has no comprehensible form, can it acquire a counterform which is human.

Beyond feeling lost outside one's own region (or estranged even within it) there should still be some reasonable alternative. A man at home wherever he happens to be carries his roots with him, is himself his own house, inhabits his own inner space—and his own time. He will also be able to inhabit, as it were simultaneously, all the places to which he is emotionally linked—in memory and anticipation, but also through mental association.

However, this requires a frame of mind quite different from the one we have burdened ourselves with in our respective societies. It also requires another kind of environmental behaviour; in fact a different kind of environment altogether. The one will have to sustain the other—assuming that a habitable world is what we have in mind!

Impervious to the spirit of ecology, society at large behaves with insanity instead of grace, like a half-wit with two left hands. A far cry indeed from the way the Dogon tend the natural morphology of their environment.

◄ BAIRD: A minor reservation admittedly, but I wonder how much hangs by the question 'if society has no comprehensible form, can it acquire a counterform which is human?' For surely there is in *our* world a sense in which incomprehensibility itself is human; indeed I see now that I am simply questioning the tone here. It is, I take it, exactly such an incomprehensibility that Van Eyck (rightly) admires in Rykwert's 'dream', where 'order and chaos, continuity and discontinuity, the determinate and the indeterminate, are gratifyingly united'.

'Everything functions, only man himself does not', Arp once said. As it happens, our dealings with the landscapes of the world (and the mind) are such that, assessing the achievement of our civilization in terms of the effects—and there is every reason to do so—Arp is proved right. Disregard the delicate intricacies of the limitless microcosm; trespass into the limitless macrocosm and frighten the angels; mess up the Mississippi and the Mekong in between.

If that is what is desired, it can soon be fulfilled (there is a limit even to the limitless) and we shall get what we are looking for: mediocosm, limitless mediocosm. It will no longer be necessary to cross-identify all things from basket to universe in order to achieve some ground of certainty within appreciated mystery, for the identity of each thing and all things will have been levelled. Man falling in line with entropy at last.

Yes, and paradise will be just like mediocosm. Nothing will be different in any way, except toothpaste, which will be smoother and softer and more refreshing, so that those in paradise may know that they are no longer in mediocosm.

Hurry, switch on the stars before the fuses go.

Lacking the Spirit of Ecology

[1] James Joyce. *Finnegan's Wake.*

[2] Aldo van Eyck, 'Bouwen in de Zuidelijke oasen,' *Forum; maanblad voor architectuur en gebonden kunsten*, VIII, 1 (January, 1953), 28–38.

[3] *Minotaure; revue artistique et littéraire*, 2 (June, 1933). A special issue subtitled 'Mission Dakar-Djibouti, 1931–1933.'

[4] Paul Parin, Fritz Morgenthaler, and Goldy Parin-Matthey, *Die Weissen denken zuviel; psychoanalytische Untersuchungen bei den Dogon in Westafrika* (Zurich: Atlantis Verlag, 1963). In a French translation *Les blancs pensent trop* (Paris: Editions Payot, 1966).

[5] Parin *et al.*, *Die Weissen denken zuviel* . . . 31.

[6] Joseph Rykwert, *Idea of a Town* (Hilversum: G. van Saane, 1963).

[7] *Ibid.*, introduction by Aldo van Eyck.

[8] Christopher Alexander, 'A City is not a tree', *Architectural Forum*, CXXII, 1 (April 1965), 58–62: 2 (May 1965), 58–61. Also in *Design*, CCVI (February 1966), 46–55.

I brought forward the leaf-tree, house-city identification at the Team 10 Royaumont meeting in 1964. Christopher Alexander was present at the meeting as a guest and joined the discussion. His subsequently published thesis that a city is not a tree but a semi-lattice is in my opinion neither a valid negation nor a valuable affirmation of the truth in mathematical terms.

I tried to replace the current false 'organic' city-tree analogy, because it is based on the sentimental, though well-meant assumption that, ideally, the man-made city should behave, and hence also be 'planned', according to the same kind of system of ascending dimension and ascending degree of complexity (with a similar one-track reference sequence from small to large – many to few – and from part to whole) as the tree's, oversimplified. The analogy is false the way all such analogies are false – and unpoetic – because it overlooks the real meaning of both city and tree. I replaced it, therefore, by two separate, autonomous though intersuggestive, identifications: leaf is tree – tree is leaf, and house is city – city is house. By their inclusive ambiguity they preclude that a city is a semi-lattice. Also that a city is chaotic and necessarily so (when we say city we imply people). Cities, moreover, as Shakespeare said of man are 'such stuff as dreams are made on'. The dream, of course, implies infinite cross reference. And so does the city. Both are as man is: This is why cities neither should nor can ever reflect the kind of order a tree wrongly suggests. Wrongly, because a tree is not a tree without its inhabitants. They – the birds, beasts and insects – see to it that a tree is also a semi-lattice. Still, a city is no more a tree than it is not a tree. That goes without saying, hence also without mathematics.

[11] Montserrat Palau Marti, *Les Dogon*, Monographies ethnologiques africaines (Paris: Presses Universitaires de France, 1957), 57–8.

[12] Parin *et al.*, *Die Weissen denken zuviel* . . . , 68.

We are grateful to *VIA*, the Student Publication of the Graduate School of Fine Arts, University of Pennsylvania, to Jared Sparks for his translations of the essays by Paul Parin and Fritz Morgenthaler, to Ortrun Niesar, and to Ella Schaap.

Meaning in Architecture

Christian Norberg-Schulz

The functionalism of the period between the wars wanted to do away with everything that had been inherited from the past. Finally the architects took courage to open buildings and cities to light and air, and they aimed at the creation of logical and practical forms. The followers of the modern movement characteristically called their activity *New Building*. The word 'architecture' was avoided because it reminded them of a time when building was considered an art. Instead of creating works of art, they wanted to explore the physical needs and functions of man, and the formal aesthetic of the past was replaced by 'clear construction' and honest materials. Although in practice these intentions were followed only in part, the secularization of architecture was in principle accomplished: it should no longer express and symbolize, but *function*. This attitude is clearly expressed in Hannes Meyer's words from 1928:

Everything in this world is a product of the formula (function times economy)
All art is composition and therefore unfunctional
All life is function and therefore unartistic.

To understand better what is expressed here, it is expedient to take a look at the manifestations of the functionalist attitude. We all know the characteristic features of early functionalist architecture: simple, cubic volumes, an extensive use of glass, white surfaces, open and airy spaces. Le Corbusier introduced the concept of *plan libre* and Mies van der Rohe carried the freedom to its extreme in the Barcelona pavilion. There all rooms were unified to form a continuous, flowing space; even the transition between outside and inside was made imperceptible. However, a clear steel skeleton created a kind of coherence. If we want to unify these features in a space-conception, we may define functionalist space as *homogeneous extension in all directions*. An open, uniform, all-embracing space

Bedroom for Erwin Piscator, by Marcel Breuer, 1927.

'Domino' scheme by Le Corbusier, 1914

was the ideal, a space without secrets or differences of quality. The tridimensional co-ordinate system furnishes an appropriate illustration. When the spaces were flooded by *light*, it was not only for practical reasons, but undoubtedly to emphasize their uniformity and logical character. Hence functionalism succeeded in creating a new formal language which expressed the desired freedom of the epoch as well as its belief in a logico-scientific mastering of reality.

The practical presuppositions of functionalism are also well known. The new needs and forms of life brought forth by industrialization, could not be satisfied by the traditional building types, and the miserable conditions in the large cities demanded a complete revision of the human environment. But functionalism is not fully explained by pointing to these factors. Basically it was a result of deeper forces. Above all we may consider it a typical expression of the post-mediaeval world.

In the Middle Ages reality was understood as an ordered cosmos. Every social role, every human product and every human action got its meaning in relation to this order. All the elements of reality thus were *qualitative* and their significance was determined by divine revelation. The mediaeval conception of the world may be compared with a building and it is natural to think of the hierarchical and differentiated form of the cathedral.

The following epochs are characterized by man's wish to free himself from this conception. Not only did he protest against the totalitarian authority of the church, but he wanted to be free to explore reality unrestricted by dogmas and traditional ideas. Instead of *belonging* to the world, man put himself rationally and critically opposite it, and the mediaeval 'building' was replaced by a growing collection of *experiences*. The real driving force undoubtedly was the dream of one day being able to face the world 'as it is'.

Architecture has reflected this general historical process. Already during the Renaissance, simple arithmetical relationships were substituted for the irrational geometry of the cathedral, and, though baroque art and architecture demonstrated a new interest in the 'supernatural', it is important to realize that its spatial dynamism points towards the 'open' space of modern architecture. Only recently, however, did it become possible to profess an empirical architecture in accordance with what Le Corbusier has called the 'natural' possibilities and conditions of man. The immense advances of science finally seemed to give the wish for a rationalistic conception of the world a firm basis and modern building technique made a correspondingly functional architecture possible.

It is not surprising that this prospect was met with enthusiasm in wide circles. Its clarity and contact with practical reality could not be rejected and, although many emotional barriers had to be overcome, it was natural that the modern

◀ FRAMPTON: Not all of the pioneer twentieth century functionalists were unconscious of our present cultural predicament; least of all Le Corbusier, who attempted to make his differences with Hannes Meyer explicit in his 'Defense de L'Architecture' published in *L'Architecture Aujourdhui*. Le Corbusier's spatial organisation was always 'hierarchic' in contrast to Meyer's theoretical homogeneity.

Ulm.

Dipoli building, Helsinki, Finland, by Riema Pietilä.

movement turned out a success. Functionalism brought architecture to terms with the general development; undoubtedly a necessary presupposition for the creation of a meaningful environment. So today the 'international style', dreamed of in the 'thirties, has become reality. Glass towers and slab-like apartment buildings dominate the city-scape, and *analysis* has become the architect's point of departure. We should rejoice: the goal is in principle reached, and although we are still fighting poverty and housing shortage, it seems to be only a question of time before man has satisfied his needs.

But in this situation of welfare and material progress, tendencies start to present themselves which have an alarming effect on the apostles of the rationalistic movement. Many leading architects again profess an architecture where the practical-functional aspect only seems to play a secondary role, and their formal language appears irrational and far-fetched. During the last years this phenomenon has become so common that we cannot any longer consider it a casual escapade from the safe road of reason.

A general doubt in the basic creed of early functionalism is obviously expressed. This doubt however hardly concerns the axiom that any building should *function*. Nor does it mean a return to the obsolete attitude of historicism and national romanticism. Rather it grasps the core of the problem: is the rational world-conception of the post-mediaeval period actually satisfactory?

The doubt in the post-mediaeval world-conception is not created by the architects. It appears in many fields and is a well known theme from literature and the daily newspapers. It is pointed out that 'enlightenment' and 'freedom' did not solve man's problems, and that our modern world has created passivity and discontent. Erich Fromm says: 'Contemporary man is certainly passive most of his free time. He is the eternal consumer. He takes in drinks, food,

◀ FRAMPTON: The degree to which slabs empirically disposed have effectively eroded the pre-existing 'syntagmatic' street format of our cities should cause us to question the attainments of twentieth century functionalism. Our achievement has been to perpetuate 'empty' forms abstracted from the totality of Le Corbusier's Utopian Socialist vision.

cigarettes, lectures, sights, books, films; everything is devoured, swallowed. The world has become one large object of his desire, one large bottle, one large breast. Man has become the eternally expectant and disappointed suckling.' Although the problem is well known, it is hardly understood. The rationalistic idea of man of the post-mediaeval epoch is still dominant and the belief that all problems may be solved if we grasp reality as it 'really is' is generally accepted.

Let us therefore take a closer look at this reality. We know that our immediate experiences have little in common with a scientific conception of the world. We neither experience atoms nor molecules, but more or less clear 'phenomena'. For instance when we meet another person, we are immediately aware of certain *properties* which produce positive or negative reactions in ourselves. These properties are of the most varied nature. Appearance and title may influence our experience. The phenomenon 'new acquaintance', thus, is put together of a series of *qualitative* components which spontaneously are mixed in a seemingly illogical manner. A scientific description of the person would not in any way be a substitute for this total experience. Even if it were possible to know another person completely and translate this knowledge into a physiological and psychological description, the description would not be exhaustive, as it can never cover the fundamental fact that qualities *of different kinds* are spontaneously mixed when experiencing. *Perception* thus functions in a way which is basically different from scientific *analysis*. The experience has a 'synthetic' nature, it grasps complex wholes where components which have no logical relationship are nevertheless completely integrated.

The so-called visual illusions demonstrate this clearly. In the well-known Müller-Lyer illusion the two horizontal lines have the same length, but they are experienced as being different, because the situation as a totality determines perception. In this particular case the enclosed *areas* influence the experience of the lengths. We *may* of course to a certain extent succeed in excluding these 'disturbing' factors, and concentrate ourselves upon the length of the lines. In daily life we often have to make such 'choices', but it is rarely expedient to take an analytic-scientific attitude, in the real sense of the term.

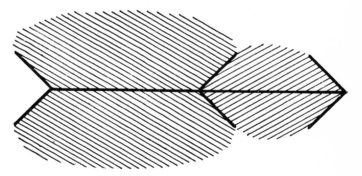

Most of us are fooled by the Müller-Lyer figure. But that does not mean that we always experience a *similar* world. From daily life we know that our agreement is rather deficient; therefore we can neither accept '*naive realism*' which assumes that the world 'is' as it is spontaneously experienced. For instance, a psychological experiment has shown that the same coin is experienced as larger by poor children than by rich. Differences in subjective value here influence the perception of a physical dimension. We also know that the same things may 'change' according to our mood. When we are depressed even what is dear to us may seem repulsive.

Our 'orientation' to the environment is therefore often deficient. Through upbringing and education we try to improve this state of affairs by furnishing the individual with *typical* attitudes to the relevant objects. But these attitudes do not mediate reality 'as it is'. They are to a high degree socially conditioned and change with time and place.

From what has been said above I must conclude that we can never experience or describe reality 'as it is', and that this term is meaningless. The nature of phenomena deprives the world of any imminent static or absolute form, and shows that we are facing an interplay of ever-changing forces.

To be able to participate effectively in this interplay man has to orientate himself among the phenomena, and to preserve them by means of *signs*. For this purpose man has developed a great variety of 'tools'. Science is certainly a very important one, but I have suggested that other types of symbol-systems are equally important. The more complex and differentiated the environment becomes, the more we need a large number of different symbol-systems.

Science takes care of one kind of symbolization. It aims at giving exact and and objective *descriptions* of reality. Through abstraction and generalization it defines laws or *objects* which are ordered in logical systems. In daily life we rarely intend the 'pure' objects of science. Rather we experience complex phenomena which are spontaneously given as synthetic wholes. As such they are not accessible to thought because they fall apart during analysis. The objects of science may be compared with a mesh having defined properties. When such a mesh is thrown over reality, only what has corresponding properties will be caught, the rest disappears through the holes. What is lost by the fishing-net of science, may however be grasped by other kinds of symbolization. Especially important for us is the large class of symbol systems known as *art*. Art does not give us *descriptions* but direct *expressions* of certain aspects of reality. We may say that art *concretizes* phenomenal complexes or *life-situations*. We may of course study art scientifically, but such an investigation is no substitute for what this symbol-system itself achieves. We may not, however, use scientific criteria of *truth* in connection with art, as our usual concept of truth presupposes a logical order of pure objects. The non-descriptive symbol-systems therefore do not give us *knowledge*, but experience and direction for our behaviour.

It is important to notice that art is able to concretize *values* and *individual situations*. The most important function of art is, however, that it may concretize *possible* complexes of phenomena, that is, new combinations of known elements. In this way it expresses previously unknown life-situations and releases new experiences. Hence it contributes to change man and his reality.

From birth on we try to orientate ourselves in the environment and establish a certain order. A *common* order is called *culture*. The development of culture is based upon information and education and therefore depends on the existence of common symbol-systems. Participation in a culture means that one knows how to use its common symbols. The culture integrates the single personality in an *ordered* world based upon meaningful interactions.

'Primitive' man does not distinguish consciously between the different types of symbolization, but merges them all into magic and myth; good and bad 'forces' are associated with everything. This of course does not happen in an accidental way, but reflects the fact that the environment really may be said to consist of hostile and friendly objects. Primitive man is never *indifferent* to the environment and he is therefore unable to 'abstract' its separate aspects. Instead he concretizes his 'synthetic' environment in relatively diffuse symbols which are expressed by magic and ritual.

Later development has tended towards a specialization of the orientations and the corresponding symbol-systems. Science has slowly purified its cognitive-analytic attitude, technology has developed as an instrumental activity on this basis, and art and religion no longer can pretend to *describe* the world. Without this specialization man would have been unable to face his ever more complex environment. It is therefore an integrating and necessary part of the development. It is less pleasant, however, that the only orientation we are today *taught* is the cognitive one. We learn that what counts is to *understand* everything. Before, an attempt was made to hold the variety of life through concretization; today we only accept 'scientific truth'. This truth may, however, be in conflict with existing values and may produce conditions we are not mature enough to master. We thus accept a fragment of culture as if it were the whole.

This destructive situation is due to some fundamental misunderstandings which have had a decisive influence on the post-mediaeval epoch. They centre upon the concept of 'freedom'. If freedom has any significance, it ought to mean 'freedom to choose between qualities', a freedom which in any society has its limits. Instead, we tend always to regard freedom more as 'freedom from form'. Modern man regards all forms as restrictions; it may be forms of human interaction, dress, language, art or religion.

The artists are also victims of the same misunderstanding. Instead of helping man to build up a common meaningful world, today they generally define their aims as 'self-expression'. Any expression, however, is only of real interest when it *transcends* the self.

The behavioural and artistic freedom certainly stems from a need for a counterweight to the rigid logic of science and the dry instrumentalism of technology. But the situation is hardly satisfactory. Giedion has defined it as 'a split of thought and feeling'. Modern thought freezes the world into pseudo-scientific schemata, and our feelings are no longer channelled by means of common forms and symbols. Rather they appear as individual and incomprehensible *outbursts*. Contemporary man is only able to communicate on a quasi-logical level, and the lack of cultural nourishment gives him little to communicate anyway. The result is that we start to consider ourselves inferior. When contemporary films and literature represent man as repulsive, amoral and corrupt, it is a natural consequence of this one-sided glorification of scientific 'truth'.

The inferior conception of man is usually defended by saying that 'honesty' is necessary to make the world get 'better', or by pointing to the demand for 'freedom'. We can only ask: Honesty to what? Honesty to 'the nature of man' is a meaningless definition, and 'honesty to contemporary man' also cannot have a precise meaning in a world with 3 billion inhabitants. We are thus continuously confronted with cultural products which make a disintegrated idea of man common: products which have a strongly destructive character.

What is said above is not intended as an attack upon thought and science, and it is not my aim to propagate a new mysticism. Specialized orientations *are* necessary, and signify a progress beyond magic and diffuse emotions. But it is dangerous to make *one* particular orientation become *dominant*. I have thus tried to show that the post-mediaeval epoch is collapsing, in spite of all material progress, because it left essential aspects of man to the arbitrariness of a misunderstood 'freedom'. The dissolution of the non-descriptive symbol-systems destroys the basis of culture and leads to human anarchy.

Seen in this light, the present tendencies in architecture get a wider perspective. When many architects cannot any more content themselves with an efficient satisfaction of man's *physical* needs, it is because of an increasing doubt in the post-mediaeval conception of the world. It is interesting to notice that the new tendencies made themselves felt already *before* the war, for instance in the work of Le Corbusier and Aalto. It is therefore superficial to see the war as the reason. The explanation lies, as we have seen, deeper. The actual confusion in architecture, thus, is basically *positive*, expressing a wish to regain a more complete interpretation of the concept of 'architecture'. We are no longer satisfied with making our buildings functional, but want them also to be 'meaningful'.

FRAMPTON: Giedion's immediate pre-war call for a 'new monumentality' has certainly found its response in post-war developments in the USA and elsewhere. Although the present confusion may be positive the problem of formalism remains. It is for this reason that I have emphasized the necessity for determining the cultural context and complex of each building task. ▶

What, then, is covered by the term 'meaningful architecture'?

As a work of art architecture concretizes higher objects or 'values'. It gives visual expression to ideas which *mean* something to man because they 'order' reality. Only through such an order, only by recognizing their mutual dependence, do things become meaningful. Such ideas may be social, ideological, scientific, philosophical or religious. We have seen that early functionalism in reality transcended the purely functional, by developing a space conception which symbolized a logico-scientific view of the world, and we understand that it stands and falls with this view. The new tendencies in architecture indicate that a new conception of the world is being formed, a conception which the architects are participating in shaping. It is still too early to describe its contents in detail, but as far as I can see, it will partially consist of a new and clarifying distribution of the roles between art and science, while politics, which recently have played

a dubious role as pseudo-science and pseudo-religion, will slip more into the background. Those countries which have let politics become dominant are actually characterized by a striking *lifelessness*, not necessarily because man is oppressed, but because the manifestations of life do not get real nourishment. The coming conception of the world certainly will take over many elements from the post-mediaeval epoch, above all the idea of an 'open' and dynamic world. We will therefore hardly experience a *break* with the space conception of functionalism. Rather we may talk about a differentiation and humanization.

The widened conception of architecture is so far best known as a rather imprecise demand for 'environmental qualities'. Experience has shown that the neutral and homogeneous space of functionalism offered few possibilities for a varied life to take place. With a certain surprise politicians and planners have had to recognize that man wilts in their 'perfectly' planned neighbourhoods. He longs for the narrow streets and irregular squares of the old town he came from, or he escapes into nature. Both tendencies offer valuable indications about the space conception which is growing out of that of functionalism. To understand better what this means we have first, however, to take a look at some earlier space conceptions.

It has been known for a long time that the phenomenal qualities of space have little in common with the homogeneous, mathematical concept of space. Aristotle pointed out that the directions are experienced as being *different*. 'Up' is something completely different from 'down', and 'backwards' is not the same as 'forwards'. All human activities are directed forward, while the distance traversed is behind. Man strives forward or draws back. He may also direct his attention upward or downward, but usually in a less concrete sense. Erich Kastner says strikingly: 'Even someone who has long ceased to believe in Heaven and Hell', will hardly confuse the meaning of 'above' and 'below'. Still we speak about 'building castles in the air' or about giving things a *basis*. The *vertical axis* as a symbol and the *horizontal plane* as a possibility of expansion, therefore illustrate the fundamental properties of human space. In this space the *way* becomes the most fundamental motive, the way towards a goal, the way between the 'stations' of life. The way is always directed from the known towards the unknown, but man always returns to the place where he belongs; he needs a *home* which designates his point of departure and return. Around this centre his world is organized as a system of ways which gradually dissolve in the distance. In the past all peoples usually considered their own country as the centre of the world. Often they defined this point exactly; for the Greeks it was the *omphalos* in Delphi, for the Romans the Capitol as *caput mundi*. For others a holy mountain may have played this role, or a totem-pole which symbolized the *world-axis*. We know nomadic tribes which always carry such a pole with them; the centre of the world is where they happen to be at the moment.

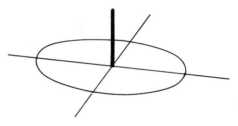

The basic structure of human space.

FRAMPTON: This is the central thesis of Mircea Eliade's book *The Sacred and the Profane*: i.e. that, for 'religious' man, space is non-homogenous.

Today we may not any more profess the religious ideas formerly connected with the conceptions of space, but psychologically space is still anything but homogeneous. And the basic structure expressed by the words 'centre' and 'way', is still valid. Above all, *home* is still connected with those values which are known to us and give us security. 'Home', 'town', 'country' therefore denote what I called 'higher objects': social attachments and cultural products. When we are travelling in a foreign country, space is 'neutral', that is, not yet connected with joys and sorrows. Only when space becomes *a system of meaningful places*, does it become alive to us. Let me express this in the words of Goethe:

> *Field, wood and garden were to me only a space,*
> *Until you, my beloved, transformed them to a place.*

What then, does all this have to do with architecture? If the place where we belong becomes meaningful just because we live there, does not this imply that architecture as an art is superfluous? Experience teaches us something different. Firstly it is essential to recognize that the 'landscape' where we live is structured *in advance*. It *contains* a system of existing 'ways' which define our possibilities of 'movement'. From childhood on we accommodate ourselves to this system,

224

and are therefore in general *conditioned* by our environment. We all know what this means. Let me remind you of cities which are divided into West and East End, or cities which are divided by a river, so that the *bridge* becomes necessary as a connecting 'way'. The phenomenal quality inherent in the latter case is expressed with intensity in the writings of Kafka, which reflect the narrow and dark streets and large squares of Prague, and not least the Charles Bridge which leads from the old town towards the *castle*.

> *Men, walking across dark bridges*
> *past saints*
> *with dim lights.*
> *Clouds, moving across the grey sky*
> *past churches*

with fading towers.
One, leaning on the parapet
looking into the evening water
his hands on old stones.

Kafka's poem from 1903 tells us that the environment only becomes a meaningful *milieu* when it offers rich possibilities of identification, when its ways lead across 'dark bridges' past 'dim lights', 'towers which fade away in the mist' and 'old stones'. Human life cannot take place anywhere, it presupposes a space which is really a small cosmos, *a system of meaningful places.*

It is the task of the architect to give the places such a form, that they may receive the necessary content. It is for instance the architect who designs the home in such a way that it offers security and peace. The 'domestic peace' is still a living idea, although functionalism tried to reduce home to a set of minimum dimensions. The investigations concerning the number of steps the housewife makes in the kitchen, are in this respect characteristic. Less alive, however, is the understanding for the urban *milieu* which was expressed in the poem by Kafka. At the most, the city of today inspires the poets to run away. The reason for this state of affairs is obviously that the modern city does not offer enough possibilities for life. Its streets and squares are no longer places for man, but simply means of communication, and the 'ways' of man have become subways. It is now time to press the demand for a regaining of urban place. The empty co-ordinate system of functionalism has to be filled. But man is not able to fill it *alone*, he has to have *forms* to aid him, that is, buildings and works of art which create places with *character*. Today man only finds places with character in nature. There he can still experience the large plains, the narrow valleys, the sombre and the smiling spaces. But even if we in the future will be able to preserve some free nature, the relatively inarticulate experience of nature cannot substitute for the urban milieu, where defined spatial characters are connected with all human activities.

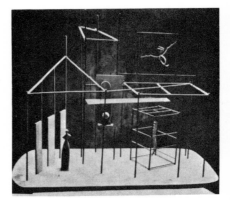

The Palace at 4 a.m., *by Alberto Giacometti.*

As suggested above it is not easy to say anything concrete about the content and forms which should make up the second age of modern architecture. We have to content ourselves with putting forward some hypotheses regarding its general properties, and perhaps pointing to tendencies which support these hypotheses. I have suggested that any space has a limited capacity for receiving life. The neutral co-ordinate system of functionalism, in a certain sense, offers all possibilities, but it is still waiting to be filled with life. The 'open' world it symbolizes is one of the great ideas of the post-mediaeval epoch. But there **is** today a danger that openness is mistaken for *emptiness*. Only by combining the co-ordinate system with what architectural theory and history teaches us about the *varieties* of space, may we hope to transform the open world into an open system of meaningful places. Evidently the architects have already faced this problem. In his later works Le Corbusier aimed at the creation of expressive spaces, and the 'cluster' structures of recent city planning show a wish to overcome the functionalist lack of urban space.

However, to get ahead it is important that we improve our theoretical foundation. We possess today highly developed logicomathematical tools, but we have hardly understood which factors these tools ought to serve. It does not help much to analyse and order, if what we are ordering is irrelevant. In my book *Intentions in Architecture* I have made a first attempt at indicating the factors which are covered by the concept of 'building task'. I have thus stressed the importance of supplementing the physical milieu with a *symbol-milieu*, that is, an environment of meaningful forms. Architecture, being an artistic activity, unifies factors of the most different kind in a single 'synthetic' form. As a synthetic activity it has to adapt itself to the form of life as a whole. Only recently has one tried to specialize architecture by reducing it to a mere practical activity. It is not easy either to understand or to practise a synthetic activity in a period of emphasized specialization. But synthetic activities are essential for interaction and cultural development.

The chapel at Ronchamp, by le Corbusier.

POST SCRIPTUM

The purpose of this article (written three years ago and given as a lecture at Cambridge University in spring 1966) was to explain certain 'expressionistic' tendencies which have dominated the architectural scene during the last decennium. It was not intended as an attack upon functionalism, but aimed at the establishment of a basis for an extension of this idea, taking the *whole* of man into consideration. In addition to the physical milieu which was outlined by the modern movement between the wars, comes the demand for a *symbol-milieu*—a meaningful environment.

The idea has been met with a certain suspicion. It may seem 'romantic' and unrealistic in an epoch characterized by incessant change and quick consumption. The demand for a symbol-milieu has not, however, been created by pretentious architects. It stems from a general and healthy reaction to the lack of real psychic nourishment in our pragmatic world (and psychic nourishment should not be confused with superficial stimuli). In fact, the idea of a symbol-milieu is much more *realistic* than the ideas of certain Utopians who, having lost their foothold, want to tell us that the world is just as 'mobile' as themselves.

What, then, is the basis of such a symbol-milieu? Meaning consists of relations. All objects are experienced as part of situations; they are connected with other objects. These relations make up their structure as well as their meaning. We usually abstract certain 'inner' relations as the structure proper, and 'outer' relations as the meaning. According to the importance of the relations in life, they are assigned different values. Values are subjective, public and objective (scientific). The public values have primary importance in society, as they enable us to interact and reach beyond our individual limitations. Any action or 'life-situation', therefore, has a structure ahd a meaning.

In the period between the wars one mainly studied the physical aspect of the life-situations. Today we also want to include psychological and social structures and meanings. The environment becomes meaningful when it offers rich possibilities for the occurrence of different and repeated situations. In practice this presupposes that the actions are related to *places*. Traditionally these places had names such as 'room', 'house' and '*piazza*'. Public values, therefore, presuppose a certain stability in the physical environment. In a chaotic and mobile world the relations between objects tend to dissolve and meanings become transitory.

Meanings are transmitted through means of communication. The means are perceptual schemata which are learnt from childhood on, as well as 'artificial' symbol-systems and forms (statements) which make description and expression possible. It is just as important to develop adequate perceptual schemata, as it is to learn to manipulate symbol-systems. In both cases the goal is an 'intentional depth' which integrates the individual with the culture (set of public values etc.) he belongs to.

Perceptions and symbol-systems are not always adequate. The fact that many find a sufficient range of meaning in the present 'flatscape', does not prove that the 'flatscape' is satisfactory or necessary. A form has to be judged on the basis of its '*capacity*'. An ordered environment with relatively defined properties ('character') will necessarily have a larger capacity than a chaotic and mobile 'flatscape'. Man can only perceive (give meaning to) order, and his orientation and identity depend upon the existence of defined structures in the environment.

The capacity of a symbol-system (form) depends on its ability to fit the 'content' it has to receive; the inner consistency and its degree of articulation. A symbol-system and a particular statement thus have a limited range of possible interpretations. The capacity of a symbol-system (form) depends upon its type of structure. A symbol-system (form) has a relevant capacity when its type of structure fits the structure of the 'content'. This fit is established by casual connection, structural similarity (isomorphism) or convention. (Conventions are usually abstracted from isomorphisms.)

Experience shows that life-situations do not find their form automatically. One has to *learn* to express oneself. We should therefore study man and his needs, and abstract the physical relations implied in any situation. A form with corresponding properties would fit the situation. (Psychic content is always mediated through physical manifestations.)

Although the symbol-systems as such are 'empty', there is evidence to support the belief that they imply certain basic isomorphisms. In the article above, I have tried to indicate this by introducing polarities like 'up-down', 'forward-backward', 'closed-open', etc., that is, basic types of relations. These basic relations imply a certain range of possible meanings. It is one of our tasks to define a system of basic relations which has a capacity to cover any type of process (life-situation).

Even in our pluralistic society the possibility for a common basis to the different symbol-systems (forms) therefore exists, making it possible for us to

FRAMPTON: This approximates to my conception of the necessary architectural 'responsibility and tolerance', also advocated by George Baird.

▶ communicate in a generally understandable way in spite of our different sets of values. Man needs to be offered organizing ideas and forms which bring his life-situations into a meaningful whole. The task of the architect is not to 'do as little as possible', but to create forms with an adequate capacity. The capacity of the forms defines their range of meaning.

SILVER: As before, one can be staggered by Christian Norberg-Schulz's erudition, descriptive scope and shrewdness, and still take issue with his prejudices. Prejudice appears in his strict beliefs as expressed by phrases like 'conditions we are not mature enough to master', 'a disintegrated idea of man [in our cultural products is] common', 'a symbol-system . . . [has] a *limited range* of possible interpretations' [italics mine]. Yet recent experiments in education should show, if nothing else did, that we habitually and grossly underestimate our ability to assimilate schemata. So given the time lag between theory and practice, I would suppose Norberg-Schulz's conservatist underestimation likewise to be timid, even dangerous, in discussing architecture's cultural properties and prospects. Therefore, two questions. Can forms contain their *fullest capacities* of meaning if challenging, potentially drastic modifica-

tion by new principles, even by ephemera, is *discouraged*? (For I take it that 'to build up a common meaningful world' will require some retrenchment.) In answering this, remember that even everything we call architecture plays only a small part in the changing environment which we perceive and rapidly absorb into culture, so the up-to-date information would always be 'leaking'. Second, if we were ever again to achieve such a 'common meaningful world' (which presumably means *world*, not neighbourhood) except by subversion, reduction of values or tyranny, wouldn't the politics which Norberg-Schulz thinks lifeless be precisely the means, the sole means, of bringing it about? (Isn't politics simply the procedure of advocacy to overwhelm differences, essential to any plurality – and change – of meaning?) I suggest the answers no and yes.

'*Flatscape with containers*'.

Part 3
Forms of Meaning

The Sitting Position - a Question of Method

Joseph Rykwert

Everybody's first action is to get up. When the child stretches its legs inside the womb it enters on the shocking experience of birth; in the womb we all spend the beginning of our existence in a sitting or crouching position. Every time we get up, therefore, we repeat—more or less consciously, more or less significantly—that original shocking experience; and every time we sit down we retreat into it.

All over the world nowadays people perform the action of sitting down and getting up with the aid of such commonplace objects as chairs, sofas, stools and so on. A great deal of attention is devoted to their exact shape since—notionally at any rate—the user demands comfort of such objects and the aim of all designers engaged on producing them is comfort. But comfort is a complex notion, which varies from person to person, and from social group to social group; varies for the individual throughout his life; more important, it goes through very violent changes independent of our physical constitution but directly connected to the inconstant pattern of convention. The dependence of comfort on social convention is one of the factors which trips up writers on ergonomics[1] when they attempt to define comfort and prescribe the conditions under which it can be obtained. Two writers recently attempted to refine the static results provided by anthropometry into a more accurate description of sitting in comfort by suggesting that comfort is the product of the greatest possible relaxation of the largest number of muscles. It is quite clear, however, from the briefest study of the positions described as comfortable that the situation is relatively independent of the measurements and materials which they use to attain comfort. So for instance in Yoga the primary aim of the different meditation positions is to achieve the greatest relaxation of the Yogi's muscles so that he becomes unaware of his body. This is usually achieved without any mechanical aids or supports, but through internal bodily balance and the control of breath.

Clearly the achievement of this kind of comfort is limited to a small minority—and for relatively short periods of time at that. The many will find it in postures from sitting on the ground with legs fully extended and back unsupported (a position adopted frequently in Asia and Polynesia, particularly by women) to standing upright on one leg with the other one thrust into the crutch (a position favoured for rest by certain tribes in Central Africa). The continuing, elaborate research on human measurement and the publication of such data as if they were of vital importance indicates a sharpened awareness in the mind of the observer of the mechanical complexities involved in the sitting position, also of his inability to appreciate the meaning of the term comfort as it relates to the whole personality rather than any real difficulty in obtaining satisfactory measurements. Anthropometric measurement is not a new technique in any case. A rude form of it interested the Egyptians in relation to canonic proportion; stories about classical artists who attained perfect beauty in the human figure through an aggregate of measurements taken from various subjects admired for their beauty, already implied the difficulties which are met by the practitioners of anthropometric ergonomics. The inclusion of the human figure in square and circle by Vitruvius suggests a further attack on the problem at a higher level, that of reducing the measurements to a total function which would fit all cases. A millennium and a half later Dürer, in his *Unterweysung der Messung*[2] measured a number of human subjects: fat men, thin men, tall men, small men, women of all sizes, babies, dwarfs and so on—but he was unable to reduce the measurements to a formulated canon. The lesson to be learnt from Dürer and his successors is that the variety of human physique cannot with advantage be reduced to a single systematic statement.

In considering objects for human use however, the designer cannot cater for the whole range of these varieties but must seek the type. Even in the days when patrons commissioned the artisan directly, such objects as chairs and tables were not intended for the patron himself but for any number of users. So that in the past, much as now, it was the average for which the designer had to cater, he could not hope to mould the object to the individual.

The great period of furniture design in Western Europe, when there was any number of great individual cabinet makers—Chippendale, Sheraton, Jacob,

Two negroid skeletons, Grotte des Enfants Grimaldi, prehistoric burial in foetal position.

The French cyclist F. Lecocq resting during the Tour de France in 1930.

Oeben—and the first manuals on furniture design appeared, was also a period in which the human posture was investigated scientifically. The first to do this, perhaps, was Nicholas Andry who, in his *Orthopédie*,[3] pointed to the relationship of the postures habitually taken in work and leisure to postural defects; he also noted basic anthropometric facts needed for the design of work and leisure chairs. It is interesting that at least one recent publication specifies a good chair height as being between 8 inches and 12 inches, which is hardly any indication at all, while Andry had already got it more closely to between 9 inches and 11 inches, the usual chair height adopted by cabinet makers and joiners in his day; a lumbar support strictly recommended by Akerbolm in his *Sitting Posture*[4] is already mentioned as being desirable by Andry. The only notable difference between the two is Akerblom's suggestion that the seat should be a little lower and slope backwards; but even this last recommendation has now been put in doubt by more recent writers. In spite of our very sophisticated measuring techniques and highly specialised approach to the problem we cannot reduce these indications to a formulation tighter than had been available to the 18th century cabinet maker. We have only one advantage over him: our superior technical achievement allows us adjustable elements in furniture; these, however, are only used in working furniture by people who occupy the same seat habitually. They have never been adapted (in spite of the attempts of some designers) to leisure furniture. The considerations which guide a designer, therefore, are not refined anthropometric data but the much coarser considerations of material and fabrication, as well as the persistence of certain traditional shapes from which little departure is made.

The dream of certain Utopian designers who thought that the time would come when the anthropometric and technical data would simply be fed into a computer to be processed into a complete specification for a chair is turning out to be chimera. Given a set of data of the kind I mentioned, the computer could—in theory—produce an infinite number of specifications; which means that it is pointless to feed this kind of information into a computer at all. What a computer can do for a designer is to produce a rapid check of a given specification in terms of cost in relation to material and manufacturing process. The mechanised analytical proposition, therefore, does not narrow down the designer's field of decision appreciably; particularly since a specification must be made before it can be checked and, for the sort of purpose that is being considered here, the specification is the design. The computer, therefore, operates on the design once it has been formulated. This situation is not likely to alter in the foreseeable future.

Although I am considering the chair as a useful instance, what I say about chairs is equally true for any other object which needs to be designed. In

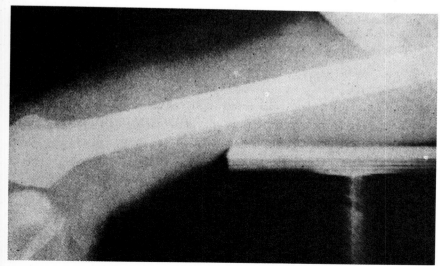

Relation between skeleton and muscle in sitting position; after Ackerblom.

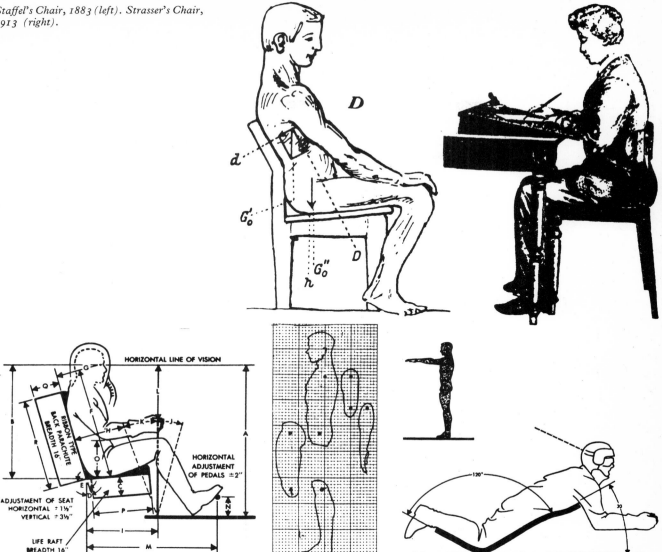

Left and right: seated and lying down positions of pilots of combat aircraft; centre: mannikins used by furniture designers.

spite, then, of the promise which the 'functionalist' theoreticians of the last generation made, the functional solution of problems will not lead to an ideal situation where the arbitrary aesthetic choices will be relegated to a marginal exercise. On the contrary, it appears that the ergonomic study will be entirely permissive and that within the norms that it proscribes—which will not depart much from those we already use—no surprising conclusions will be forced on us. It is inevitable, of course, that this should be so, since the subjects of ergonomic enquiry are entirely conditioned—we all are—by the norms of comfort which our environment proscribes. Ergonomic study based on a statistical sample must inevitably sanction the norm. It is highly unlikely to suggest, for instance, that the cross-legged sitting position (known as the 'tailor' position) should replace our way of sitting on chairs with the legs hanging down. Or even that the standing position is inherently more comfortable than the sitting one. Many functionalist designers have thought of avoiding the problem through turning to intangible factors which they label 'invention' or 'intuition' and leave the final choice which the designer must make to these unquantifiable operations. When the designer comes to exercise his craft, therefore, he is left without the support of a method in spite of the elaborate operations by which his decision has been hedged about. The whole ergonomic discipline can only narrow the field of

235

The Hardoy Chair.

action for the designer; rational discourse about his specific formal procedure is excluded.

I have already observed that little help is forthcoming from the study of materials and manufacture. They again can only provide the designer with points of reference for each individual job. Of the large number of new chairs which appear on the market most are still made of timber and leather; a few of metal and cloth or leather. Among the most popular of post-war models—particularly so with the design conscious public—has been the Hardoy chair, a cheaper but more rigid descendant of the old folding wood and leather chair which was devised for the Italian army as a camp chair in the '20's. Anyone familiar with ergonomic literature, or just willing to think sensibly about posture in relation to furniture, will know the hazards which someone using the chair must meet. And yet this discomfort does not appear to have deterred prospective buyers. The chair as it is now marketed consists of a rigid metal rod frame so bent that it provides four vertical hooks on points for a canvas seat slung between them. This means, of course, that the seat, which is loosely suspended, will mould itself to the thighs and buttocks, and that support will not be concentrated, as is thought desirable, on the ischial tuberosities; also that there will be no lumbar support so that the spinal erectors will never be completely relaxed. The hard edge of the canvas must always press on the under side of the thighs and cause considerable discomfort. What is worse, the fixed form framework and its high protuberances make any changes of position very cumbersome. The popularity of the chair—it continues to be a standard production line in several countries— clearly indicates that the buyers who choose the chair cannot do so on rational grounds. We must therefore assume that the buyers of the Hardoy chairs, like many other customers for design goods, are guided in their choice by promptings quite different from the dictates of reason. The very fact that they do so should be a matter of interest and not of regret to the designer: nothing human should be alien to him.

I have already pointed out that any statistical enquiry, particularly if it is unsupported by sufficiently detailed anatomical information, could only lead to the sanctioning of prevailing norms; the difficulties which attend an anatomical enquiry into such a matter as the sitting position were alluded to many years ago in that fundamental essay of Marcel Mauss on the techniques of the body.[5] It is curious that, although the linguistic and the social anthropologist has a vast area of comparative material on which he can operate, in such matters as techniques of the body, interest is concentrated on extreme situations: Yoga, Polynesian and Bushman tribes, workers in highly stressed situations such as aircraft gunners, etc. But in fact the material available includes the whole range of historical documentation from all civilizations, particularly as it is recorded in memoirs, folk tales, works of fiction and above all (from the designer's point of view) in works of art. A beginning has been made by certain social anthropologists: Gordon W. Hewes, for instance, has made a preliminary attempt to sort out the thousand or so comfortable human postures which have been adopted in various societies.[6] But neither he, nor as far as I know anyone else, has made an attempt to relate these positions to the emotional charge which they must carry or to relate them to the various forms of seat with which they are connected. The seat in particular is a more complex object than is usually realised.

In the West, and I mean from Asia Minor to the Pacific, it has for instance always been associated with authority: so a professor is only properly appointed when he has ascended his chair or *cathedra*; the central church of a diocese bears the name of cathedral because it is the place where the bishop has his seat or *cathedra*. Papal pronouncements which are to carry the full weight of his authority are in fact delivered *ex-cathedra* from his throne and the seat of the first bishop of Rome, St Peter, is enshrined in Bernini's enormous bronze reliquary in the West End of St Peter's, which is known as the altar of the chair.

The western church even celebrates a special feast-day of this great relic on January the 18th; as well as another one of St Peter's throne at Antioch on February the 22nd. Judges and magistrates give judgment also from their seat or bench and in English the collective noun describing magistrates is a bench of magistrates.

To continue with English examples, the coronation throne of the British Sovereign is a large mediaeval construction supported by four lions on the corners and containing a shelf underneath. On this shelf rests a large piece of stone from Scotland known as The Stone of Scone which King Edward I carried off from Scotland. It was on this piece of stone that the Scottish kings were crowned in mediaeval times and the stone, rather than any other emblem, represents the authority of the British king. Edward I and his successors on being crowned sitting on this stone could claim to be king of Scotland. The Stone of Scone is variously reputed to be the pillow stone of St Columba, one of the Irish saints, or the pillow of Jacob on which he dreamed the famous dream at Beth-el.[7] To sit on a holy stone or otherwise to obtain contact with it so as to contact unseen powers is an action which is familiar not only from scripture and the legends of saints and martyrs but seems to be a permanent feature of Indo-European folklore. But the fascination of the holy stone and the way in which the stone is a concentration of earth has been studied at length by certain historians of religion[8] and they also have remarked on the extraordinary way in which the sitting position has come to be associated with authority. This is so in civilizations where sitting on the ground is customary, amongst the Ashanti for instance, and certain other West African peoples. But power of the great chief resides in the stool on which he is enthroned and the stool itself is one of the relics of the nation. In a country where no seats were employed except under Western influence the sitting position is still associated both with authority and with the ground. In the Seiroyo-den of Kyoto Imperial Palace the Emperor sealed his authority by pouring out a libation to his Imperial Ancestors into a large piece of gypsum

which was let into the timber floor so as to allow him direct contact with the soil: the stone block stood for the soil of Japan.

Sitting, authority and the earth are closely associated. The emperor or king, professor or bishop, sitting on their thrones, are therefore sitting on what they rule. The more despotic or repressive the rule of authority the more distorted and mis-shapen the supporters of the seat will appear: which accounts for the violent grotesques which support so many misericords in mediaeval cathedrals; or the wildly gesticulating *papier mâché* seats of 19th century France and England.

The seat puts a distance between the bulk of the body and the ground and it seems that in that vital space gather the mysterious creatures which inhabit our more frightening dreams. It is under the bed that we always look for the burglar; women frequently raise the skirts of a chair to see if there are any of those imaginary mice which nibble on their ankles. These anxious gestures betray fears which often direct and may distort our ways of thinking.

JENCKS: But this expressionist interpretation confounds the importance of convention mentioned above: haven't some of the most despotic rulers sat on a streamlined throne?

RYKWERT: My wording was careless: I did not wish to suggest that despots would order their throne-makers to build them the kind of supports I describe, but that in excessively rigid hierarchical situations, or in very repressive societies, the kind of figuration I speak of may be expected to appear.

Christ and the Apostles, Dome of the Arian
Baptistry, Ravenna. Christ is represented
by the empty throne surmounted by a
jewelled cross.

Throne of Charlemagne, seat of the Holy
Roman Empire, Aachen, 805.

Symbolism, said J. J. Bachofen (overstating his case) begins in the tomb.
Symbolism springs from the way the three fundamental experiences of man,
birth, copulation and death, stress his description of the outside world. Inevitably the sitting position can be associated with the position of the child in the
womb. During the early ages of mankind most peoples buried their dead in that
position, so that by returning them to the womb of that mother from which all
things are born their dead might be born again to a renewed life. Every chair is,
therefore, in some sense a comment on our conception of authority and/or our
conception of birth and rebirth. This is true both for the designer and for the
purchaser.

The Hardoy chair is an obvious instance for examination. Its success as I have
already said, must be based on considerations which have little or nothing to do
with ergonomic choice. On the other hand it would help very little if we were to
enquire from purchasers or owners of the chair why they were moved to buy it
in the first place, since we must assume that here considerations of a symbolic
nature—which are in conflict with ergonomic—or as some would say 'functional'
or even 'rational' ones—must be unconscious. In the context of what has already
been said one aspect of the chair at least is obvious. A concave sack, despite the
physical discomfort it inflicts on the user of the chair, is very much a womb and
offers, if not the physical protection at least the material semblance of the protecting womb. In an age where the relationship with one's mother is so much
discussed (one need only open a psychological text book of any school to see how
true that is) a chair of this nature was bound to have a success, particularly among
the intellectual public, where this question poses special difficulties. It is also this
section of the public which is particularly distrustful of any imposed authority
whether political or religious and prefers authority reduced to a minimal structure like the cage supports of the Hardoy chair.

The Hardoy chair, moreover, divides flexible from rigid elements with great
clarity, which implies that a statement is also being made about the essential

239

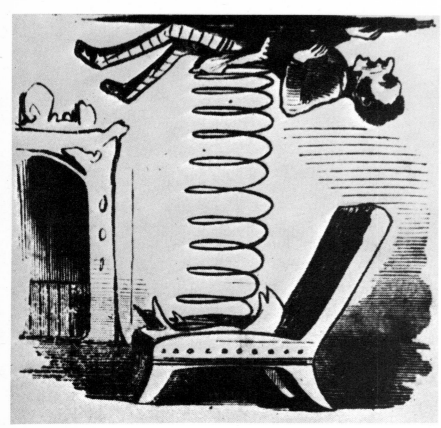

Bergère Brisée, French, circa 1740.

Springs Used for Exercise: Thomas Sheraton, Chamber Horse, 1793. The great cabinet-maker designed this 'chamber horse' for the gentleman who wished his riding exercise regardless of the weather. Since Sheraton could only obtain springs of very limited travel, he used several layers separated by thin boards. (*Quoted from* Mechanisation Takes Command.)

Capitone Stool, French or Italian, circa *1840.*

structure of the object. On examination this turns out to be a pseudo-statement; since it is only one about the articulation of the materials and not about differentiated functions: the ham-fisted joining of the cloth bag to the metal frame is a curious indication of intellectual imprecision.

My account is necessarily *post facto*: my elaborate analysis of an agreeable if arbitrary shape will seem gratuitous to some, absurdly over-literary to others. The enormous success of the Hardoy chair, however, both in terms of sale and prestige, is such a sharp contrast to its operational failure that it requires a rational explanation; particularly so, as it exemplifies the situation (I might even say the failure) of modern design about which enough has not yet been said. This situation arises out of the unarticulated need which most designers and many members of the public feel for shapes whose vitality would have that suggestion of modernity which fashion requires and the change in visual language dictates; but with it also the charge of meaning weighty enough to fill out the visual discourse. This can only happen when the charge is compounded of emotional and intellectual elements. In fact, such a mixture will occur inevitably whether the designer is aware of it or not; a designer who ignores this and attempts to work as if the objects he is producing are not emotionally charged statements, will find that the charge may backfire on him as has happened in the case of the Hardoy Tripolina.

Memory is to a person what history is to a group. As memory conditions perception and is in turn modified by it, so the history of design and of architecture contains everything that has been designed or built and is continually modified by new work. There is no humanity without memory and there is no architecture without historical reference. In a critical situation such as ours where collective memory is continually being denied and its relevance to the contemporary situation questioned, we approach (collectively) the malaise of the psychologist's patient who represses his past in order to justify his irrational behaviour in the present. It is obvious that in such a situation a chronological account of the patient's past would have relatively little value, particularly if it is obtained from the patient himself. What needs to be examined is the twisted or hidden memory of an experience which will illuminate the current malaise. This must, therefore, be the nature of any historical study which would attempt to relate memory to present experience, history to current design. Such redirection of historical study will take time. Its most conspicuous example is Giedion's *Mechanisation Takes Command*, but one or two other writers are beginning to follow suit. However, in *Mechanisation Takes Command* Giedion had not quite (to my mind) drawn the final conclusions which appear by implication in his more recent *The Eternal Present*. Of *Mechanisation Takes Command* one might make the criticism which Claude Lévi-Strauss made of Marcel Mauss' attempt to produce a social theory or symbolism. What Mauss did not realise, and Lévi-Strauss did, was that the attempt was bound to fail because society itself was a symbol.[9]

The great lesson which designers have to learn from Freud is that even the extremes of wilfulness are the products of some form of motivation: and motivation can always be discussed in rational terms. As the psychiatrists have extended the area of responsible moral decision through exposing the pseudo-motives with which we rationalise our approval and disapproval, so they have also expanded the area in which rational discourse about design problems becomes necessary through making us aware of the strong emotional charge which symbolic forms carry. It is no excuse to think that only certain areas (as, for instance, the fronts of public buildings) can be carriers of symbols. The whole of environment, from the moment we name it and think of it as such, is a tissue of symbolic forms: the whole of environment is symbol. To understand how the situation can be managed we are forced to look to the past; no contemporary guide can offer any real help here. This burdens the historian with a task to which he is not altogether used: that of acting as a psychoanalyst to society.

Historiography, particularly as it applies to the history of art, will have to be radically modified if the historian is to perform this kind of function. The grand classification of styles which handbooks teach us will become the immaterial

SILVER: Is the Hardoy chair supposed to be a lousy chair because it is badly detailed? And not because it compromises comfort (which is culturally determined) to provide a mildly original form, and thus a new taste frontier? Joseph Rykwert can't have it both ways. It would be as easy to argue, as David Pye has, that details are relative as that comfort is relative. Then with Olympian detachment one can say that the designer and user may have what they like through the exercise of their civil rights. But from that particularly rarified sitting position, creative invention appears to be just as plastic as human adaptability, so I wish Joseph Rykwert had used his critical method instead of only invoking it.

The figures on the sides of the throne-stool represent the union of Upper and Lower Egypt.

skeleton. But iconology by itself will not provide an adequate substitute: the history of environment must take account of the total person's moving in a social and temporal context. The value of individual works of art or even of overall iconological themes must be studied by reference to the general form of discourse to which they belong: the way in which their makers wanted to address their fellows, to communicate within the given context; also perhaps how this kind of communication can be transformed as the context changes; which suggests that the grand perspectives and the metaphysical speculations of a Riegl or a Wölfflin will decrease in relevance, and the sort of work which will turn out to be relevant will sometimes appear more like the moralising of the 16th century rhetorician than the pseudo-objectivities of our contemporaries. A knowledge of history on this showing can no longer be treated as a cultural ornament or extra curricular pastime: nor even as a useful substitute for theoretical thinking: it is clearly a central part of the designers equipment and of his method.

This article was first published in Italian in Edilizia Moderna no. 86 in 1965. This translation into English has been specially prepared for us by the author.
[1] W. Floyd and D. Roberts: *Anatomical, Physiological and Anthropometric Principles*, in *The Design of Office Chairs and Tables*. London, 1958.
[2] Nuremberg, 1525.
[3] Nicholas Andry de Boisregard: *L'Orthopédie, ou L'Art de prévenir et de corriger dans les Enfants les Déformités du Corps*. Paris, 1741. Andry constructed the word 'orthopédia' from the Greek 'orthos', upright, and 'paidos', child.
[4] Bengt Akerblom: *Standing and Sitting Posture*, 1948.
[5] Marcel Mauss: *La Technique du Corps*, reprinted in Marcel Mauss: *Sociologie et Anthropologie*. Paris, 1958.
[6] Gordon W. Hewes: *The Anthropology of Posture* in 'Scientific American'. February 1957 page 122 following.
[7] Genesis XXVIII, 10–22.
[8] Cf. for example, Mircea Eliade: *Traité d'Histoire des Religions*. Paris, 1953. In particular on the Throne of Stone, cf. Jeanine Auboyer: *Le Throne vide dans la Tradition Indienne*, in *Cahiers Archéologiques*, VI. Paris, 1929.
[9] Claude Lévi-Strauss: *Introduction à la Méthode de Marcel Mauss*, in Marcel Mauss: *Sociologie et Anthropologie*. Paris, 1958.

History as Myth

Charles Jencks

This history wants to show only what really happened. Ranke.

The one duty we owe to history is to rewrite it. Oscar Wilde.

A short time ago, in November of 1966, the noted architectural historian Nikolaus Pevsner gave a radio talk on the current state of architectural culture and the condition of man at the present moment in time. This talk, significantly entitled 'Architecture in Our Time', was even more significantly subtitled 'The Anti-Pioneers' and was meant to summarize the present spirit of the age and, presumably, what we should all do about it. If the listener was in any doubt at the beginning of the talk, it was not due to the subtitle which was clearly meant to show that the present spirit of the age was opposed to the one Dr Pevsner had previously espoused in his conspicuous book *The Pioneers of Modern Design.* By the end of the talk, it was also clear that Dr Pevsner disapproved of what was going on around him; only in the middle did it become slightly difficult to apprehend, when he said of the style of the anti-pioneers that it was: 'the legitimate style of the nineteen-fifties and nineteen-sixties'. Quite how it was legitimate (or morally sanctioned for birth) Dr Pevsner did not make clear. But he did say clearly that his whole argument was based on a building which he saw clearly: (Fig. 1)

> '. . . I want to take as a test case one new English building. Wherever I have been abroad recently, the young know and praise the engineering building of Leicester University by James Stirling and James Gowan. I saw it for the first time last July and had a good look at it. It consists of a low, oblong range with ridge-and-furrow skylighting throughout and, attached to it, two towers, one higher, one less high, set in a staggered way so that they only touch at one angle. Both have, low down but not at ground level, lecture theatres jutting out. These are of exposed concrete; the rest is faced with blue engineering bricks.' The Listener, January 5, 1967.

How could Dr Pevsner, a trained observer, see red tiled lecture theatres become suddenly turned into exposed concrete; how did this red engineering brick also change to blue; by what extraordinary judgment did the style which was so clearly the illicit offspring from the one 'true' style become legitimate? Before an answer is attempted to these rhetorical questions, it is charitable to point out that this error in perception and confusion in judgment is not monopolized by Dr Pevsner, but constitutes the rule rather than the exception: the history of history is in one very important sense nothing but the history of seeing certain objects in terms of other objects and there is no historian, or hominid, who is capable of anything less, a fact which will become clearer and clearer as we analyse the recent history of the modern movement. But although all perception is influenced by conception and thus the spirit of the age tends to waddle back and forth because of these conceptions, it is not inconceivable that the present *Zeitgeist* will be immeasurably aided in its wavering step by a theory of value which can transcend the usual pitfalls of ideology and style.[1] Whatever the future state of architectural culture may be however, the past views of the critics will remain of interest not only because they show what an age happened to believe, but also because they have intrinsic and final worth. What these recent views were and how they succeeded one another will be considered here, by analysing in depth the major historians and placing the other critics in their overall context, starting (as is appropriate) with the formulation that led up to Dr Pevsner's.

In 1923, in *Vers une Architecture*, Le Corbusier crystallized the myth of what was later to be called the heroic period of modern architecture, the 'twenties. The reason for this epithet 'heroic' lay in two places: first and most important there was '*Esprit Nouveau*', the new spirit which was speculative and passionate rather than cautious and compromising as the prevailing academic spirit was supposed to have been. Secondly, there was a new syncretic idealism which was positively aggressive. Corbusier's formulation brought together in a new unity several traditions which had been running separately and were thought to be antagonistic—to wit a belief in social utopianism (he ended his book with the exhortation 'Architecture or Revolution. Revolution can be avoided') and a belief in Purism (the formal beauty resulting from the precision of the automobile and the Parthenon) (Fig. 2). This last equation, the beauty of the Parthenon=

DELAGE. FRONT-WHEEL BRAKE

This precision, this cleanness in execution go further back than our re-born mechanical sense. Phidias felt in this way: the entablature of the Parthenon is a witness. So did the Egyptians when they polished the Pyramids. This at a time when Euclid and Pythagoras dictated to their contemporaries.

EYES WHICH DO NOT SEE

III

AUTOMOBILES

automobile beauty, was perhaps his most significant contribution because it fused the constant architectural value of precise form seen in light with the ability of reason and standardization to produce exactly such crystalline forms. This equation proved inexorable: it established a necessary connection between simple, Platonic forms—engineering design—and a natural evolution toward perfect standards. And it lasted, theoretically at least, for thirty years until it was finally refuted by Banham in a series of articles on the machine-aesthetic which reversed the postulated connections. Banham pointed out how objective, engineering design may lead to ephemeral, complex forms which are the reverse of perfect standards, as in the Buick V–8. But his refutation fell on partially deaf ears, because Corbusier's equation seemed so perfect. In any case, the aggressive element, the belief that reason and mass production could solve urban problems, distinguished Corbusier from the prevailing spirit. The common denominator in his new equation was logic, clarity and light.

'We must aim at the fixing of standards in order to face the problem of perfection.

The Parthenon is the product of selection applied to a standard.

Architecture operates in accordance with standards.

Standards are a matter of logic, analysis and minute study: They are based on a problem which has been well "stated" '.

And then Corbusier went on to say: 'Architecture is the skillful, accurate and magnificent play of masses seen in light'. Lest there could be any doubt that this was the eternal value of architecture, he illustrated the primacy of pure form from the 12th century B.C. to the present and finalised the superiority of this constant tradition with his new marriage to social Utopianism and mass production: his own Citrohan House of 1921. The key building which later embodied this myth, in idea if not in fact, was the Villa Savoye, and the only failure of this masterpiece was that it was not a literal result of mass production and was not for a whole society, but rather just the *image* of such an intention.

However, in intention the balance of conflicting traditions was perfect: man could have the eternal value of the Parthenon with the modern reality of mass production. The only thing stopping him was 'Eyes which do not see' the beauty latent in industrialization. But the answer to this was the architect who did see. It was not just an evolution toward beautiful standards, but above all 'a pure creation of the mind'. In other words, evolution projects, the individual selects; he is the only one responsible.

'It is a question of pure invention, so personal that it may be called that of one man: Phidias made the Parthenon . . . Phidias, Phidias the great sculptor made the Parthenon.

There has been nothing like it anywhere or at any period. It happened at a moment when things were at their keenest, when a man, stirred by the noblest thoughts, crystallized them in a plastic work of light and shade.[2]

Only with the man of genius constantly alert to evolutionary forces could a masterpiece be snatched from the mass production process. And this man naturally had to be a cool but passionate rationalist, for no expressionist would have the nerve or sensibility (a point quite likely true). The other polemicists of the heroic period were equally aligned against Expressionism and equally committed to Corbusier's new hybrid of rationalism/social utopianism/Purism (Diagram I–I).

DIAGRAM I MYTHICAL TRANSFORMATIONS

			MYTHEME A		MYTHEME B	
			rationalism	social utopianism	Purism	Expression-ism
I–I	CORBUSIER	(1923)	+	+	+	–
	Gropius	(1925)	+	+	+	–
	Hilberseimer	(1926)	+	+	+	–
	Platz	(1927)	+		+	
	Giedion	(1928)	+	+	+	–
	B. Taut	(1929)	+	+	+	
	Sartoris	(1932)	+	+	+	
I–II	Mumford	(1924, 1931)	–	–	–	+
	Hitchcock	(1929)	–	–	+	+
	Cheney	(1930)			+	+
	HITCHCOCK & JOHNSON	(1932)	–	–	+	+
I–III	Kaufmann	(1933)	+		+	
	P. M. Shand	(1934)	+		+	
	PEVSNER	(1936)	+	+	+	–
	Behrendt	(1937)	+	+	+	
	Richards	(1940)	+	+	+	
	GIEDION	(1941)	+	+	+	–
			rationalism	cultural interpretation		
I–IV	Zevi	(1945, 1950)	–	+	+	+
	Rowe	(1947, 1950)		+	+	+
	Summerson	(1949)		+	+	+
	Wittkower	(1950)		+	+	
	Mumford	(1952)		+	+	+
	Dorfles	(1954)		+	+	+
	Jaffe	(1956)			+	+
	BANHAM	(1960)	+	+	+	+
			rationalism	social utopianism		
I–Va	Whittick	(1950)		–	+	+
	Hamlin	(1952)		–	+	+
	Sartoris	(1957)		–	+	+
	HITCHCOCK	(1958)		–	+	+
	Joedicke	(1959)		–	+	+
			rationalism	cultural interpretation		
I–Vb	Benevolo	(1960)		+	+	+
	Kidder-Smith	(1961)		+	+	+
	Banham	(1962)		+	+	+
	Hatje En.	(1963)		+	+	+
I–VI	V. SCULLY	(1961)		+	+	+
	MAS Sym.	(1964)		+	+	+
	Collins	(1965)	+	+	+	–
	N.-Schulz	(1965)		+	–	+
	Jacobus	(1966)			+	+
	Sharp	(1966)		+	–	+
	BANHAM	(1966)	+	+	–	+

However, parallel to this heroic period there was a counter tradition in America which was extolling somewhat different virtues, less concerned with the machine age and more concerned with the quality of life that an architecture implied. Lewis Mumford's work during the 'twenties left out all the recent developments in technology and concentrated on architecture as a reflection of the social values implicit in any building (i.e. if an office building were over-sized and caused congestion, it was an evil, however much it was the Purist essence of business and verticality). Yet the major part of the American tradition was neither socially conscious nor Utopian, like the Europeans, but rather more rigorously aesthetic in its interests. It reduced the modern architecture that was created in Europe to three stylistic principles. Architecture was seen as volume, regularity and undecorated surface. Hitchcock and Johnson's metaphor 'The International Style' was conceived for two main reasons: to introduce America to some stylistic principles fashioned in Europe during the 'twenties and to slice these from the extreme functionalism of those such as Hannes Meyer who claimed that style did not (or rather should not) exist. The key building was Mies van der Rohe's Barcelona Pavilion, of which the authors Hitchcock and Johnson insisted 'aesthetic rather than functional considerations determined the plan'. Their description of this building was characteristic of the way the modern movement was to be looked at in America for the next thirty years, a cool, aesthetic way which enraged certain Europeans: (Fig. 3).

> 'The walls are independent planes under a continuous roof slab which is supported on light metal posts. The absolute regularity in the spacing of the supports does not prevent wide variety in the placing of wall screens to form separate rooms. Rich materials: travertine, various marbles, chrome steel, gray, black and transparent glass'.

They ended their polemic with an excited repudiation of opposite extremes and came triumphantly down in favour of a sensible moderation.

> 'Those who have buried architecture, whether from a desire to continue the past or from an over-anxiety to modify and hurry on the future, have been premature: we have an architecture still'.[3]

Thus, in spite of some differences over the importance of social concerns, American critics were united in favour of a romantic attitude toward style (as expression) and united against extreme functionalism and standardization, two of the driving themes of the European movement (Diagram I–II).

3

Barcelona Pavilion by Mies Van der Rohe, 1929.

250

It was the European movement which was loosing some of its Utopian drive in the 'thirties because of the rising Fascism which tended to support only that kind of architecture which was classical and Nationalist. Nazism in Germany, Fascism in Italy and Communism in Russia were all combined in a single bureaucratic style to quash the modern movement. Almost the best things to come out of this period, as a result, were the new formulations made to justify the failing heroic period and its philosophy of design. Nikolaus Pevsner, a German refugee in England, was the first to crystallize modern architecture into the one and only 'universal style of our century'. His object was to marry the social responsibility of the English tradition stemming from Morris with the rationalism of Gropius and to contrast this with a decadent, personal Expressionism: a formula that Behrendt, Giedion and Richards who followed him also adopted in part (Diagram I–III). Thus the 'classic' interpretation of the movement was forged into a consistent whole of logic, health and standardization, contrasted with irrationality, disease and individuality. This was one of those clear periods in history (such as the French Revolution) when all the usually contrary traditions coalesced and came into one focus, so that any one part of the equation inescapably implied the others and anyone who was not irresistibly drawn to the right answer was either dull or reactionary (or quite likely both). It was one of those periods like the 'twenties when architectural form carried a meaning that had great coherence and even greater morality. Modern Architecture was as simple and right as the Periclean Greek style and as opposed to Nationalism as the High Gothic (that certain modern architects were both nationalistic and Nazi was passed over in silence by these historians). The key building for Pevsner was Gropius' Fagus Factory with its open corners of glass and steel, and he ended *The Pioneers of the Modern Movement* with his myth of agnostic realism:

> 'It is the creative energy of this world in which we live and work which we want to master, a world of science and technique, of speed and danger, of hard struggles and no personal security, that is glorified in Gropius' architecture'.

What interested Pevsner most (as could be seen from his other works) were those moments in history when a style had reached a certain stage of development that might be called 'classic' and clear, those moments of impersonality when the sensual delights and easy gratifications of expression are renounced for more important, cognitive values. Thus in his book on the Pioneers, he constantly referred to 'the style', by which he meant the rational, anonymous style of the Bauhaus. The way the book was written suggested that history moved toward this style with an unusual single mindedness, as if the 'spirit of the age' were particularly strong minded and intelligent at this time. Thus:

> 'There was no question that Wright, Garnier, Loos, Behrens, Gropius, were the initiators of *the style* of the century and that Gaudi and Sant'Elia were *freaks* and their inventions fantastical rantings. Now we are surrounded again by fantasts and freaks, and once again the validity of the style is queried to whose prehistory this book is dedicated.' (My italics.)

There is no question here that Pevsner is writing a certain kind of myth accentuating the rational style and leaving the 'freaks' Sant'Elia and Gaudi in the footnotes until the 1960 edition when they were, as he put it, 'resurrected' to the main text. The omission of the expressionists is consistent both with his interpretation of history and the recurring themes, or mythemes, which orchestrate the book:'rationality, *Sachlichkeit*', etc. (Diagram II). He ended this recent edition of the book much as he started it, having to account for a negative spirit of the age that is present today:

> 'Expressionism was a short interlude . . . we are now in the middle of a second such interlude . . . the structural acrobatics of the Brazilians and all those who imitate them or are inspired by them are attempts to satisfy the craving of architects for the surprising and fantastic, and for an escape out of reality into a fairy world.'[4]

Now these last two quotes are particularly interesting not only because they show that architecture is experienced morally but also because they are bound to provoke an equally expressionistic stance, whatever it might happen to be. But the point here is not my reaction but the fact that the tone of historical writing has once again become moral and personal. And the reason for putting it this way is that historians often become most personal when they claim 'objectivity'. Thus Pevsner can say, ending his most recent attack on the present Expressionist 'Interlude':

'. . . what irks me lies open to attack on objective grounds . . . It (Expressionism) is ill suited for most architecture now because the majority of buildings are built of industrially produced—i.e. impersonal—materials, because the majority of buildings are built for large numbers of anonymous clients and because the first concern of the architect must therefore be with their practical and emotional needs, and not with the expression of his own personality.' The Listener, January 5, 1967.

Of course in our scientific age there is nothing so emotionally charged as the word 'objective', so we are immediately prepared in this case to answer Dr Pevsner with equally 'objective' arguments from sociologists who condemn anonymity and industrialists who show that every machine-produced form can be completely unique and personal. However, whether sociologists are more or less 'objective' than Dr Pevsner is not the point at issue either. What is at stake is the whole question of morality in architecture.

There is sufficient evidence that almost every experience of architecture has a moral component to it; certainly the polemicists of a style and the leading architects use moral terms to describe it. As is well known, the protagonists of the International Style justified their work in terms of metaphors such as health, restraint and objectivity which they contrasted with disease, confusion and subjectivity. Not only do these metaphors show a correct experience of some work in the International Style, but they also point to a common centre of value, a synaesthetic centre, where values converge—where purity reinforces restraint and they are together indicative of the higher value of 'honesty' (which refers to the balance of contending values where none is unduly usurping the function of the whole[5]). Further than this, we find that critics like Pevsner or Ruskin or Mumford write some of the best criticism precisely because it is highly moral. Precisely because they are moral their experience is concrete, because it is concrete it is (for moments) acutely faithful to the work. Yet their own particular morality is too limited (whether Puritanical or social) because it makes them condemn great artists whose beliefs they do not share. Because Pevsner believes so strongly in social responsibility he misunderstands Michelangelo, Gaudi and Corbusier (that is to say significant figures) which is quite surprising when one considers that he is the most renowned (if not influential) historian writing today. But I should be more exact. Pevsner does not misunderstand these great architects; rather he writes very perceptive criticism about them that also happens to be exactly wrong in its final verdict. His final judgment blends his own beliefs in a restrained style into the observations and thus he comes up with a verdict that is absurd—that Gaudi is a 'freak' etc. Clearly what is needed is a morality which can distinguish beliefs embodied in a work from their expression, a morality which could say 'this is a great work which fails because the beliefs are trite' (even granting a final convergence of expression and belief). Because, for instance in architecture, a prison may be a great work even though designed by a madman and containing an inhuman program—that is a great failure. The critic must be able to make this distinction if he is to keep his own morality. Clearly then what is needed is a theory of value which is supra-ideological,[1] or failing this we will have to put up with the continuing imbalances and following corrections that come from a limited morality and now constitute the historical dialectic (Diagram I).

The next major historian to consider the modern period in terms of 'the spirit of the age', although a slightly different spirit than Pevsner's, was Sigfried Giedion. In his *Space, Time and Architecture*, Giedion spent at least half his introduction preparing the reader about how subjective history writing is and has to be, and the other half justifying his particular, subjective approach: the 'universal outlook' which seeks to reconcile the schism that has developed since the 19th century between thinking and feeling:

'The historian, the historian of architecture especially, must be in close contact with contemporary conceptions. Only when he is permeated by *the spirit of his own time* is he prepared to detect those tracts of the past which previous generations have overlooked.

History is not static but dynamic. No generation is privileged to grasp a work from all sides . . . This is not an invitation to prophecy but the demand for a *universal outlook* upon the world . . . Our period is a period of transition . . . Ever since the opening of this transitional period, our mental life has been without equilibrium . . . We have behind us a period in which *thinking and feeling* were separated . . . The degree to which its methods of thinking and feeling coincide determines the equilibrium of an epoch. When these methods move apart from each other there is no possibility of a culture and a tradition. These are not deliberations remote from our subject. We shall soon see that it was just this unfortunate schism between its thought and feeling which struck down the magnificent power of the 19th century . . . The historian is not solely a cataloguer of facts; it is his right and indeed his duty, to pass judgement . . . it is the business of the historian to distinguish accurately between (constituent and transitory facts).'[6]

We see immediately what Giedion is up to: he is writing history based on certain interpretations with which he seeks to change the course of future history. With his perception, no doubt true in one sense, that the 19th century was a tragically divided age, a schizophrenic age, he goes on to preach the unification of the artist with society and the scientist. Every architect he considers is considered from this viewpoint, and every architect he omits is omitted from this viewpoint: for the same reason that the architect failed to achieve an equilibrium between thinking and feeling (for instance the Expressionists Gaudi and Scharoun, see Diagram II).

Thus there is a consistent relation between the major interpretation (that we must have a universal, balanced outlook), the various themes which orchestrate this interpretation (that we have balanced and unbalanced artists which lead to periods of tradition or schism), his theory of history (that only constituent facts are important) and his omissions (the transitory facts or Expressionists). Far from these consistent relations dismaying us we say, as we say of the musician, that his tone has integrity.

Actually the tone of Giedion is achieved by a film technique of cutting and splicing bits of information together in a continual sequence of movement. His book, like a myth, is not so much a logical argument as a sequence of technical information, art, sociology and morality strung together on a linear belt— like a film—to unwind in a staccato of cuts and contrasts which show like a metaphysical poem the strange correspondence between things different. And like the Metaphysical poet, he tries to achieve the resolution of art and science by yoking and tying them within a single tone. If one sensibility handles all this disparate material, it becomes reconciled precisely because of a single tone; and the virtue of Giedion is his discovery of a tone which could handle a large amount of commonplace facts, the dull everyday objects which fill our environment (for instance the development of the bath tub in his 'anonymous' history *Mechanization Takes Command*). In this sense, Giedion performed the service for historians that Picasso and Eliot had performed for artists: the sanctification of the banal through a single shifting tone.

In fact it is a shifting tone which allows both Giedion and Pevsner to transcend the limits of their own conscious position; in spite of their professed intentions, they both incorporate themes counter to their major myth which do justice, although slight, to the Expressionists. Thus Giedion, in an apparent reversal of position, praises Aalto for 'irrationality' and Pevsner treats Art Nouveau in a somewhat sympathetic way. Many examples could be given of this counter

Sigfried Giedion's equation in Space Time and Architecture *which allied ideas of simultaneity and transparency in Cubism with a space-time concept in architecture to produce another effective conjunction.*

theme—or mytheme B in Diagram II—which, with mytheme A, mediates between two opposites: for instance thinking and feeling or standardization and ornament. And it would be wrong to think that either historian considers mytheme B entirely derogatory, although it tends to be negative. What we do find in both historians is the mediation between opposites we find in a living myth where the purpose is to resolve such irreconcilables as the living and the dead. And also as in a living myth the reconciliation is achieved in a similar way through the introduction of convergent terms which contain enough of both opposites to achieve a symbolic resolution (Gropius serves this purpose for both Pevsner and Giedion). In Giedion's case the polar opposites are incorporated into his position in the belief that the methods of art and science either are or should be alike, and in Pevsner's case they are presented together with the belief in a 'high tension' between poles which results in the High Gothic or the International Style. Unfortunately this resolution of opposites by mediation is presented only in parts and their conscious position favours mytheme A.

However, when Giedion does achieve a resolution it is through his favourite theme, the space-time concept, and the key building which illustrates this

concept, the Bauhaus. Giedion's space-time theory called attention to a new experience of inner and outer space experienced together, as well as pointing to the new way to experience modern architecture—as continuous movement around asymmetrical, hovering volumes rather than as stationary, staccato points of view in front of symmetrical façades. The transparent corner of the Bauhaus was compared to the transparency in Picasso's *L'Arlésienne* (Fig. 4) and the space-time concept was also found in every significant twentieth century development from Cubism to relativity theory to city planning with its long vistas and isolated buildings (confirming the idea that the historian can project all sorts of theories on to works which he later seems to have found in them). Perhaps Giedion went too far in his enthusiasm for this metaphor, but it did serve one incidental purpose: it provided him with a means to cut across the usual stylistic and ideological barriers and write the most articulate history of the modern movement. That Giedion's formulation is the deepest and most effective we have to date can be seen by the continual attempts to refute it—first with Zevi's 'Organic Architecture' which was conceived as a foil to the extreme, rationalist position of the 'thirties.

DIAGRAM II   THE MAJOR HISTORIANS——

HISTORIAN	MYTH	MYTHEME A–MYTHEME B	RESOLUTION	CONSISTENT OMISSION
PEVSNER	SPIRIT OF THE AGE 'the style'	RATIONALITY–EXPRESSIONISM clarity–fantasy standardization–ornament *Sachlichkeit*–confusion social responsibility–art for art	GROPIUS	CHOISY Guadet; until 1960 Gaudi, Sant 'Elia
GIEDION	SPIRIT OF THE AGE 'balanced outlook'	TRADITION–SCHISM balance–imbalance unified artist–dissociated society cons. facts–trans. facts	BAUHAUS	EXPRESSIONISTS Gaudi, Scharoun, Mendelsohn, Dutch Exp.
BANHAM	FUTURISM 'entirely radical'	FUTURIST DYNAMISM–ACADEMIC CAUTION change–symbols technology–convention speed, danger–stasis mechanization–classical trad.	NO resolution, presents opposites	GAUDI Scharoun English Garden City Movement
SCULLY	EXISTENTIALISM 'image of democracy'	ROMANTIC CLASS–ROMANTIC NAT. Baroque order–Fragmented Eclecticism Rationalism–continual flux	CORBUSIER Kahn	SHORTNESS precludes pattern of omission

IV

Zevi used the example of Wright's organic architecture to show what he hoped would be the movement's liberation from the first 'programmatic phase', from Fascism, from Nazism and from the tendency of 'closed minds' to accept Classicism as a substitute for 'thinking and feeling'. He was the first historian after the War to document the close alliance between these negative forces which had combined to break the back of the movement; and thus, like Mumford, he interpreted architecture in cultural terms and saw it (when 'modern') as an expression of man's spiritual freedom. Organic thus meant for him what it meant for Wright: a formative approach to art, the natural product of the shaping powers of imagination. The key building which unfolded according to the laws of imagination (not the rule of convention or will) was Bear Run by Wright—the antithesis of all that was mechanical and Fascist (Fig. 5).

Concurrent with Zevi's revaluation were other more scholarly attempts to deal with the movement. But they all had one significant new contribution in common: they tried to interpret the movement in terms of the cultural situation facing the architect rather than the *Zeitgeist* (I–IV). Colin Rowe found some parallels of the movement both in Palladio and Mannerism, Summerson traced the roots to the ugliness and morality of Butterfield, and Mumford traced the roots to the functionalist philosophy of Greenough. This search for wider influences culminated in Banham's scholarly metaphor 'Theory and Design in the First Machine Age'—a book whose title explains clearly the new mixture of an academic and machine-oriented mythos.

Banham's main contribution was to resuscitate the Expressionists and more especially to bring to life the Futurists such as Sant'Elia. The motorcar was suddenly more beautiful than the Victory of Samothrace; speed and danger were more real in the modern world than art. Sant'Elia's image of the 'New City' with its multi-level circulation, swooping towers and diminutive people, was the most natural (as well as imitated) expression of our age (Fig. 6). Banham quotes the proto-Futurist Rosso: 'we are all of us merely lighting effects'. Light and movement dissolves mass, man dissolves as well; everything is expendable, perishable, shifting, illusory; the only constant is change. It seems at first that we are here close to the secular realism of Pevsner, but there is a positive difference—destruction. Destruction not only makes one momentarily value what one is removing, but it also makes one move beyond all the temporal values of this world without being compromised by convention. Perhaps it would be more accurate to say that distortion is valuable, as the metaphysical painter Francis Bacon has shown, because it makes one see and revalue the norm. A shocking metaphor stretches the world out of shape and we reassert its worth by pulling it back together. In an analogous way Marinetti's insistence on destruction, which Banham notes approvingly, makes us insist that change is only half the question:

> 'We who insist that a masterpiece must be burned with the corpse of its author . . . against the conception of the immortal and the imperishable we set up the art of becoming, the perishable, the transitory and the expendable.'

Or rather Marinetti insists that without the conception of the imperishable his art of the perishable would have no meaning, no enemy. Here, in Banham's book, we have his main position of insistent, Romantic change coupled with transcendental technology. This ascetic equation is similar to the heroic myth of the 'twenties in which most European architects saw all the symbols of this world as corrupt and illusory. And this equation will be later used by Banham, like St Bernard's God, to chastise all the symbolic values of this world—the Pioneers, the Brutalists—even those whom Banham defends, because they are essentially traditional.

But oddly enough, in method, Banham is closer to the tradition of humanist scholars than any other historian; he seeks to connect the stated intentions of an architect with his design, whereas most of the historians considered here are more interpretive. Banham is, like Panofsky and Wittkower, interested in tracing the relation between ideas and forms and he uses at length the scholarly methods

5
'Falling Water' at Bear Run, Pennsylvania, by Frank Lloyd Wright, 1936.

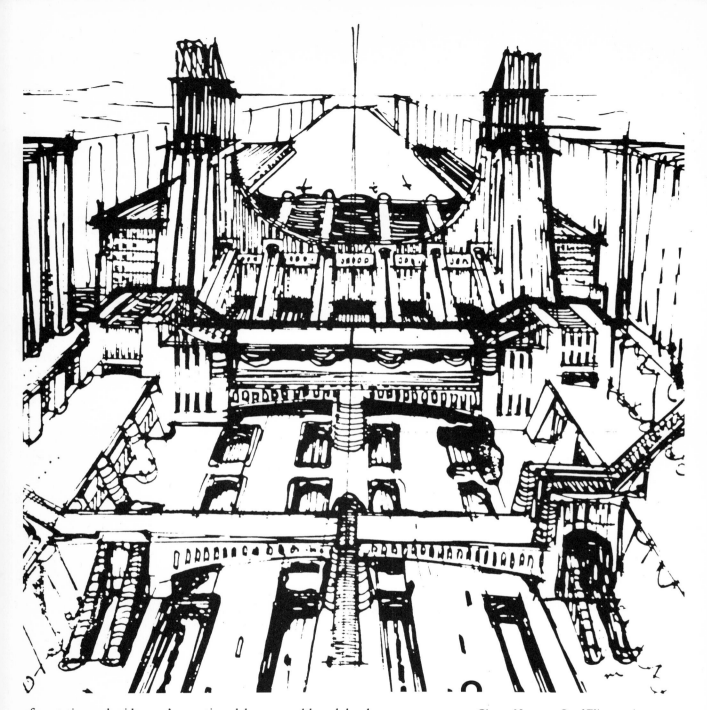

Citta Nuova, Sant'Elia project 1913. Movement dramatized and frozen in reinforced concrete; five levels of traffic segregation, exposed elevators and escalators.

of quotation and evidence. As mentioned, however, although he shares a common method he has an opposite philosophy. Where Panofsky suggests that one should learn as much about one's own position in cultural history as possible, understand one's own limitations and 'cultural equipment', Banham suggests that perhaps one might discard this 'cultural load' and travel light with the fast moving train of technology.

However, like Pevsner and Giedion, much of his book is concerned with mediating his own conscious position or myth. What he shows, beautifully at times, are the variegated strands of tradition interweaving through the years and brought together tightly by a syncretic genius such as Oud (in his polemic) or Corbusier (in his Ville Radieuse which interweaves most of the 19th century).

258

Banham unravels the strands and thereby exposes the language of tradition. What he shows is that in spite of the modern movement's wish to be totally new and radical it was renewing old ideas of the academy. He shows that the architect uses and re-uses ideas and they use him; when they become too explicit like 'functionalism' or 'formalism', he discards them, but only to have them appear again in a new form as unsupportable as his nature.

However, this, like Pevsner's and Giedion's Expressionism, is contrary to what he wishes history to be, and a moral imperative is allowed to emerge explicitly in the first and last chapters:

'At one extreme, the Futurists proposed to dump their cultural load, and rush forward equipped only with a new sensibility; at the other extreme, men like Perret and Garnier in France felt that the new should be, in Paul Valéry's phrase, subject to the old, or at least the outlines of the old. Between Futurist dynamism and this Academic Caution the theory and design of the architecture of the First Machine Age were evolved.'

In the last chapter he uses a critique of Buckminster Fuller's to criticize the Pioneers for their symbolic intentions, and he implies that Fuller's use of technology is somehow more pure and free from such preconceptions:

'The Dymaxion concept (of Fuller) was *entirely radical*, a hexagonal ring of dwelling-space, walled in double skins of plastic in different transparencies according to lighting needs, and hung by wires from the apex of a central duralumin mast which also housed the mechanical services . . . The structure does not derive from the imposition of a Perretesque or Elementarist aesthetic on a material that has been elevated to the level of a symbol for "the machine", but is an adaptation of light-metal methods employed in aircraft construction at the time.'

Actually, as Giedion shows,[7] the Dymaxion concept was not radical at all, since the mechanical core and central mast go back to the 19th century. But the interesting thing about Banham's critique is that it is based on the assumptions that Fuller's work is not as symbolic as the Pioneers' and that there is some absolute realm of beatitude removed from critical appraisal where forms are honest and completely true to technology. This place of grace it turns out is where there is an '. . . unhaltable trend to constantly accelerating change'.

'It may well be that what we have hitherto understood as architecture, and what we are beginning to understand of technology are incompatible disciplines. The architect who proposes to run with technology knows now that he will be in fast company, and that, in order to keep up, he may have to emulate the Futurists and discard his whole cultural load including the professional garments by which he is recognized as an architect. If on the other hand, he decides not to do this, he may find that a technological culture has decided to go on without him.'[8]

As already mentioned, Banham spends the major part of his book showing how language and tradition have made it impossible for man to be completely radical and dump his cultural load, however much he may want to; and aside from the nature of reality changing, he shows how this will continue to be the case. The major themes which recur in his book mediate between the opposite poles of Futurist dynamism and Academic Caution, and Banham presents both with equal regard for sources. In fact, of all the historians discussed here, he is the only one to show sufficient interest for architect's intentions to quote and discuss them at length; he is the only one to take Corbusier's theories seriously enough to dispute them. Through the obvious paradox of critical attack, he shows more appreciation for Corbusier than those who would dip him imprecisely in praise. And Banham, like Jane Jacobs and other iconoclasts, affirms tradition in the very process of denying it and rather than this critical tone being negative it is positively exhilarating at times, particularly when it is aimed at an orotund reputation. However, like Pevsner and Giedion, Banham would reset the polar opposites so that they balance around his first major theme, and like these historians he tends to omit Expressionists who do not have a Futurist sensibility such as Gaudi and Scharoun (Diagram II).

PAWLEY: Surely all he meant was that a house conceived according to such (at the time) alien concepts was immune to fine arts criticism. As far as I know no one has disproved him.

JENCKS: Nothing is immune to fine arts criticism, least of all technolatry. It can and does attack everything – witness for instance Banham's own application of Panofskian iconology to the *Man, Machine and Motion* exhibition of 1955. As for what he 'meant' as distinct I suppose from what he 'said', this, as the New Critics said, is between the author and his putative depth psychoanalyst; the critic can only go on what the author says. What this continually amounts to here is a quasi-ideal realm where things are 'entirely radical' with 'no cultural preconceptions', the realm of technutopia.

PAWLEY: After many years it has finally dawned on me that when Banham writes 'technology' he means 'engineering'.

V

Parallel to this new insistence on a situational interpretation was an encyclopaedic reaction, if it may be called that, which hoped to balance the distortion caused by interpretation (Diagram I–Va). These historians implicitly substituted the metaphor of 'no interpretation' at all and this tradition culminated in Hitchcock's neutral metaphor 'Architecture Nineteenth and Twentieth Centuries'—a large compendium of disparate forms. These works were probably indicative of the uncertainty of the 'fifties: where dogma and style seemed inadequate as a basis for selection, the only hope lay in amassing enough works so that they might hopefully speak for themselves. Significantly there was no key building or architect of the moment, unless the group firm of Skidmore, Owings and Merrill. The myth was formulated in terms of number and size. The sheer plenitude of facts was a value (a possibility not alien to the structure of myth). Out of this developed a more delicate tradition, a series of encyclopaedias which tried to determine value through criticism (Diagram I–Vb).

VI

Following this in the American aesthetic tradition, Vincent Scully sought to refute Giedion and the *Zeitgeist* again; and he offered an interpretation of the movement based on 'the image of modern man'. The key building which embodied this image was not only Corbusier's Chandigarh, but also Louis Kahn's Medical Laboratories (Fig. 7):

'. . . Kahn's design enforces human recognition of an environment both meticulously realistic and heroic in itself: one which is intended to make the scientist feel not in command but both mysteriously and comprehensively challenged. So Kahn's buildings are reverently built, monumentally constructed of toughly jointed parts. They reject the easier releases of spatial continuity and neo-classicism alike, and most architects seem to regard the method which is producing them as the most potentially creative, truly "objective" one in use today. The movement carried on by the "Brutalists" in England, most particularly by Smithson, is symptomatic of the trend: first toward Mies, then toward Aalto, now in the direction of Kahn.'

Although Scully's book is subtitled 'The Architecture of Democracy' it is more an interpretation of buildings in terms of the image of Existentialism:

'The old, *Christian*, preindustrial, predemocratic way of life has progressively broken away around him [Modern Man] so that he has come to stand in a place no human beings have ever quite occupied before. He has become at once a tiny atom in a vast sea of humanity and an individual who recognizes himself as being utterly alone . . . Like all art, it [architecture] has revealed some of the basic truths of the human condition . . . First we might travel backward in time until we reach a chronological point where we can no longer identify the architecture as an *image* of the modern world.'[9]

We travel backward quickly to about 1750 when the absolute order of the Baroque is broken up into fragmented extremes: Romantic-Classicism and Romantic-Naturalism (Romantic because a single aspect of reality is exaggerated in both cases). Then we travel forward at quite a breathless rate (the book has only thirty-eight pages for two hundred years) while the two polar concepts intertwine with a new series of antitheses in a 'continued flux of becoming'. Neo-Platonism and perfectionism are contrasted with freedom and escape to the suburbs and are synthesized in Picturesque Eclecticism, and so on in a never ending flow of felicitous *aperçus* and images.

Actually, in agreement with the other historians, Scully finds those architects who created a tension between the polar concepts he uses to be the best and so he confirms the judgements of the others from yet another position. He bases his position on metaphysical ideas and sees architecture as an image of a changing metaphysics of man due to 'the disappearance of God'. Architecture is thus interpreted as revealing a new image of man's position on earth, his new relation to the cosmos and death with God. This is probably the most legitimate single way to treat architecture (if one is reduced to single ways)—as iconology—

Medical Research Building, Pennsylvania, Louis Kahn, 1961.

but also the most dangerous because it is so highly interpretive and removed from the architect's conscious intentions. Thus Scully sees architecture since 1750 as a search for a democratic, open form and an image which will embody the existential act that gains meaning through being made; and it doesn't much disturb his history that most of the architects he considers have been anti-democratic and consciously believed in God. He has the unenviable task of making Mies, Wright and Corbusier existentialists of some sort when according to Sibyl Moholy-Nagy they all 'transcendentalized' their work and believed in God.

But that doesn't matter. The strictly iconological interpretation of architecture doesn't rely just on the conscious intentions of the creator; as Panofsky shows, the underlying symbols and meaning (iconology) may in fact be contrary to the conscious intentions (iconography), so the historian has the interpretive licence to contradict all the facts and intentions as long as he makes a plausible argument for his interpretation. Scully's case for existential democracy fluctuates with each architect; sometimes it is convincing as in the case of Corbusier, other times he gives it up and switches back to the old concepts of Romantic-Classicism and Romantic-Naturalism. But of the major historians, Scully is the one who does not consistently omit one type of architect due to a moral commitment. Perhaps because his history is so condensed that no pattern of omission can appear, for he is just as committed as the other historians to an interpretive position (which would actually seem to slight the European rationalists).

Scully's work, although often consciously opposed, is similar to Banham's *The New Brutalism* in that it concentrates on a cultural interpretation of architecture (through the image). Banham's recent work, however, places the architect

261

more deeply in his social situation so that the value of his intentions is made apparent. For instance, the Smithsons' Hunstanton School with its evocative open drains (Fig. 8) gains its honesty only by being placed in a cultural situation where compromise and romanticism had flourished for a moment:

'No mystery, no romanticism, no obscurities about function or circulation . . . But what caused even more profound shock, not only to architectural romantics but to educational sentimentalists as well, was the attitude of the architects to the materials of which the school is constructed . . . Walls that are brick on the outside are brick (the same bricks) on the inside, fairfaced on both sides. Wherever one stands within the school one sees its actual structural materials exposed, without plaster and frequently without paint.'

If Giedion was the first historian to invigorate his book with personal reminiscence, Banham was the first to base his on the delicate tool of first hand gossip—the only tool which can replicate the emotions and tone of a movement. His book starts off with a discussion of how the concept of Brutalism was born behind the scenes of the London County Council as a Swedish import dropped on to an ideological situation where it could grow into a strong counter-attitude (counter to the attitude which Pevsner was upholding, among others). Of course, the elevation of gossip and who called who 'Sandy' where and on what occasion brought out the intended reactions. For instance, Pevsner countered the counter attack by insisting that the genesis of the term Brutalism did not determine its legitimate meaning any more than the first insult of '*maniera gothica*' determined the legitimate meaning of Gothic.

But insult, gossip and other annoying methods of Brutalism were very effective because they opened the clogged channels of architectural dialogue and showed that critical attack could be more stimulating than praise. If it had always been known that a critic could damn a man by faint praise, at least the Brutalists were some of the first to show that a critic could praise a man by faint damnation. After elucidating the Brutalist myth for his whole book, Banham becomes so attached to the idea of a real '*architecture autre*', having nothing to do with any symbolic values whatever, that he ends the book with a final barrage:

'The Johnsons, Johansens and Rudolphs of the American scene were quicker than I was to see that the Brutalists were really their allies not mine; committed in the last resort to the classical tradition and not the technological.'[10]

This has the net effect of bringing round the Smithson guns into action (to use their metaphor of architectural war). The Smithsons lobbed a bitter-sweet shell into Banham's camp, saying: 'For the period up to 1958 Banham is well up to *Time* standards. He was engaged and it shows. From 1958 onwards he seems not to have been paying attention.' (The Smithsons are explicitly answering Banham's last volley.) There are two main points to these minor hostilities which the vituperation may obscure: for one thing the Smithsons are using particularly modern tactics and techniques consistent with their position of realism towards modern society. The double-edge reference to *Time* magazine, their treatment of Banham as a war correspondent, their reference to his writing 'instant history'. But the Smithsons' real contribution in extending contemporary possibilities was in the format and intention of their counterblast: it was designed for insertion in the front part of Banham's book so that errors could be corrected and the historical myth could take on a deeper, collective dimension—thus creating in this way the open dialogue of the open society which they have so often proclaimed and thus confirming Wilde's precept that the one duty we owe to history is to rewrite it. The other point of this aggression was its limited honesty toward a technological society. The Smithsons, often reiterating the indifference which characterizes a technological society, have found like so many artists of their generation that the one attitude which can penetrate this apathy is hostility. They have said that a technological world is characterized not by opposition to the artist or belief in anything at all, but rather by mere indifference. If anything positive is to be accomplished in this situation it is always in the face of overwhelming pressure, the pressure of boredom and neutrality. In this sense any positive act is by nature a battle. And the influence of Brutalism as an attitude of

8

Hunstanton School, washbasins in cloakroom, Alison and Peter Smithson, 1950/54. Literalism at its most metaphorical.

battle must have gained greater currency among architects, because they too felt the fundamental truth toward the situation must be one of anger. It seems natural that anger would become prominent, because anger is an emotion most easily conveyed and sustained in the face of indifference; it is an emotion we presumably feel most at home and natural with. Of course it has its limits, as the Smithsons show: it is abrupt, short-winded and epigrammatic; it never reaches any great intellectual or emotional heights (unless perhaps in *Caligula?*). Our appetite is no more satiated by war bulletins than it is by *Time* magazine. But it does have a limited relevance to the present moment as can be seen by the way it communicates and opens the channels of debate. Almost all the architectural critics got into the act responding, correcting, clarifying, preaching, gossiping, shocking, firing, shelling and generally behaving with a fine distemper.

Parallel to this new awareness of architecture as a cultural statement (or embattled dialogue) was the interest in Kahn and Van Eyck, precisely because they asserted a relation between meaning and form. And for the same reason also, Norberg-Schulz's book *Intentions in Architecture* became relevant. It developed both the theoretical aspects of meaning in architecture as well as defining the intentional relation of a building to its cultural context. It was suddenly as if the architectural polemicist could explain why Corbusier's Poissy was a valid statement even if not a literal result of mass production: the intentional aspect of architectural meaning was suddenly made explicit. Norberg-Schulz described how the meaning of a phenomenon, particularly an art object, consists in its relations to other phenomena and how if it is not related to a coherent set of 'higher intentional poles' then we remain uncomprehending. Thus intention was not only important in architecture, it was determinant of meaning. But the joker in the pack was us: our ability to shift the intentional poles in the object by shifting our set of intentions.

'Perception, therefore, is anything but a passive reception of impressions. We may change the phenomenon by changing our attitude. Brunswik used the word 'intention' instead of attitude, to underline the *active* character of the act of perceiving . . . If we intend the real length, the intermediary object will approach this; if we instead intend the projective length, the intermediary object will move in this direction. In both cases, the intermediary object is a product of the two possible intentions, with the intended one dominating.'[11]

Or thus, the shape of myth depends on a transaction between our intentions and those of the object. Finally, from an architect within the movement, the mythical nature of reality was made explicit from a psychological point of view as it was shown how our experience of architecture is effected by attitude, knowledge and belief. And we could thus understand why Pevsner, who believed passionately in the International Style and believed that the Leicester building was Expressionist, could then see it as blue and concrete rather than as red and brick. But Schulz's exposition was not entirely unique, because with his metaphor of 'intentions', Scully's of 'Democracy' and Banham's of 'Brutalism' we are really back to the old cycle of cultural interpretation (Diagrams I–II, IV, VI).

When we generalize this inquiry strange conclusions appear about the possibilities within history and the modern movement. We notice that architecture is always experienced morally and that its very meaning is dependent on this: a fact which I have tried to exaggerate here in order to bring out its undeniable presence so that some of the problems which it raises can be faced. If architecture is experienced morally, then at any moment in time there will be certain meanings which are dependent on sequence, on what has gone just before and what exists in the present culture. To take a well known example, Alberti's appeal to purity and whiteness could only be understood as a negation of the easy gratifications in such preceding architecture as Suger's where gold and brilliant jewellery had been an appeal to the sensual symbols of divine light. And this appeal of Suger's could only be understood when sanctioned by the mysticism of light and seen in contradiction to the white asceticism of Saint Bernard's architecture; and Saint Bernard's noble simplicity could only be appreciated both as an affirmation of religious control and a denial of sensual expressionism at Cluny; and Cluniac expressionism etc.

Now if we step into this time dependent dialectic of meanings a strange thing will happen: we will become persuaded of each world in turn and understand the beautiful actualization of meanings in each architecture. If on the other hand we decide to remain outside and detached and decide that since meaning is not fixed once and for all it is therefore nonsensical or irrelevant (a reaction not unknown in the 20th century), then we just remain uncomprehending. In this sense it is better to be prejudicial and know one set of meanings well, rather than open minded and unknowledgeable. But this alternative is spurious. What we can do is project into each world only to leave by the other side: we must experience Corbusier's architecture as clean and rational, Wright's architecture as heavy and strong, Futurist as light and flexible, Brutalist as tough and honest, because all these terms define the meaning and point to a common centre of moral experience. This centre where meanings converge however, is not a place of mutual exclusion: no one set of meanings or myth is sufficient for man or even final.

There is a tendency, which we can see in the historians discussed, to regard one type of building and myth as absolutely superior. As a result, each historian excludes certain architects and those he includes, he considers in terms of a limited morality (that is the architecture always transcends what he can say about it). As a result of this, each historian is forced to contradict his own conscious position, include counter-themes, redress a former imbalance and add the previous historian's omissions, just as in a living myth counter-themes are embodied across time to resolve irreconcilable aspects of life. There seems to be no escape from this dialectic unless perhaps a theory of value is adopted which is supraideological. One might point here to the fact that the historians are already in relative agreement about the value of architects for reasons which appear quite different, but which have an underlying common base in the resolution or tension of opposites, so that they are already implicitly using a theory of value in any case.[12] But whether they could or should make this explicit is another case. Their first obligation probably goes toward defining the limited set of meanings which is concretized in any movement, because someone must be responsible for the actualization of coherent possibilities. Then, *mutatis mutandis*, the following generation will work out further possibilities and reset some of the more dogmatic positions. In any case, the one thing that is removed from the historian's possibility is to carry out Ranke's dictum that he must write about 'what really happened'. This dictum, which Pevsner quotes at the end of his European history, can only lead to the dangerous assumption that historical meaning is fixed and determinant, a fact which the succeeding views of historians do much to eclipse. Architects make architecture, historians make history and what they both make is myth.

[1] See last part of *Semiology and Architecture*, pp. 24–5.
[2] These quotes are from Le Corbusier, *Towards a New Architecture*, The Architectural Press, London, 1946, p. 122, 202–4.
[3] H. R. Hitchcock and P. Johnson, *The International Style*, W. W. Norton and Company, New York, 1966, p. 183, p. 95.
[4] N. Pevsner, *Pioneers of Modern Design*, Penguin Books, London, 1960, reprinted 1964: quotes from p. 17, p. 217.
[5] See E. H. Gombrich, 'Visual Metaphors of Value in Art', in *Meditations on a Hobby Horse*, Phaidon Press, London, 1963, pp. 23–7.
[6] S. Giedion, *Space, Time and Architecture*, Harvard University Press, Mass., 1967, pp. 5 to 18.
[7] S. Giedion, *Mechanisation Takes Command*, Oxford University Press, 1948, p. 711.
[8] Reyner Banham, *Theory and Design in the First Machine Age*, The Architectural Press, London, 1960, p. 12, p. 326, p. 329.
[9] Vincent Scully, *Modern Architecture*, George Braziller, Inc., New York, 1961, p. 10.
[10] Reyner Banham, *The New Brutalism*, The Architectural Press, London, 1966, p. 19, p. 135
[11] C. Norberg-Schulz, *Intentions in Architecture*, Allen and Unwin, London, 1964, pp. 31–4.
[12] The theory of value developed at the end of *Semiology and Architecture*.

Typology & Design Method

Alan Colquhoun

During the last few years a great deal of attention has been given to the problem of design methodology, and to the process of design as a branch of the wider process of problem solving.

Many people believe—not without reason—that the intuitive methods of design traditionally used by architects are incapable of dealing with the complexity of the problems to be solved, and that without sharper tools of analysis and classification, the designer tends to fall back on previous examples for the solution of new problems—on type solutions.

One of the designers and educators who has been consistently preoccupied by this problem is Tomas Maldonado. At a recent seminar at Princeton University, Maldonado admitted that, in cases where it was not possible to classify every observable activity in an architectural programme, it might be necessary to use a typology of architectural forms in order to arrive at a solution. But he added that these forms were like a cancer in the body of the solution, and that as our techniques of classification become more systematic it should be possible to eliminate them altogether.

Now, it is my belief that beneath the apparently practical and hard-headed aspect of these ideas lies an aesthetic doctrine. It will be the purpose of this paper to show this to be the case, and, further, to try and show that it is untenable without considerable modification.

One of the most frequent arguments used against typological procedures in architecture has been that they are a vestige of an age of craft. It is held that the use of models by craftsmen became less necessary as the development of scientific techniques enabled man to discover the general laws underlying the technical solutions of the pre-industrial age.

The vicissitudes of the words 'art' and 'science' certainly indicate that there is a valid distinction to be drawn between artefacts that are the result of the application of the laws of physical science and those which are the result of mimesis and intuition. Before the rise of modern science, tradition, habit and imitation were the methods by which all artefacts were made, whether these artefacts were mainly utilitarian or mainly religious. The word 'art' was used to describe the skill necessary to produce all such artefacts. With the development of modern science, the word 'art' was progressively restricted to the case of artefacts which did not depend on the general laws of physical science, but continued to be based on tradition and the ideal of the final form of the work as a fixed ideal.

But this distinction ignores the extent to which artefacts have not only a 'use' value in the crudest sense, but also an 'exchange' value.

The craftsman had an image of the object in his mind's eye when starting to make it. Whether this object was a cult image (say a sculpture) or a kitchen utensil, it was an object of cultural exchange, and it formed part of a system of communications within society. Its 'message' value was precisely the image of the final form which the craftsman held in his mind's eye as he was making it and to which his artefact corresponded as nearly as possible. In spite of the development of the scientific method we must still attribute such social or iconic values to the products of technology, and recognise that they play an essential role in the generation and development of the physical tools of our environment. It is easy to see that the class of artefacts which continue to be made according to the traditional methods (for example paintings or musical compositions) have a predominantly iconic purpose, but such a purpose is not so often recognised in the creation of the environment as a whole. This fact is concealed from us because the intentions of the design process are 'hidden' in the overt details of performance specification.

The idolisation of 'primitive' man, and the fundamentalist attitude which this generates, have also discouraged the acceptance of such iconic values. There has been a tendency since the 18th century to look on the age of primitive man as a golden age in which man lived close to nature. For many years, for instance, the primitive hut or one of its derivatives has been taken as the starting point for architectural evolution, and has been the subject of first-year design programmes, and it would not be an exaggeration to say that frequently a direct line of descent is presumed to exist from 'primitive' man, through the utilitarian crafts to modern science and technology. In so far as it is based on the idea of the noble savage, this idea is quite baseless. The cosmological systems of primitive man were very intellectual and very artificial. To take only kinship systems, the following quotation from the French anthropologist Claude Lévi-Strauss will make the point clear: 'Certainly', he says, 'the biological family is present and persists in human society. But what gives to kinship its character as a social fact is not what it must conserve of nature; it is the essential step by which it separates itself from nature. A system of kinship does not consist of objective blood ties; it exists only in the consciousness of men; it is an arbitrary system of representations, not the spontaneous development of a situation of fact.'[1]

There seems to be a close parallel between such systems and the way modern man still approaches the world. And what was true of primitive man in all the ramifications of his practical and emotional life—namely the need to *represent* the phenomenal world in such a way that it becomes a coherent and logical system—persists in our own organisations, and more particularly in our attitude towards the man-made objects of our environment. An example of the way this applies to contemporary man is in the creation of what are called socio-spatial schemata. Our senses of place and relationship in, say, an urban environment, or in a building, are not dependent on any objective fact that is measurable; they are phenomenal. The purpose of the aesthetic organisation of our environment is to capitalise on this subjective schematization, and make it socially available. The resulting organisation does not correspond in a one-to-one relationship with the objective facts, but is an artificial construction which *represents* these facts in a socially recognisable way. It follows that the representational systems which are developed are, in a real sense, independent of the quantifiable facts of the environment, and this is particularly true if the environment is changing very rapidly.

No system of representation, no meta-language, however, is totally independent of the facts which constitute the objective world. The modern movement in architecture was an attempt to modify the representational systems which had been inherited from the pre-industrial past, and which no longer seemed operable within the context of a rapidly changing technology. One of the main doctrines at the root of this transformation was based essentially on a return to nature, deriving from the romantic movement, but ostensibly changed from a desire to imitate the surface of natural forms or to operate at a craft level, to a belief in the ability of science to reveal the essence of nature's mode of operation.

Underlying this doctrine was an implied belief in bio-technical determinism. And it is from this theory that the current belief in the supreme importance of scientific methods of analysis and classification derives. The essence of the functional doctrine of the modern movement was not that beauty or order or meaning was unnecessary, but that it could no longer be found in the deliberate search for final forms. The path by which the artefact affected the observer aesthetically was seen as short-circuiting the process of formalization. Form was merely the result of a logical process by which the operational needs and the operational techniques were brought together. Ultimately these would fuse in a kind of biological extension of life, and function and technology would become totally transparent. The theory of Buckminster Fuller is an extreme example of this doctrine.

The relation of this notion to Spencerian evolutionary theory is very striking. According to this theory the purpose of prolonging life and the species must be attributed to the process as a whole, but at no particular moment in the process is it possible to see this purpose as a conscious one. The process is therefore unconscious and teleological. In the same way, the biotechnical determinism of the modern movement was teleological, because it saw the aesthetic of architectural form as something which was achieved without the conscious interference of the designer, but something which none the less was postulated as his ultimate purpose.

It is clear that this doctrine contradicts any theory which would give priority to an intentional iconic form, and it attempts to absorb the process by which man tries to make a representation of the world of phenomena back into a process of unconscious evolution. To what extent has it been successful, and to what extent can it be shown to be possible?

It seems evident, in the first place, that the theory begs the whole question of the iconic significance of forms. Those in the field of design who were—and are—preaching pure technology and so-called objective design method as a sufficient and necessary means of producing environmental devices, persistently attribute iconic power to the creations of technology, which they worship to a degree inconceivable in a scientist. I said earlier that it was in the power of all artefacts to become icons, no matter whether or not they were specifically created for this purpose. Perhaps I might mention certain objects of the 19th-century world of technology which had power of this kind—steamships and locomotives, to give only two examples. Even though these objects were made ostensibly with utilitarian purposes in mind, they quickly became *gestalt* entities, which were difficult to disassemble in the mind's eye into their component parts. The same is true of later technical devices such as cars and aeroplanes. The fact that these objects have been imbued with aesthetic unity and have become carriers of so much meaning indicates that a process of selection and isolation has taken place which is quite redundant from the point of view of their particular functions. We

Geodesic Dome by Buckminster Fuller. Is it possible that the futurist imagery latent in the geodesic dome is the unintentional result of engineering necessity?

must therefore look upon the aesthetic and iconic qualities of artefacts as being due, not so much to an inherent property, but to a sort of availability or redundancy in them in relation to human feeling.

The literature of modern architecture is full of statements which indicate that after all the known operational needs have been satisfied, there is still a wide area of choice in the final configuration. I should like to quote two designers who have used mathematical methods to arrive at architectural solutions. The first is Yona Friedmann, who uses these methods to arrive at a hierarchy of organization in the programme. In a recent lecture, in which he was describing methods of computing the relative position of functions within a three-dimensional city grid, Friedmann acknowledged that the designer is always after computation, faced with a choice of alternatives, all of which are equally good from an operational point of view.

Philips Pavilion, Le Corbusier, 1958. The Philips Pavilion demonstrates the freedom that the designer has in manipulating the hyperbolic parabola.

The second is Yannis Xenakis, who, in designing the Philips Pavilion while he was in the office of Le Corbusier, used mathematical procedures to determine the form of the enclosing structure. In the book which Philips published to describe this building, Xenakis says that calculation provided the characteristic form of the structure, but that after this logic no longer operated; and the compositional arrangement had to be decided on the basis of intuition.

From these statements it would appear that a purely teleological doctrine of technico-aesthetic forms is not tenable. At whatever stage in the design process it may occur, it seems that the designer is always faced with making voluntary decisions, and that the configurations which he arrives at must be the result of an *intention*, and not merely the result of a deterministic process. The following statement of Le Corbusier tends to reinforce this point of view. 'My intellect', he says, 'does not accept the adoption of the modules of Vignola in the matter of

Ronchamp. 'Free plastic events' whose effect none the less depends on their power of reference (ironic or otherwise) to known forms.

building. I claim that harmony exists between the objects one is dealing with. The chapel at Ronchamp perhaps shows that architecture is not an affair of columns but an affair of plastic events. Plastic events are not regulated by scholastic or academic formulae, they are free and innumerable.'

Although this statement is a defence of functionalism against the academic imitation of past forms and the determinism it denies is academic rather than scientific, it nonetheless stresses the release that follows from functional considerations, rather than their power of determining the solution.

One of the most uninhibited statements of this kind comes from Moholy Nagy. In his description of the design course at the Institute of Design in Chicago, he makes the following defence of the free operation of intuition. 'The training', he says, 'is directed towards imagination and inventiveness, a basic condition for the ever-changing industrial scene, for technology in flux. The last step in this technique is the emphasis on integration through the conscious search for relationships. The intuitive working methods of genius give a clue to this process. The unique ability of the genius can be approximated by everybody if one of its essential features be apprehended: the flash-like act of connecting elements not obviously belonging together. If the same methodology were used generally in all fields we could have *the* key to the age—seeing everything in relationship.'[2]

We can now begin to build up a picture of the general body of doctrine embedded in the modern movement. It consists of a tension of two apparently contradictory ideas—biotechnical determinism on the one hand, and free expression on the other. What seems to have happened is that, in the act of giving a new validity to the demands of function as an extension of nature's mode of operation, it has left a vacuum where previously there was a body of traditional practice. The whole field of aesthetics, with its ideological foundations and its belief in ideal beauty, has been swept aside. All that is left in its place is permissive expression, the total freedom of the genius which, if we but knew it, resides in us all. What appears on the surface as a hard, rational discipline of design, turns out rather paradoxically to be a mystical belief in the intuitional process.

I would like now to turn back to the statement by Maldonado which I mentioned at the beginning of this paper. He said that so long as our classification techniques were unable to establish all the parameters of a problem, it

Concorde and Lockheed SST. The iconographic power of such 'artists' impressions' suggests that there is some 'slack' in the performance specification even for devices radically controlled by their environment.

might be necessary to use a typology of forms to fill the gap. From the examples of the statements made by modern designers it would seem that it is indeed never possible to state all the parameters of a problem. Truly quantifiable criteria always leave a choice for the designer to make. In modern architectural theory this choice has been generally conceived of as based on intuition working in a cultural vacuum. In mentioning typology, Maldonado is suggesting something quite new, and something which has been rejected again and again by modern theorists. He is suggesting that the area of pure intuition must be based on a knowledge of past solutions to related problems, and that creation is a process of adapting forms derived either from past needs or on past aesthetic ideologies to the needs of the present. Although he regards this as a provisional solution—'a cancer in the body of the solution'—he none the less recognizes that this is the actual procedure which designers follow.

I suggest that this is true, and moreover that it is true in all fields of design and not only that of architecture. I have referred to the argument that the more rigorously the general physical or mathematical laws are applied to the solution of design problems the less it is necessary to have a mental picture of the final form. But, although we may postulate an ideal state in which these laws correspond exactly to the objective world, in fact this is not the case. Laws are not found in nature. They are constructions of the human mind; they are models which are valid so long as events do not prove them to be wrong. They are models, as it were, at one remove from pictorial models. Not only this. Technology is frequently faced with different problems which are not logically consistent. All the problems of aircraft configuration, for example, could not be solved unless there was give and take in the application of physical laws. The position of the power unit is a variable, so is the configuration of the wings and tailplane. The position of one affects the shape of the other. The application of general laws is a necessary ingredient of the form. But it is not a sufficient one for determining the actual configuration. And in a world of pure technology this area of free choice is invariably dealt with by adapting previous solutions.

In the world of architecture this problem becomes even more crucial because general laws of physics and the empirical facts are less capable of fixing a final configuration than in the case of an aeroplane or a bridge. Recourse to some

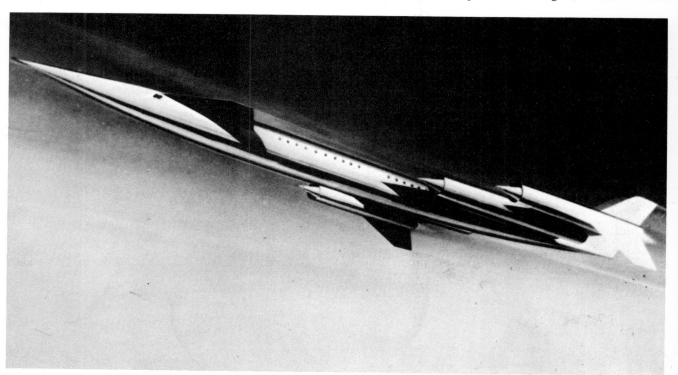

kind of typological model is likely to be more necessary in this case.

It may be argued that, in spite of the fact that there is an area of free choice beyond that of operation, this freedom lies in the details (where, for instance, personal 'taste' might legitimately operate). This could probably be shown to be true of such technically complex objects as aeroplanes, where the topological relationships are largely determined by the application of physical laws. But it does not seem to apply to architecture. On the contrary, because of the comparatively simple environmental pressures that operate on buildings, the topological relationships are hardly at all determined by physical laws. In the case of Philips Pavilion, for example, it was not only the acoustic requirements which established the basic configuration, but also the need for a building which would convey a certain impression of vertigo and fantasy. It is in the details of plan or equipment that these laws become stringent, and not in the general arrangement. Where the designer decides to be governed by operational factors, he works in terms of a thoroughly 19th century rationalism, for example in the case of the office buildings of Mies and SOM, where purely pragmatic planning and cost considerations converge on a received neo-classic aesthetic to create simple cubes, regular frames and cores. It is interesting that most of the projects where form determinants are held to be technical or operational in an avant-garde sense, rationalism and cost are discarded for forms of a fantastic or expressionist kind. Frequently, as in the case of 'Archigram', forms are borrowed from other disciplines, such as space engineering or pop art. Valid as these iconographic procedures may be—and before dismissing them one would have to investigate them in relation to the work of Le Corbusier and the Russian constructivists which borrowed the forms of ships and engineering structures—they can hardly be compatible with a doctrine of determinism, if we are to regard this as a *modus operandi*, rather than a remote and utopian ideal.

The exclusion by modern architectural theory of typologies, and its belief in the freedom of the intuition, can at any rate be partially explained by the general theory of expression which was current at the turn of the century. This theory can be seen most clearly in the work and theories of certain painters—notably Kandinsky, both in his paintings and in his book *Point and Line to Plane*, which outlines the theory on which his paintings are based. Expressionist theory rejected all historical manifestations of art, just as modern architectural theory rejected all historical forms of architecture. These manifestations were held to be an ossification of technical and cultural attitudes whose *raison d'être* had ceased to exist. The theory was based on the belief that shapes have physiognomic or expressive content which communicates itself to us directly. This view has been subjected to a good deal of criticism, and one of its most convincing refutations occurs in E. H. Gombrich's book *Meditations on a Hobby Horse*. Gombrich demonstrates that an arrangement of forms such as is found in a painting by Kandinsky is in fact very low in content, unless we attribute to these forms some system of conventional meanings not inherent in the forms themselves. His thesis is that physiognomic forms are ambiguous, though not wholly without expressive value, and that they can only be interpreted within a particular cultural milieu. One of the ways he illustrates this is by reference to the supposed affective qualities of colours. Gombrich points out in the now famous example of traffic signals, that we are dealing with a conventional and not a physiognomic meaning, and maintains that it would be equally logical to reverse the meaning system, so that red indicated action and forward movement, and green inaction, quietness and caution.[3]

Expressionist aesthetic theory probably had a strong influence on the modern movement. Its application to architecture would be more obvious than to painting because of the absence in architecture of anecdote and representation and for this reason the style for which the term 'expressionist' is usually reserved should be regarded as a special case of a more general phenomenon. If, therefore, the objections to expressionist theory are valid, they must be taken to apply to some of the more fundamental tenets of the functionalist movement.

If, as Gombrich suggests, forms by themselves are relatively empty of mean-

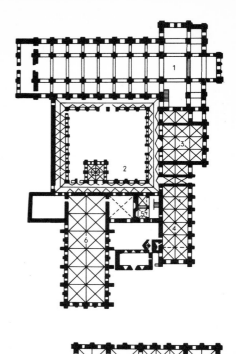

Cistercian Monastery of Fontenay, 1140.

'France'.

La Tourette, Le Corbusier 1957/60.

The mediaeval monastery and the liner offer stereotypes for the 'collective', whether the programme is traditional (La Tourette) or modern (the Unité).

ing, it follows that the architectural forms which we intuit will, in the unconscious mind, tend to attract to themselves certain associations of meaning. This could mean not only that we are *not* free from the forms of the past, and from the availability of these forms as typological models, but that, if we assume we are free, we have lost control over a very active sector of our imagination, and of our power to communicate with others. It would seem that we ought to try to establish a value system which takes account of the forms and solutions of the

past, if we are to gain control over concepts which will obtrude themselves into the creative process, whether we like it or not.

There is, in fact, a close relationship between the pure functionalist or teleological theory that I have described, and expressionism, as defined by Gombrich. By insisting on the use of analytical and inductive methods of design, functionalism leaves a vacuum in the form making process. This it fills with its own reductionist aesthetic—the aesthetic that claims that 'intuition', with no historical dimension, can arrive spontaneously at forms which are the equivalent of fundamental operations. This procedure postulates a kind of onomatopoeic relationship between forms and their content. In the case of a biotechnico/ determinist theory the content is the set of relevant functions—functions which themselves are a reduction of all the socially meaningful operations within a building—and it is assumed that the functional complex is translated into forms whose iconographical significance is nothing more than the rational structure of the functional complex itself. The existent facts of the objective situation are the equivalent of the existent facts of the subjective physiognomic situation, in expressionism. In both cases the resulting forms are assumed to obey national laws, in the one case physical and in the other psychological. But traditionally, in the work of art, the existent facts, whether subjective or objective, are less significant than the values we attribute to these facts or to the system of representation which embodies these values. The work of art, in this respect, resembles language. A language which was simply the expression of emotions would be a series of single-word exclamations; in fact language is a complex system of representation in which the basic emotions are structured into an intellectually coherent system. It would be impossible to conceive of constructing a language *a priori*. The ability to construct such a language would have to presuppose the language itself. Similarly a plastic system[4] of representation such as architecture has to presuppose the existence of a given system of representation. In neither case can the problem of formal representation be reduced to some pre-existent essence outside the formal system itself, of which the form is merely a reflection. In both cases it is necessary to postulate a conventional system embodied in typological solution/problem complexes.

My purpose in stressing this fact is not to advocate a reversion to an architecture which accepts tradition unthinkingly. This would imply that there was a fixed and immutable relation between forms and meaning. The characteristic of our age is change, and it is precisely because this is so that it is necessary to investigate the part which modifications of type solutions play in relation to problems and solutions, which are without precedent in any received tradition.

I have tried to show that a reductionist theory according to which the problem/ solution process can be reduced to some sort of essence is untenable. One might postulate that the process of change is carried out, not by a process of reduction, but rather by a process of exclusion, and it would seem that the history of the modern movement in all the arts lends support to this idea. If we look at the allied fields of painting and music, we can see that, in the work of a Kandinsky or a Schoenberg, traditional formal devices were not completely abandoned, but were transformed and given a new emphasis by the exclusion of ideologically repulsive iconic elements. In the case of Kandinsky it is the representation element which is excluded; in the case of Schoenberg it is the diatonic system.

The value of what I have called the process of exclusion is to enable us to see the potentiality of forms as if for the first time, and with naïvety. This is the justification for the radical change in the iconic system of representation, and it is a process which we have to adopt if we are to keep and renew our awareness of the meanings which can be carried by forms. The bare bones of our culture— a culture with its own characteristic technology—must become visible to us. For this to happen, a certain scientific detachment towards our problems is essential, and with it the application of the mathematical tools proper to our culture. But these tools are unable to give us a ready-made solution to our problems. They only provide the framework, the context within which we operate.

◀ JENCKS: But exclusion is less potent as a principle than selection for the reasons which E. H. Gombrich has outlined in his *Norm and Form* (London, 1966, p.97). Radical exclusion, so prevalent in modern polemics, has the tactical advantage that it can be easily understood but the strategic disadvantage that it is quickly exhausted simply because too many values are being clipped away for the sake of too few. Besides, exclusion is dictatorial in that it refuses to admit the value of what it cuts away – whereas selection will only sacrifice one value for a more important one. While exclusion may allow us to see 'the bare bones of our culture as if for the first time', selection could as well. In any case, this would be just one more 'typology' and not an 'essence' as Alan Colquhoun points out above. I take the recommendation at the end of this article to be the statement of intent by a practising architect and not the necessary conclusion of the argument.

SILVER: The necessity of relying on form types doesn't wreck the principle of authentic functionalism as I understand it; neither does an abundance of unclassifiable information in a design programme mean that the design therefore has to be in any way unsystematic. Values, which can be fathomed through 'intuitive' methods, also have systems which can be objectively discussed (though of course a designer doesn't discuss, he short-cuts to a solution). Alan Colquhoun makes me realize that infallibility in an architectural design would be an empty aim, yet he should acknowledge that objectivity – by means of which values can always be ordered at *some* critical level – is a logical goal, no matter how many people try mathematical analysis and become disillusioned with it. By the way, where is the functionalist who would maintain that the functional complex can be 'translated into forms whose iconographic significance is nothing more than the rational structure of the functional complex itself'? Since Hannes Meyer, that is.

[1] Claude Lévi-Strauss. *Structural Anthropology*. Basic Books, New York, 1963.
[2] L. Mohoy-Nagy. *Vision in Motion*. Paul Theobald & Company, Chicago.
[3] It is interesting that, since his book came out, the Chinese have in fact reversed the meanings of their traffic signals.
[4] For the study of language as a system of symbolic representation see Cassirer, *Philosophy of Symbolic forms*. Yale University Press, 1957. For a discussion of language in relation to literature (meta-language) see Roland Barthes, *Essais Critiques*. Editions du Seuil, Paris, 1964.

Architecture without Buildings

Nathan Silver

When Le Corbusier said, in 1923, 'architecture can be found in the telephone and in the Parthenon,' he was speaking principally about the relation of a task to a form. The author of this essay believes that today such a statement has become more apt and profound than in 1923, partly because (the essay holds) what has previously been understood as a 'task' in architecture should now be called a form, and sometimes the reverse.

I.

At the end of 1964 the New York Museum of Modern Art held an exhibition called 'Architecture Without Architects', a photographic anthology. The pictures showed many of those primitive or ahistorical developments which are usually classified Folk, Vernacular, Spontaneous, Indigenous or sometimes even Autochthonous architecture, that is, architecture aboriginal and native to the soil. Bernard Rudofsky, the compiler of the exhibition, called it 'non-pedigreed' and 'anonymous'. From anonymous he was led on to call it 'without architects' (overlooking a critical distinction there).

Anonymous architecture, nameless name. It implies buildings only; no 'style', no creator. The phrase would fit a ghost town, or a man-made landscape. Landscape is the word we use for raw nature when we choose to see it as an ikon, and in photographic archives one also finds Folk or Vernacular or Autochthonous architecture as iconography instead of mundane brickmaking and roof thatching. Click! Shelter becomes art in a frozen sixtieth of a second.

James Marston Fitch and others have written about such conceptual distortions inherent in architectural photography; also about our habit, generally, of seeing buildings as pictures. I want to investigate what I think may be a more fundamental quarrel between architecture as it is, and architecture as we see it.[1] At the moment I can choose sides, but I have only a rehearsal for an argument, because it will take time and careful investigation to become more certain. However if one could eventually be reasonably satisfied about the truth (or advantages) of my argument, we would have a conception of architecture that I think would lead us on to understand how architecture is changing now and what it holds for the future. This is an urgent problem, because our limited view of architecture has become unaccommodating to the extent that we need place markers to serve consistency; dummy principles, like phlogiston, or the Bohr atom. Of course *beauty* to us is like the ideal Bohr atom ('I put a great deal of emphasis on abstract beauty in a plan,' says Ralph Rapson. 'Purpose is not necessary to making a building beautiful,' says Philip Johnson). And, judging also from the words of prominent architects, *nobility, refinement, demonstrations of high culture* are the burning qualities that matter for us, to be sought for but never really isolated, like phlogiston ('Architecture begins where engineering ends,' says Walter Gropius. 'The Pyramids, the Towers of Babylon, the Gates of Samarkand, the Parthenon, [etc.] . . . the Invalides—all these belong to Architecture. The Gare du Quai d'Orsay, the Grand Palais do not belong to Architecture', says Le Corbusier. 'All buildings do not belong to Architecture. A work of architecture is presented as an offering to Architecture and to its Treasury of spaces', says Louis Kahn).[2] Our buildings reflect this too: everywhere now (and especially in America) we are confronted with bad beautiful design (sometimes beautiful bad design also, as in Las Vegas). 'Bad design' alone certainly can't explain why so much of everything we now build as architecture has come to seem so uncongenial and make-believe. An architect working today could be a sharp design boy, even a first-rate problem solver, but his sense of purpose would be stunted by what, it appears, we are content to settle for.

Clearly we need a richer understanding of what we are doing, because we seem to be willing to side-step the enormous development challenges we are faced with. Architecture as a social science lags behind other social sciences in programmes and hopes. Is it because we insist on calling it an art? If that is why we are lagging, we shall either have to stop thinking about building as art at all (which is what we have already allowed for in our most unselfconscious—and successful—building),[3] or we will have to find a better set of principles than

JENCKS: This is the classical argument of those who attack style and form in architecture – from Hannes Meyer to Reyner Banham. First, the imputation that 'beauty' is an irrelevance, a non-existent fiction like phlogiston; secondly, the characterisation of those who proffer such values in their more ridiculous moments (characterised later as 'trivial exercises in plastic manipulation'); and finally, the switch to the symmetrically opposite position as if this guaranteed a certain kind of relevance. But it is in no sense proved that Levittown, Las Vegas and functional solutions are 'most successful' (see footnote); it is just asserted. And, as if to underline the fact that this position is based on personal taste, that phlogiston 'beauty' is allowed to enter in the last paragraph – escorted of course by 'function'. In other words, one might equally well argue for an architecture based entirely on 'form' and jettison 'function' altogether, because this would be a comparable and symmetrical reduction.

abstract beauty and self-expression.

It would be nice to suppose that I could make a suggestion which would promote such immoderate gains. Here I will only try to find a reassurance that there is no predisposition anywhere in art that rules out architecture being a social science, nor rules out any ambitions and values we feel architecture should be respecting. In the interests of a fair presentation, I shall try to keep my own formal prejudices out of it. Indeed I won't say much in any specific way about form, essential to the whole though it is, because many people have written about that exclusively. What I am after here is a more productive and up-to-date conception of content. Briefly, what I have in mind is this: the notion that architecture is fundamentally a people-system, not a thing-system; and that (incidentally) architecture without architects is impossible, since intention of use is everything, but that architecture without buildings may be quite possible, since use-situations can exist without buildings for them.

One can begin with a critical look at the architectural theory that is around. In terms of aesthetics, maybe architecture's medium, its basic abstraction (its 'primary apparition', as Suzanne Langer calls it), is not *space*, as Giedion, Pevsner, Langer and others have believed. Architecture as the manipulation of space was largely the conception of non-architects (even non-clients, one is tempted to think) who were forgetting the worth of shelter, security, comfort, and organization. Fortunately no quarrel is needed about this any more. In *Feeling and Form*,[4] Dr Langer herself decided that architecture's basic abstraction must be 'ethnic domain', an admirable designation. Then, more recently, Christian Norberg-Schulz expended great energy and scholarship in resisting all one-note theories: instead of blather about space or even form exclusively, Norberg-Schulz concluded that architecture was a complex fabrication of both tasks and built objects, both aspects to be taken together. (A considerable piece of understanding, though a reasonable one from a practising architect.) Yet while he was discarding old formal notions in his book *Intentions in Architecture*,[5] Norberg-Schulz almost negligently applied new ones. While showing respect for the landmark ideas about signs and symbols in aesthetics, he wound up half-proposing new, unmistakably representational buildings, as if symbolism had to mean some formal style. He also insisted that one must distinguish between elevated and mean works, of which only the first could be called architecture. Once Alberti dreamed that the simplest geometrical forms should be reserved for the most important buildings; once Borromini carried out strict iconographic programmes—and Norberg-Schulz's formal and hierarchical biases would keep architecture faithful to such past performances.

Norberg-Schulz certainly has provided strong, previously missing links between architectural invention, and art historians' and aestheticians' notions about it. He accounts for the complicated tendrils that root an artificial body in nature. But now man-made environment is becoming dominant, really the norm for most people. It is an unremitting experience. We have no longer the remarkable few artificial things but a familiar continuum. Architecture appears now in a different order of magnitude from the past; we live in the man-made world so completely that one can well suspect a qualitative shift in our experience. One might also suspect that a theory useful for explaining works of Alberti and Borromini may not now be relevant.

Maybe some professionals just aren't looking. Aestheticians, art historians, and architects occasionally sound as if they are referring to three different matters when they talk about architecture. Of course that's in the nature of academic specialization; in another recent book, Robert Venturi wants to win all hearts when, like a proud craftsman, he asserts: 'I try to talk about architecture rather than around it.'[6] In other words, I won't take away someone else's job. Professional trade-unionism is familiar. Sometimes it comes complete with three closed shops and mutual sympathy strikes. The architect Venturi quotes the architectural historian Sir John Summerson with approval as Summerson complains about architects' obsessions with 'the importance, not of architecture, but of the *relation* of architecture to other things'. Clearly an architect should

◀ NORBERG-SCHULZ: Nathan Silver gives me credit for having resisted all 'one-note theories' and for having concluded that architecture is 'a complex fabrication of both tasks and built objects'. That is right, and that is why I have not discarded formal notions. Formal notions obviously are a necessary part of the 'complex fabrication'. (I have not, however, maintained that symbolism means a formal style. Neither have I used the term 'symbol' to designate a literal representation [Abbildung]. My use of 'symbol' refers to the fact that meaning consists in relations, and that objects 'mediate' each other.) The form I am talking about is a concrete physical system which corresponds to a system of human actions. Although the architect ought to know and may even influence the latter, his main professional concern obviously is with the former. *Reducing* architecture to the system of human actions, Silver returns to another 'one-note theory'. But the note he sings is so general that it makes our field dissolve and disappear. The title of his article, therefore, is well chosen, although 'architecture without architecture' would have been still more appropriate. As far as I can see, Venturi warns against this self-destructive attitude when he says that we should concentrate on our own job. Rather than being naive, he thereby shows a sense of responsibility.

SILVER: Did I go too far at the finish of my article? Perhaps I did if Christian Norberg-Schulz doesn't recognize his own thinking as a prime source for it. I've got no room here to quote places where *Intentions in Architecture* is indeed equivocal on symbolism – that is, where Norberg-Schulz's abstract symbolism starts to become old-time formalism. Yet how will we ever get free to take on the responsibilities that matter now, if we restrict ourselves to museum notions about architecture? Clearly we can't be free on the present understanding of what architecture is, and that's why I flirted with the idea (before rejecting it) that architecture isn't art. My saying nothing about built form doesn't mean I don't accept responsibility for such as the architect's main job, which of course it is willy-nilly, by virtue of the architect's training, opportunities and disposition. I was addressing others as well as architects. And whether my argument is valuable or destructive remains to be seen. I think nothing could be more destructive, or discreditable to what architecture can offer, than an insistence on buildings as architecture's sole or even primary formal product. I doubt that architects would be enervated or hung up if they started believing that the programme might be more beautiful than any solution. If I helped inspire confidence in that notion, I didn't go too far.

JENCKS: But the parallel is not exact. It would have to be sound is to music as form is to art or architecture as phonemes are to speech etc. All sign systems are at least doubly articulated and although Nathan Silver saves the formal articulation (by shifting it to 'pattern choosing') he does so at the cost of denying physical objects or 'things'. But why must one deny 'objects'? It would seem because they are associated with 'virtuoso architects' and 'trivial exercises in plastic manipulation', monumentality and the more obvious excesses of cultural bombast. But they needn't be; one can think of much 'non-trivial plastic manipulation'.

just build and shut up, or if he talks, he should certainly not 'talk around' architecture. And architects shouldn't trouble themselves with worrying about things beyond them, like interconnectedness, proximities, or total coherence (yet in one sense, architecture is about nothing but coherence, 'relations'). I wonder where Venturi thinks the aroundness begins. Imagine talking about literature, solely with reference to pages of composed type!

What Venturi really means is that architects shouldn't talk about architecture at all, but about buildings instead. He becomes, I think, more than a little naive when he concludes that 'the architect's ever-diminishing power and his growing ineffectualities in shaping the whole environment can perhaps be reversed, ironically, by narrowing his concerns and concentrating on his own job. Perhaps then relationships and power will take care of themselves.'[7]

Unfortunately the architect-as-pure-craftsman (or artist) probably won't be able to do much of what we want him to do in the future. Suppose we try, contrary to the above, to talk about architecture *without* talking about buildings— not at first, nor indeed ever in the slowly increasing number of cases where architectural tasks are solved without buildings. And do it even if such a policy gives a poor account of Alberti's or Borromini's work, though I suspect that historical architecture also might be profitably discussed this way (as yet I have thought through and will speak for only contemporary architectural problems). This different approach should be worthwhile if of good use empirically, from where we are standing now. I hope it is proof against, though I can't yet defend it from, theoretical or methodological prejudice. I speak as an architect.

II.

If we try to talk about architecture without buildings, we should find it no more difficult than talking about literature without typography and speech, or music without musical instruments. Now the form of music actually occurs in sound and time, so it seems a poor parallel to compare musical instruments— mere formal *agents*—with buildings. But maybe buildings are mere formal agents too. Or largely so. To examine the parallel more deeply: in musical performance there is a correlation between instrument and sound. The entrance of a horn chorale impresses as much for its addition of energy, or manpower, as for quality of sound. Recordings don't spoil this impression for sophisticated listeners—stereo recordings make it very real. Clearly musical instruments are more than hardware; as formal agents they are surrogates, or in the same sense the 'objective correlatives' (Eliot's term) of the sounds (because playing them is the formula for hearing particular sounds). Fortunately for music, but curiously, the importance of musical instruments is underrated in musical form just as buildings are perhaps overrated in architectural form. *Musique concrete* has blithely introduced totally different formal agents (e.g. natural sounds on tape), presumably without aesthetic collapse.

Buildings are the usual formal agents which transmit architectural values; like musical instruments, but even more strongly, they impress us with their correlative presence. They are often so handy for keeping us dry and warm that we perhaps forget they aren't necessarily the *form* of architecture; that is, maybe the form is predominantly, or partly, invisible. A band shell, a triumphal arch, a viewing platform, a scenic highway, a car or plane aren't simply *forms* but formal agents; they provide for larger, integral forms in our 'ethnic domain': a concert, a parade, a spectacle, a journey. The things are merely surrogates. Of course my examples aren't 'buildings', therefore, according to common use of the words, they have nothing to do with 'architecture'. Yet couldn't my same argument be extended to the invisible agency of organization and its relationship with a church, a railroad station, a meeting hall? I am trying to get at a very tricky proposition: that what we have been accustomed to thinking is form in architecture may be partly content, and what we have assumed was content may sometimes suffice for form. But here all sideward glances at other arts must stop, because I want to try to show that in architecture the formal agents, strictly speaking, may be people.

Of course *everything* lies in people, in the sense that all perceptible objects in the external world can be metered where they are perceived inside us, somewhere in the central nervous system. It is not just that. It is an apersonal phenomenon. Just as the human body in ballet arguably becomes a *thing*, an art object, in architecture the art *thing* must be a pattern of human actions. Thereafter, an act of creation, if it occurs, is what it takes to turn the pattern into a system. Construction of a building may or may not follow.

JENCKS: It seems to me that Nathan Silver is coming perilously close to the glorification of Buckminster Fuller's 'Universal architect' (God=the mediaeval architect with compass in hand laying out the universe). And although Silver is careful to reiterate that the architect would be only *one* of the pattern choosers, he would seem to be the main one: 'human adaptability is the design material'. Now even granting a hierarchy of pattern choosers, the problem with this view is that the architect is now very badly equipped to lead such a venture, Fuller's 'Universal architect' even less so, because of a chronic distaste for politics – that essential arena of pattern choosing.

SILVER: 'Close, but no cigar'. Please let's have no misunderstanding about this point: I *don't* think all this is the architect's job and it is exactly to show non-architects how essential their roles are in design that I wrote this piece. And see my questioning of Norberg-Schulz on the subject of politics.

From my window I can see a Cambridgeshire farmer ploughing his field. He goes west as far as a ditch, then turns east as far as a road, then repeats with another furrow. Back and forth. At the end of the day he leaves his tractor where he has stopped and walks home. I could think of hundreds of more interesting patterns than the one the farmer is making; so could he probably. Chinese farmers plough along terraces. Elsewhere in England, where the landscape isn't so flat, ploughing is done along the earth contours. Interesting pattern or dull pattern, we have learned to consider that if someone like Ansel Adams photographed any of these ploughed fields, his picture would be a work of art. That is because he would have chosen the subject; the picture would be design revealed in graphic art, a photograph. But in this case I saw the Cambridge pattern first. It revealed itself as a system to me. I *chose* the pattern as it lay on the ground. That design was revealed to me as architecture. The farmer chose the pattern twenty years ago when he bought the field. That was architecture. A ploughed field is architecture without building. A ceremony is another example of architecture without building.

The classic evasion in architectural aesthetics is the introduction of that slippery word 'architectonic', which means 'pertaining to architecture'. It could be otherwise held that the ploughed field is architectonic, not architecture. Well, yes and no. If neither the farmer nor I recognized his pattern as a systematic one, if neither of us and no one else actually *chose* his pattern, so to speak, then I would concede that the pattern was merely architectonic, like the bee dance: no choice; intelligence without Intelligence. But we chose and we therefore created. The creative event occurred at this early point. If we change the scene from a ploughed field to a complicated modern building, the pattern-choosing occurs at relatively the same point. Although, in a building, the more refined, complicated architectual pattern would be the whole general *ordering of use* which can be read with sensibility (and, within the pattern, perhaps use would be determining order, order determining use, or anything in between).

It sounds strange. If this is what architecture is about, who is then responsible for it—the user? Partly. Norberg-Schulz believed that the task and the built object together make architecture: I would say the task ordered into a system is sufficient. But inclusion of the task means people are involved. To use Norberg-Schulz's language, there is architecture as long as an 'intention' exists. Now 'intention' can have several meanings, which is what is so appropriate about the use of the word in this context. It refers to the attitude of the architect towards the work of his creation, the totality of meaning he invests in the pattern or built form. It also refers to the orientation of the user, and his fullest capacity for knowing what has been created. The architect's intention means design; the user's intention means inclination, ambition, or wish. Either of the two who 'intend' makes architecture, so there can be architecture without architects (professionals), though not without someone who has the pattern-choosing intention. Even in primitive society, and *even if there are no buildings*, a pattern once recognized becomes a system, a system reveals an intention, and that is architecture. There is always an 'architect'. The man in the street makes the city.

III.

I said earlier that such a notion should be promising if it had empirical advantages. Therefore, let us look at some practical matters:

1. If henceforth architecture can be seen not simply as something where content always refers to people (their tasks, culture, values) and form always refers to things, if instead it looks suspiciously like a highly complex communications system involving people and things together on both sides, then searches for 'a new symbol-system of forms' and other similar appeals to architectural improvement no longer have to be interpreted as cues for trivial exercises in plastic manipulation.

2. An opinion: what contemporary architects ought to be searching for now is not the renewal of visual form (Norberg-Schulz's and Venturi's basic concern), but something beyond. In a sense, even the radicalism of the Modern Movement —the Bauhaus and Mies van der Rohe and the 'heroic period of modern architecture', as the Smithsons recently called it—was a phase which I personally believe was more closely connected with the past than with the future, since the overriding preoccupation was still with renewing the visual symbolization of architectural form. What lies ahead is the need to take responsibility for the entire normal human state. Certainly professional architects haven't this vast responsibility alone; everyone has. Is it likely that these responsibilities would be discharged even if we got to know all there is to know about the art and craft of building? No. It is necessary to seek much further.

3. Once we architects managed to free our minds of the stifling assumption that architecture means buildings (and, by the way, Le Corbusier put it much

more cruelly: he said 'the entire history of architecture is concerned, exclusively, with openings in walls'), we could devote ourselves to the essential task of becoming good pattern-choosers. This requires seeing man as the measure, *literally*. The design material isn't brick or concrete (or tracing paper), but human adaptability. The 'subject matter' of architecture is the life situation (in contrast to the limited 'subject matter' of dance, which is the body in motion).

4. This proposition could structure complex problems with critical acuity. For example, we can suddenly understand what 'monumental architecture' is—that puzzling classification of building we no longer seem to create well. It is a special kind of architecture where built order needs to invent use entirely.

5. As a further example, we can understand why new urban building seems relatively inharmonious, compared, say, with the serene façades of nineteenth-century cities: new needs reveal themselves largely as opportunities for new patterns, and we have developed highly specialized 'building types' without reflection about whether concordant building matters or not any more. That is, new patterns seem to us only opportunities for specialization. By not being aware of the scope of pattern-choosing as the essence of architecture, we don't often choose between the alternating advantages of specialization and generalization.

6. A corollary of my whole proposition is that human adaptability is the design material. Therefore 'expression' comes to mean a variation from the normal human state (what is 'normal' in the culture, that is), which state must be explored and, as far as possible, decided for guidance. Whole libraries of information on perception (the shelves are now almost empty) ought to be the only factual basis for expression in architecture. It depends on values too: what is our view of normality? If we had something more than the intuition of architects for data on what constitutes normal existence and experience, we might be able to face architectural tasks better—to make ourselves a world where the environment issues formal instructions only in terms of use-situations or potential use-situations. This would be a truly relaxed and free architecture, because often the best policy would be no instruction. That is a choice hardly open to virtuoso architects now.

◀ BAIRD: Generally speaking, I support Silver's argument, but I ask for a little irony here vis-à-vis the past, and architecture *with* buildings. For one of the things those 'libraries of information about perception' will tell us, is just how irremediably *historical* it is.

By currently failing to see that what we think of as new form is mostly new content, we restrict the evolution of new use-situations through mismatched policies, such as rulebook zoning and conventional taste.

So, in fact, the problem of expression, not form, may be the most urgent one that we must now solve, because no comprehensible plurality, diverse interconnectedness, or enlarged system of coherence—I hope we are all convinced that this is what architecture must evolve towards—is possible as long as, on the one hand, Jones' office building haphazardly upstages Smith's, or, on the other hand, zoning and building laws merely limit the disposition of continuity and change. These situations would be less likely if we calculated works of architecture as patterns of use before they were buildings.

7. The best architecture according to this new proposition would be that which defines, with a chance of high sensibility, normality without uniformity (because the human normal state is not uniform), and formality without deformity (meaning inappropriate exaggeration).

IV.

Following my line of reasoning to the finish, a telephone conversation is architecture too. (It becomes architecture when *that* is the pattern chosen; at another time the conversation might have occurred in a city square.) There couldn't be an example more provokingly destructive to the fine-arts, visual, historical old-aesthetic conception of architecture than this, and surely anyone who is sceptical about the whole proposition slams down his own 'phone here. It's the *reductio ad absurdum*, the utter-nonsense limit, but consistency requires it, even if supporters won't flock to it. Certainly modern communications have changed the pattern of life fundamentally, and that by itself tends to sustain a communications explanation in new architectural theory.

Can we really bear to admit that architecture is an art which may be without forms or spaces? Without the 'masterly, correct, and magnificent play of masses brought together in light'? Well, if consent could only be gained by giving ground somewhere, I would grant that the architecture I choose to talk about may not be art at all. That is the alternative, which, in a sense, we have already chosen (when we decided that only *important* buildings are architecture).

Perhaps 'architecture isn't art' should be our position.[8] Clearly great changes in professional objectives are now being met. You wouldn't know it from reading an old-fashioned mass of self-justifications like those published in *Architects on Architecture*, but signs of a different sort have been visible for perhaps fifteen years. As fine artists, architects are currently managing to accomplish a tiny proportion of all the building that needs to be done. Since it seems that we will have to double the size of the man-made world in the next generation and a half, ought we go on believing that there are elevated and base works, and architecture is only about the former? We thereby implicitly deny responsibility for the rest. Rather than that, it would be better to save ourselves by saying architecture is not art. Architects aren't the only pattern-choosers, nor should they be. However, my hunch remains that architecture *is* art even if it isn't buildings. The only structure necessary may be invisible, which is the pattern of use; as such it is architecture's true 'primary apparition' which finally informs the matter as art.

It would be within expectation to find that some art historians and aestheticians resist a notion which tries to undermine a conception about form long held by them. Other non-visual notions about architecture have faced prejudice. There is also a natural antagonism to such an idea among architects—I feel it burbling myself—since most architects, after all, become architects simply because they love to build. Yet a task-centered argument about architecture is as old as Socrates, and most of my proposition is merely a radical sort of Functionalism, opportunistically dressed in some of what we have begun to learn about structural relations and communications.

BAIRD: Again, I agree entirely with the ▶ substance of the argument, but I don't find it a 'radical sort of Functionalism'. Rather (and more important) it looks more to me like a speculation on a modern theory of Decorum.

In a disputation between Socrates and Aristippus, recorded in Xenophon's *Memorabilia*, Socrates finally called a dung basket beautiful and a golden shield ugly, if the one was well made for its special work and the other badly. On architecture, Socrates was succinct: 'The house in which the owner can find a pleasant retreat at all seasons and can store his belongings safely is presumably at once the pleasantest and most beautiful.' Elements of the ideas of Socrates later appeared in the writing and practice of Horatio Greenough, Louis Sullivan, Walter Gropius and a thousand others. Included were the notions that there need be only one explanation for all beauty of whatever occurrence; that, according to this explanation, beauty is relative; and that what a thing called beautiful is relative *to* are the things for which it is useful. These were revelations like dawn light. Against them we can still form our patterns, learn to read them and change them, and then make our marks upon the earth.

[1] Some parts of the discussion which ensues were raised earlier in the following articles, where I was concerned mostly with books under review: 'Klingsor's Castle', *Progressive Architecture*, August, 1966; 'The Art of Human Use', *The Nation*, 15 May, 1967; 'Social-Science Architecture', *The New Statesman*, 28 July, 1967; 'Bad Buildings are Good', *The New Statesman*, 19 January, 1968.
[2] The Le Corbusier quotation is from *Towards a New Architecture*, London Architectural Press, 1927. The others are representative quotations from *Architects on Architecture*, edited by Paul Heyer, Walker & Co., 1966.
[3] Levittown, which Gans shows is a social success, and Las Vegas, whose architecture Venturi appreciates, are some obvious examples. I have in mind any industrial development begun in metal huts or adapted urban lofts; most commercial housing, which does achieve its limited goals; and, in underdeveloped areas, most necessary building of all kinds. However, I don't believe, with Rudofsky or Alexander, that this 'un-selfconscious' building is *actually* design of a different sort, as I will explain.
[4] London, Routledge & Kegan Paul, 1953.
[5] M.I.T. Press, 1965.
[6] *Complexity and Contradiction in Architecture*, Museum of Modern Art, 1967.
[7] Note for a work on the anti-intellectual tradition: in some schools of architecture, the critics classify their students as either 'doers' or 'talkers'.
[8] Just as Jane Jacobs said that 'cities aren't art'.

Index

action, establishes public realm, 151
Alexander, C., 97, 99, 188, 213
ambiguity, 121–7
amma, 176–7
animal laborans, 154, 166
Archigram, 18, 19, 24, 101, 108
architecture, as language, 39; implies public realm, 152–3; the end of, 95, 100–18, 259, 262, 278–85; see also, Hannes Meyer
Ardery, R., 133, 148
Arendt, H., 97, 99, 151–2, 154, 162, 166, 167
avant-garde, 11–3, 24–5, 82–3, 94–7

Bachelard, G., 33
Baird, G., 7, 8, 11, 16, 17, 36, 40, 41, 44, 45, 51, 55, 61, 72, 74, 78–99, 101, 102, 108, 130, 131, 138, 144, 146, 154, 158, 162–3, 166, 167, 212, 284, 285
Banham, R., 7, 8, 13, 20, 27, 51, 55, 69, 72, 75, 80, 95, 100–18, 127, 128, 148, 168, 248, 249, 256–9, 261–4, 279
Baroque City, 32–3
Barthes, R., 11, 25, 37, 44, 51–2, 55, 74, 81, 277
Bauhaus, 27, 66, 255
Behaviourism, dangers of, 13, 18, 22, 39, 81
Bentham, J., 79
Bororo, 27–9
Boulez, P., 59–62, 65, 75
Breuer, M., 215
Broadbent, G., 7, 8, 12, 16, 17, 18, 24, 31, 35, 40, 41, 44, 50–75
Brutalism, 55, 261–3
Buddha, 238

Cage, J., 65–6, 75, 95
Cassirer, E., 40, 41, 49, 277
cereconflict, 133, 137
chain, in semiology a synonym for opposition, syntagm, metonymy, context (see context), 52
Chaplin, C., 222
change, 16, 31, 62–72, 141–4, 164, 171, 191, 257–9, 264–5
Choay, F., 7, 8, 26–37, 138, 158, 166, 167
Chomsky, N., 73, 75
Cocteau, J., 22
code/message, 48, 82–3
Coleridge, S. T., 24, 25
Colquhoun, A., 8, 80, 98, 266–77
commentary, reasons for, 7, 8, 262
computer design, 61–3, 234, 270–3
connotation, 11, 23, 44, 54, 56
context, in semiology a synonym for chain, opposition, syntagm, metonymy, 21–4, 25, 27, 29, 31, 51, 52, 91, 134–8
conventions, 16, 25, 237–8
conventional nature of the sign, 53, 55, 90
Cretan Liar, 12, 14
cultural context, as architect's task to determine, 153–4, 166
culturalist model, 36
cultural wardrobe, abandon, 101, 118, 127, 258–9
cybernetics, 61, 63, 64, 72

Dada, 16, 17
Dallegret, F., 102–18
Dama, 184–7
de Beauvoir, S., 121, 147
De Stijl, 44, 69–73
degree of surprise, 22, 83
Dogons, 7, 173–213; basket, 183; house, 195–8
Dorfles, G., 7, 8, 38–49

double articulation, 16, 17, 40, 44, 54, 74
Duchamp, M., 16, 57, 63, 75, 95
duck-rabbit, 18
Durandus, W., 16

Eliot, T. S., 96, 99, 253, 281
ergonomics, 233–5
expressionism, 17–8, 55, 216–9, 221, 227, 248–9, 251–3, 259, 274–6
expressive form, 17–8, 40–1, 54–5, 85, 167, 228, 274–6

fashion, 16, 21, 24, 52, 121
flatscape, 101–8, 228–9
Folon, 32, 34, 35
Frampton, K., 7, 8, 25, 31, 36, 91, 93, 127, 130, 138, 151–68, 216, 218, 223, 224
Freud, S., 17, 134, 242
Fuller, B., 13, 111, 112, 132, 148, 259, 268–9
functionalism, limitations of, 128–31, 142, 218; as doctrine, 17, 36, 95, 97, 215–8, 223, 235, 239, 250, 259, 266–73, 277, 285
Futurism, 256–9

Gans, H., 33
Garnier, T., 159–60, 162
Gaudi, 252–3
'Gesamtkunstler', 79, 80–2, 85, 90, 92, 93, 96, 98
Gestalt, 17, 20, 40, 41, 55, 56, 219
Giedion, S., 56, 74, 223, 242, 249, 251–6, 258–9
Ginna, 177, 181, 190
Gombrich, E. H., 17, 18, 81, 98, 265, 274–6
Gothic form, 16, 21
Greek City, 29
Gregory, R., 56, 69, 74
Griaule, M., 190, 192–3, 213
Gropius, W., 20, 254, 256
Gubbio, 42–7

Habrakan, H. J., 135, 138, 148
Hall, E. T., 48
Hardoy Chair, 236–9, 242
Haussmann, 31, 167
historian, as psychoanalyst, 242–3
history as myth, 245–65
Hitchcock, H. R., 249–50, 260
home is not a house, 109–18
homeostatic structures, 7, 101–2
homo faber, 154
Hume, D., 94–5, 99
hypersignificant systems, 27–31
hyposignificant systems, 31–6

imaginaire urbain, 35
indeterminacy, 62, 64, 65
informality, 111
information theory, 21, 39, 82, 83, 94
insecurity, 114, 116, 118
intention, 41, 42, 283
intrinsic meaning, 17–8, 40–1, 54–5, 73
isomorphism, 17, 40, 167, 228

Jakobson, R., 37, 39, 49, 53, 74, 84, 91, 98, 99
Jencks, C., 7–8, 10–25, 31, 40, 44, 47, 51, 54, 55, 56, 86, 94, 101, 146, 238, 244–65, 276, 279, 281, 282
Johnson, P., 94, 117, 249, 279

Kafka, F., 225–6
Kahn, Louis, 109, 260–1
Kandinsky, W., 58, 74, 276
Kant, I., 14, 20, 97
Koestler, A., 20, 24, 25
Kubler, G., 141–3, 148

Labour, 151–68
Langue, definition of, 81–2; langue/parole distinction, 37, 40, 44, 51, 61, 72, 81–4, 90, 94, 95, 131
language, coherent, 163, 284–5
Le Corbusier, 24, 35, 37, 56–8, 69, 74, 109, 152, 160, 162, 167–8, 215–6, 218, 223, 226–7, 247–9, 252, 259, 264, 270–5, 279, 283–4
Levi-Strauss, C., 14, 25, 27, 28, 31, 37, 52, 54, 73, 74, 81, 96, 99, 101, 121, 147, 242, 243, 268, 277
Levistrology, 102
'life conditioner', 80–2, 92–3
linguistics, 15, 17, 25, 27, 37, 39, 40, 44, 56, 73–4, 81, 90–1, 237
Lynch, K., 31

machine age, 257–9
Maki, F., 164
Maldonado, T., 267, 272–3
Mallarmé, 64
Marx, K., 21, 31, 35, 158–9, 167
materialism, 158–9
Mauss, M., 237, 242–3
meaning, inevitable, 11–3; basic architectural units of, 17, 23, 39, 40, 47, 53, 54; in architecture, 56, 214–29; intrinsic and extrinsic, 17–21
memory, 127, 138–47, 171, 242
Merleau-Ponty, M., 86, 90, 98
metaphor, in semiology a synonym for system, association, connotation, correlation, paradigm, similarity, 21–3, 37, 91
metonymy, in semiology a synonym for context, opposition, syntagm, chain, 91, 95
Meyer, Hannes, 12, 94, 95, 166, 215–6, 277, 279
Miletus, 153
mixed systems, 31–6
monumentality, 93, 101, 109, 111, 118, 128, 163, 167, 223, 284
Morellet, F., 59–61, 66
Morgenthaler, F., 173, 188, 194–203
Morris, C., 35, 39, 53, 72, 74
Morse Code, 21, 39
Müller-Lyer, 56, 219
multivalence, 11, 24–5, 174
Mumford, Lewis, 20, 35, 158, 250, 252
myth, 20, 25, 121, 254, 260, 262–5

naive realism, 21, 85–7, 216, 219–20, 245
Nommo, 176–7, 179, 193
Norberg-Schulz, C., 7, 8, 25, 39, 49, 166, 214–229, 264, 280–1, 283

Ogden, C. K., 13, 72, 75
Open systems, 31–6
opposition, in semiology a synonym for chain, syntagm, metonymy, context, 54; see context
Osgood, C., 22–5, 75

Panofsky, E., 16, 21, 37, 44, 97, 99, 257–8, 261
paradigmatic, in semiology a synonym for system, association, connotation, correlation, similarity, 36; see metaphor

parole, see langue
Parin, P., 173, 176–82, 188
pattern-choosing, 283–4
Pawley, M., 7, 8, 98, 101, 102, 114, 117, 121–47, 166, 259
Peirce, C. S., 53, 74
Perrault, C., 93–4, 96, 99
Pevsner, N., 245, 251–4, 257–9, 262
Piaget, J., 138, 148
Picasso, 11, 12, 253
Pietila, R., 217
place, meaningful, 27–31, 36, 193, 209, 212, 224–5
Plato, 14, 16, 17
politological level, 33
Pollack, J., 63
Pop Art, 16, 74
Pope, A., 151
Popper, K., 17, 21, 101
Price, C., 27, 66, 75, 79–99, 101–2, 108
'Primitive Man', 94, 112–6, 267–8
Private Realm, 7, 116, 121–47, 151–68
Progressivist model, 36
Public Realm, 7, 91–2, 96–7, 138, 143, 147, 151–68
Pure systems, 27–31
purposeful action, 18, 20, 151

radical, 12, 13, 18, 25, 91, 101–2, 108, 259
referential meaning, 14–5, 53
reflexive, 26, 35, 36
revolution, 247, 251
rhetoric, 79, 84, 92, 93, 243
Richards, L. A., 7, 13, 24–5, 73, 75
Rietveld, G., 69–73
rootedness, 36, 102, 111, 127, 138–43, 212
Rousseau, J. J., 17, 35, 37
Ruskin, J., 35, 55, 74
Rykwert, J., 8, 167, 183, 213, 232–43

Saarinen, Eero, 44, 79–99, 101
Saussure, F. de, 11, 25, 37, 44, 51–5, 72–4, 91
schemata, 18, 20, 25, 29, 219–20, 228, 264–5, 268, 276
Schräder-Schröder, Mrs, 69, 72
scientific outlook, 220, 267
Scully, V., 249, 256, 260–1
secularization, 158, 162, 215–6, 223, 260–1
semantic reduction, 34–6
semantic space, 23–4
semiology, theory of signs, 7, 11, 13, 15, 21, 25, 27, 36, 37, 39, 41, 48, 53, 55, 81, 82, 86, 90, 93
semiological triangle, 15–7, 87, 158
Siena, 155
sign, 11, 14, 15, 21, 24, 37, 39, 47, 53, 220, 242
sign-situation, 13–7
signifier/signified, 15, 40–1, 45, 47, 53–6, 86, 90–1
significant detour, 195–7, 202–3, 209–12
Silver, N., 8, 116, 151, 229, 242, 277, 278–85
sitting position, 8, 232–43
Smith, N. K., 162, 168
Smithson, A. & P., 69, 262–3
social contract, 51, 55, 83
Sotto, J. R., 67–8
Spengler, O., 33, 35
standard-of-living package, 111–4
Stirling, J., 245–6
Stockhausen, K., 48–9, 59, 66, 68–9, 75

Stravinsky, I., 12
structuralism, 101, 108
subjectivisation, 121–6, 131, 141
substitution, in semiology a synonym for system, association, connotation, correlation, paradigm, similarity, 91; see metaphor
Suger, Abbot, 56, 264
supplementary systems, 33, 36
symbiosis, 118
symbolism, 41, 44, 79, 86, 92, 179, 193, 220, 226–8, 237–9, 242
syntagm, in semiology a synonym for chain, opposition, metonymy, 29, 37, 45, 51–4; see context
system, 51, 52, 155; see metaphor

Tange, K., 41, 49
Tellem, 176, 178, 200
territoriality, 132–3
Tilbury Docks, 103–8
time, 57, 138–47, 171, 174
Time House, 143–7
twinphenomenon, 8, 190

Twiggy, 21–2
typology, 8, 266–77; see schemata

Un-house, 116–7
Utopian model, 36

value-free, almost, 101, 108, 114, 117; see naive realism
Van der Rohe, Mies, 215, 250
Van Eyck, Aldo, 7, 8, 90, 99, 170–213, 264
Venturi, R., 79, 98, 280–1, 283, 285
Vernant, J. P., 29, 37

Wampanoag, 100–3
Weeks, J., 62–3, 66, 75
Whorf, B. L., 18, 25
Wolfflin, H., 21, 40, 243
Woods, S., 164-5
Wright, F. L., 35, 117, 158–9, 162–3, 167–8, 256–7

Zevi, B., 255–7